The Invention of Hebrew

SETH L. SANDERS

UNIVERSITY OF ILLINOIS PRESS
URBANA, CHICAGO, AND SPRINGFIELD

First Illinois paperback, 2011

Manufactured in the United States of America
2 3 4 5 6 C P 5 4 3 2 1
♾ This book is printed on acid-free paper.

The Library of Congress cataloged the cloth edition as follows:
Sanders, Seth L.
The invention of Hebrew / Seth L. Sanders.
p. cm. — (Traditions)
Includes bibliographical references and index.
ISBN 978-0-252-03284-4 (cloth : alk. paper)
1. Hebrew language—History. 2. Bible O.T.—Language, style. 3. Inscriptions, Hebrew—Palestine. 4. Semitic languages, Northwest. 5. Ugaritic literature—History and criticism. 6. Ugaritic literature—Relation to the Old Testament. 7. Assyro-Babylonian literature—History and criticism. 8. Assyro-Babylonian literature—Relation to the Old Testament. I. Title.
PJ4545.S26 2010
492.4'09—dc22 2009029988

Paperback ISBN 978-0-252-07835-4

I dedicate this book to the memory of Bill Maddex,
who would have gotten something profound that I missed,
figured I'd gotten it too, and laughed conspiratorially
at the shared understanding that had just
come into being.

CONTENTS

	List of Illustrations	ix
	Preface	xi
	Acknowledgments	xv
	Abbreviations	xvii
	Introduction	1
1.	Modernity's Ghosts: The Bible as Political Communication	13
2.	What Was the Alphabet For?	36
3.	Empires and Alphabets in Late Bronze Age Canaan	76
4.	The Invention of Hebrew in Iron Age Israel	103
	Conclusion	157
	Notes	173
	Bibliography	225
	Index	251

LIST OF ILLUSTRATIONS

1 Sinai 345 50

2 RS 16.270 (KTU 6.23), alphabetic seal of Ammishtamru 51

3 KTU 1.3, tablet of Baal epic 52

4 Taanach 2 87

5 Izbet Sartah ostracon with abecedary 91

6 Beth Shemesh abecedary 93

7 RS 88.2215 (KTU 9.426), nonstandard cuneiform abecedary 94

8 "King of Amurru" arrowhead 108

9 Tel Zayit inscription 112

10 Mesha inscription 115

11 Kuntillet Ajrud ostracon 123

12 Samaria ostracon 17a 125

13 Siloam tunnel inscription 139

14 Lachish letter 3 143

PREFACE

This book arose from my attempts to understand something new to me, for which I found my preconceived categories unhelpful. This new material was the writing from Israel outside the Bible, especially the corpus of cuneiform in Canaan that I was invited to Hebrew University to help edit. Being forced to consider what sort of writing was possible in Israel, and what it meant to people, pushed my thinking outside the confines of my discipline. If Arameans wrote Aramaic, Phoenicians wrote Phoenician, Hebrews wrote Hebrew, and the like, what were people in Israel doing with all this Babylonian? And what had all of these putative different cultural and ethnic groups done for the many centuries when almost everyone who wrote did it in Babylonian? Did writing always flow from your spoken language and everyday identity, or did the relationship change? And if it did, could that change who you were?

This exciting disorientation had consequences for the rest of my work: it made the fact of the Hebrew Bible itself seem strange. For over two thousand years, people have recognized the Bible as speaking directly to them, calling them to new forms of belonging that can threaten or transform the orders in which they find themselves. But no other Near Eastern texts talk like the Bible does; virtually all other literature was by and for scribes, courts, and kings. The Bible has meant far more than a court literature to many outside of courts. The Bible's vast reach is partly explained by the history of biblical interpretation, a topic richly studied in recent years. But the history of interpretation does not explain everything. In particular, it does not explain whatever politics could be said to be *inherent* in the Hebrew Bible, a politics connected to how the Bible exercises power: through the manner in which it speaks to people, rather than through the force exerted by a state. How and when did the Bible's way of communicating become possible, and what were its politics?

The way we have studied other ancient cultures in relation to the Bible suggests why such fundamental questions may not have been asked. Cuneiform literature was first discovered in what is now Iran and Iraq, and during the early days of its decipherment it was usually placed in a subordinate position to the texts of ancient Israel. It was connected to the Hebrew Bible in two ways: texts like Gilgamesh served as backgrounds to biblical stories such as that of the flood, and cuneiform historical texts were used to confirm biblical historical accounts. These discoveries had a great impact on thought about the Bible, but they were fit into preexisting categories about what was Israelite and what was foreign. Babylonian literature was mythic and archaic; Israelite literature was ethical and shorn of myth, and the cuneiform documents were considered most interesting when they confirmed or denied the originality or historicity of biblical accounts.

Having received my college training in comparative religion and a good portion of my graduate training in Semitic philology, this reduction of a corpus that dwarfed the Bible in size and chronological sweep seemed sad.[1] I could understand, and almost sympathize with, the backlash: those cuneiform scholars who retreated into narrowness, stressing the *Eigenbegrifflichkeit,* the conceptual unity and distinctiveness, of Babylonian and other cuneiform cultures.[2] I was vaguely aware that theological apologetics played some part in this fragmentation, but I did not understand the point—where that sort of thinking came from and how it got so deeply rooted, even among scholars without strong religious motivations.

Polemics on the authenticity of ancient traditions are themselves old; already in the Hellenistic period, native intellectuals of colonized cultures claimed historical priority while Greek and Roman writers passed judgment on them. The Egyptian priest Manetho argued for the authority of pharaonic tradition by citing three thousand years of dynastic succession, while the philosopher Chaeremon ridiculed Babylonian tradition by claiming that their priests dressed up in fish costumes to swindle worshippers. The drive to confirm or deny authenticity tends to have a polemical, even political aspect.

Reading cuneiform texts from Israel itself pushed me outside this framework. The texts span nearly two millennia, from the Old Babylonian to the Hellenistic periods, roughly 1800–100 B.C.E. Israel may have been a unified state for less than a hundred years of that, and after the division of the northern and southern kingdoms, the territory was only held by any native rulers for less than three centuries. During the rest of this time, the only political institutions were city-states and empires that wrote cuneiform or imperial Aramaic. The cuneiform texts found in Israel actually reflect the norm in this region's ancient history.

But the Hebrew texts—crucially, not just the ones preserved in the Bible but the ones dug up out of the ground—tell a different story.[3] Epigraphic Hebrew texts are known only from the late Iron Age, but they speak in the same language, from vocabulary to grammar to spelling, as the classical narratives of the Bible. They refer to the same institutions: kings and armies, scribes and priests, the same units of measure and money. They map a world of local power and culture. The cuneiform texts seem to come from a different, larger world, referring to nations and institutions that existed both before and after the Israelite state. But in Israel, Hebrew and cuneiform texts can be found in precisely the same territory; sites such as Samaria and Beth Shemesh feature both. On the fundamental level of physical space—and military power—Hebrew and Babylonian written culture came from the same world.

So what did biblical Hebrew, the Hebrew Bible, and the rest of the ancient world have to do with one another? How did the idea of Israel become such a powerful organizing force when it was only the dominant state for a fraction of this time, and most cuneiform texts found in Israel do not reflect Israelite institutions? A critical answer came during the 1990s from the minimalist school of biblical studies: unlike the massive textual and physical record left by entities such as Assyria or Persia, there is little evidence of Israel as a powerful and monolithic state. Israel immortalized itself with neither royal monuments nor archaeological burn layers over the people they killed. Following in a millennium-old tradition of freethinkers and polemicists, they argued that the Bible's self-account, preserved in extended narratives rather than monuments, must be understood as self-interested myth—invented tradition.[4] They tended to share with their opponents the assumption that early meant authentic, late meant inauthentic, and the state was the most substantial and significant protagonist of history.[5] Though sometimes politically progressive, minimalism's proponents seemed not to consider the irony of this move: by debunking forms of self-representation and institutions outside the state, they too placed state power at the center of history.[6]

An alternative to an all-or-nothing approach to Israelite history is to ask, what if the state was not, even in the Iron Age, the only way that ancient Israel did politics? The gap between Israel's self-representation and the residue of bureaucracy and violence on which we base conventional political history could mean something more. Scholars have been suspicious of the way biblical traditions provided readers with a political model that was easily projected across the space and time of European history. Yet virtually all biblical scholarship is in some way motivated by this history, the way Europe itself has been molded by biblical visions. It has been considered anachronistic to project this biblical vision back onto an Iron Age state. But how far back did this projection go—could a politics based on communication have played a role already at an early stage, in Iron Age Israel?

This suggests a difficult question that is nonetheless worth asking in public: What does biblical studies have to say to the rest of the academy?

As a Bible scholar who reads both ancient inscriptions and modern social theory, I kept seeing surprising possible challenges to modern ideas of nationalism and the politics of language. I wanted to share these challenges. And more than that, I wanted to write a book I would find intellectually exciting. In a field where the methodology is sometimes simply borrowed from other fields and narrowly applied, I wanted to see what biblical studies might have to say to social thought. Ours is an area with great, but often untapped, intellectual potential: as a core model for both the New Testament and the Qur'an, the Bible has served as the authoritative text par excellence across a great swath of world history and culture. It is no accident that Thomas Hobbes and Baruch Spinoza inaugurated Bible criticism along with modern political theory. They had to, because they needed to draw on the Bible's authority in order to undermine it.[7] Unfortunately, Hobbes's and Spinoza's success was so total that the way they won it has been forgotten: since modernity began, biblical studies has unconsciously replayed their concerns, endlessly asking: history or myth? Yet these questions, posed this way, have long since lost most of their relevance to the academy.

To my surprise and delight, as I was writing this book I had the intuition that this situation was changing—that many scholars in Bible and ancient Near Eastern studies agreed that the time was ripe for rethinking the intellectual role of ancient Western Asia. I was inspired by the successful integration of anthropological and comparative historical thought with philology in the works of Daniel Fleming (2004), William Schniedewind (2004), and Peter Machinist (1991). At the same time, some extremely interesting thinkers in anthropology and literary history were reconsidering theory's "retreat into the present"—suggesting that the fixation of social theory on modernity was a major obstacle to our own self-understanding and historical consciousness. These included Richard Bauman and Charles Briggs, whose *Voices of Modernity* permitted me to rethink the relationship between biblical studies and the formation of modern social theory; Sheldon Pollock, whose work on "Vernacular and Cosmopolitan in History" provided a comparative historical framework into which I could put the ancient Near East texts and polities I study; Michael Silverstein, who taught me how to see texts as both evidence of culture and tools for making history; and John Kelly, whose fundamental questions on writing and the state underlie this book's approach to political theory. A series of conferences and talks allowed me to shape my thinking in discussions with these scholars, culminating in the *Margins of Writing* conference at the University of Chicago Oriental Institute at which I was able to bring Silverstein, Pollock, and Kelly into conversation with Near Eastern philologists like Schniedewind and Machinist. This gave me the pleasant task of editing fresh conversations with these scholars for publication even as they were shaping my thought.

This dialogue strengthens my conviction that the Bible contains remarkable answers to consequential new questions—ones we may have been too timid or hidebound to put to our texts. A task this book sets itself, then, is to consider new empirical ways of reading ancient Hebrew with the evidence on the ground, a philology confronting the modern imagination with the ancient.

ACKNOWLEDGMENTS

I thank Robin Shoaps for introducing me to linguistic anthropology and for her detailed reading of my introduction and first chapter. I am grateful to Aaron Tugendhaft for inspiration and Jeremy Rabkin and Julie Cooper for historical and theoretical guidance on chapter 1. Ryan Byrne, Eva von Dassow, and Christopher Rollston gave crucial early readings of chapter 2 and Benjamin Sommer provided rigorous and constructive comments on a later version. Its comparative thrust is suggested by the title, inspired by John Kelly's "What Was Sanskrit For?" Chapter 3 arises from the opportunity Wayne Horowitz gave me to consider the most extensive corpus of excavated texts from ancient Israel. Eva von Dassow, Shlomo Izre'el, and Dennis Pardee provided detailed and thoughtful critical readings and Anson Rainey useful fulminations. Chapter 4 was sparked by a collaborative effort with Christopher Rollston to interpret the Iron Age epigraphy to whose study he has contributed so much and my understanding of the crucial Hebrew seals is based on further collaborative work with Shira Wallach, then my Albright Institute intern, now on her way to becoming a rabbi and Biblicist. Ed Greenstein and Chip Dobbs-Allsopp provided attentive readings of the chapter and saved me from significant errors; their support and mentorship has sustained me through a number of difficult times. Allan Millard has been a thoroughgoing and generous critic of my work; his thoughtful remarks have constantly improved it. William Schniedewind chaired the panel at which I first presented this project and since then been a valuable collaborative and critical presence. While my project diverges from those of Karel van der Toorn and David Carr, both showed real generosity in granting me access to drafts of their work, and Carr also shared his rich knowledge and insights on the sources and editing of the Torah. Mark S. Smith provided cutting and helpful readings of an early version of the entire book and an equally helpful reading of a late version of chapter 4; I thank him in equal measure for his steady wisdom, disagreement, and support.

The first draft of this book was completed while I was postdoctoral fellow at the University of Chicago Oriental Institute, maybe the single best place on earth to do philology. I thank director Gil Stein for the opportunity to pioneer an encounter between Near Eastern studies and social theory (the first Oriental Institute Post-Doctoral Symposium, published as Sanders, ed.

2006) that has gone on to break more new ground. It was accepted for publication at an early stage by Bill Regier, director of the University of Illinois Press, whose interest and faith in my work has been a real help in bringing the project to fruition. Significant parts of the West Semitic and Assyriological work in chapters 2, 3, and 4 were done at the University of Chicago with the help of a National Endowment for the Humanities (NEH) Summer Stipend and an Oriental Institute Research Associateship. I made major advances in my understanding of the Iron Age Israelite and Levantine aspects of the work during my year as an NEH fellow at the W. F. Albright Institute, whose director Sy Gitin has a long track record of supporting my work. Decisive to my intellectual life there was the friendship and support of Ed Silver and Tzemah Yoreh, who showed great interest and faith in my work even as they were each completing groundbreaking projects of their own.

I finished this book at Trinity College, where Dean Rena Fraden and the Religion Department under the leadership of Ellison Findly and Frank Kirkpatrick have provided a home, equally nurturing of liberal-arts teaching and serious research. Discussions with Rachel Havrelock and Kimberly Sims inspired new thoughts and expressions. My mother, Jacquelyn Seevak Sanders, probably knows as much about this work as I do, and has encouraged me in each setback and celebrated each victory with me. Every one of these people has a part in whatever good I achieve here, and I feel grateful and blessed to know them.

ABBREVIATIONS

ALASP	*Abhandlungen zur Literatur Alt-Syrien-Palästinas und Mesopotamiens*
ARM	Archives royales de Mari
BASOR	*Bulletin of the American Schools of Oriental Research*
CAD	*The Assyrian Dictionary of the Oriental Institute of the University of Chicago.* 21 vols. Chicago: The Oriental Institute, 1956–2008.
CRRAI	Compte rendu, Rencontre Assyriologique Internationale
EI	Eretz-Israel
IEJ	*Israel Exploration Journal*
IOS	*Israel Oriental Studies*
JANES	*Journal of the Ancient Near Eastern Society*
JAOS	*Journal of the American Oriental Society*
JBL	*Journal of Biblical Literature*
JESHO	*Journal of the Economic and Social History of the Orient*
JNES	*Journal of Near Eastern Studies*
KAI	H. Donner and W. Röllig, *Kanaanäische und aramäische Inschriften.* Mit einem Beitrag von O. Rössler. 3 vols. Wiesbaden: O. Harrassowitz, 1962–64.
KTU	M. Dietrich, O. Loretz, and J. Sanmartín, eds. *The Cuneiform Alphabetic Texts from Ugarit, Ras Ibn Hani and Other Places.* ALASP 8. Münster: Ugarit-Verlag, 1997.
Or	*Orientalia*
PEQ	*Palestine Exploration Quarterly*
PSAS	*Proceedings of the Seminar for Arabian Studies*
RA	*Revue d'Assyriologie*
RS	Ras Shamra (excavation number)
UF	*Ugarit-Forschungen*
VT	*Vetus Testamentum*
VT Supp	*VT Supplement*
ZA	*Zeitschrift für Assyriologie*
ZDPV	*Zeitschrift des Deutschen Palästina-Vereins*

Introduction

Since people first read the Bible, they have felt it speaking directly to them. Sometimes it has spoken to them privately and in isolation. But most often, and most important, it has spoken to them as members of a group defined by the very fact that the Bible is talking to them.

The call of Deuteronomy 6 is "Hear, O Israel!"[1] Between "Hear" and "Israel" is a moment of recognition. From the first Jews and Christians to the kingdoms of Christendom and colonial pilgrims, to Rastafarians and U.S. presidents, people have seen themselves as Israel, not (or not just) because of blood descent but because they recognized themselves as the "we" to whom the Bible is talking. The Bible is the first text to address people as a public. It is this call that the Bible's audiences have been answering for more than two thousand years.

The way the Bible refuses to let go of us—and we of it—suggests a challenging question: What can biblical scholarship tell us about the Bible's power as political communication?[2] Seen in isolation, it is difficult to tell whom in ancient Israel the texts were addressing. The problem is the Bible's physical condition: we only have actual biblical manuscripts from centuries after the end of the Israelite kingdoms. This means we must delve through intricate, sometimes inextricable layers of editing before we can talk about original contexts. Yet inscriptions from the time of ancient Israel show striking correlations with the Bible in communicative form; both types of writings address people in a very specific new way. Modern social theory suggests a way to grasp this compelling dimension of the Bible's power by seeing it as part of a historical change. How and when did written texts first begin to speak to a public?

By illuminating the mutual creativity of texts and societies, recent works such as Benedict Anderson's *Imagined Communities* and Sheldon Pollock's *The Language of the Gods in the World of Men* suggest a point of intersection between these philological and theoretical questions: vernaculars, the deliberate writing down and transformation into literature of languages people actually spoke. In Europe and India, vernacular literatures went hand in hand with vernacular polities, as new ways for people to think of themselves as part of a community or political order. But as a rule, people in the ancient Near East did not write, or even strongly identify with, the language they spoke. For two thousand years, Near Eastern kingdoms and empires shared cuneiform, a script, not a language.[3] Hebrew, as the first widely written vernacular, changed this.

This book explores the emergence of vernacular ways of writing and belonging in Hebrew and related ancient inscriptions. By studying these texts we can actually trace the emergence of a new mode of communication to a specific time and place: the Iron Age Levant. Unlike biblical manuscripts, the inscriptions come from the time they speak about. But like the core of the Bible, the inscriptions from Israel speak in a standardized vernacular language and assume that texts can speak to a public. Seeing the invention of Hebrew as a historical event sheds light on what the Bible was for. And it opens up the question of how the deliberate choice to create written Hebrew connects to the sense of political and theological *difference*, of being called to membership in a distinctive order, which pervades the Hebrew Bible.[4] Can we understand the Bible's distinctiveness as the result of a decision to communicate in a new way?

THIS BOOK'S ARGUMENTS

The first chapter explores why these questions of political communication have not been put to the Bible, and how they can be. The intellectual origins of biblical studies in early modern Europe help explain both its strengths and its limitations. The thinkers who made the discipline possible saw the Bible's political communication as more of a threat than a promise. Early modern political philosophers such as Thomas Hobbes and Baruch Spinoza had experienced the power of the Bible through harsh religious conflicts, and they wanted to neutralize it. In the seventeenth century the Bible was the single greatest textual source of authority for church and king. It was therefore no accident that Hobbes and Spinoza produced such devastating critiques of it as part of their new political theories. They needed to draw on the Bible's authority in order to undermine it and create new sources of authority for the modern state.[5] Political philosophers argued that texts like the Bible could convey ideas or information about their own time but not legitimately lay claims on their readers. To see anything more in the texts of a long-dead society would be anachronistic.

By demonstrating that texts could not rationally be seen as having inherent authority, these philosophers starkly limited the Bible's social power for anyone who wanted to be seen as rational and modern. They made the Bible safe for criticism because it was now possible to study it as nothing more than a text. But such a cut-and-dried idea of ancient texts seems utterly inadequate to explaining, as opposed to explaining away, the powerfully creative relationships they could form with their audiences. In fact two of the greatest eighteenth-century scholars associated with the Bible were acutely sensitive to the interplay between linguistic form and social function. Bishop Robert Lowth pioneered study of the structures of biblical language, discovering the essentially parallelistic form of Hebrew poetry. And Johann Gottfried Herder argued that this poetry was not merely spiritual or aesthetic, but political, a people's way of recognizing itself. Yet both of them saw biblical poetry as the natural outgrowth of a unified ethnic culture. They gave less emphasis to the politically constitutive dimension of language—as a tool that could actually create a sense of place and peoplehood. Israel's form of language was the result of its unique historical and social situation; it reflected but did not create that situation.

Like Hobbes and Spinoza, Lowth's and Herder's discoveries were both illuminating and limiting. Fixing texts firmly in dead, ancient contexts paints a satisfying but static picture. It does not explain how new texts or contexts emerge. But if language helps create people's social contexts, then it has a fundamental dynamic dimension: people can act to change their contexts through language. New forms of communication can help make new sorts of audiences and political participants possible.

In their attention to the vital connections between linguistic and social forms, biblical studies and anthropology are Lowth's and Herder's heirs. But we can capitalize on their poetic and political legacy by combining anthropological attention to the interplay between genres and their participants with philological attention to the historical form and contexts of texts. Reuniting these scholarly traditions helps us move beyond their limits.

The second chapter takes up these questions for ancient Hebrew and its relatives. It asks what the rise of written vernaculars has to do with the distinctive ways early biblical law and narrative speak to the reader (as a "you" enjoined to hear and remember) and the way biblical texts assume "the people" as a basic unit of ritual (a feature found nowhere in older Near Eastern texts—with a crucial exception). How can we relate these literary and ritual features to the politics and culture of the late Iron Age Levant?

The chapter begins with the case of the first known vernacular literature in world history, unearthed at the ancient Syrian city-state of Ugarit. In a rich archive dating to the thirteenth century B.C.E., scholars discovered a spellbinding range of texts: epics, rituals, prayers, contracts, and letters, in the West Semitic language of Ugaritic, an earlier relative of Hebrew. Ugaritic literature had striking formal and thematic connections with that of Israel. In poetic narratives, both cultures used paired parallel phrases to praise a divine hero who appears in lightning, rides thunderclouds, and battles the sea. At Ugarit he was Baal, patron god of the Ugaritic royal dynasty; in Israel he was Yahweh, patron of the Judean royal dynasty. The cultural connection was a theological provocation. Scholarship focused on explaining how *their* ancient West Semitic storm deity became *our* God.

But we can only read the early history of God because Ugaritic and Hebrew writers chose to write it in their own, local languages and alphabets.[6] This was not normal in the ancient Near East. Culturally, the connections between Israel and Ugarit are not exceptional but part of a larger West Semitic pattern that shares both myths and political ideas. A West Semitic storm god had battled the sea and provisionally enthroned the king six hundred years earlier at Mari, and in Mari, Ugarit, and Jerusalem this god's victory provided the mythic foundation for the ruler's own power, a power contingent on his public appearance as a just judge.[7] What is special about Ugaritic and Hebrew vernacular literatures is the sheer fact of their existence—not their unique content but the distinctive written form into which that content was cast. Literature had been the exclusive domain of syllabic cuneiform, like medieval Latin the universal script of education and empire. At the time Ugaritic literature was created, we know of no other speakers of a Semitic language who tried to systematically write the language they spoke.

Why did the writers of Ugarit, educated in the cosmopolitan tradition of Babylonian cuneiform, create the first vernacular we know? A clue appears in the most widely used religious ritual from Ugarit, the "ritual for national unity." Like the Hebrew ritual of national atonement at the center of the Torah, Yom Kippur, this Ugaritic ritual addresses its audience as "you" and involves them in a collective redemption. Ugaritic and Hebrew were used to record vernacular rituals that addressed and acted on a group in their own language. While the atonement rituals of cuneiform empires redeemed kings, these Ugaritic and Hebrew rituals were done on behalf of peoples.

The chapter concludes by exploring the political thought that made this new subject possible. Evidence in cuneiform lets us trace this ideology, in which the people is a central participant in ritual and politics, farther back in time. A tribal leader's archive, preserved in Babylonian (rather than the local spoken Amorite) from the eighteenth-century B.C.E. city of Mari, reveals a widespread ancient West Semitic political theory in which kin groups, defined not just by blood but by ritual and discourse, were the fundamental units of politics. But at Mari this theory had little effect on writing: no rituals or narratives are written in West Semitic there. Something had to change so that written texts could be about collective subjects.

How did the people enter history? The second half of this book tells the story of writing's genres and uses in the Levant in the centuries around the invention of Hebrew. It explains why Ugaritic was a singularity, but Hebrew was part of a wave. The third chapter shows how writing during the Late Bronze Age reflected a pervasive divide between local and imperial cultural worlds. Then the fourth chapter explores the Iron Age changes that led to the sudden and nearly simultaneous appearance across the Levant of written local languages during the ninth century B.C.E.—and how they made biblical literature possible.

In the Late Bronze Age, the Levant was ruled by the Egyptian empire, which used Babylonian cuneiform as an administrative tool there, not a form of expression. This cosmopolitan writing system's lack of inherent connection with spoken language was an advantage for the empire, with its far-flung outposts and linguistically unrelated agents. It was the only way everyone involved could communicate. The known genres of writing from Canaan are all narrowly specialized: school texts were used to train scribes in the dead languages of Sumerian and Old Babylonian. Scribes used writing to list people and things the empire owned and to write letters for officials who could not have understood each other in person. Local language and culture peeks through unintentionally in the letters, a remarkable hybrid of Babylonian words and forms in local West Semitic grammar, with little effort to systematize them. A second type of writing system, the alphabet, had been in casual use here since the beginning of the Late Bronze Age. Alphabetic texts played a role that was very different from cuneiform but even more narrow: they talked about little more than the objects they were written on. So short that we have yet to recover a single complete sentence, these inscriptions show no deliberate effort to record language or literature; their main use was to mark property. And unlike at Ugarit, alphabetic writing in the southern Levant shows no influence from Babylonian or its genres of imperial administration. Two worlds, local and cosmopolitan, existed side by side with no interest in what the other was writing.

The final chapter charts how imperial power began to speak to the Levant in different genres of writing—monumental inscriptions of conquest and collective rituals of vassalship—and how local cultures reacted in a new way. The situation began to change around 1200 B.C.E., when the Egyptian empire collapsed along with the city-states that served it. It was not missed: alphabetic writing persisted in the limited uses it had since its invention. But in the early ninth century, a new power imposed itself on the Levant. The Assyrian empire began to erect cuneiform monuments, speaking in the voice of the king, around the territories he had conquered. "I am Shalmaneser, king of all peoples . . . king of the universe . . . " Subjects he did not destroy had to take elaborate ritual oaths of loyalty. By contrast with the administrative genres of the Late Bronze Age, these genres of sovereignty claimed to address the peoples the king conquered. Assyrian surrogates translated them into local forms: we have both bilingual Assyrian-Aramaic and Aramaic-only monuments to Assyrian power.

Local courts did not just read these inscriptions; they interpreted them audaciously, rethinking them in their own cultural terms and taking over the inscriptions' form and content for their own purposes. Levantine kings and scribes absorbed imperial genres of sovereignty and began pirating them, creating linguistic forms they could literally own. Local languages like Hebrew, Aramaic, and Moabite had been spoken for centuries before they were written. But they were "invented," as the distinct property of royal courts, when rulers hired scribes to write them with carefully standardized grammars and scripts. Aramaic writing and grammar was deliberately made to look as distinct as possible from Hebrew, and vice versa. For the first time, local kings sponsored monumental inscriptions in West Semitic, public accounts of their own historical events, written in their own distinctive script-languages. They adopted but relocated the voice of the imperial ruler: the first known royal inscription from the southern Levant proclaims, "I am Mesha, king of Moab, man of Diban." Rather than claiming to be king of the universe Mesha claims to be a native of his hometown. Vernacular language entered politics when Levantine courts borrowed the superimposed genres of an empire to communicate in a new way: kings addressed the first accounts of history in the alphabet in local language to local communities.

But Levantine communities spoke back. They had inherited other political traditions and communicative genres, old West Semitic ideologies of collective tribal power and prophecy in which divine authority spoke to peoples, not just kings. Alphabetic writing, low-budget and easier to learn and produce, circulated outside the court. On both sides of the Jordan, local writers began to inscribe things they had not learned from empires: prophecies addressed to a people, letters of protest and complaint, monuments by workmen, graffiti from fugitives. History began to speak in a non-monarchic voice. And it is in this voice that we can see distinctive biblical discourses—of history, law, and prophecy—being configured. These new ways of speaking had political implications: a history with a people and prophets, not just kings, as the main actors; law that directly addressed a collective "you," not third-person imperial subjects; and prophecy, claiming that ultimate authority was mediated directly from God's messengers to a public. Each of these discourses resulted from a shift visible in Iron Age inscriptions, which had its greatest impact through the Bible.

LIMITS AND GOALS

This book is not a history of biblical literature, but a new kind of prolegomenon to it: an explanation of how such a literature became possible. By showing how writers began to speak in a deliberately local way and address a people, not a king or his subjects, this book documents a shift in communication and argues for seeing it as a major historical event. It explores fundamental connections with ritual in Leviticus, law in Exodus, covenant in Deuteronomy, and prophecy in Isaiah. But it is part of this book's point to avoid reconstructions of the history of biblical literature that cannot presently be based on external evidence.

One of this book's main methodological goals is to consider what would be distinctive about written communication in the Iron Age Levant if we based our viewpoint on securely dated primary sources. We thereby deliberately avoid a traditional and valuable, but problematic, practice of biblical scholarship. This is the attempt to project centuries (five hundred, six hundred, or even eight hundred years) back from our existing biblical manuscripts to reconstruct the hypothetical ancestors of biblical texts at the times of kings Josiah, Hezekiah, or Solomon and then, on the basis of this reconstruction, to reconstruct the scribal culture that produced them. This is not an implausible project—the Hebrew Bible gives clear signs of having emerged from a distinctively Iron Age culture of communication, and it is part of this book's task to investigate those signs. The recent historical investigations of Nadav Na'aman and William Schniedewind agree that archaeologically, the most plausible context for a thriving scribal literary culture is the late Judean monarchy (late eighth through early sixth centuries). Yet we do not yet have a single edited Hebrew literary manuscript from before the Hellenistic period.[8] We can be sure that scribes were writing them, but we cannot know precisely what they wrote or when.

What we can study more confidently is how vernacular writers came to speak to their audiences. We have explicit evidence for the language, genres, physical distribution, and modes of address of Hebrew and its relatives from the Late Bronze and Iron ages. We give this material priority, first because it is the most direct evidence of early written Hebrew culture, but even more because it has never been studied as a whole.

The value and limits of reconstructing scribal culture are explored in major recent works by Karel van der Toorn and David Carr. These scholars resourcefully use virtually all available information to paint a picture of a scribal ideology that stands behind the Hebrew Bible. We know that such an ideology, put into practice through editing, brought us the biblical books.[9] But we face the daunting problem of a total lack of contemporary evidence for advanced scribal education or editing of alphabetic texts in the Iron Age Levant.[10] The only school texts we have are the simplest possible ones: casually executed abecedaries and ostraca with a few repeated words, many found far outside the palaces or temples where it is often assumed scribes were trained.[11]

Given the lack of direct evidence, we are faced with a second danger: that of imagining Hebrew scribal culture on the basis of the richly documented empires that destroyed it, thus filling in our database and ironing out its distinctiveness at a stroke. Because there is no direct evidence for the alphabetic scribal culture of a small kingdom in the Iron Age Levant, van der Toorn and Carr turn to the non-alphabetic scribal cultures of large empires outside the Levant. This requires assuming that Mesopotamian and Egyptian written traditions, spanning thousands of years and hundreds of sites with dozens of local cultures, reflect a more or less uniform Near Eastern scribal culture. This provides a detailed and compelling model to apply to Hebrew. But this direct application is problematic on its face: we know Mesopotamia and Egypt so well precisely because they were so different from Israel. These cultures left so many more documents because they were the seats of geographically large empires, richly productive economies that could support many scribes, and long continuous written traditions on the scale of three thousand years, as opposed to the less than three hundred years for which we have continuous Hebrew epigraphic texts.[12] None of these are features of Israel or Judah. But since we have no Iron Age evidence of complex Hebrew scribal activity to compare with that of Mesopotamia or Egypt, we do not know whether it is safe to use them as a model, or whether instead we risk treating scribes across the entire ancient Near East as a kind of vast, three thousand-year-long monoculture.[13]

Reconstructions of scribal culture are also better at explaining how the Bible was edited than why people cared about it. They necessarily focus on elite circles of text producers, rather than how they could connect with an outside audience, placing the Bible in a tight and circumscribed circuit of communication. As van der Toorn writes, "Scribes wrote for scribes" (2007:2). The implication is that the Bible's writers were their own, and almost their only, meaningful audience. The problem of the constituents and politics of biblical texts is less urgent if alphabetic writing was a fundamentally closed system. But any account of scripture as a way for scribes to legitimate or enculturate themselves for each other is shadowed by the question of why they bothered. If the texts were for scribes alone, who else was listening to their legitimating stories? With little meaningful connection to the non-writing majority it becomes difficult to claim, as van der Toorn does, that "literacy is a mark of social distinction inasmuch as the illiterate majority holds the written word in high esteem" (2007:106). How can we know what the illiterate majority thinks if they left so little trace in the texts?[14] To the extent that this type of argument makes it easier to explain how the Bible was constructed, it makes it harder to understand how it worked in the world.

Focusing on the Bible's vernacular address to a public, a collective "you," lets us avoid two of the risks involved in reconstructing a poorly attested Hebrew scribal culture: it does not depend on a universalizing Near Eastern model, and it helps explain how Hebrew, even in an elaborately edited form, came to be seen as directly addressing every member of "Israel." A vernacular theory based in Iron Age sources provides a viewpoint that is independent of, but complementary to, a view from scribal culture. And it holds out the promise of a future synthesis: a more richly historical account of biblical literature.

This book is also not a complete history of West Semitic literature. Because not all of the evidence has survived, alternative histories will need to be written when more evidence appears.[15] This is especially clear for the later Iron Age, when clay seal impressions, but not the papyrus documents they sealed, are preserved, evidence that whole genres of official and legal writing have vanished. The problem is less serious for earlier periods, since the disparate scraps of alphabetic writing from outside of Ugarit show no sign of standardization, official use, or literary application. But we cannot say with certainty what was not written. This book therefore studies existing patterns of evidence, not the possible worlds that new discoveries will one day illuminate.

The provisional quality of our knowledge has two consequences. First, the claims here are not exclusive: that West Semitic kingdoms began to create local monuments and standardize their languages around the ninth century is certain. But such use of writing could have happened in other local languages, or decades earlier, or in other circumstances unknown to us (though we do not yet have reason to believe it did). Second, the patterns the evidence forms can only be challenged by further discoveries, not their mere possibility.[16]

As Ludwig Wittgenstein says, "What we cannot speak of, we must be silent about." No one would claim that theories should not be based on existing evidence because conflicting evidence *could* emerge, an argument that could apply a fortiori and devastatingly to the Bible, where not a single manuscript exists contemporary with the Iron Age, Babylonian, or Persian period events it describes. History reconstructed from epigraphic sources is a more secure place to begin thinking about biblical literature than the other way around.

FURTHER POSSIBILITIES

What this book intends to do is show how the Hebrew Bible could come to be the first text to imagine a public. Deuteronomy represents a community that is addressed in its own words and called into existence through the circulation of texts. The Torah's narrative represents both its own acceptance and rejection, presupposing and imagining the reactions of both its audience and the God it voices. The Hebrew Bible's covenants draw on both tribal (rituals of unity going back to ancient West Semitic traditions known from Ugarit and Mari) and imperial (the vassal treaties of the contemporary Assyrian empire) ritual to performatively enact a bond that is not allied to a state.[17] Hebrew models a political belonging through texts.

Ultimately, this book hopes to offer a way of understanding the Bible's astonishing fertility as a communicative form. As West Semitic tribal political thought reshaped alphabetic writing technology, the Hebrew Bible became foundational to a politics of recognition, where people saw themselves addressed by texts that called them together.[18] Ironically, this aggressively vernacular literature worked even more effectively in translation. This was because the ideology behind it lent itself to reproduction outside the language created for it. Vernacular form was only one vehicle for a larger goal of public address. The Bible's potential became bound up in a canonical literature whose meaning could be unpacked differently in different times and places.

In the European Renaissance, vernacular Bible translations explosively reactivated this ideology. Luther's Bible translation spoke, and forged, German; imitated, it challenged the church's Latin empire across Europe. Divine revelation spoke directly to the people. This biblical ideal helped make new kinds of unities possible, including that aspiration to linguistic, ethnic, and political unity that we call nationalism.

Arabic represents an alternative set of possibilities, also rooted in a West Semitic ideology of kinship-based politics and sharing a legacy of political communication with Hebrew. Like the Bible, the Qur'an is framed as a set of public pronouncements directly addressing a community as "you," the recitation and recognition of which helps call that people into being. Yet the language of the Qur'an seems never to have been anyone's vernacular. Qur'anic Arabic was not a language of place, but aspired to a kind of cosmopolitanism from the start. Thus classical Arabic mediated between an old ideology of kinship (reflected in the way the adjective *ʿarabī* refers to both a language and a people) and a new, trans-local political theology.[19] Speaking through Muhammad to anyone, anywhere, who was willing and able to hear, the Qur'an's text-mediated divine sovereignty became another way for texts to speak to, and generate, a community.

Both Europe and the Islamic world share a mode of political communication that emerged with the Hebrew Bible, the first vernacular literature designed to persuade a public. Documenting the invention of Hebrew helps illuminate a paradox of both the Bible and culture more generally: how the broad appeal of this mode of communication springs from its very specificity in directly addressing its audience as a people.

CHAPTER 1

Modernity's Ghosts: The Bible as Political Communication

Covenants, without the sword, are but words.
—Thomas Hobbes

THE TROUBLE WITH TEXTS

Accounts of biblical scholarship tend to begin with its fundamental assumptions already in place: they narrate the fragmentation of the text into sources, initiated in the eighteenth century and developed in the nineteenth. But the Bible was only vulnerable to source criticism because it could be seen as just a text, in a time when all texts had become fair game. What we need to understand is how it became possible for the Bible to be "just a text," how this sacred text lost its seemingly inherent power to make binding political claims on its audiences. This is the prologue to our investigation of where that power began: the question of what Hebrew and early Hebrew texts were for.

At the dawn of modern social thought, the Bible was a linchpin linking written language to political power: royal sovereignty and religious authority were thought to flow from its words. The stakes of biblical criticism were so high for seventeenth-century political philosophers that a work like Baruch Spinoza's *Tractatus Theologico-Politicus* could become at once "the philosophical founding-document of both modern biblical criticism and modern liberal democracy."[1] Spinoza and his contemporaries cleared the way for a new regime of thought and politics by showing that the biblical text was a historically relative product of its times. Its words were addressed to members of an ancient culture, subjects of a long-vanished kingdom, and therefore could not be binding on us.[2] They broke the Bible's link between language and power, exposing it as "but words."[3] By the nineteenth century this link had been so thoroughly shattered that the major task of biblical scholarship was to stratify its pieces. This deconstruction was intellectually liberating because it made the Bible newly available to historical and comparative thought.

But in throwing off the chains of the text's authority scholars lost sight of an important human phenomenon. This is the socially creative dimension of how a text speaks, not just what it says. Different ways of addressing people can put speakers in very different relationships with their audiences. This power goes beyond commonplace notions of rhetoric, in which speakers dress their arguments up in persuasive forms that their audiences will accept. While texts must draw on preexisting forms to communicate to their audiences, they can be politically creative by addressing audiences in new ways, thus helping bring new sorts of audiences and participants into being through their language. Any reader of the Bible can experience this by encountering the command to "Hear, O Israel!" (Deut. 6:4) and asking who was supposed to hear it and why people still can.

In creating the intellectual tools we use to study the Bible—philology, the opposition between orality and literacy, the very idea of "ancient" or "traditional" cultures—European scholarship also obscured the creative relationships between language and power. One of the great achievements of twentieth-century social theory has been to illuminate this relationship. We can examine how this modern way of studying ancient texts began, in hopes of correcting some of its errors and expanding its limits.

THE DISCOVERY OF THE NON-MODERN

The problems and potentials of biblical studies are often traced to the source criticism of the nineteenth century and the monumental works of its German founders such as W. M. L. de Wette and Julius Wellhausen. But their work, decisive as it was, would not have been doable before other conceptual shifts made the very idea of biblical studies possible: the biblical documents, which had once been thought to be authoritative and unified revealed texts, could only be effectively assigned to diverse ancient sources and cultural contexts after their nature had been rethought. This rethinking occurred in two major movements, one in seventeenth-century political philosophy, the other in eighteenth-century folklore and philology.

Biblical studies began as part of the intellectual work of modernity itself. It is no coincidence that biblical criticism was inaugurated along with modern political theory and developed along with folklore, ethnography, and philology, our premier ways of understanding the other.[4] This is because in order to imagine themselves as modern, Western European intellectuals needed ancient and traditional others to define themselves against. Our sense of the Bible's ancientness helped us forge our own modernness, and vice versa.

It is valuable to both biblical studies and social theory to see the role of each in the development of the other—particularly today, when much social theory accepts the premise that everything interesting begins with modernity, printing, and the nation-state. Current social theory's focus on the modern (the consequences of mass literacy, advanced capitalism, colonialism) and lack of interest in what comes before it tends to produce superficial accounts of the pre-modern, making modernity itself difficult to explain.[5] But before modernity became an unquestioned fait accompli, earlier social theorists had to construct the pre-modern; they only became modern by reflecting on what they were not.

This story or origin myth of modernity has been convincingly challenged. The extent to which modernity was *ever* accomplished is open to question, since scholars to this day cannot agree even on the century in which European modernity "really" began (cf. the anthropologist Bruno Latour's claim that *We Have Never Been Modern* [1993]). Richard Bauman and Charles Briggs have recently clarified the role the discovery of the ancient and primitive played in European intellectual self-understanding. Their *Voices of Modernity* details how scholars developed their understanding of the non-modern. Biblical and Homeric philology, folklore, and ethnography let early modern scholars discover a Great Divide between oral and literate, rural and urban, non-modern and modern, with "us" united on one side. But this "Great Divide could only be projected if *pre*modernity was itself constructed, shaped as a primordial realm that existed apart from modernity; indeed, it was premodernity that seemed to make modernity necessary" (Bauman and Briggs 2003:x).

Crucial to creating the modern was the idea of Language in the abstract. Language—meaning language in general as a scientific object of study, as opposed to different concrete languages—is something scholarship has discovered or constructed in a number of times and places.[6] Starting in the seventeenth century, European scholars began to differentiate various others from us through their use of Language. Writing and speaking became "literacy" and "orality," not just ways of communicating but ways of life: "literate societies" versus "oral societies." The two types of society had different characteristic genres: epic and poetry versus scientific essays and prose. They also had different politics: tribes and chiefdoms had oral poetry, nation-states and republics had written prose. The idea of Language helped European scholars define a clear gap between the modern and the non-modern. As the science of texts, philology helped render the boundaries between us and them precise and authoritative.

Early modern study of textual form had political consequences because it discovered a gap between authoritative modern knowledge, which belonged to European scholars, and traditional texts, which belonged to the various non-modern others who inhabited "oral societies." These enchanted but backward cultures included the peasants of contemporary Europe, modern Arabs, as well as Homer and the Israelites. Traditional texts were aesthetic and cultural sources, but could not transmit valid authority or knowledge. Philologists could show their insight by transporting us to these lost worlds where people talked and thought so differently, bridging the gap of tradition to recover antique survivals and fossils of our heritage. But modern scholarship highlighted the gap precisely by illuminating it: it made the ancient/modern divide visible.

The Discovery of the Gap between Ancients and Moderns

As natural as it seems to us today, people in the Middle Ages did not generally believe in a systematic difference between ancient and modern. The gap between ancient and modern ways of communicating began to be visible to scholars in a battle over sacred texts that took place in the fifteenth century, during the Renaissance, and in the sixteenth-century Reformation. In the Renaissance, humanists like Lorenzo Valla devoted gigantic rhetorical energies to what we would now call historical context. In violent conflicts, both verbal and political, they discovered and deployed the concept of anachronism.[7] Basic tools of philology were forged in conflicts about the claims of texts: Valla produced the first great historical criticism of a text in order to vivisect the Catholic Church's territorial claims, showing through linguistic and historical arguments that they were based on a forgery. The so-called Donation of Constantine, granting the Church massive territory in Europe, could not have been written by Constantine because it was phrased in language he never would have used, expressed concepts alien to him, and violated the most basic tenets of his policies.[8]

In the next century, during the Reformation, a series of similarly fundamental conflicts took place around religious communication: the notion that the senses could communicate authentic knowledge of the divine. No theological move highlights this revolution better than Ulrich Zwingli's reinterpretation of Christ's statement, of the bread at the Last Supper, that "this is my body" (Matt. 26:26; Mark 14:22; Luke 22:19). For centuries this had served as the proof text for transubstantiation, the doctrine that the bread of the Eucharist actually became Christ's body, and hence for the most important public ritual of medieval Christianity.[9] For Zwingli, however, Jesus' "is" (*est*, in the Vulgate) really meant "means" (*significat*), thus, "this bread *signifies* my body." In this move from direct *presentation* of the divine to its *representation* through signs, the bread of the Eucharist "now entered the semantic realm of representations rather than serving as a vehicle for the presentation of God to humanity."[10] The question set out by humanists like Erasmus "became less how the Word assumed flesh . . . than how the Word assumed meaning, as it did through preaching, prayer, and study."[11] Traditional texts and rituals could not directly present what is divine and authoritative; they could only signify it. The Eucharist became a text, subject to interpretation. Modern humanistic scholarship was inaugurated in this rethinking.

The intellectual and political stakes of these debates about communication were intertwined. The historical study of texts and the Protestant churches emerged together in debates about how tradition and writing can transmit truth. Their common concern was the attempt to access texts in their most original, and presumably therefore truthful, form. The humanists worked to establish accurate editions, while Protestant translation and printing of scripture promulgated access to the "original" word of God. Biblically based religion was a foundation of medieval European kingdoms.[12] It was called "Christendom" for a reason, whether reflecting the geopolitical reality of Charlemagne's short-lived empire or an aspiration as it did during most of the Middle Ages.[13] What would happen with broad access to the original word of God?

Fault lines between ancient tradition and modern authority, opened in the sixteenth century, split in the seventeenth. As humanists and reformers argued against the Church's political and economic power, European rulers acted violently to seize it.[14] What followed the Reformation were the Wars of Religion, a century of catastrophically bloody conflicts in France (1562–98), Spain and the Netherlands (c. 1567–93), and Germany (1618–48). Their horrors suggested to a new generation of thinkers that the word of God by itself could not transmit any unifying truth—perhaps the opposite. Thus in 1651, Thomas Hobbes published the *Leviathan* in the wake of the religiously based English Civil War in which the king himself had been tried and executed for treason.

Political Philosophy: The Destruction of Scriptural Authority

The study of the Bible in the seventeenth century was faced with an urgent question of political theology: Precisely where does scripture's authority—over the Israelites, over the later Christians, and over us ("us" being, quite pointedly, Christendom)—come from? Scholars tried to answer the question of scripture's authority by asking about its authorship: it examined anachronism, context, and logical consistency. Could the Five Books of Moses have been written by Moses when they say that nobody knows where Moses is buried? Could the self-described "humblest man in the world," as Numbers 12:3 calls Moses, actually be the most humble man in the world? Such passages implied that scripture was either absurd, inauthentic, or very complicated. The result—not unintended by thinkers such as Hobbes and Spinoza—of the early use of philological methods was the transformation—perhaps the destruction—of the question itself: "Where does scripture's authority come from?" became "Where does scripture come from?"

The turn to questions of sources—of traditions rather than of authority—was decisive. With its theological edge blunted, as the historian Jonathan Sheehan argues, "culture would be the new rock atop which the legitimacy of the Bible was built" (2005:xiv). But this diffuse and watery "legitimacy" was not the same as authority.[15] The central concern of biblical studies became the verification of documents, and the central question in the nineteenth and twentieth centuries became the decipherment of the Hebrew Bible as a representation of ancient Israel. No longer a political charter with claims on its readers, the most it could aspire to be was an authentic cultural document, somebody else's political charter. And perhaps it was not even that: the debate reached its extreme at the end of the twentieth century in the "maximalist/minimalist" polemic, with "minimalists" arguing that the Hebrew Bible was essentially a nostalgic false memory, forged in the Persian or Hellenistic period, and the "maximalists" emphasizing an authentic Iron or Late Bronze Age "historical kernel," the ghost of a once mighty biblical authority.[16]

With its arguments over this relatively feeble legitimacy, biblical studies could be seen as replaying the beginning of modernity for ever-decreasing stakes. But what if the game is over and the stakes have been taken off the table? It is of more than theoretical interest, therefore, to revisit that point at the beginning of the modern study of the Bible where modern philology and political theory were configured together. It is in books such as Hobbes's *Leviathan* (1651) and Spinoza's *Tractatus Theologico-Politicus* (1670)[17] that fundamental problems of biblical studies were conceived—or perhaps misconceived.

We will focus on perhaps the single most devastating passage in Hobbes where he both sets out a question that will occupy biblical studies for the next 350 years and warns that it is precisely the wrong one. A look at the question he offers in its place suggests that, for Hobbes as much as for later thinkers like Max Weber and Michel Foucault, problems of power are always shadowed by problems of communication.

Hobbes lays out the stakes for the early modern criticism of the Bible when he says that "the question of the Scripture is the question of what is law throughout all Christendom" (*Leviathan* 33 [260]).[18] Hobbes begins with the common assumption that the Bible provides the otherworldly foundation not just for political theory but for political authority. It is not that a king's immediate power to tax or kill is at stake, but a king's ability to give an account of what kings have in common that empowers him to tax or kill. What is at stake, then, is the source of the king's "monopoly of legitimate force," as Weber would later define the modern state. In question is not physical power but the account of its foundation: what Weber would call "legitimacy."

The strategic goal of Hobbes's biblical criticism is to give a competing account of state power. He wishes to replace the false old account of scripture as a source of legitimacy with his own superior account of the state's legitimacy, in which people collectively agree to cede their sovereignty to the "leviathan" of state power. Like the early modern philologists, he wants to clear away the unreliable old foundations of traditions and texts. Hobbes therefore explains that there is a crucial problem with biblical foundations, because divine law can only be known through documents promulgated by humans.[19]

> *For he only is properly said to reign that governs his subjects by his word* and by promise of rewards to those that obey it, by threatening them with punishment that obey it not. Subjects therefore in the kingdom of God are not bodies inanimate, nor creatures irrational; because they understand no precepts as his: nor atheists, nor they that believe not that God has any care of the actions of mankind; because they acknowledge no word for his, nor have hope of his rewards, or fear of his threatenings. They therefore that believe there is a God that governeth the world, and hath given precepts, and propounded rewards and punishments to mankind, are God's subjects; all the rest are to be understood as enemies.
>
> *To rule by words requires that such words be manifestly made known*; for else they are no laws: for to the nature of laws belongeth a sufficient and clear promulgation, such as may take away the excuse of ignorance; *which in the laws of men is but of one only kind, and that is, proclamation or promulgation by the voice of man.* (*Leviathan* 31 [246], emphasis mine)

Hobbes's problem here is that you cannot really obey God through the Bible; you can only believe him. While the Bible provided a political identity for "Christendom" through *belief,* it was manifestly not law. This is because law can only be promulgated by humans, communicated through documents, and backed by physical force. As he writes, "he only is properly said to reign that governs his subjects by his word." All creatures and things are ruled by natural law, the irresistible physical rules that order the universe, but some are either unable or unwilling to obey God's word. It is obedience to words that defines God's kingdom, leading to the harsh political distinction Hobbes says the Bible makes: "They therefore that *believe* there is a God that governeth the world, . . . are God's subjects; all the rest are to be understood as enemies."

But being believed is not sovereignty. Sovereignty is having one's words both known and obeyed, and that requires communication: the only politically relevant way to come into contact with God's words is to read documents. This is because, as Hobbes argues in chapter 32 [256], even if God communicated directly to an individual, the person would have no way to convince anyone else that it was God who spoke.[20] "To rule by words requires that such words be manifestly made known" and that requires "promulgation by the voice of man."

Here, Hobbes says, we must reconsider what is the essential political question of scripture: Where does its authority arise?

> It is a question much disputed between the divers sects of Christian religion, *From whence the Scriptures derive their Authority,* which question is also propounded sometimes in other terms, as, *How we know them to be the word of God or, Why we believe them to be so.* And the difficulty of resolving it, ariseth chiefly from the improperness of the words wherein the question itself is couched. For it is believed on all hands, that the first and original *Author* of them is God; and consequently the question disputed is not that. Again, it is manifest, that none can know they are God's word (though all true Christians believe it) but those to whom God himself hath revealed it supernaturally; and therefore, the question is not rightly moved of our *Knowledge* of it. Lastly, when the question is propounded of our *Belief,* because some are moved to believe for one, and others for other reasons, there can be rendered no one general answer for them all. The question truly stated is, *By what authority they are made law.* (*Leviathan* 33 [267], emphasis in original)

Hobbes shows that the question of the Bible's authority is the wrong one: it does not matter whether it is the word of God. He reaches this startling conclusion by breaking the supposed question down into two things people actually mean when they ask it. The first is how we "know" the scriptures to be the word of God; the second is why we "believe" them to be so. He says these are the wrong questions: "it is believed on all hands that the first and original *author* of them is God"—everybody believes it. But "it is manifest that none can know they are God's word (though all true Christians believe it) but those to whom God himself hath revealed it supernaturally"—and

Hobbes has already shown at length (in chapter 32) that supernatural revelation cannot compel assent. Not only does nobody know it, but if they were to know it, it would not matter. It makes no difference whether or not the Bible is the word of God.

In his plainspoken way, Hobbes has made it seem evident that revelation cannot matter politically. "The question truly stated is: *By what authority they are made law.*" The only question is why—or if—anyone obeys a text. The fact that it may come from God is irrelevant: as soon as a text is promulgated by humans—and the only politically relevant documents are ones promulgated by the "voice of man"— it becomes just another text, no matter who wrote it. Scripture can have no power to compel assent; it takes a state to make them law. So there is nothing in scripture that makes it scripture: the state's decision to compel obedience is the only thing that makes a difference.

At this founding moment of biblical studies, Hobbes has made a series of deft moves to shut it down, to prove the debate would be politically fruitless. All the philology in the world cannot change the essential fact that the text is just a text. Because of the private nature of revelation, which can never be mediated between people without losing its certain link to God, the word of God is *inherently* not a public matter. It only becomes public when it becomes human, published and enforced by the state. No matter what history lies behind the Bible, the document it produced should be understood in the same way as any other document.

These powerful arguments are based on a Hobbesean theory of language, which is that everything words can do must first be defined by human authority.[21] Texts cannot found any legitimate authority, for example, by their persuasive force. In this theory, all texts have the same status vis-à-vis the state: they need violence to enforce them. Questions of authorship and authenticity are irrelevant because they have no bearing on the brute facts of authority: they may be interesting, but they should change nothing.[22]

Hobbes's critique is foundational but it is also crippling. To the extent that his critique founds biblical studies it also neutralizes it by showing that the Bible is politically and theologically inert by itself. It cannot connect knowledge to power, and its textual messages are by definition no different from anyone else's: as mere communication, they should not compel obedience. Once church and state are separated, the Bible is de facto not authoritative anymore, and for Hobbes the de facto realm is all that matters. If we accept the theory that all written texts are the same—that writing is a semiotic technology necessary but transparent to authority, that all texts are inherently uniform—the question of what the Bible *did* and *does* as writing is off the table.[23] "Covenants, without the sword," as Hobbes put it, "are but words."

Folklore and Philology: The Construction of Non-Modern Language

If Hobbes showed that traditional texts could not found power, John Locke and his successors showed that they could not transmit knowledge. Locke, who came of age during the English Civil War, describes his *Essay Concerning Human Understanding* (1690) as provoked by an argument in which none of the people involved could find a common ground to stand on. The topic, which Locke circumspectly avoids mentioning, was (according to the testimony of another participant) revelation.[24] Locke's critiques of traditional texts were designed to save language from the semantic indeterminacy and unreliable authority that led to irresolvable disputes, whether over revelation or politics. Thus he argues that "in traditional truths, each remove weakens the force of the proof" (*Essay* IV.xvi.10; similar arguments appear as critiques of the Torah in Spinoza). To make the world safe for rational discourse, he formulated a campaign to purify language of reliance on beliefs derived from texts and authorities, in short, on tradition. He opposed traditional textual authority to the rational, universal knowledge that could be gained independently by the thinking individual.[25] This emerging view of traditional language was what Locke drew on for his vision of "how modern subjects should *not* think, speak, write, and act."[26]

Locke made the decisive move of conceptualizing tradition as the non-rational opposite of modern rationality. But if he declared war on tradition, the enemy was a vague target: the irrational discourse of women and lower-class men in the contemporary society that surrounded educated men of reason. It took another generation of thought on the nature of tradition to locate the problem fundamentally in the past. The notion of a past oral tradition opposed to modern literacy was conceived by early folklorists like Henry Bourne (1696–1733) and his successor John Brand (1744–1806). They studied the stories and beliefs of lower-class and rural people as relics—decayed remnants of the past that persisted in the present in the sayings of peasants. The traditions of past societies became evident in the survival of oral cultures, living antiquities.

Early modern scholars' pursuit of the threads of non-modern language led them back in time to Homer and the Bible. They moved from oral testimonies of modern "primitives" in English society to actual ancient texts. While the antiquarian work of scholars like Bourne and Brand found ancient survivals in the present, philologists such as Thomas Blackwell (1701–57), Robert Wood (1717?-71), and Bishop Robert Lowth (1710–87) discovered them in authoritative texts like Homer and the Hebrew Bible. Greek and Hebrew philology began in the service of canons, from Alexandrian scholarship on Homer to the Masoretic study of Hebrew. It was humanistic philology that began to critique the form of classical and biblical texts. The eighteenth century took this critique further as the most canonical of works were radically rethought, relativized in terms of the modern/non-modern divide.

The idea of oral poetry originated in a search for a social context to explain the aesthetic power of Greek epic. Thomas Blackwell wanted to explain why nobody had done poetry as good as Homer's in more than two thousand years. To provide such an explanation, he imagined an intermediate stage of social development when people could turn fresh memories of heroic violence into sophisticated art. It does not appear, he observed, to be "given to one and the same Kingdom, to be thoroughly civilized, and afford proper subjects for poetry. The marvelous and wonderful is the nerve of the epic strain. But what marvelous things happen in a well-ordered state?"[27] His focus on composition in performance began an intellectual tradition that reached fruition in the oral-formulaic theory of Milman Parry and Albert Lord. This theory was applied to Hebrew and Ugaritic poetry by Umberto Cassuto, William F. Albright, and Frank Moore Cross. Blackwell's oral/literate divide followed a political typology: from improvised oral poetry about tribal violence to orderly, if boring, civilized prose.[28]

Robert Wood found he could actually visit examples of these excitingly violent tribal societies in the Middle East, linking Homer and the Bible to modern primitives. His travels let him encounter a kind of pre-modern time preserved in space. Discovering the link between the ancient and the primitive let him systematize the modern/non-modern gap into a typological contrast between oral and literate societies and stages of cultural development. If one traveled far enough in space one could also journey back in time, because the contemporary Mediterranean preserved living ancient culture. Wood's vision placed the past, both living and written, "in deep contrast to European modernity, not simply in terms of neutrally conceived cultural differences, but in moral, ideological terms as well."[29]

This elevation of media differences, "orality" and "literacy," into modes of thought and politics retains its vitality in biblical studies. The oral/literate divide was a feature of modernist discourse through the twentieth century, exemplified by the work of Eric Havelock, Walter J. Ong, and Jack Goody. These scholars provided theoretical resources for the way Biblicists and epigraphers like Cassuto, Albright, and Cross understood both Hebrew epic and alphabet. And they continue to provide a theoretical framework for twenty-first-century studies of writing in ancient Israel.[30]

The connection between theories of orality and biblical studies has been deep and productive. Arguably the greatest of the eighteenth-century philologists was the modern discoverer of biblical Hebrew poetic structure, Bishop Robert Lowth. His argument that Isaiah's prophecies should be understood as poetry revolutionized biblical interpretation by showing that the same critical techniques that had been applied to secular poetry could be applied to scripture. Major interpretive difficulties could be solved through the division of the text, by language and genre, into prose and poetry. Lowth posited the sacred writings of the Hebrews as central to the larger project of discovering the pre-modern, "the only specimens of the primeval and genuine poetry to be found," and thus of antiquarian as well as spiritual value.[31] His discovery that the book of Isaiah was written in poetry was part of a new view that the ancients, like rural and primitive people in the modern world, communicated differently from the way moderns do.

The Poetics and Politics of Linguistic Form

Lowth most brilliantly raised the question of the grammatical and poetic form in which biblical and other traditional texts communicate, and what this has to do with the form of the societies they come from. Even as Lowth's view led to a new understanding of biblical prophecy, it complicated its status as a perfect and revealed divine text. Isaiah was different from us in some of the same ways that both Homer and European peasant folktales were.

This understanding of linguistic difference as signifying a cultural and political gap has come to be known as the oral/literate divide, a way in which our own canonical ancient texts were connected to the living antiquities preserved by people ranging from Middle Eastern Bedouin to English peasants. Traditional texts, and the traditional societies they came from, used proverbs and poetry; we moderns had rationality, natural science, and prose. This transition between oral and literate is seen as repeated among every people whose history we know through writing; as the folk grow up, they lose touch with primitive inspiration, a process that was already occurring in ancient times. And this folk poetry, in every place it is encountered, is "inherently in a state of decay." As Bauman and Briggs put it, the *Volk* is by definition disappearing, whether through the rise of prosaic forms (like the Torah and Priestly law), or capitalism and industrialization.[32]

Lowth's attempt to reconstruct the rules of Hebrew verse set the standard followed by scholars like Cassuto and the Albright school: while later misunderstanding had garbled the pristine form, fragmentary "vestiges of verse" could be found in the text. These grammatical features included regular syllable counts, special particles, "frequent change of persons," "more frequent change or variation of the tenses than occurs in common language," and poetic parallelism, the division of a line into two (or more) grammatically and semantically analogous parts, the second of which echoes, extends, or plays upon the first. The most decisive of these features was parallelism: here Lowth perceived a poetic form in which linguistic form, thematic content, and ritual function were interrelated, laying the groundwork, as Roman Jakobson pointed out, for the first structural understanding of texts.[33]

But if the eighteenth-century discovery of oral tradition in ancient texts made them comprehensible as antiquities, it also made them primitive in a way that has continued to be problematic: the archaic biblical poems were good culture but bad history.[34] Hugh Blair (1718–1800) argued against seeing traditional texts as providing a history of "events"—no great loss, since they are often obscure and uninteresting—and focusing on a history of "manners"—what we would now call a history of Israelite tradition:

> History, when it treats of remote or dark ages, is seldom very instructive. The beginnings of society, in every country, are involved with fabulous confusion; and though they were not, they would furnish few events worth recording. But, in every period of society, human manners are a curious spectacle, and the most natural pictures of ancient manners are exhibited in the ancient poems of nations. These present to us, what is much more valuable than the history of such transactions as a rude age can afford, the history of human imagination and passion.[35]

We can see a fundamental contradiction of twentieth-century biblical studies take form here: Israelite tradition as authentic but false. Blair's focus on "manners" fits uncomfortably with the history of "events" that can only be reconstructed from dubious oral accounts or, eventually, through conjectural form- and source-critical work. Oral poetry is tied not to history but a primal political collectivity: the poems are recited at "feasts, sacrifices and public assemblies" that move them to song.[36] It was these conjectural collective institutions that biblical scholars such as Sigmund Mowinckel were to reconstruct in the covenant-renewal ceremony of the early Israelite tribal league or the enthronement ritual of the primal Davidic monarchy. The problem for Mowinckel's theory, as with Albright's and Cross's elaborations of it, was the lack of contemporary evidence; no excavated Late Bronze or Iron Age documents mention them. The early, oral, institutional structure had to be reconstructed through later written traditions. When their conjectures lost conviction and the consensus assumptions about history were questioned, the integrity of the whole became dubious.

And Lowth's discovery of Hebrew poetic structure had a surprising further effect in politics: it helped form modern nationalism through the strange case of Ossian, the supposed third-century C.E. national bard of Scotland. When James MacPherson began to publish what he described as translations of these traditional oral epics in 1760, they fulfilled a valuable role for a Scotland that still rued its loss of political autonomy and would be flattered to discover ancient traditions that could withstand historical misfortune. His work, purporting to derive from unpublished Celtic texts, became the subject of intense excitement and controversy.

And nationalism, in turn, influenced biblical studies just as the scholarly discovery of Hebrew had influenced European nationalism. Blair's adulatory *Critical Dissertation on the Poems of Ossian, son of Fingal* (1763) appeared only a year after MacPherson's *Fingal*. The *Critical Dissertation*, contrary to its name, was in fact the first extended pitch for authentic oral poetry as the great emblem of national identity. Major intellectual figures like the German Romantic philosopher Johann Gottfried Herder (1744–1803) heralded Ossian, giving the work tremendous influence across eighteenth-century Europe. Ossian's poetry became "a charter document in the great movement towards vernacularization of literature in the Western world, which was fundamental, in turn, to the coalescence of nationalist ideologies and the formation of modern nation-states."[37] Herder was then able to assume, and promote, the seamless unity of language, culture, and politics—especially in ancient Israel.

This eighteenth-century nationalism helps explain why the writing down of Hebrew has generally remained invisible as a significant historical event. We have come to consider national written literatures natural—widespread, tending toward egalitarianism, "popular"—to the extent that we assume that just as French people naturally read French texts, so Israelites read Hebrew ones. Not only was this far from the case in the ancient Near East (and even early modern Europe), but it required a great deal of work for this view to become natural. And this work was only possible because of prior European reflection on the Hebrew Bible.

In considering the unity of the Scottish oral epics, Blair describes Ossian as having "a remarkable resemblance to the style of the Old Testament." But the resemblance was rather more direct than Blair thought: it emerged that MacPherson, though familiar with traditional Scottish poetry, had drawn on Lowth and the King James Bible, rather than any specific Celtic text, for his "translations"![38]

Lowth's model of Hebrew poetry fed modern nationalism most brilliantly through Herder. As a model for creating a Scottish national folk epic, it provided a central inspiration for Herder's theory of folk poetry and song as the vehicle of national-historical identity. As we will see, Herder's theory then provided the core typology of biblical language and writing used by influential twentieth-century scholars such as Cross and Cassuto. Both modern biblical studies and the modern nation-state were inspired by this thinking.

Early modern antiquarian and philological thought culminated in Herder's theory of national literature, in which ancient Israel's fusion of text and authority had pride of place.[39] He described Moses as poet, "liberator and lawgiver" of the Hebrews, stating that "the greatest part of their poetry, which is often taken to be spiritual, is political." And if, in ancient Israel, the poetic is the political, Hebrew is "more poetical than any other language on earth."[40]

Herder's literary theory was inherently political: he viewed poetry's fundamental role as the constitution and self-recognition of peoples. The main function of tradition is to form groups and generate authority. "The fathers taught their children, the lawgivers and so-called wise men taught the public, which was called the people." Herder understood the power of vernacular literature as fundamentally reflexive: poetry allows a people "to portray themselves, and see themselves, as they are." People represent and recognize themselves as a unity because of the unity of their distinct group language, and "only through language can a people exist."[41]

In the early modern discovery of the non-modern, it is the two scholars of the Bible, Herder and Lowth, who offered the most productive views of the power of texts: not through a mystical idea of their inherent authority, but through their analyses of the form-function relationship. Their ways of reading texts as culture and politics reached beyond the evolutionary scheme from primitive to modern. Yet what tended to dominate the discussion was precisely this evolutionary typology that rendered the texts of the past neutral and inert, their power difficult to understand as more than pre-modern irrationality.

HERDER'S HEIRS: THE STAKES OF BIBLICAL PHILOLOGY

Herder's theory was transformed into a research project by the great Germanic philologists and folklorists of the nineteenth century, Wilhelm and Jacob Grimm. Hermann Gunkel, founder of biblical form criticism, laid his work out along lines provided by the Grimms. While his first project, *Creation and Chaos at the Beginning and End of Time,* laid out a brilliant, and equally promising, historical morphology of myth,[42] the most productive model Gunkel provided for biblical studies was (perhaps, unfortunately) his discovery of folk genres in the Hebrew Bible, e.g., *The Folk-Tale in the Old Testament (Das Märchen im Alten Testament),* on the model of Grimms' *Kinder- und Hausmärchen* (1812–15). The Grimms professionalized the collecting and editing of folk texts. They deployed the full powers of their Germanic and Indo-European research to recontextualize the traditions they discovered, turning scattered manuscripts and interviews into authoritative evidence for the history of folk culture. They made textual scholarship into a linguistic science, carving out an autonomous realm of specialist expertise.[43]

The philological recovery of Israelite culture, undertaken in biblical studies by scholars like Gunkel and Wellhausen, reached a similar pinnacle of professionalism by the middle of the twentieth century. With the discoveries of an actual ancient West Semitic archive at Ugarit and early biblical manuscripts at Qumran, the database had grown radically. The philological apparatus of Albright's and Cross's articles was part of their message, manifesting itself graphically in a swelling sea of footnotes supporting the raft of the main text. These displays of erudition were no mere decoration—their insights flowed from extensive philological work—but they also served to create a visual authority, impressing and intimidating students and colleagues alike.[44] Albright's and Cross's work of dating pots, scripts, and—most important for our purposes—poems by typology arose from a morphological technique pioneered by Johann Wolfgang von Goethe and configured by the Grimms.[45]

The tools of philology, guided by evolutionist typology, allowed them to re-create texts from early, oral stages of Israelite society. The legendary double-dissertations of Cross and Freedman put Albright's more scattered, article-length statements on the development of spelling and poetic texts into an extended, disciplined form: the second, *Studies in Ancient Yahwistic Poetry* (1950), built on the conclusions reached in the first, *The Evolution of Early Hebrew Orthography: The Epigraphic Evidence* (1948), to precisely reconstruct just the sort of religion imagined by Romantic folklorists and philologists. The first paragraph of *Studies in Ancient Yahwistic Poetry* describes its subject:

> In this small body of literature are preserved the oldest expressions of Israel's faith. It reveals a conception of God at once intuitive and concrete, born of vividly direct experience and participation in his mighty acts, a conception devoid of the sophistication and formalism which results from centuries of theological speculation. The language of the poems is rich and exuberant, the imagery is picturesque, the figures of speech extravagant. The compositions are marked by a strong rhythm, with a regular musical beat, frequently organized into strophes of considerable complexity. Altogether, they are the product of the most dynamic and creative era of Israel's literary enterprise. (Cross and Freedman 1975:3)

Here philology comes full circle, hinting at renewed access to God through just those irrational elements of language Locke hoped to expunge: a poetic conception "born of vividly direct experience and participation in his mighty acts." Their linguistics and epigraphy ended up as excavative tools, digging through the current forms of the texts to gain access to the folkloric and theological sources of Israelite religion. A quarter century later, they insisted that "the reconstruction of early Israelite religion, whether of the Fathers or of Moses and his followers, requires equal attention to backgrounds: cultural, linguistic, mythological, and historical" (afterword in Cross and Friedman 1975:186).

Today, as less technically formidable studies of the literary form and interpretive afterlife of biblical texts have taken center stage, we can gain perspective on the Albright school's Germanically inspired philology. Their techniques of epigraphy and historical linguistics remain powerful and productive intellectual tools. But we can reconsider the Romantic and evolutionist presuppositions that made the primary linguistic and historical data into "backgrounds" for development. Philological tools can tell us new things if we are willing to listen to the linguistic and historical "backgrounds" they uncover.[46]

Social Theory in Philology: Nationalism, Antiquarianism, and Modern Biblical Scholarship

Of the oppositions between ancient and modern that early modern scholars discovered, the one most central to twentieth-century biblical scholarship was the oral/literate divide. In this view, non-modern societies are characterized by forms of oral poetry, now dying or lost and beginning to be misunderstood even in ancient times, which are opposed to modern literacy (what Bauman and Briggs call the *gap-making* function of modernity). On the other hand, oral tradition can persist, albeit in decayed form, through traditional texts and ceremonies. In this view, it becomes the task and defining privilege of scholars to present tradition as the legacy of a national or cultural "us" (the gap-bridging function of modernity).

Seeing Israelite oral poetry as Canaanite and ancient Near Eastern tradition, part of a misunderstood or lost past, falls under the gap-making rubric. When this tradition is imagined as continuous with later culture, the mature "Hebrew epic" we can still read in the Bible, it falls under the gap-bridging rubric.[47] Not only Herder and the brothers Grimm but also Gunkel and Wellhausen continued to imagine Israelite oral tradition as the primeval opposite of a rational, prosaic culture, whether that of "late" Judaism or of our own era. It is in the scholar's power to remind us of the text's strangeness and recover its traditional context. This political-literary typology continues to resonate throughout biblical studies in the evocative titles of Cross's books, *Canaanite*

Myth and Hebrew Epic and *From Epic to Canon* as well as Tamara Eskenazi's work on Ezra and Nehemiah, *In an Age of Prose.*

Cross's work, with its integration of every dimension of philology from historical linguistics to source and textual criticism, is the most impressive example of how scholarship productively built on the eighteenth-century developmentalist typology of Blackwell and his peers. His work implies a typological passage from *Myth* to *Epic* to *Canon* like Blackwell's, in which "the appreciation of epic poetry . . . locates it at a point in the developmental trajectory of nations between the beginnings of society and language and the modern condition, though nearer the former than the latter. Epic—poetry in general—is an historical hybrid, affecting and powerful but of the past."[48]

The stakes were different in the modern nation-state of Israel. In the mid-twentieth-century, Israeli scholars applied oral-traditional theory to the Bible practically, as part of the revival of both the Hebrew language and *Volk.* Studies in this topic were carried out by the Israeli comparative school represented by Cassuto and his student Samuel Loewenstamm.[49] Cassuto's "The Israelite Epic" appeared in 1943 in Hebrew, the newly revived ancient national language.[50] Cassuto's essay arrived a scant eight years after the discovery of the Lachish letters, the first ancient Hebrew correspondence discovered from the last days of Jerusalem's autonomy in the 580s B.C.E., and five years before the foundation of the State of Israel. Writing in a nation that was itself being formed along Herderian and biblical lines, Cassuto sensed the potential of the newly discovered Ugaritic epic for the reconstruction of the original Israelite folk literature.

Had Herder written in Hebrew, the lines could have been his:

> That prose-writings should begin to appear after poetry is a common phenomenon in the history of world literature. Poesy issues from the youthful strength of young peoples, whereas prose is the product of the experience and reflection of adult nations. As for narrative prose, it forms among various peoples a continuation, as it were, of epic poetry, in conformity with the new requirements of a maturing public, which still clings to certain elements of epic discourse.[51]

Cassuto sums up modernist antiquarian thought almost eerily. But again, he encounters the problem that none of this youthful poetry is preserved in actual epics. So the task is to excavate "fossilized expressions" of epic in prose, Wood's and Blackwell's antiquities within the text. Cassuto sets about to reconstruct an Israelite version of the Pan-Near-Eastern epic of the "revolt of the seas" preserved in biblical fragments. He begins with two striking allusions to God's victory over a cosmic monster. The first, from Isaiah 51:9–10, is cited as: "Arise, arise, clothe yourself in might, Arm of the Lord! Arise as in days of old, as in ages past! Are you not he who cut Rahab, who pierced Tannin? Are you not he who dried up Sea, the waters of the great Deep?"

As his second example, he cites Psalm 74:12–15: "But God, (you are) my king of old, who makes victory within the land. You split Sea with your might, shattered the heads of the dragons on the water. It is you who crushed to pieces the heads of Leviathan, who made him food for the people of the desert. It is you who split open spring and wadi, you dried up the perpetually flowing rivers!" The two texts share parallels with Baal's battle with the Sea in Ugaritic epic (KTU 1.2 IV).

But Cassuto must make delicate choices, not only with respect to these texts' archaism but with respect to their gender. The parallels are real, as these two texts manifestly share grammatical features with each other and lexical and thematic items with Ugaritic. But Cassuto pointedly does not mention another striking feature of the texts: both explicitly set themselves in the sixth-century B.C.E. Babylonian exile, the period after the death of Israelite autonomy and kingship. That is, these are explicitly late compositions. Second, the first text is actually addressed to a personified *female* being (despite the translation "he" in English, the Hebrew uses the third-person feminine singular pronoun and feminine singular participles in a sequence of addresses to a personified female being), and thus shares its closest grammatical and thematic affinities with addresses to an Ugaritic goddess.[52] In other words, these Israelite epic texts are both problematically late and problematically pagan.

Cassuto's moves exemplify how philologists carry on the work of Blackwell and Herder, recognizing and producing antiquities by extracting them from literary context. Even more interestingly for his role as a national philologist, Cassuto purifies these texts from foreign religion:

> The Israelites saw in the ancient saga . . . a symbol of *ethical* and *national* concepts.
>
> The Torah then came and made use of the material of this poem in its own way; it refined and purified this material; it was careful not to accept such features as were foreign to its spirit—for instance, anything that was grossly corporeal or smacked of mythology.[53]

Like Cross, Cassuto does more than just replicate Herder: in place of the modernist's oral/literate gap, there is now also an epic/canon gap. For twentieth-century philologists—interestingly, both Protestants like Albright and Cross and Jewish nationalists like Cassuto—the Torah purges this *volkisch* heritage of myth.[54]

After providing evidence for no less than eleven other possible ancient epics (1975:103–9), Cassuto implicitly connects the recovery of these antiquities to a national revival. "Our ancestors possessed a complete epic literature till after the Babylonian Exile and the Return to Zion." He concludes with the hope that just as excavation has uncovered epigraphic evidence of the last generation of the First Temple at Lachish, "so may it be granted to us to behold, through some fortunate discovery in the near future, relics of the ancient epic poetry of the people of Israel" (1975:109). The national revival resurrects the folk epic through philology.[55]

Toward Philology in Social Theory

Herder exalted the political creativity of ancient Hebrew: not only did it allow Israel "to portray themselves, and see themselves, as they are," but "only through language can a people exist."[56] Scholars like Bauman and Briggs debunk as based on hidden inequality the sort of deep horizontal comradeship Herder exalts.[57] Yet people continue to live and die for entities and ideas that extend beyond themselves in space and time. Is self-representation through language just a Romantic nationalist myth? Such questions are precisely where political thought begins, and why we reread writers like Hobbes.

In the twentieth century, Michel Foucault was most prominent in putting the relationship between power and knowledge back on the table. Jürgen Habermas, in his famous 1962 *Habilitationsschrift* (Habermas 1989), argued more specifically that a new political world, which he called the public sphere, arose when public texts began to speak in the voice of citizens, not just the king. Benedict Anderson's 1983 study of the modern nation-state as something in the first instance *imagined* through the textual forms of newspapers and novels also put this thinking in a concrete historical shape. And Michael Warner, most recently (2002), has compellingly argued that the public, that group from which both governments and markets derive legitimacy, is itself called into being by the circulation of texts. Yet the notion of texts' political power has been retained in biblical studies mostly in the diminished form of "ideology" and "legitimation" (often in scare quotes), the notion of traditional authority as hoodwinking and propaganda.[58]

Biblical criticism and its subject have played a crucial part in this history and may have more to offer. Discussions of the linguistic form in which the Bible transmits authority have solidified around the oral/literate opposition, with positions staked up along the two poles of an early authentic oral core (preserved in linguistically archaic or archaizing texts such as Exodus 15, Deuteronomy 32 and 33, and Judges 5, which Biblicists categorize as Archaic

Biblical Hebrew) or a late synthetic scribal creation (Late Biblical Hebrew, in which books like Ezra, Nehemiah, Esther, and most of Daniel are written). The only other positions available seem to be compromise formations in which the two are blended together.[59]

How can we draw on the insights of the scholarship we have reviewed while rejecting its evolutionary prejudices? First, this book looks at a body of textual evidence—early alphabetic writing in Israel—that is peculiarly suited to challenging the oral/literate opposition and the evolutionary typology it is based on, reopening the early modern question of the relationship between textual medium and political authority. The problem with scripture has always been a problem with tradition, transmitted from a distant past. What would happen if we addressed this foundational question of biblical studies to texts that were actually from Iron Age Israel, as opposed to scripture in its distinctively Late Antique form? How did the language of the Hebrew Bible communicate when it was first written down?

Even Hobbes admitted that texts are essential to sovereignty: a sovereign is the one whose words are obeyed. But how are those words communicated? Everyone would agree that political ideas and activities do not spread through thin air, but require some kind of medium to be passed on, and in many cases the medium is part of the message. The public that Habermas's, Anderson's, and Warner's new printed newspapers and novels addressed was a new kind of political actor, a collective of modern citizens: the literary "we" of the novels and newspapers became the political "we" of "we the people." The answers of theorists like Anderson and Warner are specific to the modern period, but their questions—about the historical connections between the concrete ways people produce texts, the literary forms they take, and the political situations their texts presuppose and help create—encourage us to trace the political engagements of texts without flattening literature into "ideology" in the weak sense, transmitted from elite propagandists to passive audience. Epigraphic evidence now allows glimpses into the historical relationship between the forms in which ancient West Semitic speakers wrote, the genres they used, and the political forms they imagined in writing and enacted in history.

Second, then, this book asks if the originality of ancient West Semitic texts can be understood not in terms of their faded archaism but in terms of their innovation as political communication. As with Hobbes's question of political theology, the question that might arise is whether our current framework is even suited to doing this—can we ask political questions of Iron Age texts that philology can answer? Currently, little theoretical attention is focused on epigraphic texts or historical contexts. Much of the field's intellectual energy seems devoted to either the importation of decades-old trends (especially the canonization of brilliant but already canonically subversive literary theorists) or the replaying of battles over the authority of scripture in a form already old in the seventeenth century.[60] This is perhaps why the polarizing debate between "maximalists" and "minimalists" in the 1990s could captivate so many scholars within biblical scholarship and relatively few outside of it.[61] Strikingly absent is theory developed through thinking about the Bible.[62]

CONCLUSION

It is never enough to simply point out the limits of scholarship. Bauman and Briggs emphasize the horizons that philological thinking opened up: a genuinely relativist understanding, in which empathic projection and cultural context are key to entry: Blackwell's dictum that we must "put ourselves in the place of the audience" implies "commensurability, the potential for translation from one culture to another" (2003:96).[63] The problem with the critique of scholars like Cassuto and Cross we have just finished making is that, while they are Herderian in important ways, they also may be right in important ways. Cassuto and Cross cared deeply and attended carefully to the forms in which the texts communicated, and connected them with their continuing productivity and power. So they may be most right in precisely the ways that they are most Herderian. This explains much of the impact of Anderson's work: while many intellectuals examined and debunked nationalism, Anderson, like Herder, encourages us to think historically about the ways art and language help make forms of self-organization possible, without reducing them to mere ideological hoodwinking. Each in his own way, Foucault, Habermas, Warner, and Anderson represent productive revisitings of Herder's insight into the power of media and linguistic form to produce belonging. This book hopes to participate with these scholars in rereading the folk-poetic foundations of biblical studies.

Due to a combination of long-running interests and recent politics, some of Herder's heirs in anthropology are now deeply occupied with the question of political communication in "non-modern" Semitic-speaking cultures. Contemporary Arabic political poetry in Yemen "requires expanding our notions of textual culture beyond the kind of literate, formally educated domains typically foregrounded in studies of public culture" (F. Miller 2007:31). Such scholarship pays "special attention to the construction of audiences as 'addressees'" through poetic and grammatical forms and examines "the ways in which both artists and audiences collaborate in crafting new witnessing subjects whose ratification underscores new forms of collectivity" (F. Miller

2007:30). It is this agenda in linguistic anthropology that the present study will pursue in philology. Studying language in context lets us grasp the founding power of words Hobbes excluded in favor of the sword.

When we ask about the political creativity of texts, all of us—political theorists, anthropologists, and philologists—ultimately stand in a tradition formed by Hobbes, Lowth, and Herder. The ancient epigraphic evidence now available provides a strategic place to reopen early modern questions of interest to all three disciplines. Early alphabetic texts, and the history of Hebrew writing, have a particular historical significance as political communication. As deliberately local culture, made by people familiar with multiple modes of writing, they constitute a new form of self-representation, in ways Herder would have recognized and in others he might not have. The Bible's mode of address assumes participation in a polity that spans time and space, letting us examine perhaps the most durable way people imagined communities beyond empires or nation-states. Epigraphy provides a starting point to examine the claims of ancient texts as something more than either sacred truth or premodern error.

CHAPTER 2

What Was the Alphabet For?

Das große Gefühl . . . daß wir Ein Volk sein,
Eines Vaterlandes, Einer Sprache.
The great feeling that we are one people,
of one fatherland, one language.

—Johann Gottfried Herder

A sprach iz a dialekt mit an armee un flot.
A language is a dialect with an army and a navy.

—Max Weinreich

THE RISE OF WRITTEN VERNACULARS

Hebrew as a New Possibility

The existence of Hebrew writing, and the resulting possibility of a written account of Israel, has been largely taken for granted.[1] We assume that, once they reached a certain level of development, it would be natural for Israelites to use the language they spoke to write about themselves.[2] But the very idea that each people should have its own written language, let alone its own history, turns out to be a parochial assumption with a very limited basis in the ancient Near East. Only with the rise of European nation-states in the eighteenth century did the idea of national literatures spread: that the French should speak and write French or the Germans speak and write German. In most documented times and places, including the ancient Near East, writing, speech, and political order did not have any necessary relationship with each other.[3]

Not only did people in the Iron Age Levant not expect to write their own languages; history was not supposed to be about them. Previous historical narratives centered on kings, so that the idea of writing the history of a people would hardly have been natural. Indeed, there is no evidence that Israel's cultural ancestors had any interest in this topic. As Mark S. Smith has pointed out (2007:8), among the varied and abundant texts produced by the earlier West Semitic-speaking city-states of the Levant, we find no evidence of histories or chronicles. This is despite the fact that these city-states were intimately familiar with Mesopotamian high culture, where chronicles and historical inscriptions had long been central. But Mesopotamian history was for kings; collective groups played a marginal role as docile subjects or hostile marauders.

The Bible's impact requires us to consider the deliberate writing down of Hebrew as a significant historical event. The invention of Hebrew opened up possibilities at once linguistic and political: a literature could now be both addressed to, and written about, a people. These new possibilities, made concrete in the Bible, demand explanation. It is a well documented fact of European history that now-familiar written languages like French, German, and English were actually invented at specific times and places starting around the tenth century C.E.. For centuries nobody thought to write them; then, a series of deliberate choices was made to turn these spoken vernaculars into written ones. Each written language's form took sustained work: honing, or hacking, a varied spectrum of spoken dialects down into a single standard form. In no case were they made up out of thin air, but in every case they were the result of creative effort to bring something new into being, evoking a place and a community through language. It is in this sense that we will explore the invention of Hebrew: neither as a fraud without existing basis, nor as an effortless, natural reflection of culture, but as a historical process that created new historical possibilities.

The invention of Hebrew gives us a new way to look at the relationship between the literary Israel of biblical texts and the material Israel of archaeology, because writing helped produce both of them. Archaeologists only began looking for a unique material culture within the borders of Israel because the Bible described Israel as unique and defined its borders. Ironically, the only excavated artifact that strictly fits biblical borders is written Hebrew itself. Careful study of the epigraphy shows that its tight fit within biblical borders was not a natural outgrowth of Israelite culture but the result of deliberate effort. The Hebrew Bible itself does not assume the existence of a unified, unique national language: it never refers to "Hebrew" as a language, and only has a name for the southern dialect, "Judean."[4] Both epigraphic and biblical texts were tools for creating a unified language in writing.

The invention of Hebrew also helps explain how the Bible continues to be understood. The idea that languages and ethnicities should correspond tightly to state borders is a European ideology that came to have a powerful influence on biblical studies.[5] But this European ideology emerged in the first place out of profound reflection on the Bible by philosophers such as Johann

Gottfried Herder. Herder's ideas, though new, had a basis in the Bible itself. Israelite writers in the Iron Age did not have a national language handed to them: instead, they created a form of political communication that could address a group called Israel, narrate its history, and let its audience see itself as part of that group and that history. Embodied in the Bible, this ancient invention endures as a productive model for political community. Asking how it became possible will help us understand its enduring productivity.

THE FIRST VERNACULARS The decision to put a local spoken language into writing is not a unique anomaly but part of a large-scale historical pattern, and useful insights have been gained from its study.[6] The Sanskritist Sheldon Pollock was the first to point out that not only Europe but also South Asia experienced a vernacular revolution around 1000 C.E.: kingdoms that had only written Latin began to write English and French, while Sanskrit was retooled to write Tamil and Javanese. Pollock detailed the phenomenon thus:

> vernacular literary cultures were initiated by the conscious decisions of writers to reshape the boundaries of their cultural universe by renouncing the larger world for the smaller place, and they did so in full awareness of the significance of their decision. New, local ways of making culture . . . and, concomitantly, new ways of ordering society and polity came into being, replacing the older translocalism. These developments in culture and power are historically linked, at the very least by the fact that using a new language for communicating literarily to a community of readers and listeners can consolidate if not create that very community.[7]

There has been a mutually creative relationship between vernacular writing and political community. People had the opportunity to recognize themselves in a new way—as the audience of texts newly written in Tamil, or Hebrew. And the medium of communication itself pointed to and provided something they had in common, a tool with which to think and act.

The creation of vernacular literatures implies a shift in horizons, of the things people can do or belong to. Familiar Near Eastern evidence suggests just such a shift in connection with Hebrew. The Old Babylonian laws of Hammurabi were not addressed to anyone in particular, laying out rules for both citizens and commoners in the third person: "If a citizen does X, the penalty is Y."[8] Applicable to everybody at once and nobody in particular, these imperial edicts were an endlessly copied centerpiece of the scribal curriculum. Yet they were never cited by name or treated as foundational for a community; they did not make anyone who they were.

The laws of the Torah share legal principles with Hammurabi but communicate differently because they speak to someone imagined as capable of hearing and responding.[9] Deuteronomy addresses a "you," Israel, which is also part of a "we" that includes the laws' speaker, Moses. The audience member who "hears" the call of "Hear, O Israel" in Deuteronomy 6 joins a group for whom "the Lord is our god, the Lord alone." Deuteronomy's address to all Israel may have begun as an attempt at a national charter in the seventh century, but the tool that made it possible was older. A standard written Hebrew had been circulating all over Israel and Judah, on rough-hewn walls and palace steps, potsherds and monuments, for well over a century.

The creation of local literatures in the Levant entailed a vernacular revolution, a shift in what texts could mean to people. Understood this way, it becomes the oldest body of evidence for a vital contemporary debate about language, culture, and power. Pollock's work represents a pre-modern response to the politics of modern written vernaculars conceptualized in Benedict Anderson's *Imagined Communities* (1991 [1983]). Anderson's work raises immensely fruitful questions by connecting communication and political form, exploring the power of address and recognition. But he ties written vernaculars and their publics uniquely to capitalism, based on the technology of mass printing and its resulting commercial genres, newspapers and novels.[10] It was through print-capitalism that the new written vernaculars of the eighteenth and nineteenth centuries addressed, and helped create, a new audience: the self-conscious modern nation.[11] As people read about the experiences of their nation in newly standardized vernaculars, they recognized themselves in both the language and the political community. As yet another attempt to explain modernity Anderson's work is limited by its chronological horizons. His insights follow a long line of social theory that isolates its phenomena in the last three hundred years, rendering the rest of the past almost invisible and practically useless.[12] A political community addressed through vernacular texts is nationalism, or it is nothing.

It is high time to challenge this isolation of pre-modern evidence from modern thought. How did it become thinkable in the Late Bronze or Iron Age for a people to "have" a language and a history? What political correlates did vernaculars have, and were they different from those in medieval or modern Europe? Is there a political theory implied in the very form of the Bible? Empirical work can not only answer our questions but improve them if we are willing to let it.[13]

New Directions in the History of the Alphabet

As a new awareness of the political stakes of writing—exemplified by Anderson and now Pollock—has spread among historians and theorists, epigraphers have opened up remarkable news about the alphabet's early history.

During the second millennium B.C.E. the alphabet had two major forms: the oldest type, called the linear alphabet, originated in pictographs and still resembled abstract drawings. The first letter, *alef,* evoked the sign it originated from, the head of a bull (*ʾaplu*). The second type, the cuneiform alphabet, first known from the Syrian city-state of Ugarit, completely readapted the linear shapes to the cuneiform system of writing on clay. Until the end of the twentieth century, the genius of the alphabet was touted as part of a history of progress: it had been assumed that the alphabet evolved in an increasingly simple and efficient direction, ultimately leading to Hebrew and then Greek. Alphabets were also joined to peoples, imagined as direct forms of ethnic and linguistic expression.

The emerging evidence washes away the image of the alphabet's rise as naturally reflecting evolution or ethnicity. Linear alphabetic inscriptions discovered in the 1990s at the *Wadi el-Ḥol* ("gulch of horrors") in Egypt dated to the nineteenth or twentieth century B.C.E. and fixed the origin of the alphabet at the earliest point anyone had imagined.[14] But they did more than this: they showed that the best candidates for the alphabet's inspiration were relatively crude Egyptian desert inscriptions, which the inventors may not have even fully understood. The earliest known alphabet was not the creation of erudite scholars but a hybrid improvised in a contact situation on the desert fringe. The second blow to the idea of the alphabet's history as one of linear progress came with the decipherment of a cuneiform alphabetic tablet from Israel that had mystified generations. The Beth Shemesh abecedary revealed that from an early time there was more than one alphabetical order—the well-known *ʾabgad* order, which we have inherited, and a *halḥam* order, which survived in South Arabian.[15] At the same time, it became clear that these alphabetical orders were not connected to any one language or writing system: Egyptologists noted the presence of the *halḥam* order in texts from the mid-first millennium B.C.E., demonstrating that this order was not necessarily connected to the alphabet at all.[16] Finally, Ugaritic studies confirmed that the diversity of early alphabets was not ethnic.[17] The alphabetic cuneiform texts from south of Ugarit did not represent an "Arabian" or "Phoenician" alphabet (as the one book on the subject argues[18]), but rather a standardized alphabet, created by the Ugaritic state chancery, and a variety of unstandardized ones outside it. Scribal discipline, not unselfconscious ethnic expression, drove the early alphabet's order.

Together these discoveries paint a very different picture of the alphabet's history, with two major features. First, the alphabet's rise was not inevitable. For the first half millennium or so of its history, the main attested use of the alphabet was for marginal people—foreign soldiers and laborers—to write graffiti in desolate, out-of-the-way places. In the second half of this millennium the alphabet blossomed into a wide range of forms, most of which did not survive into the next. Thus, although scholars in the twentieth century presumed that the alphabet's vast later spread was due to its overwhelming technical superiority, this presumed superiority was not much help during the first thousand years of its existence.

Second, the new history of the alphabet links forms of writing with political efforts. Alone among the early alphabets, the only one we can fully understand is the alphabetic cuneiform that was standardized and produced in large quantities at Ugarit. This seems to be a direct result of efforts by the Ugaritic state. The first known major cultural project done with an alphabet had the purpose of creating a native Ugaritic literature. Ugaritic scribes were trained in the classical Mesopotamian curriculum, but declined to translate any of this into Ugaritic, nor is there any Ugaritic literature translated into other languages.[19] Yet this fledgling vernacular died out for political reasons: Ugarit was destroyed around 1200 B.C.E., when the Late Bronze Age system of city-states and empires collapsed.

The past two decades of epigraphy have made clear that the alphabet's history is less one of linear progress than of cultural projects done by particular historical groups: its development was driven by writers who used it for particular ends under particular circumstances. The early alphabet's cultural success lay not in itself but in the work institutions did to canonize it. As we will see, there was a multitude of letter inventories, script styles, directions, and orders available at the end of the second millennium. This diversity makes the restricted, predictable forms of standard Ugaritic and Hebrew stand out as the fruit of deliberate intellectual labor. But to what end?

Scholarly Models and Epigraphic Discoveries

The major works of twentieth-century scholarship on the early alphabet understood it according to sweeping general presuppositions. The most prominent view, well-suited to rich, panoramic treatments like David Diringer's *The Alphabet: A Key to the History of Mankind* (1968 [1948]), saw the alphabet as the culmination of a history of progress:

> The alphabet is the last, the most highly developed, the most convenient and the most easily adaptable system of writing. Alphabetic writing is now universally employed by civilized peoples; its use is acquired in childhood with ease. There is an enormous advantage, obviously, in the use of letters which represent single sounds rather than ideas or syllables . . . Thanks to the simplicity of the alphabet, writing has become very common; it is no longer a

> more or less exclusive domain of the priestly or other privileged classes, as it was in Egypt, or Mesopotamia, or China . . . It is this simplicity, adaptability, and suitability which have secured the triumph of the alphabet over the other systems of writing. (Diringer 1968:13)

After a series of cumbersome experiments, humans arrived by trial and error at the best possible way to communicate. As Diringer's references to its "common" and "adaptable" nature suggest, his is a universalist model, close to the concerns of John Locke and the Enlightenment. It views the alphabet as a technology that promotes progress, a democracy of knowledge in which every citizen can read and write (and must read and write in order to be a productive member of a democracy).[20] But the universalist model of the alphabet shares with Locke the implication that those backward enough not to share in alphabetic literacy, whether through ignorance or attachment to backward, non-alphabetic systems, remain in a kind of dark age. This model projects modern European notions of literacy back in time, positing our political culture of literate citizens as the natural end point of historical development.[21]

An alternative view of the alphabet saw forms of writing, like styles of pottery, as "traditions" expressive of particular ethnic identities.[22] This is a Romantic model whose assumptions can be traced back to Herder. Its great advantage is its emphasis on the alphabet as culture, but to this insight is attached the assumption that alphabets have ethnicities. The Ugaritologists Manfred Dietrich and Oswald Loretz correlate the structure of an alphabet (its inventory of consonants) and associated mnemonic devices (orders of letters used to learn the alphabet) with specific language varieties, ethnic groups, and ethnic homelands. Rather than modular cultural tools or semiotic systems, alphabets are branded with the cultures of specific peoples.[23]

Neither the Romantic nor the universalist models explain what happened in the ancient Near East.[24] The problem with the Romantic-ethnic model, exemplified by Dietrich and Loretz's work, is that it assumes that language, culture, territory, politics, and sometimes "race" naturally go together: Herder's "one people, of one fatherland, one language."[25] In this case the model identifies alphabets with abstract genetic classes of language—not even concrete, historically attested varieties—such as "Northwest Semitic" and "South Semitic," and with political and ethnic groups on the ground. But ancient peoples did not identify themselves with languages or scripts in anything like the modern way.[26] The complex linkages that ancient writers made between language, script, and culture are important, but they were the result of deliberate creative effort, not a natural, uniform, or spontaneous phenomenon. Ernest Gellner's quip (1996) about nations—that they don't have navels—is true of alphabets as well.

An archaeological maxim states that it is a mistake to equate pots and peoples: ceramics do not necessarily have ethnic meaning. The Romantic theory makes this error with respect to written language. It assumes what we need to investigate: the role of institutions in creating unities of language, culture, and power. As the Yiddishist Max Weinreich shrewdly implied, the achievement of such unities involves extensive work on the part of native thinkers, bureaucrats, and even armies.[27] If people decide to equate a particular feature such as a dialect, only spoken by some members of the community, with a whole territory, state, or culture, this choice is a historical act that can fruitfully be studied. But scripts have no more inherent relationship with peoples than do pots.[28]

By contrast, the universalist model does not see writing as ethnic expression but as evolving technology. Writing begins with logography, the writing of whole words, advances to representing sound through syllabaries, and culminates in the simple, logical, and adaptable alphabet celebrated by Diringer. This model parallels the evolutionist social theory we examined in chapter 1. In archaeology, neo-evolutionist theory projected these old presuppositions onto prehistoric evidence, seeing society's political evolution as beginning with small bands, moving to chiefdoms, and culminating in the bureaucratic state. During the 1980s and 1990s archaeologists recognized crippling flaws in this unidirectional model. Drawn from old ethnographic theory, it did not fit Near Eastern data.[29] Norman Yoffee proposed the need for new theories of political development that were "contextually appropriate" for archaeology in linking "archaeological problems to the archaeological data available for their investigation."[30] Just so, the universalist model of writing as culminating in alphabetic literacy is no longer accepted by anthropologists, historians, or scholars of comparative literacy. We need a model that both fits and illuminates our data.

Current epigraphic models have the same problem as neo-evolutionist theory: they do not let us productively connect the rich data we are discovering to larger issues. It is often argued that, in the first millennium B.C.E., the technology of the alphabet revolutionized communication and cognition by democratizing writing. Frank Moore Cross, the most accomplished scholar of the West Semitic alphabet, echoes Diringer in saying that its impact on "the evolution of human civilization is difficult to exaggerate": "The older elitist and relatively static and hierarchical societies of the Near East gave way to new, dynamic societies, *alphabetic societies* which reached their pinnacle in the ancient world in Israel and Greece: egalitarian Israel with its prophetic critique of state and church, democratic Greece with its gift to humanity of logical thought and skepticism."[31]

The contrast is between a situation before the invention of the alphabet where "only a scholar with years of arduous training and high intellect learned to read and write with facility" and "inevitably, literacy remained the exclusive possession of a small, powerful elite," followed by the "rapid" and "broad" spread of literacy, a matter of "centuries rather than millennia," after which "a person could now learn to read and write in a matter of days or weeks."[32]

Cross is in good company: while the oral/literate Great Divide is a relic of eighteenth-century modernist thought, the view that widespread literacy is an essential determinant of the difference between "civilized" and "primitive" people became a basic tenet of work in anthropology, sociology, and psychology, appearing in the work of scholars such as Edward Burnett Tylor, Claude Lévi-Strauss, Emile Durkheim, and Lev Vygotsky.[33] Literacy was defined as "a more or less exclusive feature of Western life," as the anthropologist Niko Besnier puts it:

> Where it existed in the non-Western world, [literacy] had characteristics that gave it an inferior quality: for example, it was thought that learning to read and write in China required years of apprenticeship because of the apparently complex and unwieldy nature of the writing system. Similarly, in much of the Islamic world, literacy was described as being in the exclusive hands of a social elite, which prevented it from giving rise to an enlightened society.[34]

This model was most richly elaborated from the 1960s through the 1980s by the anthropologist Jack Goody, whom Cross cites,[35] and the intellectual historian Walter J. Ong. Goody argued that "inherent properties of literacy, especially alphabetic literacy, caused basic changes in the structure of societies, the makeup of cultures, and the nature of individuals." Ong similarly argued that "more than any other single invention, writing has transformed human consciousness."[36]

But this technological determinist view has been abandoned by anthropologists and historians of literacy. As his model was subjected to scrutiny, Goody's stance became more tentative.[37] Two types of problem emerged: the first, noted by anthropologists of literacy, was the failure of its predicted correlation between literacy and social types; no one has found "alphabetic societies" that are all broadly different from non-alphabetic ones, and classicists have argued that the arrival of writing did not revolutionize Greek life and thought, but instead "the new technique was grafted onto long standing uses in magic, ritual, and memorial."[38] The second, emerging in more recent work by historians, is that the correlation between writing and culture may actually be the opposite of what Goody described; that is, it is only *after* a culture has undergone certain changes in its attitude toward texts that literacy can become significant.[39]

The cognitive divide predicted between alphabetic and other societies did not appear, and scholars realized that even defining a literate society was difficult because people use writing in so many different ways.[40] For example, literacy rates in rural Sweden reached 90 percent by the mid-eighteenth century without formal schooling, but the only texts read were the Bible and catechisms. They were read to be memorized for religious purposes, with no necessary ability to write.[41] These Swedes did not read novels or use newspapers to participate in the debates of the day. In Thai villages of the 1950s, literacy for purposes of rote memorization of Buddhist texts coexisted with the use of reading and writing strictly for accounting purposes.[42] Through writing people participated in very different kinds of communities, both religious and economic, but in neither of these cases did they do anything like what Americans expect of literacy today. As Besnier concludes, "most societies of the world in fact fall between the categorical cracks" of the old model (1995:4).

Biblical scholars often still rely on Goody.[43] But can we speak, in a meaningful way, of "alphabetic societies" in ancient times? While "alphabetic/logo-syllabic" suggests a more complex opposition than "oral/literate," it is based on a similar type of binarism—and it does not really work. If we posit a radical divide between alphabetically literate, egalitarian societies and their rigid, cuneiform-bound opposite numbers, what does one do with alphabetic societies such as imperial Rome or the medieval Catholic and Byzantine kingdoms? With their massive hierarchies and endless circulation of Latin and Greek texts, the same writing that made these societies "alphabetic" was one of the greatest tools of central state power.[44]

From the point of view of education, the radical ease of learning the alphabet is a myth: nowhere in the modern world does it take an average child "days or weeks" to learn to read and write. Regardless of the writing system, the visual, cognitive, and motor processes of reading take months or years of repetitive effort for normal children to master, whether with alphabets or logo-syllabic scripts like Chinese.[45] Skilled readers of alphabetic and syllabic writing recognize whole words in much the same ways.[46]

Modern literacy's spread is inseparable from the modern nationalism Anderson illuminated: the political goal of standardizing a language for a people across a native territory. Controlling how people read and write is part of creating a particular kind of ideal people in a particular kind of ideal political space; the Czars did not care that the peasants of Russia could not read, write, or speak French as well as they could. Widespread literacy, in the modern sense of the term, requires uniform state-sponsored schooling, whether in China or England, which presupposes a nation-state and a standardized national language. It is the state sponsorship of logo-syllabic writing, rather than factors inherent in its script, that has led to strikingly high literacy rates in Japan and China.[47] The political question here is so central, yet so seemingly obvious, that it needs to be emphasized: universal literacy means reading a standardized written language—but whose? Who chooses that one dialect that will become that most-valued language taught in schools and used as an index of status and intelligence? Spoken language varieties tend to vary significantly and overlap irregularly across space.[48] The arbitrary imposition of a single written language over a large region takes work.

France provides the most powerful modern example. In his influential *Peasants into Frenchmen,*[49] Eugen Weber showed that until the end of the nineteenth century, most of France did not speak French. Weber details how city-dwellers were shocked to realize that they could not understand what people in the provinces were saying. Instead of Parisian French, they spoke Breton, Languedocienne, Armagnac, Gascon, and other relatives of French, Spanish, German, Celtic, English, and various often mutually unintelligible dialects. Only a dedicated government program, teaching the language of Paris and devaluing and stamping out the local dialects and traditions, permitted peasants to become Frenchmen. A century after *liberté, egalité, fraternité,* nothing short of an extended culture war was required to make the majority of France into the kind of citizens who could read French and vote. If widespread linguistic uniformity and literacy is an artifact of the modern nation-state, not the alphabet—and if it is only a century old even in France—it can hardly be assumed as a model for the alphabet's early history.[50]

Rethinking literacy raises the stakes for scholars of the ancient Near East. We can explore how writing plays out in particular ancient cultures instead of expecting yet more of the same, some universal divide between alphabetically literate societies and others. Anthropologists and historians now argue that meaningful "generalizations are much more likely to be discovered in the relationship between literacy and its sociocultural, political and ideological context than in the inherent properties of literacy itself."[51] Our data can lead beyond the Romantic or Enlightenment models.

In the case of ancient Israel the question of how a written language could be standardized across a geopolitical space is provocative, because here the nationalist model seems to be strangely inverted. As we will see in chapter 4, a uniform style of Classical Hebrew spread across the territories of Israel and Judah during the late Iron Age, violating state boundaries but fitting cultural borders. Scholars tried, and failed, to identify ancient Israelites archaeologically. If the signs of the Hebrew script are the only consistent archaeological signs of Israelite territory, did something other than ethnicity or a state make them Israelite? If this uniformity was not achieved by a state, what led Israelites to write in precisely the same script across more than one political space? Rather than merely illustrating universal truths about writing, the epigraphic and historical facts here demand a rethinking of what writing was for.

Vernacular Literatures in Near Eastern History

Consider the most striking new datum in the history of the alphabet: if the alphabet did indeed serve to spread literacy in Israel and Greece, why did it take more than a thousand years to catch on? After *Wadi el-Ḥol* has made clear the antiquity of the alphabet, the question of its use over time becomes even more glaring. Exactly what was this naturally superior, easily learned system doing during the entire second millennium? Technology by itself cannot explain the alphabet's ancient history. The important questions become those of use and meaning, engineering and rethinking. We will seek our answers in the relationships between writing, state politics, and local culture during this period.

The fundamental fact about writing in the second millennium B.C.E. Near East is the dominance of syllabic cuneiform. Sumero-Akkadian cuneiform was an extremely culturally cosmopolitan writing system, much more so than Greek or Hebrew was in the first millennium. Cuneiform was used to record members of no less than six genetically unrelated language families: it provides us with our earliest examples of Indo-European, in Hittite, Luwian, and Indo-Iranian; Semitic (Babylonian, Amorite, and Canaanite); Hurrian; Sumerian; Elamite; and Kassite. Ancient scribes could use cuneiform to record any language they encountered, and they did.

Yet cuneiform cosmopolitanism had equally impressive limits: despite syllabic cuneiform's adaptability, it was only used systematically to write a single variety of Semitic during the second millennium—the East Semitic Babylonian. "In Syro-Mesopotamia the cultural hegemony of Babylonia signified . . . that writing a Semitic language meant writing a Babylonian-based language, and writing literature meant writing Babylonian literature or an imitation thereof."[52] Seeing the variety of Semitic languages that left traces in syllabic cuneiform clarifies both its range and limits: the first major example in this period comes from Assyrian traders living in Anatolia. During the nineteenth century, they streamlined the cuneiform writing system, producing a stripped-down but effective communicative form for receipts, business letters, and the occasional nagging family harangue. From the Old Assyrian caravan archive we learn of tormenting ghosts, pig bites, and living, non-Babylonian, grammar.[53] A century later at Mari on the upper Euphrates, a profusion of local political and kinship terms appeared in the Babylonian letters of tribal leaders. As we will see, these eighteenth-century examples of West Semitic Amorite language and culture attest a politics very different from that of the Babylonian state—one that reemerges in ancient Hebrew. A third major example occurs in the Babylonian letters written by West Semitic-speaking rulers of Levantine city-states such as Jerusalem and Byblos during the fourteenth century. At a time when Babylonian was used by a multitude of non-Semitic-speaking empires—Egyptian, Hittite, Hurrian—we find letters from Canaan in an anomalous hybrid writing. Their grammar is mainly West Semitic, written with frozen Babylonian vocabulary and occasional glosses where West Semitic words emerge fully written. But we still do not know what they thought they were doing: Were the letters imperfectly learned Babylonian, or were they actually meant to be read out in Canaanite? Each outbreak of non-Babylonian Semitic in the second millennium was exceptional, unique to its time and place.

What determined the writing of Semitic was not peoples but institutions: Old Assyrian, Mari Amorite, and Amarna Canaanite vanished from writing because none were systematically taught. Babylonian had achieved a prestige equated with that of cuneiform itself, and as long as the Assyrian and Babylonian empires lived, Babylonian was the official language of diplomacy, culture, and law. This form of culture was cosmopolitan in the Indologist Lloyd Rudolph's terms, "an invitation to those who are different . . . to become like us."[54]

We know this enchanted system's users, because they wrote so much. Writing in the second millennium was dominated—though not, as Old Assyrian suggests, monopolized—by scribes. The experts responsible for the maintenance of this universal culture mastered Babylonian to varying degrees, but few of them ever spoke it: they were themselves the main examples and agents of Babylonian cosmopolitanism.[55] At a minimum, scribes were always at least bi- or triliterate, since they had to learn Sumerian and Babylonian—and since by the middle of the second millennium, nobody spoke the Babylonian that was being written anymore, even Babylonians existed in a classic state of diglossia. Scribes also wrote the local literary language such as Hittite or Hurrian, which could itself become a high literary standard.[56]

This cosmopolitan situation is already clear in the Old Hittite empire by the seventeenth century. The early Hittite king Hatushili I alludes to texts of the Akkadian king Sargon—in order to brag that he has outdone him. By the fourteenth century Hittite scribes had produced their own translation of the definitive Mesopotamian epic of Gilgamesh. But the scribes of the fourteenth-century Levantine city-states—many of whom may have learned to write from Hittite-trained scribes—were perhaps the greatest icons of this cosmopolitanism and its predicaments. A Ugaritic scribe could be literate in at least four languages: we know that some of the same people who copied Sumerian and Akkadian texts also wrote Ugaritic, and Ugaritic texts sometimes contain passages in Hurrian while a large number of people at Ugarit, including one king, had Hurrian names.[57] This multilingual cosmopolitanism extended to Syria-Palestine in the Late Bronze Age. At Taanach, Hazor, Ashkelon, and Megiddo we find trilingual lexical texts, names in Hurrian, Indo-Iranian, and East and West Semitic, and a Babylonian fragment of Gilgamesh.[58]

During this period the alphabet is no threat to the hegemony of Babylonian cuneiform. By contrast with the sophisticated corpus of Sumero-Akkadian, the *Wadi el-Ḥol* inscriptions are typical graffiti. All we can decipher of the oldest alphabetic inscriptions are short, unevenly written blessings, such as those found near the turquoise mines in the Sinai desert. More extended texts, of up to four short columns, may imitate the informal personal rock inscriptions left by hundreds of ordinary Egyptians during this period.[59] These inscriptions suggest the quick and dirty tool of foreign workers, scratched in desolate places: the mines, the gulch of horrors. There is no high culture here. While it may have been used for low-budget record-keeping, the alphabet's first known uses boil down to basic, even touching forms of communication: one early inscription's writer claims to be *mʾhbb ʿlt*, "Beloved of the Lady." This Lady, the parallel Egyptian texts clarifies, is the Egyptian goddess Hathor, who watched over the mines and miners.[60]

The decisive political feature of the oldest alphabetic inscriptions is that, unlike Babylonian, they are not standardized. The varying, improvisational nature of the earliest alphabetic writing has the political correlate that it did not yet represent an official language. The larger city-states of the Levant had scribes who were trained to produce standardized cuneiform writing in large quantities. The elaborate lexical lists from which they learned to read and write Sumerian and Akkadian were sometimes actually called "language" (*lišānu*) itself. By scribal standards, the short, haphazard alphabetic inscriptions might not qualify as language at all. No one had yet systematized alphabetic writing, or developed rules or a curriculum.[61] In contrast to the voluminous and crisply organized texts pumped out by the Babylonian schools, no scribes had bothered to define the alphabet. Its writings were not language in a formal sense because the alphabet did not yet belong to an institution with the will to formalize it.

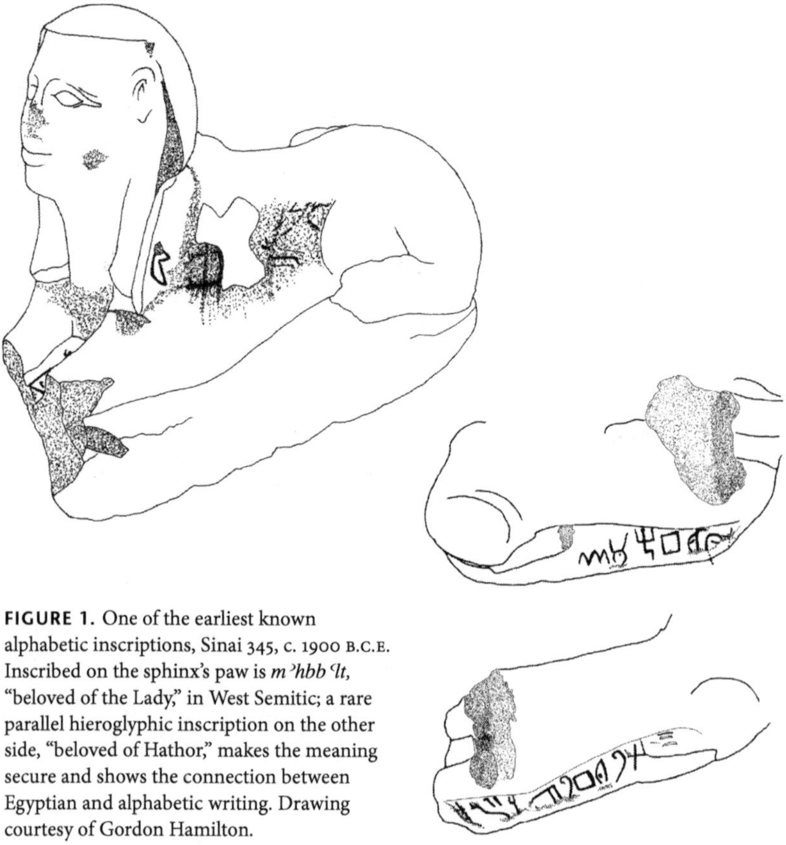

FIGURE 1. One of the earliest known alphabetic inscriptions, Sinai 345, c. 1900 B.C.E. Inscribed on the sphinx's paw is *m ʾhbb ʿlt,* "beloved of the Lady," in West Semitic; a rare parallel hieroglyphic inscription on the other side, "beloved of Hathor," makes the meaning secure and shows the connection between Egyptian and alphabetic writing. Drawing courtesy of Gordon Hamilton.

THE INVENTION OF UGARITIC A state first claimed the alphabet in the thirteenth century B.C.E. In the middle of this century, the personal seal of the king of Ugarit, Niqmaddu, was written in Babylonian, in the standard international cuneiform syllabary.[62] But during his reign, the epic of Baal was recorded in alphabetic cuneiform, a hybrid writing system that used the same clay and wedge-shaped marks of the Babylonian system to inscribe a radically different type of writing: an alphabetic system of twenty-seven consonants.[63] By the end of the century, the royal seal of Amishtamru, Niqmaddu's successor, was written in Ugaritic.

The Baal epic was the first West Semitic myth written in a West Semitic language, and it inaugurated a new, distinctively local literature in both form and content.[64] The epic tells the story of the storm god's struggles with the

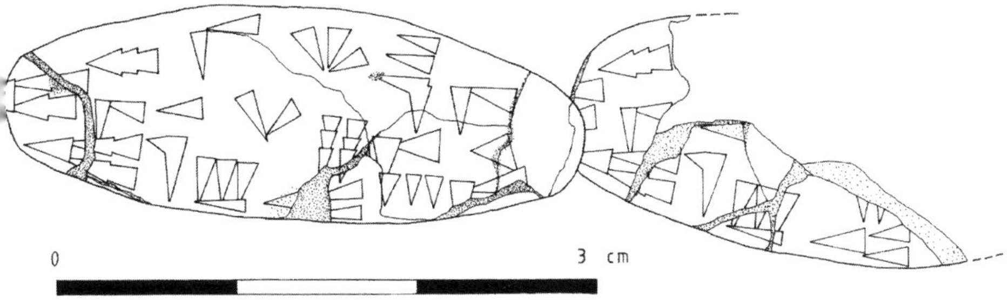

FIGURE 2. The impression of the royal seal of Ammishtamru, king of Ugarit (RS 16.270, thirteenth century B.C.E.) is the first royal seal in an alphabet. Drawing courtesy of Dennis Pardee.

Prince of the Sea, his death within the (literal) jaws of Death himself, and his rescue by his violent little sister Anat.[65] There is nothing really like it preserved in contemporary Babylonian culture, with its unified councils and victorious high gods. Most obviously, this type of myth had never been recorded in complete form before.[66] But its plot is also unknown in Babylonian literature: the divine warrior actually suffers greater and greater humiliation as the story progresses, to be rescued in the end by a goddess who is easily his equal in combat. Indeed, in the epic Baal does not actually achieve a single one of his legendary victories on his own: in his first battle his smith, Kothar-wa-Hasis, creates two magic weapons that are also incantations. It is the sentences themselves that smash into Baal's opponent when Kothar shifts them from dormant imperfectives into skull-crushing imperatives. Kothar utters the commands, while Baal literally does not lift a finger.[67] To gain a palace, the crucial prerogative of kingship, Baal must again ask for help, this time for the approval of the patriarchal god El. In his second battle, with Death, Baal is even more dependent. He descends "like a lamb" (Death describes the event using the Ugaritic words *imr* ["lamb"] and *lli* ["kid"] [1.6 II 22–23]) into his foe's open mouth. It is his sister who unleashes an orgy of violence on Baal's gastric captor, slashing, burning, grinding, and scattering Death's body to rescue her brother.

Sovereignty in the first alphabetic epic is negotiated in speech as much as it is won in battle. Baal wins power through the words and acts of kin and peers: the virile storm god's rise depends on a magical smith, his stronger sister, and the ruling patriarch. A comparison with the contemporary Babylonian *Enuma Elish,* based on the same myth of the young storm god's triumph over the sea, is instructive. In the Babylonian epic the sea is an angry mother, matriarch of the old regime who now threatens to destroy the entire community of gods.

Called on to kill the creatrix, Marduk gains a cosmic mandate: he demands and receives total submission from the assembled pantheon. He achieves absolute authority, represented first by his ability to create and destroy a constellation with his word and finally by his butchery of the sea, building the present universe with her corpse. Baal lives in a universe he did not make: the cosmos has been created by his elders, while he struggles merely to build his own palace. And by contrast with Marduk and his weaponsmith Kothar, Baal's words do not act by themselves. Baal neither asks for nor receives supreme power: if he wants something to happen, he must persuade others who can either grant or deny his requests.

If the Baal epic's plot is peculiarly West Semitic, so are its politics. The Baal epic reflects an old political theology in which the West Semitic storm

FIGURE 3. The third tablet of the Baal epic from Ugarit, KTU 1.3, containing Baal's feast and Anat's bloody recreational battle. It is the only known copy of the epic. Photo courtesy of Wayne Pitard.

god's defeat of his cosmic enemies recapitulates the king's this-worldly power to defeat his foes.[68] This theology was first made explicit five hundred years previously in a set of eighteenth-century texts from Mari. The epic of the West Semitic tribal king Zimri-Lim speaks of the storm god Adad "marching" at his left side. Adad speaks, through a remarkable letter from a prophet, of granting the king "the weapons with which I battled the Sea," which will ensure the king's future victory.[69]

In this old West Semitic political theology the ruler's power is provisional, earned through repeated acts of loyalty to more powerful helpers. In the continuation of the prophet's letter from Mari (less frequently cited by scholars) Adad himself makes clear to the king that his sovereignty is dependent on his loyalty to Adad: "I gave the whole land to Yahdun-Lim, and because of my weapons he had no rival. (But) he abandoned me and I gave the land I had given to him to Samsi-Adad . . . I returned you to the th[rone of your father] and I gave you the weapons with which I battled Sea and I anointed you with the oil of my splendor. No one can withstand you!"[70]

But the storm god defines piety as a limit on the king's behavior, not just aggrandizement of temple or palace: "Only hear this one word! Whenever anyone appeals to you for judgment and says 'someone has wronged me,' be there to judge his case! Answer him justly! This is what I desire from you!" (5–9, 1'–10').

A narrative pattern, reflecting an ideal of sovereignty, appears in West Semitic texts from Mari to Ugarit to the Bible, spanning over a thousand years and including the genres of epic, history, letters, and prayers. In this narrated political theory, the ruler must prove that he is the legitimate sovereign by taking a stand in public and favorably judging the cases of the weak and wronged. If he fails to do this, he will fall from the throne.[71]

This theology is one of political communication as well as power-sharing. If in both Mari and Ugarit rulership is earned through repeated acts of loyalty to one's divine protectors, then there is a second, communicative, point in common: the question of whether the ruler has to listen to anyone else. At Mari, the king attends anxiously to divine messages, which include admonitions. That the king be just is a standard Near Eastern monarchical ideal (found, for example, in the prologue to the laws of Hammurabi v 14–24, contemporary with this letter) but in the Old Babylonian dynasty no one ever *tells him* to be just. There is no evidence that anyone, let alone a god, demanded that Hammurabi make good on his claims. Shamash, the god of justice, never dared to speak to the king the way Adad speaks to Zimri-Lim, threatening him with defeat if he fails to judge justly. Babylonian royal justice is a first-person boast, cast in the king's own voice on royal monuments, not commanded to him in a private letter from a god. Indeed, we must wait for the Deuteronomistic history to encounter such a political theory in writing again.

The Ugaritic dynasty inherited this old West Semitic political theology, and Baal was its patron god. By the time Niqmaddu's successor Ammishtamru had his name written on his personal seal in alphabetic script, the alphabet in which Baal's tenuous climb to kingship was narrated had become a state emblem.[72]

Ugaritic is the first known standard alphabet. Why was it at this historical moment that the scribes of Ugarit reengineered the old linear alphabet, taking it over for the state chancery? No founding moment—a royal command in Akkadian to start writing in Ugaritic—has been preserved for us. The change in royal seals has to have *followed* the adaptation of alphabetic writing for official documents, since Niqmaddu's Babylonian seal is itself found on a document in alphabetic cuneiform (Virolleaud 1957:18). Yet this switch confirms that some such decision, whether at one stroke or incrementally, was made. The answer is probably not in the sheer simplicity of the Ugaritic alphabet. Because it added three new signs to the inventory of the linear alphabet, the cuneiform alphabet actually marked an *increase* in complexity.[73] Indeed, any explanation must begin with precisely this complication: it is not just that Ugaritic put local content—the Baal epic, the regional language—into writing, but that it took the cosmopolitan form of cuneiform on clay. Rendering the alphabet into cuneiform complicated, and dignified, it with a new physical format.

Why adapt a linear alphabet to cuneiform? Here it is important to consider the dominance of Babylonian cuneiform as both politics and communication. The medium of cuneiform on clay had a pedigree of more than a thousand years of hegemony over writing. In the Late Bronze Age the game of international relations was played via letters in cuneiform. By sending Babylonian letters to their "brothers" and vassals, kings created and reinforced their status in a long-distance community—a community in which the Ugaritic king was a subordinate vassal.[74] By adapting Ugaritic into cuneiform, the alphabet usurped Babylonian's cosmopolitan status. Amishtamru's seal may thus stand for Ugaritic as a whole: the presence of a local alphabet in a universal form is a literal emblem of the Ugaritic city-state's attempt to inscribe its own distinctive place in a larger world.

But the first written vernacular died with its writers. The Ugaritic archive was sealed around 1200, when invaders called the sea peoples destroyed Ugarit, baking the tablets in the city's flames and cleanly stratifying them beneath the rubble of its smashed walls. From the viewpoint of the cities and empires, the destruction was caused by a rabble of foreign invaders and local refugees who had cut ties (Akkadian *ḫabāru*) with the civilized world.[75] For those outside the city-states, this looked more like a mere shift in the balance of power (a view visible in the statements of those who took over or destroyed the old city-states such as Aziru and Abdi-Ashirta in the Amarna archive).[76] This shift marked the end of the plural, local uses of cuneiform and the rise of plural, local uses of the linear alphabet.

Outside Ugarit, political groups' use of alphabetic writing appeared for the first time around the eleventh century along the Levantine coast, but the texts encode a political status different from Ugarit's. We find two arrowheads of Zakar-Baal, "king of Amurru," one of a "commander of a thousand," one "ruler" (*mšl*), and six "retainers" of aristocrats (denoted with the formula *ʾš* PN).[77] As at Ugarit, these texts' owners were prestigious, not marginal workers, soldiers, or slaves. But the writing appears on arrowheads, emblems of military power and wealth, used by people who claimed kingdoms and armies but not literary compositions. Their scribes had not decided which direction to write: the direction varies from right to left, in the uneven tone of local craft production.

In Weinreich's playful definition, the West Semitic of these arrowheads could almost qualify as a language: they belonged to kings and commanders, and thus certainly had an army.[78] But the script, with its varying directions and letter stances, came from outside a chancery. This was unstandardized writing, not produced in mass quantities or attached to a bureaucracy. It seems that the scribal craft was neither professionalized nor enmeshed in a network. In the Late Bronze Age the Ugaritic state is the only one we know to have standardized an alphabet, and a form of local speech, in writing.

It is the systematic production of alphabetic texts by a state—the tight fit between a political institution and a literature—that made Ugaritic special. Local mythology had been recorded before, but the Hittites recorded their myths in syllabic cuneiform. Prosperous contemporary West Semitic-speaking city-states such as Emar had similar high cultures, and, as we will see, similar political theories and rituals. But Emar did not see fit to develop its own writing system. The scribes of Ugarit were just as conversant with the dominant international high-cultural script as Emar was—but they chose to abandon it and write their own language.

The first known vernacular literature was created under strikingly cosmopolitan circumstances. Far from a uniform or tightly unified folk culture, Ugarit with its Egyptian, Hurrian, Hittite, Babylonian, Sumerian, and Canaanite traditions was perhaps the most diverse Near Eastern site in the entire second millennium B.C.E. And Ugarit's very cosmopolitanism, combined with its relative political marginalization, might help explain its vernacular creativity. Anthropologists such as Michael Silverstein and Simon Harrison have remarked on the tendency for ethno-nationalism to arise in cosmopolitan contexts, situations "where self-differentiation *becomes* essential."[79] That is, a broad political program based on ethnic difference requires that some members of a group have a refined awareness of ways their group *can* be different. These possible signs of difference are then packaged together—into a literature, for example, which has been made systematically different from all other known literatures in its content, language, and writing system.

For in creating the first known vernacular literature, Ugaritic writers set it systematically apart. The scribes who began to use the alphabet made a clear and sharp split: "Ugaritic literature is not written in syllabic cuneiform, nor is Babylonian literature written in alphabetic cuneiform."[80] Foreign cosmopolitan texts were written in the foreign cuneiform syllabary they had inherited. For native texts—local myths, letters between members of the royal family, bookkeeping within the court, texts designed for internal consumption and originating in the native language—a unique native script was to be used. The scribes even set about producing abecedaries and school texts, standardizing their local vernacular over against the cosmopolitan system they were trained in. The cosmopolitan scribes of Ugarit deliberately made their writing system local. They were the only culture in the second millennium to do so.

And the first West Semitic speakers to systematically write their own language made this choice in a geopolitical context. For most of its history, Ugarit was a vassal of the Hittite empire. The city-state of Ugarit was a strategically placed dwarf among giants, balanced between the Hittites to the north, Egypt to the south, and the Babylonians and Assyrians to the east. These empires communicated with Ugarit and each other in Babylonian cuneiform.

The early alphabet was not universalizing, but particularizing—precisely the opposite of what we would expect from the conventional story of the alphabet. It would have been difficult, even impossible, to use this alphabet anywhere but home.[81] Rather than being universal, the texts were designed to be read within a strictly limited region. The writers of Ugarit did not send their alphabetic texts abroad.

Vernacular writing was developed by groups on the margins of the cosmopolitan empires, and there was a relationship between their writing and their marginality. In the Late Bronze Age, scribes mediated between two very different worlds: an international one that had been handed down to them and a local world they brought into being. In Late Bronze Age Ugarit, the same scribes produced both local alphabetic and international syllabic texts.[82]

The daily work of these scribes was to manage two separate and very different flows of information, using the same wet handfuls of clay. The first was a flow between Ugarit and the larger world: the king of Ugarit had to communicate with Egyptian, Hittite, and Babylonian kings, but we have no evidence that he spoke any of these languages. To these kings, separated from him by hundreds of miles of desert, he was alternately a vassal, a feeble ally, or prey. The second flow of information was within Ugarit: it is in this language and writing system that his subjects professed loyalty to him, claiming to cast themselves to the ground "fourteen times on my face."[83] In this language he was the key player in rituals that redeemed Ugarit from disaster; in this language he sent his ancestors to the grave in rituals that simultaneously divinized them; in this language he would become a god when he died.[84]

Ugaritic rendered the king's traditional sources of authority visible and meaningful. Rituals and letters in Ugaritic articulated the native king's authority, in his traditional terms and in a code his foreign overlords could not read. One sacrificial list could create a lineage tracing the current king back to divine patriarchal ancestors, divinized in writing and ritual (Pardee 2002:195–210; cf. 2002:85–88). Native writing made the foundations of native politics evident.

There were other cuneiform alphabets, but none show evidence of being used for ritual or politics. At the same time as the Ugaritic alphabet was only found within Ugarit, variants appeared in dribs and drabs at Ugarit and in scattered locations to the south—they represent at least one language other than Ugaritic, sometimes with a smaller inventory of consonants and different basic vocabulary, and unlike Ugaritic they are sometimes written from right to left like Hebrew.[85] They share letterforms with Standard Ugaritic and thus seem to have been written in awareness of Ugarit's adaptation of a linear alphabet, but suggest the independent adaptation of at least one other linear alphabet into cuneiform.[86] The texts in these minor alphabets include dedications on luxury objects, but also economic notes and abecedaries. We see here not just one attempt but multiple competing attempts at transmitting, and perhaps even standardizing, local languages.

The new native writing in Ugarit and the Levant draws a line between the cosmopolitan and the vernacular. By excluding the global, it argues for the local. Central Ugaritic texts make new assumptions about what it means to be a native, to participate in this local way of being. These texts can shed light on the Ugaritic motivations for creating a new type of written language.

THE IDEOLOGICAL BACKGROUND OF WEST SEMITIC VERNACULARS

The People in Ritual

How did written vernaculars matter? To understand what a local literature could mean in the ancient Near East, we need to look at the participants it assumes. Written Ugaritic shares intriguing features with the products of modern cultural nationalism. Its deliberate fusion of language, polity, and culture, more than three thousand years before Herder, is striking.[87] But what kind of relationship was intended between Ugaritic texts and people?

Anderson's theory of linguistic nationalism is based on modern models of mass communication: printing and capitalism were the way written vernaculars found audiences. Large-scale commodity production of local texts and their consumption through private reading let people read themselves as nations.[88] Anderson evokes the continuity between reading and political publics by asking, "What is the essential literary convention of the newspaper?" (1991:33). What connects the hodge-podge of local and global events on any given day's front page of the *New York Times* is their relevance to an assumed U.S. reader. Scanning the page implicitly but powerfully orients the reader as a member of the American people, in a world of nations, at a specific moment in history.

But there were no publics at Ugarit based on mass consumption of texts. As Karel van der Toorn (2007:18–19) has clearly shown, texts did not circulate as commodities in the ancient Near East. Ugaritic literature drew on old traditions that were widely known: the Baal epic's theme of the battle between the storm god and the sea appears in West Semitic cultures five hundred years earlier at Mari and a thousand years later in the biblical book of Daniel.[89] But the written texts themselves did not circulate through a literary audience at Ugarit; they were crafted by experts, used, then deposited. The three most extensive Ugaritic literary texts, the epics of Baal, Kirta, and Aqhat, were all found in one location, the "House of the High Priest," in a single copy each.[90]

Ugaritic texts may assume their own models of participation, which must be explored in detail if they are to tell us anything new. The modern nationalist model assumes a political public based on consumerism, inconceivable without the sale of highly engineered texts like the *New York Times* to a sophisticated readership. Herder imagined that oral poetry is "the archive of the folk," but his agenda as an editor of folk literature was to turn this unwritten archive into mass-produced texts for a reading public.[91] In every case where we can tell, Ugaritic literary texts were produced in single copies for the king. If the people were not addressed through mass-produced texts in Ugaritic, what community was this vernacular for?

AN UGARITIC RITUAL FOR NATIONAL ATONEMENT AND UNITY

Our single copy of the Baal epic can be contrasted with a ritual found in diverse versions and locations at Ugarit. This text, KTU 1.40, is by simple empirical standards the most important ritual known from Ugarit. Its understanding has been illuminated by the two recent comprehensive studies of Ugaritic ritual (the analysis by del Olmo Lete 1999 and the definitive edition by Pardee 2000), which agree on its essential purpose and central role. Intriguingly, it has been characterized as both a "ritual for national atonement" (del Olmo Lete 1999:159) and a "ritual for national unity" (Pardee 2002:77).[92] These two modern titles lead us to reflect on what "atonement," with its etymological roots in Old English *at on*, "to agree, to be reconciled, to be at one" (OED *s.v.*), might mean here, and why both scholars recognized it as somehow "national."

Pardee explains that KTU 1.40 was the most broadly reproduced ritual at Ugarit.[93] Unlike the epic of Baal, present in just one manuscript of uncertain function, we know the ritual attested in KTU 1.40 was *used* repeatedly because the text is not just present in multiple copies but in multiple versions: there appear to be at least six manuscripts of the text, and in one the king's name is replaced with another name, apparently non-royal.[94] The ritual involved a confession of sins and the slaughter of sacrificial animals for the purposes of atonement. Since its publication, scholars have noted that its ritual mechanisms parallel those of the biblical Day of Atonement, described in Leviticus 16.[95]

What has not been emphasized is that both these West Semitic rituals revolve around a new type of participant. Both Leviticus 16 and KTU 1.40 are done on behalf of a community, not just a leader. Within the Ugaritic ritual corpus, KTU 1.40 is characterized by its uniquely broad sweep and high level of repetition, addressing male and female inhabitants of the city, and, again uniquely, including both foreigners and natives, sovereign and citizens.[96] It is composed of a set of three paired invocations and expiations, the first of each pair addressing men, the second women. And it names a spectrum of ethnic and social groups within the city, against whom sins are confessed.[97]

The first set of sacrifices involves the slaughter of a donkey—an act unknown elsewhere in Ugaritic, but common in earlier West Semitic ritual at Mari. This is significant because, as we will see, the slaughter of a donkey was the proverbial act for bonding two Amorite tribes together. A donkey-slaughter was a paradigmatic ritual for forming new unions in earlier West Semitic culture.

A representative part of the middle invocation reads as follows, first in the male version, reconstructed with extensive parallels, and then in the preserved female version:

> [Whether you {men} sin . . . according to the statement of the Hurrian, according to the statement of the Hittite, according to the statement of the Cypriote {a total of seven groups are mentioned} . . . according to the statement of your oppressed, according to the statement of your impoverished; whether you {men} sin in your anger or your impatience, or by the quarrels you might have, whether you {men} sin concerning the sacrifices . . . the sacrifice—it is sacrificed, the offering—it is offered, the slaughtering is done!][98]

> Whether you {women} sin . . . according to the statement of the Hurrian, according to the statement of the Hittite, according to the statement of the Cypriote . . . according to the statement of your oppressed, according to the statement of your impoverished; whether you {women} sin in your anger or your impatience, or by the quarrels you might have, whether you {women} sin concerning the sacrifices . . . the sacrifice—it is sacrificed, the offering—it is offered, the slaughtering is done![99]

Two things set this ritual apart from other known rituals from the second millennium: first, it addresses a broader group than the king, as indicated by its male and female plurals. Second, it makes both ethnic and social groups outside the palace into central players in a ritual of redemption. It exists in an implicit tension with the bulk of Ugaritic rituals, in which the king is the protagonist, and the major literary texts like the epics of Baal or Aqhat, which each focus on one or two heroes. The text's lack of parallels in Mesopotamian or Hittite culture suggests a distinctively Ugaritic political theology.[100] That is, it provides a divine grounding for a particular type of human order, because it treats violations against the city's constituent groups through the same ritual used for transgressions against the gods—expiation. The idea that such a ritual of expiation for sins against a community of different ethnic and social groups would be *necessary* is unknown to other cuneiform literatures; at Ugarit it predominates over all other attested rituals.[101]

The Ugaritic ritual for national unity shares a fundamental feature with its West Semitic-speaking neighbors at Emar. The central rituals of Ugarit's contemporaries at Emar were also conducted on behalf of the city's populace, rather than a king. The ritual for the installation of the high priestess of Baal begins "When the sons of Emar elevate the high priestess to the storm god . . ." and stipulates that the daughter of any citizen of Emar may be chosen.[102] At Emar the ritual itself is described as initiated by the sovereign decision of the people.

The Ugaritic ritual for national unity is thus the most explicit example of a pattern we see in more than one West Semitic society in the Late Bronze Age: rituals on behalf of the people. If this ritual has no other parallels in the second millennium or cuneiform, its continuity with a curious but central

Israelite ritual is powerful. Since its publication in 1929 scholars have noted the parallels to the Hebrew Yom Kippur ritual in Leviticus 16.

A JUDEAN RITUAL OF NATIONAL ATONEMENT AND SALVATION

The widely scattered copies of the Ugaritic ritual for national unity testify to its prominent role in Ugaritic practice. The Judean Priestly editors who shaped the Torah gave similar importance to a related ritual. This atonement ritual was already both old and sacred to them, but they systematically intensified its power. The ceremony of Leviticus 16:2–28 (termed elsewhere, but not in the text itself, *yôm hakkipurîm* "the Day of Atonement")[103] receives the lengthiest and most detailed description of any ritual in the Bible. Its editors placed it at the center of the Torah, at the structural midpoint of the middle book.[104] In the Priestly calendar, it was assigned to the beginning of the year. Positioned at the center of the Priestly text, time, and space, it redeems the center of the ritual universe. In its current form the atonement ritual not only redeems the entire people (16:17, 20–21) and purifies the very sources of purity—the sanctuary and priesthood (16:16–17)—it also causes God himself to appear. And this honor was granted to a text full of baldly alien features: it uses a terminology found nowhere else in Priestly writing and places an otherwise unknown god named Azazel on par with the Lord by presenting him with a sacrifice, offered in a way unknown elsewhere in the Torah.[105]

Formally, the Day of Atonement rite stands out because its most distinctive public act, the scapegoat ritual, violates two fundamental patterns of the Priestly ritual system. In the Torah, sacrifice is always silent and typically bloody. By combining a bloodless animal sacrifice with a speech at its climax, the scapegoat ritual breaks the bounds of its editors' own system.[106] The cumulative weight of these distinctive features has long convinced observers of its independent origins—if not its total incomprehensibility.[107]

Interpreters have generally placed the scapegoat in an ahistorical and apolitical framework (as with Priestly ritual in general): it is to be understood typologically, as an expiation ritual. Yet this has not helped: whatever system writers have sought to find, the scapegoat has ended up outside it. While its features seemed pagan and magical to writers like Yehezkel Kaufman[108] and Israel Knohl in search of coherent forms of Israelite religion, they seemed equally far from primitive Semitic sacrifice to William Robertson Smith in his portrait of the archaic "religion of the Semites."[109] Most entertainingly, two of the twentieth century's most influential theorists of sacrifice, James G. Frazier and Rene Girard, each wrote books called *The Scapegoat* that avoided this text entirely.[110]

When seen historically and politically, Leviticus 16 shows a more coherent aspect. Comparing the scapegoat ritual with its predecessor in Ugaritic reveals a clear but apparently heretofore unremarked process by which *the people* become a fundamental ritual actor in a ceremony of communal salvation.

In Leviticus, the Day of Atonement ritual is framed as a command from the Lord to Moses about how Moses' brother Aaron (referred to consistently in the third person as "Aaron" or "him") is to enter the innermost chamber of the sanctuary without dying. This place, referred to here (and nowhere else)[111] as *haqqôdeš*, "the Holy," is normally lethal to humans because of the divine presence within. The Lord reveals that he regularly becomes visible inside the sanctuary: "I appear in a cloud over the Atonement Place" (Lev. 16:2). Aaron is thus to risk death and prepare to enter the innermost chamber. First he dons priestly clothing and, acting as the representative of all Israel, takes animals provided by "the assembly of the Israelites," including two goats, which he will divide between the Lord and another being:

> He will take the two goats and he will stand them before the Lord at the entrance of the Tent of Meeting. And Aaron will cast lots over the two goats: one lot for the Lord and one lot for Azazel. And Aaron will bring near the goat on which the lot for the Lord fell and make it a sin-offering. And the goat on which the lot for Azazel fell he will stand alive before the Lord, to atone through it, to send it to Azazel, into the desert. (vv. 7b–10)

This passage is nothing short of astonishing for the aggressively monotheistic Priestly source, which nowhere else seriously contemplates other divine powers. Here a god named Azazel receives offerings matching those for the Lord. This is not easily assimilated to Priestly theology, as medieval Jewish interpreters still recognized: How can Israelites atone by sacrificing to a being that is not God?[112] Azazel's divine power continues to demand explanation. The most plausible one is that the Priestly writers considered the ritual too sacred to remove and too dangerous to leave out: Judeans believed it worked. There is a substantial scholarly consensus that the scapegoat was already ancient and prestigious in the Priestly writers' time. Erhard Gerstenberger exclaims that it is "simply inconceivable" that the Priestly theologians, "loyal to YHWH as they were, could have allowed this kind of 'polytheistic' idea to pass through. The wilderness demon Azazel must also be appeased, and not only YHWH, the only lord of the world!"[113]

After preparing to sacrifice to two different gods, Aaron now undertakes a second task: to see the first of these gods without dying. He is to bring the materials for creating the cloud, coals, and incense, into the Holy Place. "And he will put the incense on the fire before the Lord and the cloud of incense will cover the Atonement Place that is above the Testimony, but he will not die" (Lev. 16:13). Like the polytheistic sacrifice, the divine revelation passes without comment; were it not for the remark that Aaron "will not die," it would be possible to forget exactly what would otherwise be expected to kill him (Exod. 33:20) and miss the second theologically unique dimension of the ritual. Alone of all Priestly acts, the Day of Atonement ritual allows God himself to appear.

> And he will atone for the Holy Place from the pollution of the Israelites and from their transgressions {*pešā ʿîm*, used as a technical term here and nowhere else in the Priestly source}, all their sins, and he will do thus for the Tent of Meeting {used only here to refer to the sanctuary as a whole}, which resides with them in the midst of their pollution.. . . . and he will atone on his behalf and on behalf of the whole congregation of Israel. (vv. 16–17)

The ritual atones for the Holy Place, Aaron, and the congregation at once, tying priest, sacred center, and people together as protagonists of a single ritual action. Next Aaron brings the live goat to the altar.

> And Aaron will put his two hands on the head of the living goat and he will confess over it all the misdeeds of the Israelites and all their transgressions and all their sins and he will put them on the head of the goat and send it into the desert, at the hands of a man who is prepared for the occasion. And the goat will bear on it all their misdeeds to the cut-off land, when he sends the goat into the desert. . . . And he will go out and make the burnt offering for him and the burnt offering for the people and atone on his behalf and on behalf of the people. (vv. 21–22, 24)

Here the Israelites are seen as a single agent. The ritual makes their responsibility collective and material, fused together in a single utterance and then located in an animal. What makes the ritual so special, then, is not the mechanism of expiation but the people on whose behalf (*ba ʿad* in 16:24) it acts.[114] The distinctiveness of the ritual's new participants is apparent from a careful reading of Jacob Milgrom's massive Leviticus commentary, which collects and compares a large corpus of similar rituals in cuneiform, spanning one and a half millennia.[115] In enumerating a series of differences between biblical and Mesopotamian expiation rituals, he comments in passing that "there are no group transfer rites in Mesopotamia; the biblical scapegoat, in contrast, removes the sins of the entire nation" (1991:1079).

The difference from the cuneiform empires is decisive. From Babylon to the Hittite realm, rituals never involve the people as a collective agent—the protagonists of the Babylonian and Hittite rituals are the king, his army, or his territory. This is a stage inhabited by an old and limited cast of characters, dating at least as far back as the third millennium in which old Near Eastern principles of sacred kingship are rooted. It is the king's actions that matter to the gods; they determine the identity and destiny of the kingdom.

There is, of course, a second ancient Near Eastern expiation ritual with collective subjects: the Ugaritic ritual for national atonement and unity. The Ugaritic text and the core of the Leviticus passage share a common pattern: they represent West Semitic group salvation rituals, and each held a central place in a new local writing. What explains this is not the distinction between a unique monotheistic Israel and a common pagan Near East, but between vernacular and cosmopolitan cultures.

In the last portion of Leviticus 16, the transmitters of the tradition speak, setting the ritual in its new place at the center of the Priestly cycle. The diction switches without warning into the second person and Priestly language: unlike the ritual itself it distinguishes sharply between the tent of meeting and the sanctuary, as everywhere else in the Torah.[116] Summarizing the ritual, it adds completely new directions. No longer do the instructions concern Aaron, referred to in the third person, but a collective "you"(second-person plural), separate from "the priest" (who has been referred to consistently as "Aaron" up until this point) who is to perform the duties:

> For you this will be an eternal edict: on the seventh month, on the tenth of the month, you will engage in self-denial; you will not do any work, neither the native nor the visitor who lives with you. For on this day he will atone to purify you; from all your sins before the Lord you will purify yourself. It is a day of complete rest for you, in self-denial you will engage: an eternal edict. And the priest, who he anointed and who he appointed to be priest following his father, will atone. He will put on the linen garments, the holy garments, and he will atone for the holy Temple and for the Tent of Meeting and for the altar he will atone. And this will be an eternal edict for you, to atone for the Israelites, for all their sins, once a year; And Moses did as the Lord commanded. (vv. 29–34)

With its arcane diction speaking of acts and gods otherwise unknown to the Bible, the ritual is now set like some weird gem at the center of the Torah. Its language is systematically different enough that three different terms contrast with the language of the rest of the Priestly work (Budd 1996:230).[117] Within the text, clearly delimited by voice and language, there is no sign of a fixed calendrical framework. This fits with the other known Near Eastern atonement rituals noted by Milgrom, which are occasional; none are designed to be performed regularly. These last lines insist repeatedly (three times in six lines!) that it is now an eternal edict to perform the atonement once a year, "instructions for regularizing the ritual as an annual ceremony" (Balentine 2002:125).

The similarities of the Hebrew and Ugaritic texts as unifying and atoning rituals of new, vernacular states is not an accident. Both address and presuppose a new kind of participant. In both the Late Bronze and Iron Age texts, the rituals conjure up the people; those who recognized themselves in it were invited to be characters in a story of being redeemed together.

The Hebrew and Ugaritic texts also communicate and imagine space in two markedly different ways that differentiate their politics. The first is geographic. Temples were central to Ugaritic ritual (for details, see Pardee 2002:228–29), but as staging grounds for sacrifice, not entities *for which* sacrifice is performed or subjects of dramatic rituals. The Ugaritic rituals preserved for us do not contrast a temple at the sacred center with a dangerous, profane periphery. While the temples of Baal of Ugarit and El are prominent, each is merely a temple, not *the* temple. By contrast the holy center in Leviticus 16, placed in the middle of the Torah, prescribes the cleansing of the sanctuary, which is centrally located and acts to found Israel's sacredness.[118] By sending the scapegoat with Israel's sins from the temple outward to the margins of the world, it reestablishes Israel as a cosmic axis, with the temple at the heart, over and against what is imagined at the margins. Leviticus 16 imagines its participants as well as its temple as monolithic in their unity: all of Israel is purified at once, their fates bound up together. The Ugaritic ritual, by contrast, neither imagines a sacred center nor casts anything out of it. Its participants are markedly diverse, naming seven different ethnic groups and addressing male and female participants. Its politics are plural.

The second difference is one of genre. Leviticus 16 is part of a complex story that mythically founds a ritual. It is multiply framed as God's direct speech, delivered to Moses during a story told by an omniscient third-person narrator, prescribing in the third person a ritual that Aaron, as the ancestral high priest (standing for all future high priests), is to perform. The ritual instructions themselves make no reference to time. This voice is then supplemented by an editorial voice speaking in the second person about the ritual that "you" as a collectivity, along with the priest, are to perform; it is this editorial voice that specifies a time frame, transforming it into an annual ritual.

By contrast, KTU 1.40 has no frame: the whole text is a speech to be read by a priest during the ritual.[119] Like the core of Leviticus 16, it has no chronological context. What distinguishes the scapegoat ritual's genre is thus the same as what distinguishes the Torah's genres from other ancient Near Eastern texts: the presence of law in narrative. Ritual law, which everywhere else in the ancient Near East comes in a discrete textual frame and genre, is told as part of a story in the Torah. Its place in a founding narrative simultaneously decontextualizes it from any other history and encourages its readers to recontextualize it through reuse.

As rites of national salvation, the Ugaritic and Hebrew texts are the first known rituals on behalf of peoples. But the very different written forms in which they come to us mark a historical shift. KTU 1.40, from the Late Bronze Age, has a rich archaeological context precisely because it died and was buried when Ugarit did; we can read its importance forensically, from the way its remains were scattered. This ritual was repeatedly reinscribed when it was necessary to invoke the religious authority of peoples. There is an implicit tension between this ritual, which evokes the authority of peoples alongside the king, and the royal myths and rituals of Ugarit in which everything depends on the royal protagonist or another central hero. Most written Ugaritic ritual was about the king; if the subjects were thought to have any stake in these rituals, it was because of the standard monarchical assumption that the king represented the people. In KTU 1.40 alone, peoples are represented.

Dating from the late Iron Age—as well as every later period in which it was reproduced—Leviticus 16:2–28 provides a striking contrast in both media form and political context. Physically, it has no archaeological context at all before Roman-era fragments appear at Qumran because it was repeatedly copied, edited, and incorporated in successively different textual wholes. Politically, there is also an implicit tension with royal political theology here, but the Priestly response is to flatly negate it. The ritual's core predates monotheism and the exile, and so must have existed alongside Judean kingship. Yet the king has no role at all. This tension was ultimately resolved by historical accident: after a period of competition between the two ideologies, native kingship fell and the people won. The kingly ideal lived on only in sporadic failed revolts and the political and theological imagination of the messiah. This old occasional rite was inscribed at the center of the Torah's ritual calendar. And the Torah's main human protagonist was a newly imagined unit: "the people" of Israel.

The two oldest known major West Semitic vernaculars share a model of participation. In this model's Late Bronze Age Ugaritic and Iron Age Judean instances a new unit, the people, becomes the subject of newly written rituals of crisis, atonement, and redemption. This book's final chapter will explore what this model entails: in Hebrew, the people become the subjects of history. The central ritual of the Priestly calendar finds its place with the collective protagonist of the Deuteronomistic history as the core of a Hebrew vernacular literature.

The People in Politics

Why is it that West Semitic cultures first write down rituals and literatures assuming this new participant, "the people"? If there is nothing natural or inevitable about seeing peoples as fundamental units of action, then this idea should not enter history from nowhere. It should have a cultural background, a prehistory that, with careful philological detective work, we may be able to trace. As it turns out, valuable evidence for such a background has emerged in recent decades, but its significance has been obscured by a tendency in Western political thought itself.

Since Aristotle proclaimed the city-state to be the supreme political form (*Politics* 1:1),[120] the state in its various forms has dominated the Western political imagination—including our view of ancient Near Eastern history.[121] Debates over the archaeology of Israel in the Iron Age have often resembled a treasure hunt for the state, whether that of the united monarchy or the less reputable but richer polities of the divided kingdoms.[122] A state-centered approach dominated older archaeological theory. Echoing Aristotle, evolutionary theory portrayed the Near Eastern state as a higher development that grew organically out of tribes and chiefdoms, just as the alphabet had grown organically out of earlier, cruder forms.[123]

But a different pattern is visible in Near Eastern epigraphic evidence, beginning in the Old Babylonian period (c. 1800 B.C.E.) and continuing through the Iron Age. In these texts far older than the polis, West Semitic peoples act as sovereign agents. Their participation in sovereignty can be seen on three levels: language, ritual, and political process. Linguistically, both Mari Amorite and biblical Hebrew have a terminology and associated grammar that defines kinship groups as political actors. Ritually, we find practices in which these groups can be joined, or perhaps even founded, when members *agree* to become kin. And people enacted this ideology: population groups assembled to fight, decide for peace, or perform essential rituals. Not restricted to nomads, tribal politics penetrated into towns and cities, cut across borders, and outlasted the collapse of ancient Near Eastern states. In the Old Babylonian-era upper Euphrates we encounter a tribal group called the sons of Yamin (a spatial term that can mean either "south" or "right"); a thousand years later in the southern Levant, we hear of a tribe called Benjamin, again, son of Yamin.[124] Yet the antiquity and viability of such orders has been mostly invisible to our political thought.

Since Aristotle, Western theory has tended to see the state as both the driving force and pinnacle of history. The absurdity of this assumption becomes self-evident in cases like Georg Wilhelm Friedrich Hegel's 1806 declaration of the end of history. This was supposed to have happened with the triumph of the liberal state, represented by Napoleon's defeat of the Prussian monarchy. History insouciantly continued. The hold of the state on the Euro-American imagination was such that less than two hundred years later, Francis Fukayama (1989) insisted that with the collapse of the Soviet Union, the liberal state had actually triumphed and history was over—really, this time. As John Kelly (2006b:161) commented about this kind of teleological thinking, "If the Nazis had gotten a little farther in their heavy-water physics, we would (if we were not dead) be discussing flimsy Neo-Hegelian depictions of the Third Reich, rather than the nation-state, as the end of history." Today the political and military complexities of Afghanistan and Iraq remind us that tribal orders never went away. But the gap in our thinking remains: while genealogies of the ancient Near Eastern state continue to thrive, there is no adequate discussion of the development of the concept of the people.[125]

Yet the state has always had competitors, and the Near East provides the earliest rich body of evidence for them. Chief among these is the tribe—an entity that seems to have emerged in parallel with the state, rather than as its primitive ancestor.[126] But up until the last few decades, tribes before Israel were mostly seen as mere barbarians. Since states were the only ones with writing, history was written from their point of view. Tribes were, almost by definition, without history.[127] When cuneiform historical sources were discovered, we gained our first contemporary view of ancient Near Eastern tribes. But because these Mesopotamian documents were written by officials within Babylonian states, they viewed the tribes indiscriminately, whether Amorites or Arameans, as an external, alien threat.[128] A new perspective became possible in the 1930s, when a rich archive of a living tribal society from the Old Babylonian period was unearthed at the city of Mari on the upper Euphrates.

As we gain more information about the role of tribes in Near Eastern history, they emerge as mutually creative with states: as the title of a recent anthropological study puts it, "tribes make states and states make tribes" (Whitehead 1992). Tribal organizations actually helped produce a number of political orders in Mesopotamia. Indeed, Dominque Charpin (2004) has argued for renaming the Old Babylonian period the "Amorite epoch," switching from an imperial language to a tribal identity to define the era. Symptomatically, Hammurabi used both to define himself: bearing a West Semitic name (*ḫammu-rāpi* ʾ, "the (divine) kinsman heals") and an Amorite genealogy (Finkelstein 1966), he became the most prominent conqueror and legislator of the Old Babylonian empire.

While Mari Amorites did not systematically write their own language, they gained military control over a city-state's language-writing apparatus, the scribal class of Mari. This is what makes the Mari materials so valuably different: they give a detailed image of a West Semitic political organization in its own terms. They were written in Babylonian (sometimes inflected by the speaker's native West Semitic) for tribesmen themselves, since the best-known king of Mari was himself a member of the Sim'alite confederacy (Charpin and Durand 1986). Thus, as Daniel Fleming writes, "for the kingdom of Zimri-Lim . . . tribal categories represented the primary structures of the ruler's own people" (2004:103). If the state's monopoly on writing made it represent tribes and peoples as threatening outsiders, the situation at Mari is the reverse. The past two decades of work[129] have shown that, for most of the eighteenth century B.C.E., tribal leaders actually ran the state. "In Zimri-Lim's realm, tribal populations do not negotiate a relationship with city-centered power. They hold the reins of power and dominate the population" (Fleming 2004:71).

The West Semitic terms in Mari texts evoke a political vocabulary shared with ancient Israel and other West Semitic societies.[130] Indeed, the only comparably rich expressions of ancient Near Eastern tribal ideology occur in the Bible: "it is only in Mari and Hebrew, of all the documentary evidence of the ancient Near East til Islamic times that tribal society manifests itself in full bloom."[131] This cannot be mainly due to direct influence: Old Babylonian Mari and late Iron Age Israel were nearly a thousand miles and more than a thousand years apart, and produced radically different types of texts.[132]

What Mari and Israel share is a cultural heritage, which is why the two corpora reward anthropologically and linguistically sensitive attention to how their politics is conducted through language (Fleming 2004; Caton 1987, 1990).[133] The Mari letters reveal that their writers shared a distinctively West Semitic notion of "the people" as an agent with a voice. In stark contrast to the vocabulary of the eastern Mesopotamian city-states and empires, where the collective mass is imagined as voiceless dependents (*nišū*) or second-class noncitizens (*muškēnum*), here population and kinship units are distinct entities with the power to speak and act.[134] We find here an ideological thread binding West Semitic cultures from the Euphrates to the Mediterranean and from the Old Babylonian period through the Iron Age.

This West Semitic political theory finds fundamental expression in the vocabulary of group belonging. In second-millennium Mari the two dominant tribal confederacies use two different terms for "tribe." The Yaminite tribal confederacy uses *li'mum*, while the Sim'alites use *gāyum*. These terms appear, resignified under changed social conditions, in the Hebrew of the first millennium. The highest level of kinship in the Yaminite confederation at Mari, *liʾmum*, "(your/our) tribe," is marginalized in biblical Hebrew to *leʾôm*, "(someone else's) people." Similarly, in Hebrew *gāyum* has developed into *gôy*, "nation (as opposed to people)," its kinship denotation fading as its political denotation comes to the fore. And now *ʿam*, "people," an earlier word for ancestor (*ḫammum*, "grandfather" at Mari, later Arabic *ʿamm*, "paternal uncle"),[135] emerges as the dominant term for the highest, most global level of "kin" in Hebrew (similarly in Phoenician). The words' syntax entails culturally specific ways for individuals to relate to larger social groups. While both Amorite *liʾmum* and biblical *ʿam* take possessive suffixes (not just "the people" but "my people," "your people," "the Lord's people") biblical Hebrew *leʾôm* and *gôy* are almost never possessed. *Gôy* is not a term of personal belonging; one can be the *gôy* of a region, but not of an individual or a god.[136]

These kinship terms reflected historical change in West Semitic institutions. The Sim'alite tribal unit, the *gāyum*, is never described as having a leadership: no patriarchs or elders are mentioned in connection with it. It cannot be owned or grammatically possessed, and there are no references to "my *gāyum*." Sim'alite pastoralism is not just an ideal but an economic fact: Sim'alite division leaders (*sugāgum*) identified by *gāyum* generally pay their financial obligations in sheep (Fleming 2004:53), while the ones identified by town usually pay in silver, as do the Yaminites. In Hebrew, *gôy* is spatialized; no longer a tribal unit, it becomes a territorially based political order that one must acquire. Thus in order to become a *gôy gādôl*, "great nation," Abraham must move from his father's house and immediate kinship associations into the new, bordered, territory of Canaan (Gen. 12:1–2). Over the thousand years separating the Mari texts from early biblical texts we witness a shift in which kinship terms with political connotations become political terms with kinship connotations.[137]

WEST SEMITIC WAYS OF CONSTRUCTING PEOPLES At Mari, West Semitic kinship terms were put into practice through ritual. This means that tribal membership was never simply a primordial blood-based form of belonging. Neither was it a nostalgic fiction, a past created purely to justify the present. The archive from Mari lets us see individual members of tribal cultures discussing kinship as a live issue, not (or not only) through the lenses of myth or memory.

A letter from the governor Sammetar to the king Zimri-Lim reports the request of the elders of Dabish, a Yaminite town. They complain of their lack of support and social connections among their current clan. He quotes them as saying, "We want, therefore, to move into the Sim'al-tribe itself, among the people of Nikhad, and slaughter a donkey-foal."[138] The donkey-sacrifice is a ritual of bonding that we meet again in Ugaritic ritual. The official's response is to question them three times to make certain of their commitment, and then to write to the king for approval of their new tribal affiliation.

All the participants in this interaction know perfectly well that tribes can be "socially constructed." Not only that, they agree on a standard way to do it, which involves killing a donkey. What the participants are negotiating is the performative creation of a tribal allegiance. Prospective tribal members do not need to share blood: a donkey's will do just as well.

At Mari the ancient tribal bonds that we still tend to imagine as either primordial or remembered are contractual, created in the present through ritual. They are made possible through *discourse*—alliance and negotiation—as much as blood.[139] It is this ideology that Cross describes with reference to Israel as "fictive kinship":

> In tribal societies there were legal mechanisms or devices—we might even say legal fictions—by which outsiders, non-kin, might be incorporated into the kinship group. Those incorporated, an individual or a group, gained fictive kinship and shared the mutual obligations and privileges of real kinsmen. In the West Semitic tribal societies we know best, such individuals or groups were grafted onto the genealogies and fictive kinship became kinship of the flesh or blood. In a word, kinship-in-law became kinship-in-flesh. (1998:7)

The idea of kinship as a binding verbal agreement pervades both historical-legal and ritual genres in the Bible. Compare Yahweh's proclamation during the covenant-ritual that concludes Deuteronomy: "Today you *become* the people of the Lord" (Deut. 27:9, emphasis added) with such straightforward—and for us, startling—performative utterances as God's speech to David in Psalm 2: "You are my son: Today I beget you!" (2:7). The donkey-slaughter at Mari and its echoes at Ugarit point to a West Semitic practice by which kinship can be created through talk and ritual. The belonging that results is no less real than that of blood.

Near Eastern states also required fictions about peoples: consider the king's claim to represent the entire population of his territory. In Mesopotamia an old myth of state origins claims that the king arose when the collective permanently ceded their power to him. In the Middle Babylonian epic of creation the divine council transfers total power to Marduk at the beginning of time; an Old Babylonian text names an otherwise unknown early ruler Iphur-Kish "(the city of) Kish assembled."[140] Neither tribes nor states were imaginary, but both needed to be imagined. This is why political communication was essential to both. The difference lay in how they imagined participation.[141]

We find the earliest examples of collective governance at Mari, but Ugarit's West Semitic-speaking contemporaries still showed a vigorous popular ideology: texts at Emar, ruled by a council of Elders, on the upper Euphrates, actually refer to a divinized people (^{d}*Lim*), and a central ritual is conducted by the people ("the sons of Emar").[142] While Ugaritic also attests terms such as *lim*, it had developed into a monarchy. Tribal ideology was only called on in crisis, in the ritual of national redemption (KTU 1.40). Here we see a historical shift: the Levantine coastal city-states detribalized more quickly than the inland communities, which retained nonurban and nomadic ties.[143] Perhaps the oldest West Semitic political monument from the Levant, the Iron Age stela of King Mesha of Moab, draws on regional and tribal ideology in order to co-opt it, building what Bruce Routledge (2000) has described as a segmentary state. Similarly in Phoenician, a Persian-period royal inscription (KAI 10) refers to the *ʿm ʾrṣ* (cognate with Hebrew *ʿam hā ʾāreṣ*), "people of the land," as an entity to be appeased along with the gods. This ideology endures through the Hellenistic period in the widespread Punic "assemblies of the people" according to whose reigns monuments are dated (Sznycer 1975).

Tribal identity provided a powerful political alternative to kingdoms because it brought not just flexibility and autonomy, but durability, the ability to participate in an order that outlasted individuals and whole regimes. Tribes could outlast states because kinship is portable; it persists at a level too deep—or superficial from the viewpoint of the state—to be subject to "collapse," the defining feature of Near Eastern political dynasties (Liverani 2001). In a world of failed or conquered states and frequent population movement, kin endured.[144]

The ritual and discursive dimensions of tribal identity let it expand symbolically to even include the state itself. Kings as well as population groups could choose clan affiliation out of strategic self-interest. Both Zimri-Lim and the town elders of Dabish seem to have chosen to emphasize or acquire Sim'alite affiliation for political reasons. For the Sim'alites appear to have constituted the majority, perhaps 75 percent, of the tribal population surrounding Mari (Millet-Alba 2004:231). This affiliation had direct military and political advantages. As J.-M. Durand put it: "In reality, the clan or tribal affiliations are not, as we would like to believe, eternal and rigid, but may be a personal decision, coming into being from one moment to another."[145]

TRIBAL DEBATE AND SOVEREIGN DECISIONS The linguistic and ritual foundations of West Semitic tribal culture produced a real politics. On an ideal level, this was conceived as a form of power emerging through verbal performance and persuasion. In both Ugaritic and Mariote myth, the sovereign power of the storm god was contingent on successful speech. Baal, patron god of the Ugaritic royal dynasty, had to negotiate power with his divine kin. At Mari, Hadad told Zimri-Lim that his sovereignty depended on his public performance of justice. But the practical basis for this culture of political communication probably lay in how it organized violence. Ernest Gellner describes a tribal democracy of force:

> [The chieftain's] armed forces were the tribe. . . . The tribal military unit was a pre-existing social group, endowed with cohesion by its shared experience and concerns and habituated by the normal conditions of its life to mobility, violence and frugality. The continuity between the social and military existences of the tribal armed forces often made them formidable; they did not need, like ordinary recruits, to be specially trained and armed with an artificial *esprit de corps*. They arrived, fully trained and *encadré*, with recognized leaders and a familiarity with the terrain in which they were to be deployed. (1995:185–86)

This "continuity between social and military existences" means that tribal affiliation was military as well as genealogical.[146] Indeed, the overlap in Mari texts between Amorite tribal units and armed forces led at least one scholar to see "Amorite" as a synonym for "mercenary."[147] While philologically dubious, there is a truth in this: military activity was an organizing principle of Mari Amorite society, and violence was at least as much discussed as performed. Indeed, belonging in Mari letters frequently boils down to who will make themselves available to whom to kill people. The very term for "general," *rab amurri* literally "head of Amorites," suggests this.

But marshaling the violence of the mobile, able-bodied males took a great deal of speech: the Amorite general could only command by persuading the army to agree to his decisions.[148] This mobile political and military group is typified as the *Ḫana*, "tent-dwellers." Political autonomy flowed from these decisions made in military assembly. This power is eloquently displayed when tribal groups made peace:[149] "In the assembly of our tent-dwellers [*Ḫana*], we decided for peace and to give up evil . . . henceforth, let us make a lasting peace; let there be no fear or terror between Yaminites and Sim'alites; let them herd in safe pastures!"[150]

Sovereignty, the power to choose and execute war or peace, was vested in the tribal assembly conceived as a meeting of tent-dwellers. The Mari archives are full of reports of the tribes assembling for political decisions.[151] Power in this form of politics depended on one's ability to persuade others in assembly. It is significant here that some of the most successful political leaders at Mari show a remarkable interest in storytelling. Jack Sasson has noted that the administrative correspondence "can be fairly long and incredibly garrulous, reporting dialogues, dispensing anecdotes, even spreading juicy gossip about the courts they are visiting."[152] These diplomatic narratives are artfully crafted, setting scenes, foregrounding characters, and deploying verbal rhythms. This interest in persuasive storytelling is not found in Mesopotamia: "these letters are rarely matched in the *Altbabylonische Briefe* series or, for that matter, in Akkadian literature. Narrative prose that tells a story, but does not report on a campaign or the like, is not particularly well-represented in Akkadian."[153]

We see here the context of the earliest known West Semitic narrative prose: as a verbal performance that addresses leaders and collective assemblies. We do not find this form in other early East or (detribalized West Semitic, like Ugarit) societies. Rather than representing a historical rupture, as Robert Kawashima (2004) provocatively argued, Hebrew narrative prose both rethinks and formalizes an old West Semitic legacy. Sasson points out another important feature of this political use of verbal art at Mari: "even the most elaborate letter found in Mari was crafted over a relatively brief interval span, often under very trying circumstances, by personalities that (we presume) had little instruction in the literary arts" (1998:109). Success in West Semitic political poetics required a healthy dose of improvisation.

The letters are the written analogue of what is reported about tribal assemblies: the political communications through which decision-making was carried out. Because of the democracy of violence in this society, an unusual degree of power could flow from the ability to involve an audience in a convincing story. If the political rhetoric West Semitic leaders used in the Mari letters was similar to the political rhetoric they used in other situations of performance, these texts are a window into how assemblies were persuaded. Unlike in Mesopotamia, order from on high would not be sufficient.

For what kind of audience was this rhetoric designed? The art of political language at Mari assumes participants who see themselves as yielding not to force but persuasion. Steven Caton argues that this ethos of speech and action is a correlate of segmentary societies. He notes the pervasiveness of such political discourse in modern West Semitic tribal societies, citing comments ranging from those of Jacob Burckhardt (1831), that "a sheikh, however renowned he may be for bravery, or skill in war, can never expect to possess great influence over his Arabs without the talent of oratory," to those of Robert Montagne (1930), that political power among Moroccan tribesman requires the ability to speak in assemblies. Most strikingly, E. E. Evans-Pritchard echoes the claim of Burckhardt that "a tribesman readily agrees to persuasion, but never accepts a command."[154] Caton concludes,

> When one examines the ethnographic record to determine what it is that Middle Eastern tribesmen are doing in political acts, one finds that they are talking to each other probably more than they are fighting, and that this has to be explained by a native model of the person as an autonomous actor in an egalitarian society, with the consequent or attendant belief that the basis of power is persuasion rather than the exercise of force. (Caton 1987:89)

The public dialogue that is the foundation of power in this West Semitic ideology entails a linguistic form: second-person address and vernacular language. The assembly must be summoned and addressed in words it can understand. The earliest detailed records of a West Semitic tribal society, with the assembly imagined as the context for political communication, provide the cultural background for the concept of the people.[155]

CONCLUSION: THE PEOPLE IN HISTORY

Hebrew and Ugaritic represent the first attempts by people in the ancient Near East to write in their own, local spoken languages. This new form of writing opened up new possibilities of participation, reflected in rituals written in Ugaritic (KTU 1.40) and Hebrew (Leviticus 16) that assumed the people as a central protagonist. The cultural background of this Late Bronze and Iron Age image of the people as an agent of ritual appears in West Semitic political thought already at Mari in the Old Babylonian period. Here the vocabulary represented tribes as unitary agents that could speak politically and actually be joined in present time through ritual. Unlike Mesopotamian political ritual and discourse, which imposed a king over a mass of subjects, imagined as a territory or a passive, voiceless group, this West Semitic ideal of political ritual and discourse bonded peoples, imagined as agents, to each other. We find here a model of political communication in which power flows from the ability to *recruit* people into relationships of alliance and fictive kinship through ritual and persuasion.

How did this West Semitic ideology enter writing? An enduring difference between states and tribal polities was their differential access to technologies of communication. Because of their bureaucratic and agricultural bases, states wrote. For two thousand years, states had exerted various monopolies on writing. The following two chapters will investigate how this situation changed. It is to this difference in access to writing that we will turn to understand why a West Semitic ideology emerged in writing when it did.

CHAPTER 3

Empires and Alphabets in Late Bronze Age Canaan

> It is only in response to a superposed and prestigious form of preexistent literature that a new vernacular literature develops.
>
> —Sheldon Pollock

Sometime, probably during the ninth century B.C.E., a group of people decided to systematically write down their local spoken language, Hebrew. This choice made possible something previously unknown in the Near East: a vernacular literature addressing a broad group of people in their own language, unifying local writing and local language to produce a kind of local politics. But people had spoken languages like Hebrew in southern Canaan for many centuries before it was deliberately written down.[1] And we know of these languages precisely because they appear in writing! Not whole texts or even complete sentences, but pieces of local dialects appear repeatedly in the writing of the Late Bronze Age. There is extensive evidence that speakers of languages ancestral to Hebrew encountered writing in Palestine over and over again. Yet among the hundreds of texts they produced there is not a scrap of native literature preserved, nor is there any sign of the kind of systematizing such a literature would entail.

This fact puts a sharp point on this book's main question. In the southern Levant, Canaanite speakers had been using writing for centuries with no demonstrated interest in using it for literature. What changed, so that at just one historical moment, and not another, a formal written Hebrew was created? We cannot hope to understand that change until we know what it emerged from. We need to track how the relationships between writing, language, and politics changed during the Late Bronze and Iron ages. This requires a history not just of scripts or writing techniques in the Levant but of writing's uses and possible users: a history of written *genres.*[2]

TWO WRITTEN WORLDS

This chapter will examine how genres and languages were represented in texts from the Late Bronze Age (here treated as c. 1500–1100 B.C.E.) southern Levant. This material is the most direct evidence for the region's culture in the period, and it forms a striking pattern. We see two different worlds of writing: an imperial world of syllabic texts, for the most part in a form of Babylonian cuneiform, and a local world of alphabetic texts, written in both linear and cuneiform scripts. The syllabic texts concern the administration and control of territory: they are tools of bureaucracy and diplomacy. The alphabetic texts are simply about the objects they are written on: they serve mainly as property markers. But neither syllabic nor alphabetic texts deliberately or consistently represent any one language. The Later Bronze Age texts, in other words, neither represent spoken language nor speak to a public, and this absence of public speech sets up a stark contrast with the Bible's picture of the period. This contrast will help us understand what changed, making vernacular literatures, including the Bible, possible.

The Bible and Late Bronze Age Writing

Both scholarly and biblical accounts describe the territory later named Israel as inhabited long before the later Iron Age culture of Israel emerged. The resulting question, since before the completion of the biblical text, has been how profound a break Israelite culture represented.[3] This question determines the story that will be told: Did Israelite culture originate through an invasion, a settlement, a revolt, or an evolution? The question has often been asked in hindsight and prejudiced by an outcome that seems inevitable.

Epigraphy lets us tell the story from a Late Bronze Age viewpoint—not where did Israel come from, but when did it become something you could write about? Where did the inhabitants of the southern Levant gain the power and desire to represent themselves and their languages in writing? Beginning the story here lets us see how Iron Age writing both flows from its past and decisively breaks with it.

Biblical scholarship has often directly contrasted biblical accounts of origins with archaeological and epigraphic evidence. This is not the path we will take, since we are out to explore not the veracity of the Bible but the very possibility of its writing. The biblical sources emphasize their difference from other local cultures, telling the story from an exclusively Israelite—and explicitly later—viewpoint. Scholars agree that the Bible's viewpoint is retrospective: any contemporary sources surviving in the Bible have been reframed and rethought. But the text itself goes even further: it is explicitly and emphatically memorial. Books like Joshua serve an explicit memorial function by acknowledging that they stand at a substantial distance in time from the events they narrate. The narrator of Joshua singles out those remarkable names and objects that have persisted from the archaic time of the Conquest "to this day."[4] Perhaps the most explicit monument to difference in biblical literature appears in the Lord's command to at once exterminate *and* memorialize not just a population but the *memory* of a population of enemy natives: "Write this as a memorial in a book and put it in the ears of Joshua, that I will utterly blot out the memory of Amalek from under heaven" (Exod. 17:14).

Modern scholarship has debunked these claims of radical difference: archaeology has not recovered the stark opposition between Israelites and others that some biblical texts proclaim. Archaeology has instead presented us with a subtler pattern of differences and similarities, and the corresponding challenge to interpret these remains without crisp, simple binarisms. Excavations show that Syro-Palestinian material culture varied mainly by region, not ethnicity. Cultural anthropology has long since begun to understand ethnic identity as an enterprise of choice and interpretation by group members and their neighbors. The great methodological contribution of Ian Hodder's *Symbols in Action* (1982) was to empirically connect archaeology to anthropology. In a series of studies, archaeologists interpreted the material remains of a culture whose natives were actually alive and available for interview. Able to ask the users themselves what the excavated objects meant to them, Hodder found that the ethnic significance of objects was decided in verbal interaction, not laid down in material patterning. In other words, the physical forms of the artifacts were not as important as the ethnic interpretation their users gave them through language.

The fact that the ethnic meaning of objects flows more from their interpretation than their inherent qualities contradicts long-standing—and ultimately Romantic—assumptions. The "Culture Area" hypothesis held that ethnic and linguistic divisions should match material culture divisions along national borders: the so-called "pots and peoples" approach. But Syro-Palestinian archaeology has borne out Hodder's argument that objects' ethnicity is something people create in interactions. Studies of the distribution of items once thought to be taxonomically Israelite, such as the four-room pillared house and the collar-rim jar, have shown that they do not line up cleanly along putative ethnic boundaries. The appearance of these items in places such as Jordan correlates with geographical and economic features, not the political or ethnic boundaries described in texts.[5] The archaeologist Elizabeth Bloch-Smith incisively points out that "not a single 'Israelite' trait identified by proponents of the Culture Area approach—pillared houses, collar-rim store jars, or pig abstinence—was exclusive to a conservatively delimited Iron I highland Israel . . . In general, Iron I highland architecture, diet, material culture, subsistence adaptation, language, and even cultic features continued Late Bronze Age practices or were attested in neighboring regions."[6]

The real problem is not that the Culture Area approach did not produce the expected result in Israel; the problem is that the result it expects is the excavation of a nation. Originating in and working to reinforce the modern concept of the nation, this archaeology's "methods appeared to enable a clear-cut territorial boundary to be drawn around discrete culture assemblages, thereby delimiting the object of study as that of a distinct ethnic culture." The scholar of nationalism Anthony D. Smith writes that "[this] presentation of a highly concrete and bounded territorial, archaeological culture seemed destined to clinch the nationalist image of a world of discrete and unique nations, each occupying an historic homeland, and each possessing its own shared memories and public culture, single economy and common laws."[7]

But if the political meaning of material culture is worked out in language (and other behavior), we need to start with the concrete, if limited, written evidence for how that meaning was created. The Late Bronze Age Levant presents a very diverse set of ways of representing language, which contrast sharply with the Bible's portrayal of early writing as an unbroken unity. The Torah remembers only one kind of early writing. It is seen as a single thing: communicatively transparent and holy. What is written is identical with what both the Israelites and God speak. There is no gap between speech and writing, and no difficulty arises from the difference between spoken and written messages.[8] Archaeological evidence presents a different universe entirely: we have not yet found a single written sentence in a local spoken language.

But after the beginning of the first millennium B.C.E. people began using the alphabet to write entirely new kinds of things: the decisive shift was an expansion in genres. In 1000 B.C.E. we find a relatively uniform Phoenician script, still mainly used to mark property—the same function the linear alphabet had served for centuries. By the ninth century this script has been adapted to serve local kingdoms in the vernaculars of Aramaic, Moabite, Ammonite, and Hebrew. And it lets the kingdoms speak in new ways: we find first royal conquest accounts echoing those of Assyrian kings, then letters and hymns. And by the eighth century, its uses have ranged far from the palace: a text in

Jordan records a divine message addressed to a people in the name of a famous prophet, Balaam, rather than a king. By 700 B.C.E. local scripts like Hebrew have escaped the royal chancery; Israelites have used the old linear alphabet to create a literature. In the late Iron Age we find extended linear alphabetic texts in a spectrum of genres: letters from all walks of life, poetry, and ritual blessings. In the kingdoms of Israel and Judah the new writing had assumed a definitive status. Yet in the very territory and history Hebrew described, the literary silence from which it emerged had been forgotten.

The most successful product of this new writing, the Bible reads as if written Hebrew had always existed, preserving no memory of its origins or what came before it. From the beginning, God had written the language that He, and Israel, spoke: Hebrew. Memory has been a major theme of recent Bible scholarship that tries to reconcile Near Eastern history with biblical literature.[9] But the Bible was also a powerful tool for forgetting: the gap in memory between Late Bronze Age and late Iron Age culture erases a decisive moment in the history of writing in Israel, the point at which written Hebrew was invented.

Why does the Bible forget the invention of Hebrew? Did no one in Israel remember earlier writing? There may have been good reason to forget or ignore it: writing in the Late Bronze Age southern Levant had very different goals than Hebrew did. Differences in writing were not just matters of style but correlated with political divisions. The syllabic systems in which most Late Bronze Age texts were written belonged to empires and city-states: few locals identified with them, and no one spoke their written languages at home. By contrast, the writing system that persisted outside these empires and city-states, the alphabet, was local. But it was not standardized to be "in" any one language: alphabetic inscriptions, as we will see, hint at a range of dialect features. Writing in the Late Bronze Age southern Levant does not display any deliberate, consistent connection with a local spoken language. Indeed, we find such a unique combination of written and linguistic elements in many of the syllabic cuneiform texts that we can read most of them without being certain what language they were in, or if they were intended to be in one specific language at all.

Language versus Writing in the Late Bronze Age Levant

Syllabic texts in the Late Bronze Age Levant reflect an intriguing gap between writing and language. Syllabic cuneiform tells us a great deal about local language, but was not intended to resemble any particular spoken variety because it was designed for long-distance political communication. It permitted unspoken conversations between imperial outposts where people did not speak the same languages: Egyptian rulers and their Canaanite- or Hurrian-speaking local representatives. To understand these conversations we must abandon modern notions of literacy, where all good citizens read the language they speak. Syllabic writing was technology with a complex infrastructure; it had to be *translated* by expert scribes and messengers into speech.

A treasure trove of Late Bronze age texts written in the southern Levant illustrates this writing/language gap by showing us the creative ways that West Semitic speakers used written Babylonian to communicate. This corpus, the Amarna letters, was actually discovered in Egypt, at Tell El-Amarna in 1887. The majority are letters from various parts of Palestine to the Pharaoh Akhenaten, supposed founder of monotheism.[10] They testify to a remarkable collision between local and imperial languages. The texts from Canaan are generally written in vocabulary from Babylonian, a variety of the East Semitic Akkadian family, peppered with West Semitic Canaanite forms. Similarly, their grammar is an intertwining of both Canaanite and Babylonian, with Canaanite often dominating on the level of word order. Hence, "Canaano-Akkadian."

Scholars do not agree on whether Canaano-Akkadian was a language anyone spoke, or whether it was even a language in any normative sense. Our evidence for it is composed entirely of a single genre: diplomatic letters. Unlike Babylonian, we have found no evidence of school texts designed to teach it.[11] The first serious sociolinguistic studies of the texts, by the Israeli scholar Shlomo Izre'el, argued that most of the letters represent a mixed language that was actually spoken by a small group of people—the scribes of the letters. But Izre'el also pointed to significant diversity in the letters' relation to language: many reflect minute local differences in both writing and speech, but at least a few were purely mental notes to the scribe, never intended to be spoken as such. And the letters' grammar does not neatly fit the cross-linguistic profile of mixed languages, which arise in situations of bilingual speech.[12] In response, Eva von Dassow (2004) established a new direction in the texts' study by viewing them as the expression of a sharp break between writing and language. She argued that the texts were composed and read out in Canaanite, but encoded in Babylonian vocabulary and writing. Rather than being read, syllable by syllable, as Babylonian words, the Babylonian signs would be taken together to stand for Canaanite words. This practice, called alloglottography, "writing in another language," was an established fact in the ancient Near East, as Gonzalo Rubio (2005) has shown.[13] In the history of Babylonian writing we find many texts written mostly in Sumerian signs, with only a few Babylonian words or endings peeking out to reveal the text's "real" underlying language. This is true from an early stage of Semitic writing at Ebla in Syria, before the dominance of Babylonian. Many of the earliest extended Semitic texts were in an East Semitic language related to Babylonian: the writing took the form of Sumerian words, but with Eblaite grammar and suffixes.

Each of the very different uses of writing scholars have observed can explain part of the evidence. What is clear is that cuneiform writing in the Late Bronze Age Levant had multiple layers, uses, and meanings. On the level of phonology, there is striking evidence of fusion between Babylonian and Canaanite forms in a single word, indicating language that was pronounced—in scribal training, if not at home (Izre'el 2005:9, examples 10, 11). At the same time, there is no explicit evidence that anyone ever read a Canaano-Akkadian letter out loud to its recipient. Indeed, the only clear evidence we have points in other directions. The pattern of note-making and erasures in one letter (EA 369) implies that it was a set of mental notes by a scribe for an oral presentation to the Pharaoh: purely written, not spoken.[14] The letters' role as essentially written communication is emphasized by the only explicit statements about how to read a letter. Four of the five complete letters from Jerusalem request not that the words of the letter itself be read, but that the scribe give a verbal performance in Egyptian, somehow based on the contents of the letter. Postscripts at the end of each of these texts plead that the scribe "present pleasing words"—rather than the verbatim text—to the Egyptian Pharaoh.[15] Those pleasing words were spoken on behalf of the Canaanite ruler of Jerusalem, but whether the message was imagined in Egyptian or Canaanite, they could not have been in the same Babylonian words as the letter itself. The four Canaano-Akkadian letters that bear clear instructions for their own reading were not intended to be read out loud, yet their grammar bears unmistakable marks of local speech.

This cosmopolitan writing system connected with local language by encoding it, translating it into writing rather than copying it and fully representing it. It is commonly stated that the civilizations of the Near East were united in this period by the common *lingua franca* of Babylonian.[16] But it is more accurate to say that the Near East was united in this period by a form of writing—the *litterae francae* of Babylonian cuneiform. These *litterae francae* encoded a variety of messages and related to language in a variety of ways.[17]

The alphabetic corpus, mainly studied for its script rather than its content, shows a different interplay between writing and language. Epigraphers, most notably Frank Moore Cross (2003), set the Later Bronze age texts in a sequence of linear progress.[18] Writing and language were assumed to evolve together in a relatively even development, moving from the earliest alphabetic writing in Egypt to the later Iron Age scripts, and from early West Semitic to the later dialects of Phoenician, Hebrew, Aramaic, and so on. Empirically, this theory encounters a critical breakdown: progress toward a simple, twenty-two-letter alphabet cannot explain the wide variety of language forms that persisted from the Late Bronze to the Iron ages (Greenstein 1976; Sanders 2006). And historically, it does not help us understand the Iron Age's radical shift in how the alphabet was used.

The syllabic and alphabetic corpora, like the texts' linguistic and social dimensions, are generally seen in isolation. But isolating the corpora from each other and their contexts prevents us from asking some obvious, and interesting, historical questions: Why did Canaano-Akkadian disappear forever with the collapse of the Late Bronze Age empires, while the linear alphabet experienced no "collapse" at all and even flowered in the later Iron Age? Why did the local writing system that blossomed at Ugarit leave no trace in the Iron Age? As we compare the written worlds of Late Bronze Age Palestine we can gain new insight into how they changed: how new, self-consciously local players reshaped writing in thirteenth-century Ugarit and the ninth-century Levant.[19]

SYLLABIC WRITING: THE EMPIRE OF CANAANO-AKKADIAN

The syllabic writing system was a cosmopolitan import: by the beginning of the second millennium, empires and city-states had brought Babylonian cuneiform from Mesopotamia through the north, via Anatolia and Syria. Cuneiform spread through both trade and conquest: it was designed to travel. Egyptian in Palestine goes back even farther, to late third-millennium conquests, and the only extended texts from the Late Bronze Age are direct instruments of imperial rule: records of harvest taxes and monuments of rulers. The syllabic cuneiform texts bear more extensive messages, written on clay tablets of a relatively uniform size and shape. The vast majority of the preserved Egyptian and Babylonian syllabic texts from this period come from garrisons established for economic and political control by the Egyptian empire. The cuneiform corpus, which dwarfs the Egyptian corpus in size and variety, will be the focus of this chapter because it contains so much valuable information about West Semitic language and culture.

Syllabic cuneiform was used by scribes to maintain the communicative networks and social roles established by the Egyptian empire in Canaan. The evidence shows three main uses for the writing system: education, administration, and communication. Self-expression and literature were not among them.[20] School texts in Standard Babylonian, not the local Canaanite or the regional Canaano-Akkadian hybrid writing, were used to teach writing; they were copied and even edited but not composed. Bureaucratic lists were written in the more contemporary dialect of Peripheral Akkadian to keep track of personnel and objects, while Egyptian hieratic was used to record taxes. Letters were written in Canaano-Akkadian (more rarely, Peripheral Akkadian) to create and maintain relationships between the texts' users. We have no writing for expressive purposes. Indeed, the only genres in which we know writers *composed* new syllabic texts in Late Bronze Age Palestine are personnel lists, economic documents, and diplomatic letters.[21] The main way we encounter verbal art is through the political rhetoric of the diplomatic letters.

The educational texts were designed to foster specialized habits of thought that radically separated writing from everyday language. They let us see how someone would have learned to produce written languages that nobody around them spoke: Sumerian and Babylonian.[22] We may consider here three examples. The first is a fragment from Hazor containing excerpts from the encyclopedic Mesopotamian school text *Urra = ḫubullu* (named after the first line, "loan with fixed interest" in Sumerian and Babylonian).[23] The series is organized by theme, and then by the initial sign of a Sumerian word, producing an organization interrupted by apparently irrelevant phrases with a fortuitous grammatical or phonetic connection to the previous ones. Our excerpt comes from the first, administrative, part of the series, designed to help bureaucrats put people and goods in order. In its original Mesopotamian context, the texts helped show the scribe how to make relationships between two very different kinds of written language: the dead but supremely prestigious Sumerian, and a formalized version of the living but less prestigious Babylonian. Dependent on peculiarities of Sumerian linguistic structure, the list's order appears arbitrary at first to anyone not steeped in that tradition. After study, it reveals its secrets: an underlying order, concealed within the signs. In the standard series, the second column contained a translation into Babylonian, originally the student's native language.

In Babylonia, the successful student could convert this text's writing into language by translating the Sumerian signs into his native Babylonian. A reward of study was that the list of alien words and ideas would become not just comprehensible but logical and transparent. This scholarly logic, pursued to its conclusion, could even assume a mystical dimension: the idea that the structure of words on a tablet revealed knowledge of things in the world.[24]

But outside Mesopotamia, the connection between writing and language that the school texts were designed to teach was complicated by a new multilingual situation. The Sumerian that ordered a lexical text like Urra was originally translated into spoken Babylonian, but when the text reached Late Bronze Age Canaan, that Babylonian had become a foreign language. The explanations now needed explaining. Thus the Babylonian, in turn, was either translated into or replaced by the state languages of other regions: as the curriculum spread new columns were added in Hurrian, Ugaritic, and Hittite.[25] As Babylonian school texts were carried to new lands, the relationship between the writing they taught and the language students spoke became increasingly complex. Study meant translating the tablets' written culture into ever-new languages.

The linguistic horizon of Babylonian receded as distance from Mesopotamia increased, producing new perspectives. This is what makes our second example, a fragment excavated at Ashkelon, so remarkable. It comes from the very same series, *Urra = ḫubullu*, as the Hazor fragment, suggesting this was part of a standard curriculum for Levantine scribes.[26] But it has an additional column translating the Sumerian into local Canaanite. Extensive parallel texts make it possible (Huehnergard and van Soldt 1999:191) to reconstruct the third line thus:

Sumerian	*Babylonian*	*Canaanite*	*Translation*
[sag.iti. šè	*ana rēš arḫi*	*li riʾšī]ti yarḫi*	until the beginning of the month

The Canaanite speech of the scribes, a language with no local written tradition in cuneiform, appears in the rightmost column. Unlike the translations into Hittite and Ugaritic, the Canaanite variety we find here is not the written language of any known city-state or empire. This may be why we find no extended syllabic texts in Canaanite. Unlike the great Hittite-using power of Hatti or the great Hurrian-using power of Mitanni, Canaanite had no political sponsor. And unlike at Ugarit in the north, no city-state chose to adapt the alphabet into the prestigious form of cuneiform. In the south, Canaanite was written down, literized, but not literarized to produce imaginative texts.[27]

Our final example comes from Megiddo and as a literary text, is telling in its isolation.[28] It is a substantial fragment from tablet VII of the Babylonian epic of Gilgamesh, narrating the ominous dream and death of Enkidu. This is the only piece of written literature found in the Late Bronze Age southern Levant.[29] As an import, it emphasizes the complete lack of native imaginative, poetic, or religious texts in the record from this period. Already prestigious and centuries old, Gilgamesh was surely adapted, as it was elsewhere, into the scribal curriculum as a classic.[30] We find no local writing used to imagine other worlds.

The lone piece of literature from Late Bronze Age southern Canaan emphasizes just how sweeping the change that occurred soon afterward was. By this time, writing had existed for more than a thousand years in the Levant, but until about 800 B.C.E., we find no local literary expression.[31] By the end of the Iron Age, evidence of Phoenician, Hebrew, Aramaic, Moabite, and other local languages is abundant.

Why has this period not yet produced a scrap of native literature? And why do we find no texts in Canaanite? Here the role of genre is crucial. As far as we know, in this time and place state-sponsored writing was used for genres of administration and nothing else. It may be that writing the language they spoke, as an end in itself, was of no interest to the Canaanite scribes of these city-states. What we know is that after learning to use Babylonian cuneiform, they used it to produce just two things: bureaucratic lists and diplomatic letters.

The administrative role of syllabic writing was to list people and things—not for their own sake, but because they belonged to the city or empire. Lists let the texts' users do the basic business of moving soldiers, workers, goods, and taxes.[32] This enumeration was conducted through letters, by far the most abundant type of text from Late Bronze Age Palestine, as well as lists of names and objects.

Probably the earliest collection of Late Bronze Age documents from the southern Levant, dated on historical grounds to the late fifteenth century, includes a "list of people called for service" (Taanach 3), with West Semitic, Hurrian, and Indo-Iranian names. This tablet was hardly written as a testimony to ancient Near Eastern multiculturalism; rather it was a device to keep track of locals who had been enlisted (note the structure of this word!), perhaps not of their own free will, to serve the Egyptian empire. The only verb in the tablet, *dekû*, "called (to service)," concludes both[33] of the preserved tallies of names, describing what has been done to the people listed. The verb's semantics elegantly encompass a broad spectrum of ways to put people in order: from making them get out of bed in the morning to summoning officials, calling up corvée workers and soldiers, and moving troops into battle.[34]

The final role of the texts, long-distance communication, is where we find the richest verbal creativity. Letters built relationships among the rulers, warriors, and bureaucrats who used them. That creativity should be found here makes sense: the far-flung empires of this period were in an important way constituted by communication. Letters could be used to coordinate: local rulers and Egyptian representatives wrote to mobilize soldiers and workers and to inform the Pharaoh of what was happening in his territories. But they could also be used to negotiate for power between local rulers, to try and convince governors to take a specific action, or to present the Pharaoh with a certain view of events. It is in the letters that we see an international order being created and contested.

The earliest extensive texts from the Late Bronze Age, the four well-preserved letters found at Taanach (1, 2, 5, 6) addressed to the local enforcer *Talwašur*, contain a nice catalogue of imperial tasks.[35] The letters demand

FIGURE 4. A letter between warlords, regarding chariots, bows, and marriage. Taanach 2. Photo courtesy of the Israel Exploration Society.

or request the movement of the instruments and rewards of conquest. By exchanging these messages, their authors built and reinforced relationships, whether symmetrical—"you are a brother and a beloved friend in that place (where you are)" (2:3–4),[36] from the warriors with West Semitic and Hurrian names (*Ahiami, Ehli-Tešub* in letters 1 and 2)—or asymmetrical, in the brisk orders of the Egyptian official Amenhotep (5, 6).

The names of the senders and recipient of these letters show that in this period, ethnicity had little to do with the use of written language. If the names bear any direct relationship to their bearers' mother tongues, a remarkable fact emerges: not only are the letters written in a Babylonian none spoke, but in three of the four letters the "underlying" Canaanite influencing the Babylonian does not even match the ethnicity of the sender, if his Hurrian or Egyptian name is any guide.[37] Not only do these men exchange goods and people acquired in Canaan; the writing they use to do it is itself a local hybrid serving the purposes of a foreign empire. We see here a communication system unique to the region, in its nature fusing heterogeneous elements of Babylonian and Canaanite into a hybrid writing that is no one's language.

As the historian Marc van de Mieroop notes, "All participants in this system knew what their place was in the political hierarchy and how to interact with others. They behaved as if they lived in a large village where communications were close and people were related to each other. In order to maintain the system, they were in constant contact with each other, sending envoys back and forth with oral and written messages" (2007:134).

The virtual village the great powers shared existed nowhere but here. These messages, moving fluidly between spoken and written forms and multiple unrelated languages, are what let the Hittite and Babylonian kings address the Pharaoh as "brother" and exchange wedding-gifts as if they were relatives. They also let vassals in Canaan "fall at the feet of the king, my lord, seven times and seven times." As far as we know, they never met.

Writing above Language

Most of the letters are written in Canaano-Akkadian, that unique code that only appears in the fifteenth and fourteenth centuries B.C.E.[38] The writing system, most of the vocabulary, and much of the morphology is a Babylonian that could only be learned from scholars or school texts. The syntax, some vocabulary, and much of the morphology is contemporary spoken Canaanite.[39] The relationship between languages is multidirectional: written and spoken affect each other on multiple levels. We find Canaanite grammatical forms attached to Babylonian stems, but more rarely also Babylonian forms alongside Canaanite ones, and whole Canaanite words alongside or instead of Babylonian ones, usually after a gloss marker. Babylonian and Canaanite grammar are layered on each other in a situation of morphological interpenetration.[40]

There is still no agreement on whether Canaano-Akkadian is best described as a single language or as a form of written communication involving multiple codes.[41] What research has uncovered over more than a century is a rich rhetoric couched in complex and sometimes clashing grammatical patterns. Scholarly literature has deployed terms ranging from "jargon" and "bêche-de-mer" (delightfully, "sea-cucumber"!) to "mixed language," "creole," or "pidgin" today.[42] Yet none of these terms fits all of the features we observe in these texts. Canaano-Akkadian does share a central feature with the well-known category of contact languages: creoles, pidgins, and mixed languages all combine one language's vocabulary with grammar from another. Contact languages show three possible specific relationships between the vocabulary and grammar of two spoken languages: creoles and pidgins inflect the vocabulary of one language, usually the dominant one, with simplified grammatical forms. Mixed languages can use the full grammar of one language with the other's vocabulary, or provide a grammatical division of labor, assigning some elements to one language and others to a second one.

But Canaano-Akkadian is both grammatically and socially more complex than any of these three. Striking features of Canaano-Akkadian—morphological interpenetration, multilingual glossing—are not found in contact languages. In these languages the morphology is either simplified or mainly derived from one language, not interpenetrated with both and rendered thereby more irregular and complex.[43] Rather than the complex French past tenses, *passé simple* and *passé composée,* which combine tense, aspect, and person in inflected verb forms, Haitian creole has a single uninflected form of the verb that does not indicate tense. Individual particles are added before the verb for the past, *té-*, or progressive action, *-ap-*; pronouns are prefixed to indicate person (Valdman 1970:149). In a typical sentence of Media Lingua, a mixed language of Ecuador, all the grammar is Quechua Mayan, but all the vocabulary is simply replaced by Spanish nouns and verbs.[44] By contrast, the mixed language of Copper Island Aleut displays a grammatical division of labor, using Russian verb inflection but Aleut noun inflection (Bakker and Matros 2003:3–4). None of these three resembles Canaano-Akkadian grammatically.

Why does Canaano-Akkadian evoke, but not fit, our category of contact languages? Our reflection should begin with this lack of fit. The fact is that "*languages* do not actually come into contact in any meaningful sense. Rather, *speakers* of languages come into contact, and they do so under a wide range of historical and social circumstances" (Garrett 2006:50).[45] To explain the structural difference between Canaano-Akkadian and the grammar of modern creoles, pidgins, and mixed languages we should consider their fundamentally different social situations. Creoles and mixed languages arise from contact between *speech communities,* two or more groups of people interacting in conversation. But nobody argues that Canaano-Akkadian arose from contact between Canaanite-speakers and Akkadian-speakers! The Canaanite-speakers who learned to write Old Babylonian studied a language whose native speakers had died centuries before. Indeed, many Canaano-Akkadian letters do not even mention anybody with a Babylonian or a Canaanite name.[46] By learning to read and write Babylonian, local writers joined an international republic of letters. The contact that produced Canaano-Akkadian was *between a speech community and a writing community.*[47]

What is special about the Canaano-Akkadian texts' grammar, then, arises from what is special about their context: the distinctive contact situation between Canaanite-speaking and Babylonian scribal culture. They are a hybrid of cosmopolitan writing and local speech. To be effective, the cuneiform system needed to work on a geographical level far above regional dialects; yet local speech nonetheless permeated it: what is so fascinating about Canaano-Akkadian is that here cosmopolitan writing could not quite escape spoken language.

Canaano-Akkadian was for communicating between city-states and empires; it is a humbler bureaucratic device, the Egyptian hieratic numeral system, which may be the only legacy of imperial syllabic writing to written Hebrew. Hieratic was mostly written for narrow administrative purposes—extracting goods from the locals—while hieroglyphic was used for a few monuments and decorations.[48] Yet it is the hieratic system that may have had the only durable local impact on writing.[49] Unlike Late Bronze Age Babylonian cuneiform, which died with the collapse of the international system, hieratic became the standard numbering in ancient epigraphic Hebrew of the ninth through sixth centuries.[50] The style of hieratic prominent in Iron Age Israel and Judah shows the strongest contact not with contemporary Iron Age Egypt but with archaic Late Bronze Age forms.[51] Sharing media with the alphabet (inkbrush on potsherd and [presumably] papyrus, rather than stylus on damp clay), a local tradition of hieratic remained from the Egyptian occupation.[52] If the hieratic numeral system persisted during the two or more stateless centuries between foreign empires and Levantine kingdoms, this is an important fact. It means that hieratic numerals were adopted for local economic uses when nobody[53] needed them to collect harvest taxes, joining an alphabetic tradition below the radar of state bureaucracy.

ALPHABETIC WRITING: THE SMALL WORLD OF CANAANITE WORDS

By contrast with the abundant Amarna letters, brimming with language and politics, we are hard pressed to find a single complete sentence in the alphabetic texts of Late Bronze Age Canaan. The Izbet Sartah ostracon is at least by dint of sheer quantity of letters the longest inscription in the linear alphabet before the Iron Age II. It contains the first known abecedary in the linear alphabet. But if it is any representative of alphabetic education, we are far indeed from a professional or standard curriculum. Paleographically dated to the twelfth century, it contains four lines of letters that do not form words in any known language.[54] A fifth line has the letters of the alphabet. This awkward and uncertainly executed abecedary is the first example of the *ʾbgd* order later inherited by Hebrew and Greek, whose first known ancestor appears in Standard Ugaritic.[55] Cross designated it "a practice tablet" (2003 [1980]:220), alluding to the wide variation in form that the letters show, the "hodge-podge of stances—which goes far beyond the confusion of stance regularly found

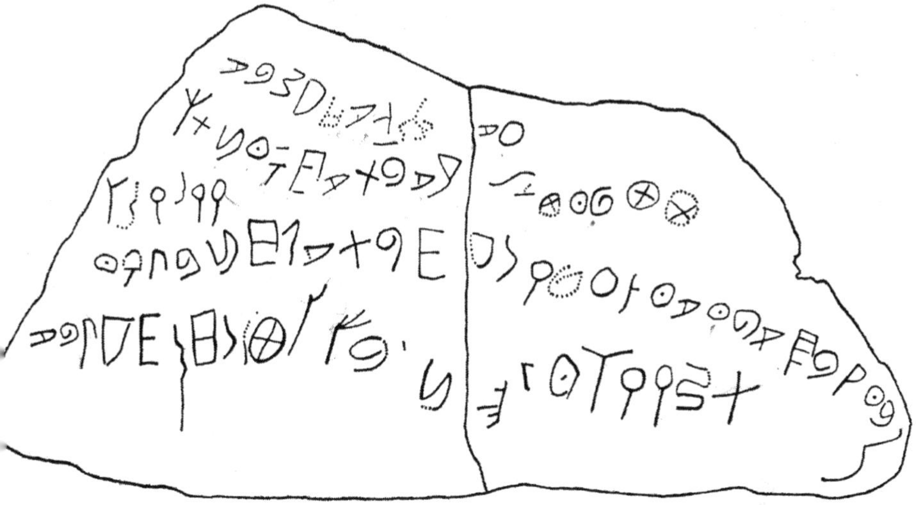

FIGURE 5. The earliest known abecedary in the linear alphabet, line 5 of the Izbet Sartah ostracon follows four lines of incomprehensible writing: random scribbling, or an unknown language? Drawing courtesy of Aaron Demsky.

in contemporary texts and common to the period of multidirectional writing," as well as several errors, including a missing or misplaced *mem* and the writing of two *qofs* in a row instead of *qof* and *resh*.[56] This humble local text stands in illuminating contrast to syllabic practice tablets such as Hazor 6, so complexly organized that Assyriologists were able to identify it from a few repeated signs, or the epic of Gilgamesh, with its twelve tablets of reflection on human limits.

The rest of the linear alphabetic texts are simply names and messages about the things on which they are written. Pragmatically, their role is deictic, pointing to the artifact itself: "this object belongs to/is for X." Their essential use has not expanded beyond the very first alphabetic inscriptions, the proto-Sinaitic texts from Middle Bronze Age (c. 2000–1500 B.C.E.) Egypt. A ewer from thirteenth-century Lachish reads "(from) Mattan. An offering to my [Lad]y Elat."[57] The task of marking human and divine property is a primordial role of writing, also found in the earliest Phoenician and Greek inscriptions. A dedication to a goddess, also known as the Lady, is the most common phrase in the earliest linear alphabetic texts from Egypt.[58]

The three alphabetic cuneiform texts from Israel provide the most illuminating contrast with the cosmopolitan world of writing. They adapt the linear alphabet to the cuneiform clay media of city-states and empires, but for much the same limited local purposes as the linear texts. They are part of a distinct body of alphabetic cuneiform inscriptions found south of Ugarit (as well as a few at Ugarit itself). Ugarit is the only known home of an alphabetic literature and a standard alphabetic script in the second millennium. But no texts in standard Ugaritic are found outside the immediate vicinity of Ugarit.[59] South of Ugarit a more varied, "southern" alphabetic cuneiform appears. This corpus has two marks: first, a script that uses distinctive forms and tends to lack word dividers. The second is the sheer diversity of its presentation. Each inscription displays some combination of nonstandard features: right-to-left direction; the collapse of one or more written consonants; syntax, vocabulary, and phonology found later in Phoenician over against Ugaritic and other Canaanite varieties. Few texts have all of these features, but each has at least one. But in their content, these texts do not depart much from the linear alphabetic inscriptions—they do little that is new. Two of our three texts belong to the well-known genres of the linear texts—an abecedary and an ownership inscription—and the third is a short receipt.

The most remarkable alphabetic cuneiform text from Palestine is the Beth Shemesh tablet, found at a cultural crossroads. Beth Shemesh ("Temple of the Sun [-God]") witnessed a steady stream of traders and craftspeople during the Late Bronze Age and Iron Age.[60] An economic ostracon in linear alphabetic script found in the same stratum as the abecedary suggests that people were using both linear and cuneiform alphabets at the site.[61]

The Beth Shemesh tablet was found in a stratum that seems to have been destroyed around 1200 B.C.E. (Grant 1934:27), and since its script is unlikely to predate that of Ugarit, a date in the thirteenth century is plausible. Unlike the uniform school tablets from Ugarit, this tablet has a unique form: a long, thin wedge tapering to a sharp edge and resembling nothing so much as an axe. It appears to have been made by pressing clay into a mold for casting metal weapons.[62]

Our alphabetic axe bears a unique type of inscription: reading from right to left, it is inscribed in a single counterclockwise arc along the outer limit of the flat of the "blade," so that it could be read continuously by rotating it 180 degrees. The letters are executed loosely and display non-canonical "southern" letterforms such as a *d* with symmetrical heads, and reads as follows:

h l ḥ m q w ṯ r t š k n ⸢ḫ⸣ [ ] ʿ ⸢ḍ⸣ ⸢g⸣ d ⸢ǵ⸣ ⸢ṭ⸣ ⸢z⸣ [ ]

The text makes no sense in West Semitic, nor does it contain the familiar West Semitic alphabetical order, and so it baffled scholars for more than fifty years. In 1987 it was discovered that the text was an abecedary (Loundin 1987),

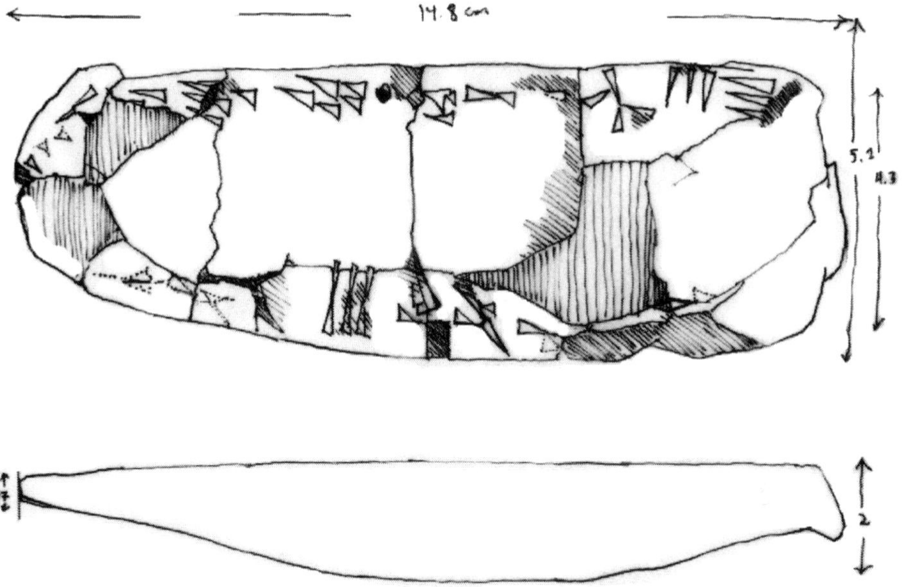

FIGURE 6. An alternative alphabet from Beth Shemesh, like the Ugaritic parallel RS 88.2215 and later examples from Epigraphic South Arabian, begins *hlḥm* rather than *ʾbgd*. Remarkably, the clay tablet it is written on was shaped in a weapon mold to resemble an axe-head. Drawing by the author.

but following an order known from South Arabian abecedaries of the first few centuries C.E.[63] This was the first trace of a second alphabetical order as old as our familiar one. It does not imply ethnic connections with South Arabian tribes[64] because linguistically it has no distinctive "South Arabian" features.[65]

The year after the Beth Shemesh abecedary was deciphered, a parallel text containing virtually the same alphabetic order was discovered at Ugarit, proving at a stroke that there were at least two alphabetical orders known across the Late Bronze Age Levant.[66] Together they let us reconstruct this second, nonstandard alphabetical order and consonant inventory, and suggest a new view of alphabetic variance.

The earliest abecedaries from Israel give us a glimpse of an entire alternate form of alphabetic writing, one that left only the slightest possible trace in the early Hebrew alphabet. Users of the order that the first millennium inherited, the *ʾabgad* order, seem to have been aware of this second, now-forgotten *halḥam* order. This is suggested by the single sequence the two orders share, *s-p-(ʾ)-ʿ*. The earliest known ancestor of the *ʾabgad* order, from Ugarit, actu-

FIGURE 7. An alternative alphabet, RS 88.2215. Ancestors of the standard *ʾabgad* alphabetical order known from Hebrew, which gave rise to our a-b-c, predominate at Ugarit, but a second order, beginning *hlḥm*, is found in one example each at Ugarit and at Beth-Shemesh in Israel. Photo courtesy of Dennis Pardee.

TABLE 1.
Comparison of the Beth Shemesh abecedary with the parallel RS 88.2215 from Ugarit, the Epigraphic South Arabian order, and the two early linear orders

Bet Shemesh	h l ḥ m q w ṯ r t š k n ⸢ḫ⸣ [ ] ʿ ⸢ḍ⸣ ⸢g⸣ d ⸢ǵ⸣ ⸢ṭ⸣ ⸢z⸣ [ ]
RS 88.2215	h l ḥ m q w ṯ r b t ḏ š k n ḫ ṣ s p ʾ ʿ ḍ g d ǵ ṭ z y
ESA	h l ḥ m q w ś r b t š k n ḫ ṣ s f ʾ ʿ ḍ g d ǵ ṭ z ḏ y ṯ [z] *
linear p-ʿ order	ʾ b g d h w z ḥ ṭ y k l m n s p ʿ ṣ q r š ś t
linear ʿ-p order	ʾ b g d h w z ḥ ṭ y k l m n s ʿ p ṣ q r š ś t

* The *z* phoneme is not represented in the attested South Arabian abecedaries according to Irvine and Beeston 1988 (correct accordingly the chart in Bordreuil and Pardee 1995:860). For ancient South Arabian phonology, see Nebes and Stein 2004.

ally contains a *s-* ʿ*-p* sequence, while the *s-p-* ʿ order is well known in the Iron Age. If the beginning of the *ʾabgad* order is indeed the least variant part (and thus the ʾ is not subject to this influence) the reversal of - ʿ and *p* in the early *ʾabgad* was most probably triggered by familiarity with the *halḥam* order, known at both Beth Shemesh and Ugarit. The most widespread variation in the alphabetical order of Hebrew, still encountered in the Bible between Lamentations 1's ʿ*-p* order and the *p-* ʿ order of Lamentations 2–4, may testify to this lost mode of writing.

What is certain is that these texts taken as a whole challenge any simple evolutionary view of how the languages and scripts of Palestine developed. It is well known that the Hebrew alphabet, adapted from Phoenician, does not itself fully represent the consonants of Hebrew! Scholars have long recognized that ancient Hebrew writing itself conceals at least one, and more probably three, consonants found in ancient Hebrew language. Not only was the double use of the *shin* sign to represent two completely distinct consonants (*sin* and *shin*), but scholars have long realized that there were likely at least two other consonants in early dialects of Hebrew, *ǵ* and *ḥ*, hidden beneath the Phoenician consonant inventory.

The fact that even Hebrew writing did not "evolve" to fit Hebrew speech makes a simple evolutionary perspective self-evidently inadequate. Yet this evolutionary view remains attractive, perhaps because of the sense of coherence it gives. Commenting on the significance of the Izbet Sartah abecedary for the development of the Canaanite dialects, Cross wrote, "[The Izbet Sartah Ostracon's] twenty-two sign alphabet is clear proof that the merger of phonemes which reduced the Canaanite stock of consonantal phonemes from about twenty-seven to twenty-two has taken place. Other evidence, including the reduced set of graphemes in late thirteenth-century Canaanite alphabetic cuneiform, dates these mergers to the end of the Late Bronze Age" (Cross 2003:225).

But this is to confuse language with writing and obscure the concrete linguistic diversity underlying the scripts. Beth Shemesh, with its twenty-seven or so letters contemporary with the twenty-two-letter Izbet Sartah abecedary shows that people in the same region could write one alphabet with twenty-two letters but distinguish five more in writing. How many consonants did they use in speech? Our data render implausible the idea that the south was evolving toward a single, reduced alphabet that was identical to the Phoenician and Hebrew scripts in its inventory.[67] We need a more sophisticated interpretation of paleographic and linguistic diversity in the early alphabets.

Scholars have tended to take the written standard as a representation of the language being spoken, relying on the dubious assumption that this single system captures the sound systems of the living languages. Yet the Masoretic tradition flatly denies this, with its two distinct sibilants *sin* and *shin* hiding under the single Phoenician-derived *shin*. We also are faced with the case of Old Aramaic, where "the Proto-Semitic phonemic inventory survives virtually unchanged," hidden again under the standard twenty-two-letter script but revealed by shifts in transcription and etymological correspondences.[68] The Hebrew and Aramaic scripts did not, even in relatively late periods, represent the full consonant inventory of all spoken forms.[69] Current linguistic analysis sees many, if not most forms of Hebrew and Aramaic in the Iron Age preserving at least twenty-five consonantal phonemes; the broad "Phoenician collapse" is an illusion resulting from the confusion of a standard script with all the varieties for which it was adapted. The linguistic diversity of the Iron Age flows from a Late Bronze Age variety so abundant that it has left clear marks even in the few texts we have seen. The Beth Shemesh abecedary indicates that the texts from south of Ugarit are not written with a single underlying phoneme inventory or in a single direction.

Our next inscription suggests that alphabetic cuneiform texts in the southern Levant were not all in a single language either. The inscription is incised on a knife blade found near the dry river bed of Nahal Tabor (Yeivin 1945).[70] Again, its meaning is essentially deictic. It reads:

> *l ⸢ṣ⸣ ⸢l⸣ b ʿ l b p l ṣ b ʿ l* "(this knife belongs) to *Ṣillī-Ba*^{a}*l*, s[on] of *Palsī-Baʿl*"

Its script style and a missing letter show how it fits into our puzzle. The inscription fits the spectrum of nonstandard alphabetic cuneiform in its letterforms, direction, lack of word dividers, and apparently reduced sibilant system.[71] Most interesting is the missing *n* in *bn* ("son"). Since the text's publication, scholars have debated whether the absence of this *n* in *b p l ṣ b ʿ l* is due to omission or assimilation, that is, a random scribal error or a significant sound change. If it is a scribal error, it would be unique in the period. But as a sound change, it fits a pattern found in the oldest extended inscriptions in the linear alphabet. This kind of assimilation is found in only one other West Semitic dialect, the Old Byblian Phoenician of the tenth century B.C.E.[72] Thus read, this text displays a distinctive feature of what would later become Phoenician.[73] Indeed, other alphabetic cuneiform inscriptions from outside Ugarit, at Sarepta and Cyprus, share distinctive features with Phoenician.[74] Displaying fewer sibilants than the Beth Shemesh text and linguistically lining up with these proto-Phoenician inscriptions, the Tabor knife implies that at least three West Semitic varieties left their mark in alphabetic cuneiform.[75]

The third text, a document of business or kidnapping from a destruction layer at early twelfth-century Taanach, postdates the Canaano-Akkadian texts discussed above.[76] It appears to be a receipt: "*KKB ʾ* (personal name), for *P ʿṢ* (personal name)": "the ransom (which was) set for him." Sloppily inscribed and difficult to decipher, it nonetheless displays sufficient distinctive features to place it firmly with the non-canonical southern texts. If the translation "ransom" (rather than "fee") is correct, we have evidence for further connections between writing and the activities of warlords.[77]

Writing below Language

Our alphabetic cuneiform texts reflect the same small-scale local political economy as the linear texts; in terms of content, little has changed since the invention of the alphabet. In the earliest known alphabetical inscriptions, West Semitic speakers in Egypt write their names and dedications to their goddess. The Late Bronze Age Palestinian alphabetic texts mark ownership (the Tabor knife) and exchange, whether from humans to gods (the Lachish ewer) or between humans (the Taanach tablet). In contrast to the syllabic system, the two abecedaries (Izbet Sartah and Beth Shemesh) display the rough, improvised remnants of an educational system with no curriculum beyond the letters themselves.

The alphabetic political economy, in contrast to the syllabic one, does not mark detailed difference in class. The level of craftsmanship and materials is moderate, not rising to the splendid heights of the gifts that cuneiform warlords and kings exchanged. In contrast to the wide range of titles and roles attested in the syllabic texts, the only titles in the alphabetic texts differentiated gods from humans: Elat is "my Lady" in the Lachish ewer. This does not imply that this society had no lords or ladies, but we find nothing like a monumental royal inscription. Of course the medium of writing itself could implicitly distinguish the powerful, when the inscribed object or script style was elaborate. But even here the alphabetic artifacts do not suggest particularly large accumulations of luxury goods. None of the inscriptions are elaborate or ornamented, and the longest, the Izbet Sartah ostracon, is also the most inept. Orly Goldwasser has recently argued that the proto-Sinaitic alphabet passed invisibly among the hieratic and hieroglyphic inscriptions as "the script of the caravans," which was also "the script of the poor" (Goldwasser 2006:153). If the owner of the Tabor knife was a military leader, we have no sign that he monumentalized his exploits through writing.

The alphabetic cuneiform texts provide a very different image of education than the syllabic ones. On current evidence the Beth Shemesh text, shaped with the tools of a metalworker rather than a scribe, represents the only example of how alphabetic cuneiform was taught outside of Ugarit. Its physical format violates common notions of scribal education, imagined to occur in highly organized settings like schools. The image of an alphabet written on an axe-head and cast in a mold for producing weapons suggests a social location for writing with no clear boundary between craftsmen and scribes. With the lone exception of the Taanach tablet, all southern alphabetic cuneiform texts found in the Levant are the irregular results of craft production, inscribed not on the standard clay tablets of the Late Bronze Age, but bowls, knife blades, or potsherds. This suggests that the institutional base of the tablet's producers was not schools but loose guilds, perhaps like those of itinerant metalworkers, and fitting the long history of movement of West Semitic speakers between Canaan and Egypt.[78]

Both the Canaano-Akkadian and the alphabetic texts show a striking lack of fit between writing and language, but for opposite reasons. The Canaano-Akkadian texts reveal an old and geographically widespread cosmopolitan written standard that is being mapped only inconsistently onto local language and culture. By contrast to the cuneiform texts, intended to work above the level of local language, the alphabetic texts represent local words and phrases on a level where "local language" was not yet a cultural and educational goal. Each alphabetic text is unique: beyond the bare fact of a (sometimes) shared inventory of letters, none shows signs of conformity with a standard beyond the momentary goals of its own writing.

WHAT WAS LITERACY?

What, then, did writing mean in Late Bronze Age Palestine, and what difference did that make for Iron Age Israel? The syllabic and alphabetic texts analyzed together present a drastic contrast in genre and power, with a cosmopolitan syllabic world positioned above a local alphabetic one. We have seen that the syllabic genres are tools for bureaucratic control over (or diplomatic negotiation for) a large geographic space. Educational texts teach a writing system beginning with Sumerian and Babylonian signs, and so not, consistently, a language. Administrative lists track people and goods. Letters served as the Egyptian empire's nerve system and a way for the city-states to talk back. The alphabetic genres are narrower and independent of the syllabic ones. They preserve essentially the same functions as at the alphabet's origins: teaching the script (but not a language) and marking objects. The patterns of writing in Late Bronze Age Palestine are political more than they are linguistic. Almost none of our texts are "in" any standard language because almost none are "of" a state in the way that Babylonian, Hittite, Ugaritic, and Egyptian texts are.[79] Yet it is the alphabetic world that endured here.

The genres and uses of writing show that the modern concept of "literacy" is not relevant to Late Bronze Age Palestine. The notion implies a free movement between genres (reading newspapers, tax forms, novels, or Bibles) and a back-and-forth between written and spoken forms of a single language: one is literate in, and can read texts out in, English, German, or French. A literate person can read literature for pleasure, compose extended texts, and, most fundamentally, render written texts directly into a spoken form. But how would the Amarna letters be read out loud? Can you be "literate" in a system, like the Late Bronze Age linear alphabet, which may never have been used to write a complete sentence? The epic of Gilgamesh could well have been read for pleasure, but it is an ancient and exotic product of a school curriculum, and it is so far alone in this regard. In neither the syllabic nor the alphabetic texts do we find evidence of direct, deliberate connection between written and spoken forms of one language. Nor do we find the composition of literature: the single literary text from Late Bronze Age Palestine was an already ancient classic, designed to be copied.

The evidence indicates that writing in Late Bronze Age Palestine was used for something both more and less than "literacy." The two writing systems had two very different relationships to both language and power, and there were strong cultural barriers between them. Syllabic writing was used for genres of administration: to build and maintain relations between city-states and empires. Canaano-Akkadian, translated into language via intermediaries, served great powers and those who aspired to their status. It is no wonder that it disappeared completely and forever at their collapse. Writers trained in the more mundane Egyptian hieratic passed on its numeral system, which was taken over when another set of states arose to tax people.

The linear alphabet reflects none of the genres being written in syllabic cuneiform. Since it contains little or no discourse, we have no reason to believe it was read in anything like the modern sense. Nor did it contain or project identity: unlike the Egyptian stelae, it did not speak from a king to an audience, and unlike the Canaano-Akkadian texts, it did not work to control territory. If it was "read" at all rather than merely recognized, the alphabet marked local belonging in the most literal way: it was written on things that locals owned.

A Very Short History of the Alphabet in Late Bronze Age Canaan

On this evidence, the likeliest scenario for how the alphabet developed in Late Bronze Age Palestine is this: the cuneiform alphabet was developed rather quickly, with no clear examples before the thirteenth century. In stark contrast to the linear alphabet, which shows no signs of standardization or scribal use before the Iron Age, the cuneiform alphabet is standardized at Ugarit a generation or so after the first examples appear. Its sudden, well-elaborated appearance suggests that it originated through engineering by cuneiform-trained scribes at Ugarit or a place much like it. Standard Ugaritic enjoyed the international high-cultural prestige of cuneiform writing and clay media but also the unique local identity of an alphabetic system. In connection with this refined form of alphabetic cuneiform a competing form of alphabetic cuneiform developed outside of Ugarit, probably at one or more smaller cultural centers in the south, of the type we know from Beth Shemesh and Taanach. This other alphabetic cuneiform is the tool of multiple ethnicities and artisans at craft sites where metalworking and writing were practiced together. Perhaps in the thirteenth century, it is created with some awareness of the Ugaritic system (at the very least, awareness of the principle of adapting the linear alphabet into cuneiform and some of the sign-forms) but without the unusual trappings of the Ugaritic city-state chancery. Peculiarities such as the three *alephs,* derived from an attempt to rethink the syllabic cuneiform system's vowel-initial syllables acrophonically on the part of West Semitic speakers who cannot pronounce a syllable onset without a glottal stop or other consonant,[80] are not adopted. The base variety for this prestige dialect is a relatively full type of early West Semitic that happens to have the same consonant inventory as Ugaritic.

Since it is conceived outside the chancery of a major city-state and used perhaps mainly for prestige, this variety is subject to less standardization than the standard Ugaritic system. As with the linear alphabet, there is vacillation in the direction of writing, and the neutralization of oppositions between gutturals, known from many Semitic varieties, is manifested in speakers' sporadic collapses of ʿ into *ǵ*, *ḥ* into *ḫ* and *ḫ* into *ḥ*, and the like. These do not necessarily represent a "reduction" in the official consonant inventory; they can as well be the spontaneous practice of speakers in an uneven scatter of subregions to whom these distinctions are no longer meaningful. The lack of standardization has another important effect: unlike Ugaritic or Standard Babylonian, this writing system is used to write more than one West Semitic language variety, including at least one and probably two dialects ancestral to Standard and possibly Byblian Phoenician.

Perhaps a century later, in the eleventh or twelfth century, a competitor arises: a version of the linear alphabet that is, for the first time, relatively consistent and carefully crafted, what Josef Milik used to call "standardized Phoenician." This variety is taken from a West Semitic dialect, probably Phoenician, which happens to have a substantially smaller consonant inventory, twenty-two versus the old twenty-five to twenty-eight letters. With the loss of Ugarit as a political and economic prestige center, and the continued vitality of the Phoenician city-states, the linear variety wins out over the next few hundred years.[81] As with our hypothetical alphabetic cuneiform system, because there is not a strong regional center directing text production, there is a period when variation in direction and language is the norm.

By the tenth century, this non-national regional linear script has won, becoming the common script of scribes and craftsmen across the Levant that we (though not, as far as we know, they) call "Phoenician." Right-to-left direction has been regularized for the linear prestige writing and the twenty-two-letter linear alphabet is in general use but there is not yet that one-to-one correspondence between script type and language variety engineered by the scribes of the later Iron Age national script-languages of Aramaic, Hebrew, Moabite, and Ammonite. In the gaps between these linguistically self-conscious kingdoms, we find remnants of this earlier period, resulting in the various languages that epigraphers refer to by place-name: Yaudic, Samalian, Deir Allian, and the like. Of course these varieties were as real and coherent as Hebrew or Aramaic, but they lack the bulky textual corpora, long histories, imagined ethnicity, and even national identities that we like to think are naturally expressed by languages and scripts but in every case are at least partly created using languages and scripts as tools.

We are now in a position to consider why the alphabet survived into the Iron Age, to flourish as the official script of the ethnic states of Israel, Moab, and Aram, the *litterae francae* of the Persian empire, and eventually the medium of the Bible and Greek literature. The alphabet during the Late Bronze Age was a local craft technique that acquired increasing prestige during the retrenchment of the Egyptian empire and the collapse of the major city-states. Indeed, for the writers of the alphabet, a low-budget and multimedia writing technology, there may have been no collapse, since it was tied to a local, less differentiated social structure that was far less vulnerable. It was only for Babylonian users that the transition between the Late Bronze and early Iron Ages was a "dark age."

CONCLUSION

Comparing the Late Bronze Age imperial texts to the alphabetic ones shows us the crucial thing that the alphabetic texts were not doing that they begin to do in the Iron Age. The Amarna letters made the empire into a comprehensible realm of communication by building long-distance relationships between rulers and their agents. This is precisely what the alphabetic texts (with the crucial but short-lived exception of Ugarit) never did: imagine an organization beyond the face-to-face. No alphabetic text from the Late Bronze Age southern Levant copied what the writers of syllabic texts were doing. The local texts did not provide the means to think about a space or belonging beyond the objects they were written on.

It is this dimension of imperial learning that distinguishes the Iron Age. After Babylonian-writing empires returned to the Levant in the ninth century, a whole set of Mesopotamian genres by which power was imagined—royal conquest accounts, chronicles of public events, codes of law—began to appear in alphabetic literature of the late Iron Age. It is by rethinking them according to a West Semitic political model (chapter 2) that they become something new: a vernacular literature. The first vernaculars resulted when the two written worlds met.

The two written worlds met tentatively for the first time in thirteenth-century Syria and then decisively in the ninth-century southern Levant. At Ugarit media, but not genres, were borrowed from the cosmopolitan Mesopotamian tradition, as clay cuneiform was adopted for the alphabet. The Ugaritic writers avoided history and law, the Mesopotamian genres of power. In terms of imaginative texts only native genres (epic, ritual, liturgy) were written; the rest was administrative. It was in the second encounter, in the ninth-century Levant, that locals borrowed cosmopolitan genres of power, resulting in the first enduring vernacular literature. What was decisive with the Iron Age Levant and most extensive with Hebrew was the adaptation of these genres, superposed by a more powerful empire. A shift in deixis—what things in the world the texts are pointing to—transformed the significance of writing; rather than being about the objects they were written on, the genres of law and history were now about Israel's collective "us," not the remote third-person "citizen" of Mesopotamian law.

In the ancient Near East, the relationship between alphabets and empires had always been productive. The alphabet began in Egypt as an imitative response to the writing system of an empire, and it is when the empire of Assyria returned to the Levant in force that we see the first extended, persuasive writing in the linear alphabet. In studying the vernaculars of medieval South Asia and Western Europe, Pollock postulates "a strong tendency, perhaps even a law: it is only in response to a superposed and prestigious form of preexistent literature that a new vernacular literature develops" (2006b:328). It is this that we will begin to see happen in the Iron Age.

The epigrapher Brian Peckham wrote of the Phoenicians, creators of the first standard linear alphabet, that their texts "share a world, but not a history" (1987:80). Creating the means for a shared history out of the Levant's local world was the Iron Age's real revolution. It was by learning from syllabic empires that alphabetic locals began to write their own histories.

CHAPTER 4

The Invention of Hebrew in Iron Age Israel

Gentem lingua facit.
Languages make peoples.
—Claudius Marius Victor

THE RISE OF WRITTEN VERNACULARS IN THE SOUTHERN LEVANT

A historical account of how written Hebrew became possible and what it was for can begin from contemporary evidence, rather than the proto-texts that biblical criticism must reconstruct from late manuscripts. While it cannot provide a complete picture, contemporary evidence can help us cut the Gordian knot of Bible scholarship: the seemingly inescapable, and often irresolvable, debate about the original dating and context of biblical sources. These primary sources allow us an independent viewpoint on the relationship between Israel's history and the literature it produced. Instead of proving whether biblical history goes back to the Iron Age, we can look at Iron Age inscriptions to gain perspective on how biblical history became thinkable. From this viewpoint, Hebrew itself was invented as a tool for making history, a new kind in which first local kings, then local people, spoke.

The inscriptions have the two-edged quality of not coming to us prepackaged, in an edited form with a moral already built into the story. On the one hand, this evidence is fragmentary; it does not claim to tell the whole story. It is tempting to delay interpreting it out of fear that there is not yet enough (yet we will always want more). On the other hand, this evidence has the advantage of coming directly, in its current form, from the times and places it is talking about. This is not true of any biblical text. The inscriptions provide a valuable new starting point. But they assume their full significance in the context of West Semitic political culture and literature, from Old Babylonian Mari to Late Bronze Age Ugarit and Canaan to the Bible, whose creation process spans from the Iron Age to the Hellenistic period.

We have seen that in the first known vernacular literatures, of Late Bronze Age Ugarit and late Iron Age Israel, rituals of collective redemption held an unusual prominence. What was distinctive about these rituals was their notion of participation: they were done on behalf of peoples, not individual clients or kings. Indeed, while no such rituals exist in the vast preserved archive of Mesopotamian cuneiform, they are the most prominent major rituals in the Ugaritic corpus and the Torah. These rituals find their basis in a widespread West Semitic culture, already well-documented at Old Babylonian Mari, organized around ideals of kinship and political communication. Important decisions involved the participation of collective groups in verbal performance: peoples, represented as hearing and speaking, were central to political action.

Collective participation was not a goal of the documents from Late Bronze Age Canaan, which served to administer empires or mark objects. Yet this West Semitic political ideal persisted in Canaanite culture: by the time that the Priestly and Deuteronomic sources of the Bible were set down, they had become central in a new way. We now find genres borrowed from Mesopotamia: history and law, as well as new forms such as narratives about prophets. But all have been rethought according to different rules of communication: they directly address a collective audience, a second-person plural "you" understood to be Israel. No literature addressed such a "you" before the Bible. For biblical literature to become possible, fundamental assumptions about writing's participants must have changed over the course of the Iron Age. But how? An epigraphic account provides clues.

To explain how the ideal of collective participation entered writing requires a new perspective, not just new data. So this account will not just be a history of scripts or languages, but also of genres and participants: the forms into which people organize texts and the roles they create for themselves in those texts. Genres are the most obvious way that communication is socially organized: knowing whether a text belongs to the genre of royal monument or graffiti, private letter or public law, gives the reader decisive cues as to what to do with the messages the texts contain. We will also pay attention to participant roles, the kinds of possible actors imagined in texts. Participant roles are where genres connect to people by setting out who is speaking: how, to whom; can they talk back? Royal conquest inscriptions speak in the voice of the king to everyone in general and no one in particular: they present him as a unique participant and everyone else as a passive audience subject to his word. Letters, by contrast, speak from one individual to another, assuming that the person being addressed can respond. They imply a conversation between multiple active participants.

Genres and their participants are not natural—their possibilities are created and limited by culture. This means that we can never safely assume the existence of a genre or use for writing without concrete evidence. As a corollary, new genres mean new things. Sumerian was written for at least five hundred years before it was used for anything but record-keeping. Then for centuries Sumerian scribes wrote hymns and royal monuments for ambitious kings without thinking to write letters. The politically subordinate Ugarit, on the other hand, produced manifold letters and hymns, but not a single royal monument. The genres and participants of written history testify to how social roles could be imagined and enacted in writing. And they give us something to watch for: when texts begin to presuppose different kinds of participants and imagine new audiences, writing begins to do new things.

Vernacular writing in the Iron Age Levant began as a medium for top-down genres of sovereignty. Royal monuments presented the king speaking in a local language. Local speakers of that language were supposed to recognize the language—and the king—as their own. Addressing the audience in a form of speech that they uniquely shared with the king was a way to imply that they were one people, and that the king's victories and inscriptions brought them together. But here is where we can detect a shift. As alphabetic genres diversify, coming to include prophecies and letters of protest as well as incantations and prayers, the possible *types* of participants diversify as well. Identifying with a language no longer meant identifying with a king. By the middle of the Iron Age epigraphic texts could be written on behalf of harvesters and soldiers—as well as God. And they could claim that a people belonged to a prophet, not a king. The expansion in genres and participants made it possible for the alphabet to speak both to and for people outside the palace. The result was a non-monarchic literature, the most decisive shift in political communication to occur in the Iron Age.

Unlike biblical literature, the Iron Age written vernaculars that made non-monarchic writing possible appear in precise archaeological contexts. This lets us trace the historical conditions under which they emerged. In the tenth century the first records of an inland script appear in Israel, but they are in an unstandardized Canaanite.[1] We have alphabetic writing and official seals from the probable period of the United Monarchy in the tenth century but the writing is not yet Hebrew and the seals are wordless.[2] Standardized local script-languages appear in monumental form hand in hand with local states in the Levant by the late ninth century. The first deliberate vernaculars are royal tools. Hebrew arose alongside these written languages and was produced in both the north and south of Israel by the beginning of the eighth century B.C.E. through the sixth century B.C.E.

While Hebrew began as a typical local script-language of inland Canaan, it had a different fate resulting from its users' contemporary historical situation and cultural past. As states developed in the Iron Age Levant, Hebrew diverged from the other state script-languages in two ways: first, it flowed beyond the geographic boundaries of a state. By the ninth century, any unified kingdom that might have existed had split. Yet it is in the period of the divided monarchy, Israel in the north and Judah in the south, that we first find a uniform Hebrew writing. This inscribed language is also the one in which the bulk of biblical narrative is written. Second, in this period epigraphic Hebrew attests a strikingly wide range of uses, going beyond genres of royal sovereignty to include forms of communication with multiple participants.

The Twelfth and Eleventh Centuries B.C.E. (Iron Age I): The Signatures of Warlords

Around 1200 B.C.E., a space opens up that will permit the rise of the kingdoms and peoples of the Iron Age. This is the point at which the system of city-states and foreign empires collapses, and their Babylonian cuneiform-based writing systems disappear. To Canaanites who lived outside of the city-states it was probably not much of a "collapse." The disappearance would have made little difference in most people's lives; it certainly did not change how they wrote. But a new opportunity was there. As the historian Mario Liverani writes, "Thus, Palestine was,—for the first time in 500 years—free from foreign occupation and from the menace of external intervention. . . . 'Little' Palestinian kings, accustomed to submission to a foreign lord, were now beholden to no superior authority apart from their gods."[3] In the absence of military dominance, new political and cultural forms could develop without fear of taxation or reprisal.

The vast majority of the writing known from Late Bronze Age Canaan was for royal courts and administrators. It was written by the employees of city-states and empires in a cosmopolitan syllabic cuneiform system. Cuneiform scribes wrote administrative genres: school texts, bureaucratic lists, and diplomatic letters. None of these texts addressed a public or a group; they were for kings, courts, and other scribes. Linear alphabetic writers, on the other hand, left almost nothing but short phrases marking property. In the alphabet, inscribed objects speak for their owners to passersby or gods; none address a court. Neither group showed interest in the genres the other wrote: the linear alphabetic texts show a total lack of influence from the syllabic cuneiform texts, and vice versa. But while syllabic cuneiform disappeared from the Levant around 1200 B.C.E., the alphabet remained as it was. From the point of view of alphabetic writing the Late Bronze/Iron Age transition is continuous with the Late Bronze: we find competing alphabetic scripts, including linear and (for perhaps a century) cuneiform, and two different alphabetical orders. Texts are written in multiple directions: right to left, left to right, and top down, with varying consonant inventories reflecting various language varieties. The grammar reflects forms of West Semitic like Phoenician, but there are no substantial texts with consistently differentiated dialect characteristics. Now that Babylonian and Egyptian have vanished with the city-states and empires, we find no signs of standardization or bureaucracy. There is no official language on this frontier.

If no state owns the alphabet in this period, violence is still key to politics, and writing is newly tied to symbols of coercion. It is in this period alone that most alphabetic inscriptions are found on weapons. A conservative estimate dates about eleven linear inscriptions on clay and at least twenty-two, probably closer to thirty, inscriptions on arrowheads. Included in this corpus is the Beth-Shemesh abecedary, an alphabetic cuneiform abecedary in the shape of an axe-head.[4] The distribution of this evidence is archaeologically significant: because the materials of the arrowheads are unusually durable, it is unlikely that their restriction to the Iron Age I is an accident of discovery.

The arrowheads put a violent twist on the old alphabetic tradition of announcing the owners of objects. The chief evidence for the employment of scribes is to write the names of local warlords, rough signatures on their weapons. As these warlords attempted to consolidate power, the means of communication was literally inscribed onto the means of coercion. Writing helped make military groups elite by distinguishing their weapons: inscribed, they could speak for them and memorialize them. Even the teaching of writing is connected to weapon production, as an abecedary is written on a clay axe-head at Beth Shemesh. This tool tangibly connects the crafts of scribe and metalworker. Alongside the chaotic Izbet Sartah abecedary, it shows that alphabetic writing was taught outside the elaborate school settings of the Mesopotamian-style city-state. The isolated settings of these discoveries also suggests that writing was distributed through travel, the communication of mobile craftsmen. We will see extensive evidence of this two centuries later when traders spread the alphabet to the Greek world.

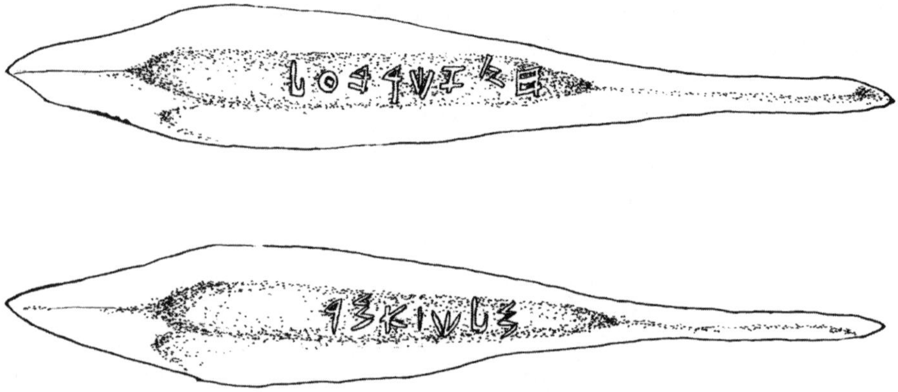

FIGURE 8. Arrowhead of "Zakir-Baal, king of Amurru" in a loosely standardized linear alphabetic script ancestral to Phoenician. Drawing by the author.

The Tenth Century: Educational Graffiti and a Bureaucratically Useless Calendar

Political consolidation in Judah emerged with little emphasis on writing. This pattern, long suggested by the absence of any inscribed seals before the eighth century, has been confirmed by recent discoveries. Excavations at Tel Rehov and the City of David have now yielded a mass of around two hundred well-stratified seals and seal impressions from the tenth through late ninth centuries.[5] Yet every excavated seal from the ninth- and tenth-century Levant is uninscribed, and the documents bearing the seals in Jerusalem were probably Phoenician.[6] This evidence stands in sharp contrast to the ever-growing body of inscribed seals and impressions of the eighth through sixth centuries, where Hebrew appears in abundance.[7]

With the seals, we witness a stark and crisply defined shift in the use of vernaculars: a decision was made by the kingdom of Judah and its scribes around 800 B.C.E. to begin using Hebrew on seals—at precisely the time we first see standardized Hebrew being written. Before this the kingdom shows no interest in using writing as an emblem. And this process precisely parallels that of the first standardized West Semitic vernacular, Ugaritic, discussed in chapter 2: Ammishtamru, the first Ugaritic king to seal his documents in Ugaritic script, was also the first king under whom we know Ugaritic literature was written down. This is true across the Levant: writing seems to have had no symbolic value for the emerging polities of the tenth century. While the late ninth century will yield a set of clearly differentiated national scripts, tenth-century epigraphy squares with archaeology: no king has yet trademarked writing.

This view is strengthened by the two significant inscriptions from tenth-century Israel, the Gezer calendar and the Tel Zayit abecedary, representing a pre-Hebrew language and script. As teaching devices, laying out the order of letters and time, we would expect them to be paradigms of standard language: the uniformity that bureaucracy requires. But they turn out to be paradigms of something else entirely: with no grammatical features and few paleographic signs to distinguish them from Phoenician, they represent a regional, non-bureaucratic writing style that vanishes from Israel and Judah by the eighth century. When the newly discovered Tel Zayit abecedary takes its place beside the well-known Gezer calendar, we can place them alongside perhaps four small inscriptions with a single name each (Tappy et al. 2007:28).[8] In script style these may be the first examples of writing in Canaan to diverge from Phoenician, up until then the only form of Iron Age alphabetic writing. An elongation of strokes suggests the emerging inland script style well known from later Moab, Israel, and Judah. Their paleography hints at the developments that will produce Hebrew and its relatives.[9]

But if the script of the tenth-century texts from Israel shows signs of evolution toward Hebrew, does their content show signs of evolution toward an Israelite state? What sort of political apparatus could have used them? We can situate our texts in the history of West Semitic literature by comparing them with what they wrote in contemporary Phoenicia, and then with the writing of the ninth through sixth centuries.

The contemporary Phoenician inscriptions serve a durable, conservative end: they elaborate a thousand-year-old linear alphabetic tradition of marking property.[10] Each of the known tenth-century Phoenician texts (KAI 1, 4, 5, 6, 7) is a royal dedicatory inscription. The kings of Byblos, Ahirom and his heirs, are only the latest in a long line to use the alphabet for nothing more than inscribing things they had made. Memorials of local rulers, they express no territorial or historical ambitions beyond immortalizing the king's piety and rule. The topic is always the dedication of the very object that bears the inscription. Each begins deictically, presenting the object itself as the first word in the sentence, followed by the relative particle *z*: "(this is) the sarcophagus/temple/wall that the king made."[11] They do not refer to broader political or military actions. Neither do they ventriloquize the king in the first person (not "I am Ahirom"), but rather point anonymously to the object ("this is what Ahirom made"). Less than a century later this will change, as linear alphabetic inscriptions begin to speak directly in the voice of the king about his conquests. By the eighth century the earliest known Hebrew texts will convey bureaucratic messages from a territorial state.

The tenth-century Gezer calendar and Tel Zayit abecedary lie outside the tight political pattern of their Phoenician contemporaries and Levantine successors. They are not royal property markers, but neither do they bear any of the well-known marks of a Near Eastern bureaucracy. The bureaucracies that produced most writing in the ancient Near East were intimately connected with the coercive tools of government: taxation and standing armies. Bureaucracy makes systematic taxation possible by counting time and things: keeping track month by month of who owes what, when. Tax collecting in turn creates the concentration of wealth needed to support the army, whose soldiers the bureaucrats keep paid and fed on a regular basis. An essential feature of every Mesopotamian city-state bureaucracy, from the invention of writing on, was the regimentation of time: breaking the year down into discrete, even units. The months may be numbered or they may be named, after local festivals, for example, but they are uniform.[12] This is precisely how 1 Kings 4:7 remembers Solomon's tax system: "And Solomon had twelve officers over all Israel, which provided victuals for the king and his household: each man his month in a year made provision" (KJV).

The Gezer calendar, unlike all other state calendars known in the history of ancient Near Eastern bureaucracy, does not break up time into even, countable units:

> A couple of months (*yarḥêw*, in the dual) of gathering
> A couple of months of early sowing
> A couple of months of late sowing
> A month of making hay
> A month of harvesting barley
> A month of harvest and finishing
> A couple of months of vine-pruning
> A month of summer-fruit

We find here eight months in an uneven order: three double months, then three single months, then a double month, then a single month. Following the flow of human labor tied to the ecology of northern Israel, it is more a calendar of seasons than months. Thus it does not give these months numbers or proper names. By contrast, the contemporary Phoenician system uses proper names: *yeraḥ bûl* (to use the biblical vocalization), "the month of Bul." This Phoenician practice reflects a common Canaanite bureaucratic system that the early Israelite monarchy also borrowed. It is only in the post-exilic Judean system that we see a system of proper names for months in regular use in biblical texts: *ḥodeš nîsān*, "the month of Nisan." But these names are directly borrowed from Babylonian. Meanwhile, the pre-exilic systems of the divided Israelite and Judean kingdoms use numbers: *haḥodeš haššemînî*, "the eighth month."[13] What all of these bureaucratic calendars have in common is the regimentation of months into twelve even units. In writing, state control extends beyond script and language to time itself.

The Gezer calendar stands outside of bureaucratic standard time, ordered by the passage of agricultural seasons. These uneven, colloquial months are not plausibly those of the biblical lunisolar calendar, with its rigid and symmetrical man-made thirty-day units and intercalary months.[14] The Gezer calendar is a fragment of cultural activity in the opposite direction of bureaucratic regimentation: the literization, the setting-down in writing, of a local culture.[15] If the Gezer calendar is useless as a bureaucratic tool, its language reflects the categories of farmers, in a common Canaanite vocabulary of timekeeping. It has the appearance of a non-scribal learning tool, teaching writing as an entertainment, not an instrument.[16]

Comparison with this inscription highlights distinctive features of early Phoenician and later Israelite and Judean bureaucratization. Both the Gezer calendar and the Phoenician inscriptions use the old Canaanite term *yarḥ(u)*, "moon/month." In the Hebrew Bible, this term only appears as a month name in three citations of the annals of Solomon in the book of Kings (1 Kings 6:37; 6:38, 8:3). The contrast between this older Canaanite terminology and the official dating system of the Israelite and Judean states is apparent in the Deuteronomistic Historian's need to translate these month names. The book of Kings glosses the old Canaanite month-names into the numbered months of Israel and Judah: *yeraḥ bûl hûʾ haḥodeš haššemînî*, "the month of Bul, that is month VIII (in our dating system)" (1 Kings 6:38). The uniform format of Kings' dating fits that of the Arad ostraca, which does not name months but designates days by number of the month. The very need to translate the old Canaanite months into "Judean Standard Time" suggests that the calendar system of Solomon is not the innovation of a new state but a relic of the then-dominant written culture: the pan-Canaanite scribal system of Phoenician. The most plausible explanation is that people were indeed writing annals for Solomon during the tenth century, but not necessarily in Hebrew: the Solomonic dating system, like the iconography of the tenth-century seals, is Phoenician.

The Zayit abecedary also reflects a relatively loose and chaotic written culture. It has two letter sequences that are found in no Israelite abecedary, one of which is known only from the earlier Canaanite alphabetical order found at Izbet Sartah.[17]

By the eighth century, most of the distinctive features of the Zayit abecedary have vanished: it has more features in common with pre-Israelite orders than with known Israelite and Judean orders. Table 2 shows how, of the three differences from the later order we consider standard, two appear in the

TABLE 2.

Comparative chart.* Note in the top row the probable consonantal inventory of Iron Age spoken Hebrew (including the three consonants that never appear in the Iron Age linear alphabet: we know ḫ and ǵ were pronounced because of transcriptions into other languages, and the Masoretic tradition still accurately distinguishes *śin* from *šin* today). The bottom two rows show that most known Iron Age Hebrew abecedaries do not follow the later order of the Hebrew alphabet in that they have *peh* come before *ayin*.

Full consonant inventory for Iron Age Hebrew	ʾ	b	g	d	h	w	ḥ	ḫ	z	ṭ	y	k	l	m	n	s	p	ʿ	ǵ	ṣ	q	r	ś	š	t
Izbet Sartah	ʾ	b	g	d	h	w	ḥ		z	ṭ	y	k	l	m	n	s	p	ʿ		ṣ	q	r		š	t
Tel Zayit	ʾ	b	g	d	w	h	ḥ		z	ṭ	y	l^{X}	k	m	n	s	p	ʿ		ṣ	q	r		š	t
Majority Iron Age IIb	ʾ	b	g	d	h	w	z		ḥ	ṭ	y	k	l	m	n	s	p	ʿ		ṣ	q	r		š	t
Minority Iron Age IIb	ʾ	b	g	d	h	w	z		ḥ	ṭ	y	k	l	m	n	s	ʿ	p		ṣ	q	r		š	t

* Reading the k-l inversion in the Zayit abecedary as an error, as suggested by the writer's large scratched "X" between these letters. For this argument, see McCarter in Tappy et al. 2007.

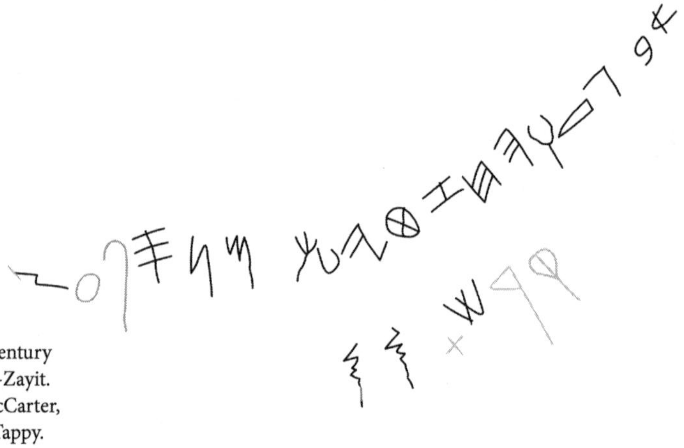

FIGURE 9. Tenth-century abededary from Tel-Zayit. Drawing by Kyle McCarter, courtesy of Ron E. Tappy.

fourteenth-century Izbet Sartah abecedary, while only one, the *peh-ayin* order, is known to have survived past the tenth century.[18] The tradition underlying the Tel Zayit abecedary harks back to an earlier way of teaching the alphabet that died out. Its letter-shapes stand in the lineage that produced Hebrew, but its order is significantly different from the one Israel inherited.[19]

Thus the only writing we have from tenth-century Israel comes from outside of a state bureaucracy. In fact, writing in this period is still most plausibly the province of regional scribes, as Schniedewind (2004) and Greenstein (1996) have argued convincingly. While the broad geographic region of the Levant, from Anatolia (Young 2002) down to Philistia (Gitin, Dothan, and Naveh 1997), used Phoenician as a standard, Phoenician was no one's national script. Indeed, the later Greek term "Phoenician" gives a false impression of unity: users of this script-language did not share an identity or even a native tongue. While Phoenician kings and citizens simply refer to themselves by city ("king of Byblos," "king of Sidon"), Luwian and Philistine rulers with unrelated heritages and identities used Phoenician freely to write their monuments. If Phoenician-speakers had a collective name for themselves, it was "Canaanite." Local kings who could afford an elegantly crafted inscription may have simply thought of the script as "writing." No tenth-century alphabet bears signs of local identity.

The known writing of the united monarchy is of a piece with the earlier Iron Age: a continuity, not a turning point. The inland inscriptions show a period of homegrown craft rather than a Solomonic enlightenment. By this point, a richly developed politics and poetics existed in Hebrew culture: as we have seen in chapters 1 and 2, biblical texts represent new permutations of long-standing West Semitic intellectual traditions. But we have no reason to believe this culture was written down in Hebrew yet; at least the writing we have from this period was not designed to convey it. If David's court did keep records, Seriah (2 Sam. 8:17), the sole scribe mentioned, may well have set them down on papyrus in the dignified Phoenician suitable to a tenth-century Levantine monarch.[20] Early medieval French courts, after all, would not have thought of writing their documents in anything but Latin. In neither case had native writing yet become a cultural goal.

The Ninth Century (Iron Age IIa): History Begins as the Voice of the King

In the late ninth century, southern Levantine courts begin to represent the world in their own vernaculars. Previously unknown languages, genres, and political orders appear together at once in writing, and the alphabet begins to address its first truly new audience. No less than three written vernaculars now emerge—Moabite, Ammonite, and Aramaic—all to write a genre previously unknown in the alphabet. Each new written language appears in a first-person royal conquest narrative inscribed on a stone monument, announcing the emergence or expansion of a local territorial state in Moab, Ammon, Sam'al, Hamath, or Damascus. Here communicative and political forms connect tangibly on massive blocks of stone.

The first extended linear alphabetic texts each lay out their territories, regimes, and languages at a stroke, on a single iconic monument.[21] The speaker is the king, who identifies himself and recounts the battles he has won and the lands he has rescued from unjust foes with the mandate of his patron god.

Remarkably, we can tell with some precision where the kings got this idea. The first narratives of historical events—indeed, the first narratives of any sort—in the local languages of the Levant are vernacular versions of the conquest narratives that Mesopotamian kings had been telling about themselves for almost two thousand years.

Historical narrative first appears in West Semitic during a broad historical moment of around fifty years, across a region from Anatolia through Syria in the North down to Jordan in the South. This early wave consists of no less than five known inscriptions, all most likely from the last third of the ninth century B.C.E. (though two may be slightly later, from the early eighth). The suddenness, breadth, and uniformity with which a new genre appears at one stroke in a set of newly written languages can hardly be an accident of discovery (Na'aman 2006:175–76, 212; Emerton 2006). At once we witness something new entering the world and recognize it as the transformation of something else.

The stela of Mesha is the first known alphabetic inscription to address an audience in the first-person voice of the king. It presents a man who claims, in Moabite, to be the king of Moab. The shift in participants from earlier alphabetic royal inscriptions is decisive. The inscription now designates itself by the speaker, not the object. No longer "(this is) *the stela* which Mesha set up" but "*I am* Mesha, son of Kemoshyat, King of Moab, the Dibonite." The inscription presents royal power by making the king present in language, ventriloquizing Mesha as if he were standing in front of us; he speaks directly to the reader without acknowledging that reader's presence: there is an "I" but no "you." And it tacitly assumes something actually quite remarkable: an audience for Moabite monuments. The content of the Mesha stela can be dated the earliest because it describes people and events known from Assyrian and biblical sources to date from around 840 B.C.E. It describes how he drove out the "men of Omri," king of Israel, consolidated territory for his personal war god, Kemosh, and built new cities. The people and territory he describes are then remembered, in the Bible, for example, as a unified "Moab," under the tutelage of a national god Kemosh.[22]

The Mesha inscription does not reflect the existence of a unified state, people, and written language so much as make an argument for one. It demands that Mesha's patchwork conquests, by which he attached territory to his hometown, be recognized as a kingdom. Bruce Routledge (2000) calls the text a turning point in the political discourse of the region, since there is no evidence of an integrated Moabite state before Mesha. His examination of the inscription reveals that Mesha himself does not describe his actual power as broadly territorial, but centering on the main city he controls, Dibon. This

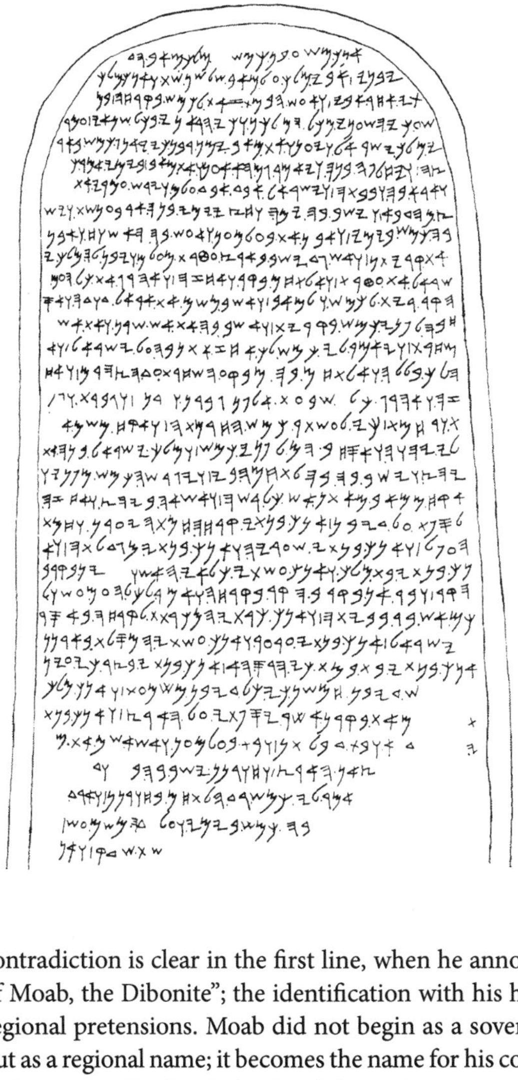

FIGURE 10. The inscription of Mesha, king of Moab, is the first known West Semitic royal monument, and hence the earliest historical narrative in the alphabet.

contradiction is clear in the first line, when he announces himself as "King of Moab, the Dibonite"; the identification with his hometown mitigates his regional pretensions. Moab did not begin as a sovereign political territory, but as a regional name; it becomes the name for his control over various cities with surrounding lands that he claims to have annexed or founded.[23]

Unlike the spoken languages they represent, the written West Semitic vernaculars did not develop unconsciously or organically. Both the written language and political narrative of the Mesha stela are tools designed to make the case for the existence of this new entity "Moab" in opposition to smaller, more complicated tribal groups within Moab (including the tribe of Gad [line 10], considered an Israelite group in the Bible!) and the external enemy kingdom of Israel to the north. The language of the stela is a West Semitic variety so close to Hebrew that it is not entirely certain whether two of the three most marked differences (the masculine plural and feminine singular nominal forms) are not merely matters of spelling.[24] The script is even closer, so much so that the Moabite inscription has been termed the first actual example of the Hebrew monumental style.[25]

The appearance of similar language and nearly identical script in Israel and Judah a few decades after the Mesha inscription implies that written Hebrew may have been created alongside Moabite and standardized with similar political and cultural goals. Each shared a process of vernacular literization—the deliberate reengineering of the generic Phoenician script into a local form of writing. The same is true for Aramaic, which is linguistically quite distinct from Hebrew and Moabite but derives its script from the same Phoenician source.

The emergence of written Aramaic exemplifies how a new, engineered kind of diversity entered the world. In the inscriptions' linguistic form, varied local dialects are honed down to a recognizable "Aramaic," in sharp linguistic contrast to Hebrew, Phoenician, and Moabite. In their religious content, varied local storm gods are recruited to play the part of violent cosmic real-estate agents: their only role is to grant the king territory, comfort him when enemies oppose his right to it, and then kill them. The four other royal conquest accounts represent two more newly written languages—Aramaic and Ammonite—and a striking reuse of Phoenician, the prestigious old script-language from which the others were derived. The first royal monumental inscription in Aramaic is the Tel Dan inscription attributed to Hazael, king of Damascus (Biran and Naveh 1995; Schniedewind 1996). Speaking, again, in the first person, he proclaims victory in throwing off the shackles of Israel, the oppressor to the south. In fighting off an invasion by the king of Israel, he claims to have killed Jehoram king of Israel and Ahaziah king of Judah. Hadad, his personal war god, marched in front of him (line 5) and he withstood (or set up) a siege (line 13). In the very language of the place he has defended, the king narrates his divinely mandated military reaction to the unjustified incursions of his neighbors. In this he becomes most like them.

Remembered as nations, each of these kingdoms seems to have begun as a gambit for power by a king or a dynasty with a personal patron god. Aramean kings did not just talk about fighting Israel; they also talked about fighting each other, with the support of various patron deities. The Aramaic monument of Zakkur king of Hamath (KAI 202) can be placed a generation later, since he states that he fought Bar-Hadad, Hazael's son (A line 4). After Zakkur was appointed king by his own war god, Baalshamayn, the king of Ạram formed an alliance against him but Baalshamayn promised through prophets that "I will deliver you from all [these kings who] have forced a siege against you" (A 14–15).[26] The first inscription in Ammonite, a poorly known regional language similar to Moabite, the Amman citadel inscription, contains a similar promise from the war god Milkom to the king that "all who besiege you shall surely die" (line 2).[27] The fact that each incipient state was remembered as a nation suggests that the inscriptions' political rhetoric did in fact have an audience: possibly through public reading (which was, as we will see, always identical with proclamation) and probably through a broader discourse—including a literature.

The Aramaic inscriptions represent the oldest known evidence in the linear alphabet of an attempt to unify written language along political lines, one that may already assume the existence of a standard Hebrew. The great Aramaist Jonas Greenfield termed the language of the early royal inscriptions "Early Standard Aramaic" because while they use common literary tropes also found in biblical Hebrew, they show a set of linguistic forms distinctive and unified enough to seem deliberate (1974:94). Drawing on Greenfield's insights, Ian Young proposed that "there is a unifying intention which characterizes this type of Aramaic."[28] He argues that if "Standard Aramaic is a conscious amalgamation of all that makes Aramaic distinct from Canaanite," "it would seem most likely that the primary stimulus was political opposition to the Israelite kingdoms and their nationalized standard language, Hebrew" (1993:57).[29] While we do not yet have evidence of standardized Hebrew in the ninth century, the very existence of carefully written Moabite and Aramaic may imply its presence.[30]

The only ninth-century royal conquest inscription not to use a newly written local Semitic language is the exception that proves the rule. The Phoenician inscription of the Luwian king Kilamuwa of Zinjirli in Anatolia (KAI 24) bears no relation to local speech or territory, but borrows the international prestige of Phoenician precisely because its meaning goes beyond the local. This text comes from a region with a tradition of writing monuments in Luwian, an Indo-European language, in a hieroglyphic script. The Anatolian practice extends back to the Late Bronze Age and is inherited from the Hittite empire.[31] This different political tradition is reflected in the inscription's rhetoric. Kilamuwa was not summoned and supported exclusively by his war god to carve out a territory; more humbly he claims to have hired the Assyrian empire to his aid and thus liberated his country. This cosmopolitan, non-Semitic-speaking king draws on an independent tradition of monumental inscriptions without national aspirations.[32]

The ninth-century royal conquest inscriptions do not presuppose nations but present the process of inventing them. Rather than evolving, we see nations being crafted: royal courts form both their languages and territories in competition with and awareness of each other. The first written evidence of conflict between the Iron Age territorial states of Moab and Israel is not over some arbitrarily inflated difference—making Israel or Moab into a demonized "other"—but rather over close and contested territory: the men of Gad seem to have held membership in both. It is this narcissism of small differences that may have impelled scribes to sharply define Aramaic and Hebrew in contrast to each other.

The inscriptions propose new kinds of political order, and they do it in a form designed to help create them. Their language and assumptions are performative, in that they entail the existence of the very things they are trying to create on the ground: a single people, language, territory, and god. This is possible because the realities they entail are more than physical. For each of these kings, peoplehood is a proposition that the inscriptions argue, not a reality they unthinkingly reflect. Each uses a similar script to represent a local language, claiming a newly defined local territory for a personal war god. In none of the ninth-century inscriptions is the god described as already that of a territory or a people. Rather, the war god helps the king gain a territory, which if accepted by the text's audience could be understood as that of a people. The script-language and the war god are being *proposed* as national. Indeed, the similarity between the vernacular media and territorial goals of each of these aspiring states is their most remarkable feature.[33] When the fifth-century (C.E.!) poet Claudius Marius Victor, writing in France, coined the phrase *gentem lingua facit*, "languages make peoples," he could almost have been speaking of our period. The line occurs in a paraphrase of the book of Genesis, so perhaps in a way he was.[34]

Where did the political rhetoric of the early Iron Age Levant come from? It is important to understand both what is new about this connection between writing and politics and what is old about it. The first vernacular histories are arguments for the first vernacular polities, and there are no previous examples of written languages being used to make peoples in this way. But the idea that politics is founded on talking directly with peoples, as opposed to giving orders to territories, is an old and widespread West Semitic concept, well documented by 1800 B.C.E. As we saw in chapter 2, a profound difference between the West Semitic Amorite rulers of Mari and their Mesopotamian predecessors and peers was their tribal ideology. Kinship groups constituted fundamental military and administrative units; ordered harshly, they could abandon or kill you. In the Amorite ideal, kinship groups were ruled through dialogue: the tribal leaders, and often the tribe itself, had to be negotiated with and persuaded. Rituals in which the people participated could performatively bond tribes together. Political power flowed from persuasion, addressed to its constituents, in the vernacular.

But to the best of our knowledge, no West Semitic ruler had ever previously felt a need to write down a public rhetorical performance. This is not plausibly a gap in our evidence: among the tens of thousands of texts written by West Semitic scribes in the Late Bronze Age, there is not a single public monument or historical account. The obvious reason is that there was no political context for such written rhetoric: a stela would have been of little use during a tribal assembly, and Ugarit's imperial overlords would not have taken kindly to monuments claiming their territory.[35]

Before the Iron Age, there was a West Semitic politics but no West Semitic imperial literary tradition—because there were no West Semitic empires. To be imperial meant to imitate Mesopotamia. The career of Hammurabi, with his glaringly Amorite name (*ḫammu-* being the cuneiform transcription of Amorite *ʿammu*, "people/elder kinsman," cognate with Hebrew *ʿam*) is an elegant example. To become the Babylonian emperor par excellence, he became a founder of Babylonian literary culture. The claim to royal first-person public address was a claim to Mesopotamian-style privilege. This is why it appears in neither vernacular nor cosmopolitan language in the well-documented West Semitic-speaking city-states of the Late Bronze Age. Neither Ugarit nor Emar produced royal monuments or historical accounts of the deeds of kingdoms. As Mark Smith recently pointed out (2007), the chronicle is simply not a native West Semitic genre.[36]

On the rare occasions when earlier Levantine kings had aspired to imperial status, they borrowed Babylonian language and forms to do it. A thousand years before the Iron Age inscriptions, the king of Mari could begin a conquest account by identifying himself directly to the audience with a typical proclamation of victory and divine support. He was "Yahdun-Lim, son of Yaggid Lim; king of Mari, Tuttul, and the country of the Hana-nomads, the powerful king, who controls the 'Banks of the Euphrates': Dagan proclaimed my kingship and, handing me a powerful weapon for destroying kings hostile to me, I defeated 7 kings."[37] But despite living in Syria and probably not speaking Babylonian himself, Yahdun-Lim had his inscription written in Old Babylonian, the script-language of Mesopotamian kings before and after him. Until the Iron Age no West Semitic speaker had chosen to address a broad audience in their own script and language.[38] The linear alphabet lived for a thousand years or more, from its invention around 2000 B.C.E. to the ninth century, without speaking for a state. Even the early Phoenician royal inscriptions of the tenth century do not make political claims; they are products of skilled craftsmen rather than bureaucrats.

The independence of the linear alphabet from the state until a relatively late period should not surprise us. The history of writing shows very different possible fits between scripts and states. First, a state is not a prerequisite of scribal production: you do not need a state to produce massive amounts of writing. In the Old Assyrian caravan archive of Kültepe we find tens of thousands of texts that merchants wrote (or perhaps had written) to each other; the texts refer to scribes not of the palace or temple but the *kārum*, the trading colony. A later ancient society in a different part of the world provides extensive further examples: Sanskrit was spread widely across south Asia and into China, ignoring numerous political boundaries, by Buddhist monasteries, not kings (Kelly 2006a). And in the modern period, Ivor Wilks's (1968) remarkable study of Islamic writing in southern Sudan shows that "nongovernmental organizations" like Islamic schools produced majority male literacy in African villages without plumbing.

Thus the real question with the history of the linear alphabet is not the state's absence but its sudden appearance in the Iron Age. To understand the invention of Hebrew we need to explain how and why the state finally did co-opt linear alphabetic writing after a thousand years of disinterest. Why in the Levant, and why at the end of the ninth century?

Imperial Imitation: Levantine Kingship as Plagiarism

History-writing arrived in the Levant in the form of imperial propaganda. It is Assyrian conquest, and the genres it conveyed, which provided the model for the wave of late ninth-century vernacular inscriptions. The historian Nadav Na'aman was the one to point out this relationship: it is in the early ninth century that we first hear of Neo-Assyrian kings placing monuments in the Levant. Beginning with Assurnasirpal II (883–859) and intensifying under Shalmaneser III (858–824), Assyrian invaders erect stelae speaking of the king's conquests in his voice, at borders and boundaries between Syria, Phoenicia, and Israel.[39] Interactions between Assyria and the Levant went beyond military action and cuneiform propaganda: Assurnasirpal established relations with local courts such as those of Carchemish, Tyre, and Sidon (Kuhrt 1995:487). Beginning with Shalmaneser, Assyria established more complex mutual political relationships with certain Levantine courts, such as those of Sam'al (Kuhrt 1995:461–62). And it is a generation after Assurnasirpal that local kings first narrate their own victories in first-person inscriptions. The vernacular monuments pirate a cosmopolitan genre of empire, the first-person royal conquest inscription, for the new purpose of asserting a local language and territory.

But exactly how did Levantine courts absorb Assyrian genres? Through what medium did local rulers receive, imitate, and rethink Assyria's messages?[40] It is telling that a series of inscriptions from the court of Sam'al, beginning with Kilamuwa's testimony to his debt to Shalmaneser, explicitly refers to its close political relations with Assyria in a shifting spectrum of local script-languages (Young 2002). But it is the ninth-century bilingual Assyrian-Aramaic inscription of Tel Fekheriye that provides our most concrete example of how a genre of state sovereignty was transmitted from Mesopotamian empires to local West Semitic rulers. This example strengthens and extends Na'aman's proposal for the origins of historical inscriptions in the Levant. In this inscription, carved on the "image" and "likeness" of the local ruler Hadad-Yis'i, he claims an almost comically mixed identity, describing himself as "king" in the Aramaic version (line 6) but "governor" in the parallel Assyrian (line 8). Generically his text is not the conquest account of a territorial king but the dedicatory inscription of an Assyrian governor. But as an Assyrian form it attests to precisely the translation of genres for which we are looking. As Greenfield and Shaffer pointed out, the text consists of two separate sections: the first is composed in stereotypical and idiomatic Assyrian, while the second has linguistic and stylistic features found only in Aramaic inscriptions.[41] Here we see an Assyrian imperial form literally translated into local Aramaic vernacular terms, and vice versa.

This translation of a cosmopolitan genre into a vernacular language finds its context in a broader new Assyrian strategy: the attempt to verbally address large groups of subjects. With the geographic expansion of the empire, Assyrian rulers encountered the need to control broad groups without the direct use of military force. The most concrete result of this was the use of the vassal treaty. To achieve its aims this imperial genre invoked new participants. It did not just present the king's power but mandated a role for local rulers and people through public performance and spoken ritual. In the oath of vassalship that the Assyrian kings required of conquered rulers, a group standing in for the whole population ritually took part in the oath, uttering scripted responses. They are addressed by the words of the treaty, commanded and threatened along with the vassal ruler. And they speak as "we" in the ritual portion, taking the treaty's political obligations on themselves as a whole.[42] Assyrian political inscriptions in this period began to address their subject populations collectively, and to require them to respond.

Assyrian imperial genres were not only translated into local languages like Aramaic—they were published in that language, publicly presented as monuments, and proclaimed. Because the oaths had very specific political stipulations, local rulers and populations would have had to understand them to participate in the ritual. Evidence for this local translation and publication appears in the eighth-century inscriptions of Sefire discovered in Syria. Written in an imperfectly standardized form of Early Standard Aramaic with local grammatical features, they closely follow the form and ritual acts of the Assyrian vassal treaties. The dimension of public reception is highlighted in the demand for a double publication, visual and aural.[43] The parties are commanded, "Let not one word of this text be silent" and concludes, "thus we have said and thus we have written."[44]

The transfer of imperial genres of sovereignty into local language was initiated by the Assyrian empire in the ninth-century Levant with unintended consequences. By translating and orally proclaiming royal inscriptions and vassal treaties, genres in which the king spoke to whole groups, the Assyrian empire could attempt to address local populations as wholes. These genres of imperial sovereignty were then pirated and transformed into genres of local sovereignty by Levantine kings: the Assyrian king of the universe became the Moabite man of Diban. With this shift, monumental rhetoric began to invoke a collective "us," not just a subjected "you," to include and persuade rather than terrorize.

Epigraphy provides concrete evidence for how local kings began to use the alphabet to take on the genres and voices of empires for their own ends. The process by which small polities borrow or steal from larger ones has been termed "imperial imitation" by Sheldon Pollock (2006a:281 and 2006b). Imperial imitation extended to ideas, not just scripts and genres. By making the king speak on a stela in a vernacular language about the people he killed, the things he built, and the god who gave him victory, the local Semitic-speaking cultures of the Levant translated the self-image of an empire to smaller places with narrower horizons. The new kings transformed an imperial genre by addressing its claims to local communities in written versions of local languages, which were to be understood as theirs. The tools had been forged to write about, imagine, and identify with the history of a place and people, an Aram, Moab, or Israel.

THE ENGINEERING OF HEBREW IN THE NINTH TO THE SIXTH CENTURIES

In the beginning only kings spoke in written vernaculars. How do we know anybody was listening? We can trace the outline of expanding audiences for vernacular script-languages as their uses and users become incrementally more diverse. While Moabite and Ammonite never significantly diversified, during the eighth century people began to express themselves in Hebrew and Aramaic in ways they had not in the ninth.

The decisive feature of Iron Age Hebrew writing is its unity: across time and space, and beyond the boundaries of any one state, people wrote Hebrew in the same way. At Kuntillet Ajrud around 800 B.C.E. the first trappings of statehood appear in Hebrew writing: not only letters between individuals in a hierarchy but prayers to a war god. On a pithos we find practice versions of the Hebrew alphabet (in both of its Iron Age IIb versions), but also a practice letter "to my lord," from a military or bureaucratic subordinate to a superior. On the wall we find a hymn praising El and Baal as military gods, who make the mountains shudder on "the day of battle." By the early eighth century, ostraca from Samaria (probably from Jeroboam II c. 770 B.C.E.; see Rollston 2006:52n15) represent the first evidence in Canaan of alphabetic record-keeping: taxation in the service of the kingdom of Israel.

By this time Israelite writing has the form of a curriculum. Kuntillet Ajrud attests a constellation of tools for *reproducing* a standard written Hebrew. Together for the first time we see practice texts: abecedaries with two variant alphabetical orders, hymns to national war gods, and practice letters that did not just reflect but enshrined social hierarchy by addressing the receiver as "lord." It is in the ninth and eighth centuries that we begin to see in the linear alphabet what Ryan Byrne (f/c) calls "the cosmetics of statecraft"—specialized items that signal the presence of a territorial political power: "the state was here."

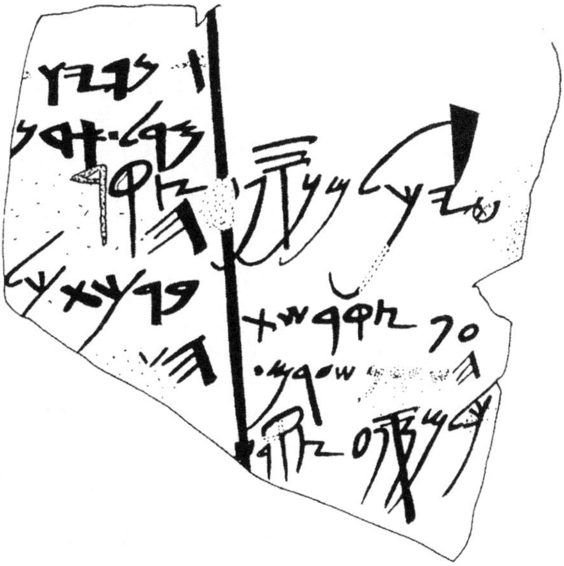

FIGURE 11. Israelite education out of school, c. 800 B.C.E.: a potsherd from Kuntillet Ajrud in the Sinai desert has three different attempts at the alphabet, with two slightly different alphabetical orders (a variation also found in biblical acrostic poems), and the beginning of a practice letter to "my lord." Drawing courtesy of Ze'v Meshel.

But the formal features of the Kuntillet Ajrud texts also exemplify how the technology of writing could flow through state borders while reinforcing cultural ones. Found in the far south, in the Negev desert, they are written by people with northern names (with the divine name written *yw*, representing the northern *yaw* rather than the southern form *yhw*, representing *yāhū*) and include a dedication to the Lord of Samaria, capital of the northern Israelite state (Ahituv 2004:232–45). What is more, the surviving building attests cultic inscriptions on its walls in the Hebrew language and northern, Phoenician-style script.[45] This small, isolated desert way station is precisely where we do not expect a school, and precisely where we do expect to see skills and goods transported over great distances. Here we find not just writing but practice texts, generative of the skill that creates writing, connected to pilgrimage and trade routes.[46]

The very uses that early kingdoms made of writing testify that it was already something more than a state tool. If written Aramaic and Moabite were created in competition with an emerging standard form of Hebrew, then they are indirect evidence for the invention of written Hebrew in the late ninth century. It is certain that by the early eighth century, Kuntillet Ajrud and Samaria attest to writing in Israel as a bureaucratic device. But early texts acknowledge different political forces, of tribal organization and trade route communication, undergirding state power.

As Mario Liverani points out, "The representation of social relations in a genealogical form is typical of the Iron Age" (2005:42). Whether they shared a bloodline (consanguinity) or simply a village (consociation), Levantine groups designated themselves as kin. At Samaria, a set of receipts of wine and oil is organized by clan regions, all named after the eponymous ancestors of the tribe of Manasseh (Num. 26:28–34; Josh. 17:1–6).[47] The archaeological evidence indicates that most of the population—and thus most of the tax base and military force—was organized in areas like these tribal regions.[48] Similarly, we find dedications to the northern Yahweh of Samaria alongside Yahweh of the South (Teman) at the desert site of Kuntillet Ajrud. As with the Mesha stela, the economic, military, and cultural resources to create this effect of a state rely on local powers that undergird the state: the Lords of the North and South. The inscriptions are not stelae, monuments of conquest, but scribal graffiti—artifacts of trade or pilgrimage. These inscriptions make visible how the powers of the state to tax, kill, and communicate float atop local orders of politics and communication.

What we find is not an Israelite state establishing writing but writing being recruited by an Israelite state to establish itself. If alphabetic scribalism is what *survived* the Late Bronze Age/Iron Age transition, it is not what the state

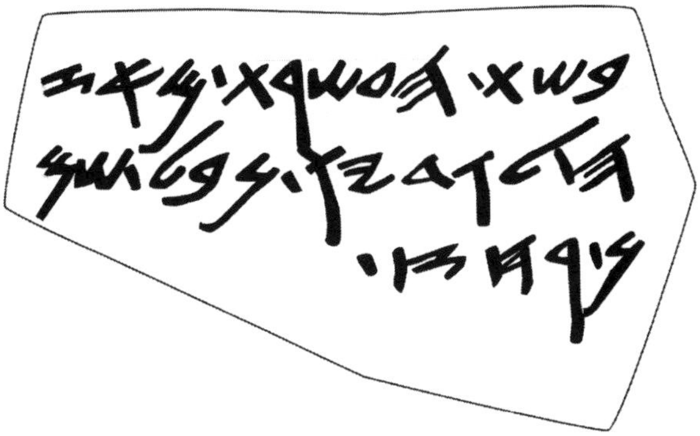

FIGURE 12. Bureaucratic writing in service of the kingdom of Israel. A record of an oil delivery dated to "year ten" of the king's reign in a neat, standardized Hebrew script, Samaria 17a. Drawing courtesy of Christopher Rollston.

created but what the state co-opted for its own purposes in order to argue publicly that it existed. As Routledge's study of Moabite writing and politics suggests, rather than simply evolving out of tribes, King Mesha used writing to persuade people with a tribal ideology to think of themselves differently, to see themselves as part of his kingdom. The state was at least as much a form of communication as it was a form of coercion or redistribution, a new way to represent local communities, not just kill people and take their things.

Thus we do not need an Israelite state to explain a complex Iron Age culture, but the other way around. What sorts of culture did the states adapt? A recent groundbreaking analysis has revealed abundant concrete evidence that Iron Age Hebrew writing was a highly ordered, but geographically scattered practice. Seeing how Hebrew was organized can give us insight into how its writers were organized.

A Deliberately Local Script

The distribution of Hebrew across space and time suggests that skilled writers outside the palace perpetuated the standardization of writing in Israel. When the first recognizably Hebrew texts containing actual sentences are found at Kuntillet Ajrud in the far south they already bear a striking resemblance to the texts from Samaria, the capital in the North. We see one script for two kingdoms.

Christopher Rollston's definitive study (2006) shows that as soon as Hebrew texts appear they share script, orthography, and numeral system across state boundaries, but are already noticeably different from those of their near neighbors in the north (Aramaic) and in the south and east (Ammonite, Edomite, Moabite).[49] The provenanced epigraphic materials suggest that a standardized written language was being promulgated across both the north and south of Israel, and that writers across Israel and Judah were trained in much the same way. Rollston demonstrated that the script has three strikingly unified features; a detailed look at this unity will help us understand what the people who standardized it were doing.

PALAEOGRAPHIC CONSISTENCY The sheer uniformity of the script in widely separated areas of Israel–Judah in the Iron Age IIb suggests that a great deal of work went into making Hebrew inscriptions the same as each other and different from those of their neighbors. Scholars have sometimes supposed that, by contrast with the exquisite formal training required for Mesopotamian and Egyptian writing, Hebrew required no technical training. But this alphabetic inferiority complex cannot plausibly explain the systematic similarities between widely separated forms of Hebrew writing. Even as the linear alphabet required less memorization and fewer layers of interpretation than cuneiform or hieroglyphic, there were more clear-cut local differences in spelling and script between regional and national script-languages. If Hebrew and its neighbors were simpler than Egyptian and Mesopotamian systems, they were also more sharply differentiated from each other.[50] Rollston has demonstrated three fundamental areas in which ancient Hebrew shows deliberate uniformity: paleography, spelling, and numeral system.

The key unifying feature of Iron Age Hebrew paleography is communication: Hebrew develops in precisely the same direction at widely separated sites across Israel and Judah. In the north and south, the script of eighth-century Hebrew ostraca from Samaria and Kuntillet Ajrud reflects the same basic script morphology. Similarly, early sixth-century texts have the same script morphology as each other, but the eighth-century and sixth-century types are clearly different from one another. The script of seventh-century Hebrew inscriptions reflects an intermediate stage between the two. In every case, they have undergone the same set of changes across a broad region. This is worth emphasizing because of its significance for Hebrew scribal institutions: variety is the rule, and people do not naturally and spontaneously write the same way; the uniformity of a script across space requires extensive effort on the part of institutions. What is more, these scripts cut off sharply at the borders of ancient Israel as a whole, rather than between Israel and Judah.

As an example, the Iron Age Hebrew *yod* in the eighth century B.C.E. consisted of a vertical shaft, a top and middle horizontal, and a bottom horizontal tail. Sometimes the eighth-century *yod* had a tick on the tail, an ephemeral feature not attested for the seventh- and sixth-century Hebrew script. The dominant form of *yod* during the late seventh century and the early sixth century was very different. It consisted of a vertical stroke and two horizontals; however, the middle horizontal exhibited a "breakthrough" and there was no horizontal foot.

The *ayin* exhibits similar morphological development. For example, all of the strokes of the eighth-century Hebrew *ayin* were fully formed; none exhibited extreme shortening. However, during the sixth century the internal strokes are radically shortened, often becoming vestigial. Moreover, the angle of the external strokes of *ayin* becomes more and more oblique during the Iron Age. Rollston estimates the average stroke angle of the left stroke of the Samaria *ayin,* in the eighth century, as between eighty and ninety degrees, while that of Lachish II and Arad VI in the sixth century is between thirty and fifty-five degrees. Similarly the average stroke angle of the right stroke of the Samaria *ayin* is between fifty and sixty-five degrees, while that of Lachish II and Arad VI is between thirty and fifty degrees.[51]

The distinctive features shared by Hebrew scripts across the territory of Israel and Judah end abruptly at territorial borders. Hebrew scribal technique must have traveled along craft networks, but unlike Iron Age pottery style (Bloch-Smith 2003), it was politically salient and deliberately local. Some letters are instantly distinguishable across small geographical boundaries. The Iron Age Hebrew *ayin* has a closed head, approximating an "o" shape, while the Ammonite *ayin* of the late seventh and early sixth centuries consistently features an open head, forming a "u."

Hebrew scripts from the eighth through the sixth centuries B.C.E. display *uniformity across space* and a *uniform direction of change across time.* This uniform transmission would require deliberate effort: it cannot have been accomplished on an ad hoc, regional basis. Why was the Iron Age Hebrew script distinct from the scripts of Israel and Judah's close neighbors? Institutions with a well-honed sense of place would have been required to produce this uniformity.

STANDARD SPELLING Early Hebrew spelling also reflects formal scribal education. It bears the defining mark of standardization: it is both consistent and arbitrary.[52] That is, the minute orthographic conventions that define Hebrew spelling over against that of its near neighbors are uniformly applied in each period, but bear no necessary relationship to the language they represent. Each of the well-attested West Semitic national scripts—Hebrew, Phoenician, and Aramaic—reflect their own particular forms of standardization.

A central feature in the history of the early alphabet is the development of vowel letters. Alphabetic writers exploited linguistic change as an opportunity to signify meaning: a phonological process of diphthong collapse (*ay* > *ê*, *aw* > *ô*) in northern and coastal dialects allowed the semivowels *w* and *y* to stand in for long *o* and *e*. The process unrolled distinctively in each script-language, sometimes exploiting morphological markers such as the final *h* that originally stood for the feminine long *a*, sometimes consonants such as ʾ and *h* that had been phonologically neutralized in certain positions. The way spelling was rethought varies by written language. Writers in the conservative tradition of Phoenician resisted borrowing from their neighbors. Iron Age Phoenician, the old prestige script, retained its original style until the end of this period, never employing internal vowel letters. By contrast, the younger Hebrew and Aramaic developed vowel letters, but at different times.

Rollston uses the example of the Hebrew word for "man," *ʾîš*. Our earliest Hebrew texts, from the eighth century, employ no internal vowel letters. Thus *ʾîš* is written *ʾš* (e.g., Siloam tunnel, line 2), without a vowel letter for the long *i*.[53] But Aramaic dialects had already begun to use these vowel letters by the ninth and eighth centuries. Texts like the Tell Fekheriye inscription, dating to the middle of the ninth century, employ them extensively.[54] As Hebrew spelling continued to evolve during the Iron Age, by the second half of the seventh century and early sixth century, Hebrew (perhaps under Aramaic influence) began to use internal vowel letters, hence *ʾîš* is now written *ʾyš* at Arad (40.8) and Lachish (3.9, 10).[55]

Hebrew orthography is consistent in its arbitrary representation of the same sounds, distinct from Phoenician and Aramaic practice, in spite of the fact that the same alphabet is used. This consistency requires a standardized training.

HIERATIC NUMERALS Rollston's third factor is a complex scribal convention: numbers. Egyptian hieratic numerals, probably inherited from the Egyptian empire's Late Bronze Age occupation, are attested at multiple Iron Age Israelite and Judean sites from the early eighth to early sixth centuries (there is no clear evidence of hieratic in other Iron Age alphabets, though this may result from the paucity of texts).[56] The first attestation of hieratic numerals and Hebrew letters together is Arad level XI 76, soon followed by Samaria.[57] Kuntillet Ajrud Pithos B also has hieratic numerals. At Lachish, a hieratic ostracon was found in the fill of the foundations of a palace, with the first line reading "tenth regnal year."[58] The use of hieratic numerals at Kadesh-barnea is particularly significant, because one ostracon originally consisted of hieratic numerical data increasing by factors of ten, from one to ten thousand, and also contained at least the beginning of another similar listing of the numbers. The ostracon bears the marks of adaptation to a Hebrew system: in the place of the hieratic for ten thousand, we see the hieratic for ten and the Hebrew *ʾlp*, "thousand." This is most naturally understood as a teaching tool.[59]

The hieratic evidence shows that Hebrew scribes were taught complex *techniques,* but also points up the absence of any remains of a complex *curriculum.*[60] The ostracon featuring the full set of hieratic numbers at Kadesh-barnea is not just an educational text: it is the longest and most complex one we have preserved from Iron Age Israel. This is surely an accident of preservation: the narrative techniques of the monumental inscriptions suggest a world of more extended texts, both spoken and written. But it means that we can make few statements about the shape of the curriculum beyond script style, spelling, grammar—and alphabetical order. And as we will see in the case of archaic Greece, it is possible for writers to produce artful texts without any curriculum at all.

ABECEDARIES The abecedaries from Israel and Judah are the most widely attested tools of scribal education, produced by either a teacher or student, and thus evidence for the existence of writing institutions in these scattered locales.[61] A good example is the abecedaries on the pithos from Kuntillet Ajrud. Surely the abecedaries are primary evidence of writers being trained to a standard. Yet such abecedaries predate Hebrew itself, and as the Izbet Sartah ostracon and Tel Zayit inscriptions show, they can exist in the absence of any sign of standardized language. Furthermore, we have no archaeological evidence for the schools in which such abecedaries would have served in a curriculum: the educational texts appear scattered rather than clustered.

In the reduction of variation in the abecedaries, we can trace the alphabet's domestication to serve Hebrew. Telling signs of standardization appear in the regularizing of alphabetical order. Between the thirteenth century, when the first known abecedaries appear at Ugarit, and the tenth century, when we find the Tel Zayit abecedary, we find variations in alphabetical order at every site where we find abecedaries. This is true of both the *ʾabgad* order known from Ugarit, Tel Zayit, and Izbet Sartah, and the *halḥam* order known from Beth Shemesh and Ugarit. The Kuntillet Ajrud orders are the first ones that we find reproduced precisely elsewhere: by 800 B.C.E. an alphabetic scribal culture shows broader spread and tighter control.

This control was not (or not only) bureaucratic. There was certainly bureaucratic use of writing: a number of inscriptions are administrative, such as the Samaria ostraca detailing the receipt of commodities like wine and oil. The Arad ostraca refer to distributions of supplies to troops, including what appear to be Greek mercenaries. Some of the Lachish ostraca deal with troop movements and military logistics. The *lmlk* ,"belonging to the king," jar handles, dating to the late eighth and early seventh centuries, also demonstrate the existence of an administrative hierarchy. Yet the system of each is unique and ad hoc, and none of these limited collections constitute the massive, systematic archives we find elsewhere in the ancient Near East. Writing was adapted for different forms of royal administration, producing varying relationships between writers and states. Scribes may have been hired to make records, without being defined institutionally by this role; there is no need to assume an extensive administrative apparatus at each site. The evidence is ambivalent as to the scale and nature of Hebrew bureaucratization.

Who Standardized Hebrew?

Hebrew inscriptions show a distinctive unity of form and an intriguing breadth of content. This standard script-language served the kingdoms of Israel and Judah in the bureaucratic ways that writing served other small Levantine kingdoms, as the Samaria and Arad ostraca show. Yet from the eighth century onward we find an increasing range of voices and social locations in Hebrew. Strangely, in some places where we would expect a royal voice, we see it elided—not flatly rejected but subtly pushed aside. It is at this time that we begin to find non-royal monuments: in Jerusalem, the Siloam tunnel inscription is the only example in ancient Near Eastern history of a monumental building inscription that does not mention the ruler. In Hebrew letters we see reports of prophecy circulating beyond the palace. Outside the realm of standard Hebrew, but intimately connected to the culture and memories of prophecy in the Bible, is the Deir Alla inscription from just across the Jordan. This text, contemporary with the Siloam inscription, is the first known written prophecy in Near Eastern history addressed not to the king but to the people. It is interesting that we have not yet found any stelae set up by kings of Israel or Judah, though our evidence is too limited to rule it out. What is certain, and important, is that no biblical text reads like a royal monument, using the royal "I" that we have seen in other Iron Age inscriptions. While some biblical records of royal accomplishments may plausibly derive from inscriptions (Parker 1997; Na'aman 2006:211–27), these prose accounts show no trace of a direct royal voice in the way the inscriptions of their neighbors do. The inscriptions are signs of a new way of writing that we find elaborated in biblical history and prophecy.

Who was responsible for Hebrew's unity and breadth? Hebrew formed a regional order that is difficult to explain as the work of a single state apparatus. Yet the thesis that Hebrew scribes were trained in an isolated way, for example, in the home by the male head of the household, cannot account for the uniform spread and manner of change in the Hebrew alphabet during the Iron Age IIb. Neither can it account for the way Hebrew writing follows the knife-edged territorial borders outlined in the main document of Classical

Hebrew, the Bible.[62] Decentralized training could not plausibly have produced the paleographic and orthographic consistency of the Hebrew inscriptions, or the extensive use of the complicated hieratic numeral system. The epigraphic evidence implies coherent training: Hebrew writing was not just a style, it was an institution.

But there is no reason to assume that this institution was a school, in the modern sense. Scholarship has moved away from the idea that scribes must have been trained in a specially designated building alongside people from different families, and toward a more kinship-based model. There are no archaeological remains of dedicated structures to house multiple students.[63] Just the opposite: as Menachem Haran (1988) has shown, the majority of physical contexts in which the best evidence for learning to write—the abecedaries—is found are just those places least suitable to be schools: tombs, desert shrines or way stations, palace steps, and caves. Neither can the uniformities of the texts be explained by the authority of a single state chancery, since if such a chancery existed its demise already lay at least two hundred years before the flourishing of the inscriptions.

The epigraphic evidence points to Hebrew scribes working outside of large institutions, which makes them less like monks or clerks and more like potters or metalworkers. Such well-known forms of craftsmanship are hardly exclusive of state power: taxation and armies were not possible without storage jars and swords. These skills were taught at scattered sites and communicated over time and distance through trade networks and family traditions. Like pottery and metallurgy, this sort of scribalism could easily be brought into the service of the state but did not require the same massing of people and resources as a chancery. Craft scribalism could be turned toward the state's purposes but was not bonded to it.

In their relative independence, Hebrew scribes were part of a long tradition in the ancient Mediterranean. The long history of the movement of artisans in the ancient Near East was sketched by Carlo Zaccagnini (1983). Zaccagnini read Late Bronze Age diplomatic correspondence that shows how scribes were classed alongside skilled artisans of all sorts, including, for example, doctors, singers, and craftspeople. They were loaned from one ruler to another and taken captive as valuable sources of material and cultural goods. From this strictly palace-centered viewpoint, artisans simply circulated between palaces. But Zaccagnini neglected the extensive archaeological evidence for the existence and movement of craft producers outside of palaces. In Israel, Late Bronze Age sites like Taanach and Beth Shemesh, which produced no diplomatic texts at all, attested both bronze forges and texts in local alphabetic writing.

The persistence of alphabetic scribalism during the total collapse of the palace economy around 1200 (Bryne 2007) and the spread of Phoenician to Greece along trade routes prove that Zaccagnini's palace-based view is incomplete. The craft of writing thrived outside royal courts, traveling far and wide in the Late Bronze Age and Iron Age Levant. Unlike the royal economy detailed by Zaccagnini, this economy was not terminated by a dark age or change in settlement patterns: while cuneiform entirely disappears during the transition from the Late Bronze to the early Iron Age, linear alphabetic texts are attested in every century.

The diffusion of alphabetic writing in the Iron Age is an excellent example of the way that artisanal activity can be organized around trade networks independent of a palace economy. Phoenician scribes worked for whoever paid them, including kings. The Phoenician script-language achieved universal prestige in the early Iron Age Levant without ever being tied to a single ruler or a central state chancery. Yet by the eleventh century, the linear alphabetic texts already show consistency, with a uniform right-to-left direction, in a script modern scholars can consistently identify as Phoenician. In concrete historical terms this script has no national or ethnic identity: before it was used in the tenth century by the Phoenician-speaking kings of Byblos (to identify themselves by patronym and city, not as "Phoenician") it had already been used in the previous century to designate arrowheads owned by "the king of Amurru." Two hundred years later a Luwian ruler at Karatepe commissioned what is in fact the longest known text in the Phoenician language.

The disconnect between alphabetic script and state was essential to the script's initial success. The early prestige of the Phoenician script-language is connected to its cultural and political neutrality, so that Luwian kings who may not have spoken a word of Phoenician could still hire Phoenician scribes. And it was precisely Phoenician's archaic and unmarked character that let later written languages originate by differentiating themselves from it.[64] Unlike Ugaritic we cannot explain the first standardized linear alphabetic scripts as flowing purely from the autocratic decisions of state chanceries: our national-sounding designation "Phoenician" is a purely modern convenience, with no basis at all in contemporary Phoenician sources. Neither can the standardization of linear scripts be understood along the lines of the "standardization" of a pottery or decorative style, the result of a myriad of organic, small-scale decisions on the part of a multitude of individuals.

A powerful economic analogy for such an independently created standard system of communication in Israel is the weights and measures of Judah. Raz Kletter (1998) has shown that a system of weights was in use at the end of the Iron Age that was highly uniform throughout the region of Judah. Yet there is little sign of direct influence from the palace: official inscriptions almost never appear on the weights (2 out of 434 instances), which are mostly found in private contexts (Kletter 1998:143–46). Here we find a highly developed nonlinguistic standard connected to a specialty—trade—which seems to have been developed through negotiation and circulated along with the merchants who used it.

If Hebrew was not a palace monopoly, it was also not the exclusive property of skilled writers. Typologically there existed, beside the formal register of scribes used for official documents, a semiformal style used for daily activities and personal messages by nonprofessional writers.[65] This style was widespread in Iron Age Hebrew and shows the same orthographic and paleographic discipline as the formal register. Farther down the scale from the formal products used in archives, we have a third type: the Hebrew engraved on stones and clay vessels. At Lachish, we find the first five letters of the alphabet engraved on the steps of a palace, and the first four imprinted on a clay jar before firing. Haran (1988) has convincingly argued that these artifacts, which neither communicate messages nor represent educational practice, are the work of craftsmen familiar with the alphabet and the use and function of writing, who nonetheless did not compose extended texts themselves. The excavated evidence attests a spectrum of relationships to formal writing, from scribes, craftsmen whose trade was writing, to nonprofessionals capable of using writing to produce extended (if not literary) texts, to a third group of craftsmen who were familiar with writing, in the sense of being able to recognize and reproduce letters.

Hebrew, then, was engineered and spread but not monopolized by a geographically wide-ranging group of skilled artisans. The epigraphic evidence shows a spectrum of ways to write in Iron Age Israel, ranging from scribal to non-scribal. These uses include what we would recognize anachronistically as "literacy"—the ability to read and produce extended texts in a high-cultural register—to a pragmatic familiarity with the use of writing: the artisan's ability to engrave letters, the ability of the owner or official to recognize a name on a stamp-seal. It is in this pedestrian, non-scribal use of writing that ancient Israel outstrips its contemporaries and neighbors.[66] And it is through non-scribal writers that the alphabet had its greatest historical impact. The early uses of the Greek alphabet demonstrate the wide promulgation of alphabetic writing and the production of artful texts far from schools.

Talking Cups and Dirty Graffiti: The Example of Early Greek

The clearest and best-known example of the linear alphabet's spread by nonprofessional writers, not scribes or states, is that of the archaic Greek scripts.[67] As in the Iron Age Levant, the alphabet was spread to Greece by contact with

Phoenician craftsmen, in this case through contact along the Mediterranean coast. The first known Greek inscriptions match Phoenician closely in both letterforms and script direction, with inscriptions running both right to left and in the snaking, boustrophedon style. Yet when we first see it, Greek already exhibits a crucial development: vowels. The Phoenician consonants that lack a corresponding sound in Greek have been reused, extending the ways the alphabet could represent spoken language.[68] This innovation happened early in Greek and was promulgated everywhere Greek-writers traveled. While the date of adoption is debated, all evidence appears in the second half of the eighth century and later.

The earliest genres of Greek writing suggest that it was a technology operating without elite control. While the products of Greek writing were easily as complex as Hebrew, they were less uniform. The Greek alphabet took on varying shapes as it reached each new region. Separated by islands, the local scripts exhibit diversity in letterforms and sometimes even in letter inventory.

As it spread across the Aegean, Greek alphabetic writing in its first century showed no influence from a professional class or a monarchy. This is evident from the three main genres of the late eighth and early seventh centuries: poetic lines for drinking parties, names on property (often, not coincidentally, drinking cups), and obscene graffiti. Perhaps the oldest Greek inscription, from Pithecusae around 740, literally identifies itself. That is, the cup speaks in the first person, saying it belongs to an individual (whose name is broken off): "I am of . . ." (Jeffery 1990:453, A, pl 76). It is paralleled by first-person graffiti on a cup of the eighth century, "I am the cup of Korakos" (Jeffery 1990:356, no. 1). The role of these inscriptions in competitive performances is signaled by items like the jar from Athens dating around 740–730, "(belonging to?) he who of all the dancers now performs most daintily" (Thomas 1992:58; Jeffery 1990: 68, 76 no. 1) The festival context and the property-marking functions are brought together in a cup from Pithecusae dated around 730–720, which seems to already parody a curse formula. In hexameter, it warns: "I am the delicious cup of Nestor. Whoever drinks from this cup the desire of beautifully crowned Aphrodite shall seize" (Jeffery 1990:239 no. 1). The participants are defined by their roles in merrymaking.

Most startlingly nonprofessional is the third genre: obscene graffiti. Beginning at the end of the eighth century, we find a profusion of inscriptions, often in hexameter, on Thera: "Everywhere on the rocky plateau of the ancient town there are casual graffiti" (Jeffery 1990:318). Near the gymnasium all the inscriptions concern dancing and sex: statements range from "Barbax dances well and he's given [me] pleasure," in hexameter, to the playful "Krimon, best in the 'whanger bop,' has warmed the heart of Simias."[69] The inscriptions abandon euphemism, becoming straightforwardly obscene when Krimon himself adds, "By Apollo, right here did Krimon fuck [so and so], the son of Bathykles, brother of [so and so]."[70] The wordplay and use of hexameter reveal skill in verbal art, but the decidedly amateur performances invoked here could not be farther from the ponderous scholarship and archives of Near Eastern scribal production.

The Greek adaptation of the alphabet demonstrates the radically different contents and forms writing can take on when a culture encounters and reshapes it for new goals. If Levantine kings adapted the alphabet for genres of power, local Greeks adapted it for genres of pleasure. Greek displays departures in form as well as content: unlike their West Semitic predecessors, the Greek cups actually talk about themselves, uttering formally unspeakable sentences (unlike Korakos's cup, Mesha was at least physically capable of speaking). And just as there are no public monuments in the Greek alphabet during the first century of its existence, there are no southern Levantine alphabetic texts from the first thousand years of its existence that speak of dancing or sex.

The riot of early texts is followed not by royal inscriptions but urban laws and private funerary monuments. In Greece the state only took on the power of writing after individuals had used it extensively for their own purposes. The first official use of writing, for city-state law, emerges a century or more after writing's arrival, in the second half of the seventh century (Thomas 1992:65).[71] Rosalind Thomas argues that the monumental legal inscription may have begun as a rear-guard action: "an attempt to give new political and procedural laws the weight and status—and, most important, divine protection—that was already accorded the unwritten laws. In this, the main and most prominent use of writing by the archaic *polis,* the impact of writing may initially have been largely that of lending monumental weight and perhaps religious authority to the new political organization of the developing city-state" (Thomas 1992:72). The state co-opted writing in archaic Greece as well as in the Levant, but here it did not speak in the king's voice.

As with each new instance of alphabetic writing, Greek funerary monuments add voices we have never heard before to our story. The oldest Greek inscription accompanying a statue is the funerary marker of Phrasikleia, an otherwise unknown girl who died around 540 B.C.E. An ancient Greek reader, reading it out loud, would undergo a remarkable transformation. He would begin by talking about the self that is speaking in the neuter, as the monument refers to itself through him: "I, the *sêma* ["gravestone/sign", a neuter noun] of Phrasikleia, shall always be called girl, since instead of marriage I received this name from the gods." He ends by proclaiming that he will be addressed, in the feminine, as *korê,* "girl." The presumably male Greek participant becomes a sort of transgendered ventriloquist's dummy, as Phrasikleia speaks through him.[72]

This sketch of the genres of early Greek writing shows that the linear alphabet did not need schools or states to spread widely or be used in complex new ways. The Greek alphabet was adopted from wide-ranging traders to serve the purposes of competitive dancing, drinking, and loving. In the centuries that followed it was used not only to consolidate the Polis but to ventriloquize dead girls. The Greek case is important for us because it shows that there was no single set of rules for the genres and participants of the alphabet in the ancient Mediterranean: alphabetic writing did not have a predictable set of users, forms, or voices. So when new ones speak, we must listen.

THE RISE OF NON-MONARCHIC WRITING IN ISRAEL

The impetus to adapt Phoenician script to write Hebrew may have arisen from the political conflicts of the late ninth century. If the standard Aramaic and Moabite script-languages known from that period were indeed created in competition with an emerging standard form of Hebrew, this would be a major irony. It would not be out of radical difference but fundamental similarity with its neighbors that Hebrew literary culture became possible.

The idea of a standard alphabet did not need any kind of royal chancery to create it because it had already been conceived outside of a kingdom. The standardized alphabet was already a few centuries old in the Levant, forged by the non-national scribes of Phoenician. These scribal artisans were commissioned not only by the kings of the various Phoenician city-states but by the Luwian-speaking rulers of Anatolia. And the contemporary Early Standard Aramaic of the Iron Age was also crafted for uniformity, and also was not the property of any single kingdom. The bond between alphabet and state was uneasy: the Aramean kings, who each attempted to kill and conquer each other at their gods' instigation, all wrote about it in Early Standard Aramaic.

What was decisive for Hebrew was what Israelite and Judean writers, not just their kings or chanceries, did with it. The boundaries of Hebrew writing never fit the boundaries of any state but they were made consistent with the biblically defined territory of Israel. And Hebrew's users put in extensive work to make sure that their texts were done in a way that made them the same as each other and different from those of their neighbors. The success of Hebrew was a result of the decisions of wider groups to address people outside the palace, in forms the court may never have contemplated. In its origins Israelite writing shares an important feature with Israel's political constituency: just as the kingdoms of Israel and Judah were made up of preexisting tribes, so the Hebrew script was built from a preexisting independent order.

"This Is the Story": From the Presentation of the King to the Presentation of the Text

The Levantine national script-languages were doubly pirated: the writers of the earliest royal inscriptions got their alphabets from Canaanite scribes and their genres from the Assyrian empire. If the local scripts were engineered to be royal tools, how did they come to speak for so many people? The answer may be that people literally took the king at his word. We have seen that the earliest Iron Age vernacular inscriptions had the king speak a language he shared with the people he was addressing. To the extent that Moabite speakers recognized themselves as part of the "Moab" that King Mesha had rescued (not, of course, "conquered"), they were part of one people for whom, and in whose tongue, the king's monument spoke. Inscribed monuments transformed local speech into written language, a valuable thing that the king owned. In some places, the texts' addressees came to believe that this newly written language really belonged to them.

We should keep the ultimate outcome of this process in mind: Hebrew's Iron Age history resulted in a drastic expansion of written participant roles. The Bible, the most influential result of Iron Age Hebrew, created roles for its readers far beyond those of king or mute subject. In the case of law, where abundant closely related material lets us compare biblical and Near Eastern genres, the single clearest biblical change is in the participant roles of lawgiver and audience. In Mesopotamia, laws are declared by a king to a non-speaking third-person subject, "a citizen." In Exodus and Deuteronomy, precisely this kind of law is addressed by a prophet, speaking on behalf of God, to a collective "you."[73] And it was fundamental to the entire enterprise that "you" "listen" and respond: at issue is something far beyond mere legal punishment. Only by accepting and enacting (typified in Hebrew as *šmʿ*, "hearing/heeding") the biblical laws can the audience become who they are, the "you" addressed as Israel. Whereas Mesopotamian law is aimed at the static identity of a citizen of the king's territory, biblical law is founded in a dynamic identity that emerges through engagement with the text of the law itself. The deictic shift in person is one way biblical law rejects a foundation in royal sovereignty and founds itself instead through participation in discourse: the words of the law and their reception.

Biblical law makes a decisive political break through its linguistic framing: its deictic markers that point to what it is and whom it is for. Yet without dated sources, we lack a historical background for this change, and cannot further locate its social context. But a suggestive, and analogous, deictic shift takes place in the inscriptions. And we can specify how and when this shift happened over the course of the tenth through eighth centuries.

As we have seen, the first extended texts in the linear alphabet, the Phoenician royal inscriptions of the tenth century, continued an archaic alphabetic tradition of marking property. Rather than merely naming the object's owner, "(belonging) to PN," the Phoenician inscriptions point to the object they are written on: "(This is) the temple which Yehawmilk, king of Byblos, built" (KAI 4:1). In every Phoenician royal inscription of the tenth century, the object bearing the inscription is the topic of the first sentence, with the king's name following inevitably.

The first deictic shift in West Semitic inscriptions occurs when the vernacular inscriptions begin to point to the king himself, instead of the object inscribed. While the older deictic forms continue, a possibility is now added. All known royal conquest accounts of the ninth century begin by presenting the king as the speaker: "I am Mesha, king of Moab." This generic feature is borrowed from Mesopotamian royal inscriptions, which have presented rulers for millennia, but transferred to a vernacular form. The beginning of the inscription no longer highlights the mute object on which the text is written but presents the speaking person of the ruler. By beginning the inscriptions with this self-presentation the king emphasizes the pragmatic fact that it is he himself speaking to the audience in the very language and script of the region he claims.

The eighth century reveals a second deictic shift: from the king to the message itself. Not "I am the king" but "this is the story." New genres of monument emerge in Israel and in very close proximity, Transjordan, which point to neither the mute object nor the vernacular-speaking king but to the discourse that the inscription contains. This contrast emerges when we compare the beautifully executed ninth-century building inscription of Mesha with the beautifully executed late eighth-century building inscription of Siloam, from Jerusalem. That we have only one well-preserved inscription from Moab and one from Judah is an accident of preservation: tiny fragments remain of four Israelite and Judean monumental inscriptions, each of which could be that of a king.[74] But the Hebrew inscription represents a genre and form of address with no prior parallels anywhere in the ancient Near East, while the Mesha inscription speaks in the same form as its contemporary Iron Age royal West Semitic inscriptions.

The Siloam tunnel inscription's newness is apparent in its first sentence: "[This] is the tunnel, and this is the account of the tunnel."[75] Although the

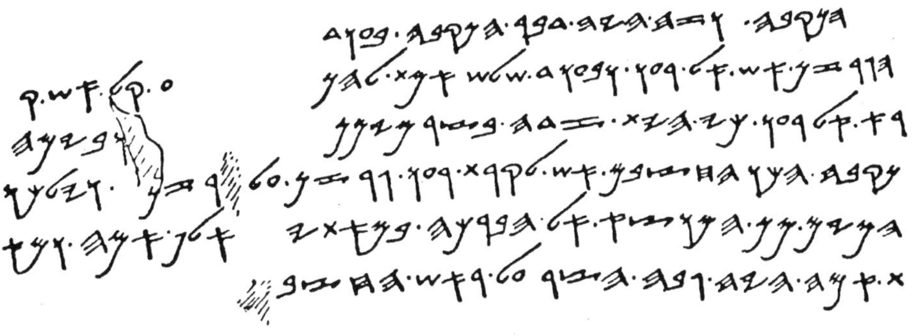

FIGURE 13 The Siloam tunnel inscription describes Hezekiah's building project in preparation for the Assyrian siege of Jerusalem (701 B.C.E.), but from the viewpoint of the workmen.

inscription describes a project commissioned by King Hezekiah, there is no "I am Hezekiah, king of Judah" here; the inscription points not just to what has been built but the *story* of what was built. In all other instances of ancient Near Eastern building inscriptions, the king or an official claims responsibility.[76] Here he is absent. What it commemorates was certainly a royal building project—biblical sources quite plausibly describe the tunnel as ordered by Hezekiah (2 Kings 20:20; 2 Chron. 32:2–4, 30). But the inscription does not mention the king once.

Instead, the "account of the tunnel" attributes responsibility for the achievement to the people who actually made it: the dramatic climax comes when two groups of stonecutters, working their way toward each other from opposite ends of the tunnel, finally hear the sound of "each man ca[ll]ing to his fellow" and realize that they have succeeded in connecting the two halves (lines 2–3). Not only does this inscription grant no role to the king, it describes none of the things that ancient Near Eastern building inscriptions commemorate, from the unprecedented nature of the project to the benefits it will confer on the populace. Instead, the Siloam tunnel inscription dramatizes the experiences of the workmen, the thrill of their success in an immensely difficult work of engineering. A kind of inverted royal inscription, it is carved within the depths of the tunnel. Rather than dominating the landscape, it is inscribed in a place that would be difficult for anyone except people who worked in the tunnel to see. As a hidden memorial to anonymous collective experience, rather than royal fame, it is also remarkable. Monuments that the public could not see, such as the Mesopotamian foundation inscriptions or the Behistun inscription, were designed as secrets to be shared between the king and the gods.

A second such eighth-century interior monumental inscription is emphatically public: its purpose is distribution of a prophet's vision to "his people."

This inscription is written not in standard Hebrew but in a local version of the high poetic language common to the southern Levant. Sharing more distinctive features in vocabulary and verbal system with the language of biblical prophecy than it does with the narrative prose of the Siloam inscription, it represents the professional tradition of visionary speakers, not scribes.[77] Inscribed on the wall of a way station or shrine just across the Jordan from Israel, the inscription describes the vision of Balaam, son of Beor (recognized as a famous foreign prophet in Numbers 22–24).

Marked in red as a title for the whole text, we read "[this is the] message {*spr*} of [Balaam, son of Beo]r, seer of the gods."[78] The vision produces great distress in Balaam (weeping, fasting, and despondency) and he reveals its content in response to a question from "his people," who approach him out of concern for his condition. While *spr* can refer to a physical document as well as its content, the inscription is presented as a circulating message, rather than an object. This is demonstrated by the striking model it provides of its own publication: the second section highlights a command to make the *spr* known orally.

The Siloam and Deir Alla inscriptions show a regional southern Levantine trend: monumental writing that asserts its role as communication, not as a built object or an icon of its royal builder. The inscription designates itself with a word for "message," rather than "king" or object, at the beginning of the first sentence. The text now points not to the item on which it is inscribed or the king who is supposed to be speaking it, but the account it contains. And these accounts no longer assign primary responsibility to the king: their protagonists are craftsmen and prophets. This trend finds its most extensive expression in biblical narrative, which is never authored by the king and where people and prophets assume new prominence as agents.

Over the course of the Iron Age, we can observe a concrete shift in how inscriptions are designated, from things to kings to messages. Beginning by pointing exclusively to the inscribed object itself, by the eighth century a significant expansion has occurred in how inscriptions can be designated. This expansion matches a shift in the text's content and participants. Both the Siloam and the Deir Alla inscriptions tell a story that is not initiated by a king or focused on military activity. Key to the drama is the speech and actions of a collective group. Alphabetic inscriptions now imagine people as participants.

Prophetic Monuments

As the only excavated prophetic text from the Iron Age Levant, the Deir Alla inscription gives us a view of what an authority independent of a state might look like. Balaam's prophecy is instigated by the gods, not the king of Moab, and he addresses it directly to his people (*ʿm*) rather than a royal employer. It begins with the rubric "[This is the] message of [Balaam son of Beo]r, the man who sees visions of the gods: The gods came to him at night and he s[aw a vis]ion, a signal from El."[79] The inscription presents the text, with the first words of the gods marked in red, of the divine council's judgment against the world, including the command to cover up the sky forever. Though damaged, it is clear that the text describes an apocalyptic vision of hierarchies reversed and the world turned upside down. A second portion contains an enigmatic underworld vision, in which the king's fate seems to be being decided. The last rubric in this text commands the reader to transmit the words of the inscription itself (combination ii:17, following Ahituv 2004:406).

The very same prophet appears in the Bible in a revealingly different role. Balaam's international renown is shown by the account in Numbers 22–24, in which Balaam is hired by the king of Moab to deliver a prophetic curse against the people of Israel, because the Moabite king knows that "who you bless is blessed indeed, and who you curse is cursed" (Num. 22:6). The plot revolves around the king's inability to make the prophet do his will; as the messenger of the divine rather than royal realm he ventriloquizes the god of Israel, pronouncing a series of poetic blessings. What is most interesting about Balaam's role, though, is that it seems that even Israel's patron god Yahweh is concerned about Balaam's ability to mediate otherworldly power. In the account of Numbers 22:22–35, Yahweh sends a divine warrior to block the prophet's path to the Israelites. The implication is that if Balaam had not been intimidated by Yahweh's threat of violence, he could have doomed Yahweh's people regardless of their national god's will.[80]

Both the Iron Age inscription and the biblical account reflect a genre that had not previously existed: a narrative about a prophet who conveys divine messages and power regardless of a king's desires. In the biblical account, his autonomous religious power is such that he requires the threat of divine force to be brought into line. In contrast to Near Eastern royal monuments, the writing of Deir Alla marks not the conquest of space by armies or architects but the circulation of a message to the people on the interior of an ordinary building. And they command, as part of the divine judgment, that they be read aloud. But in what language?

When they were published, the Deir Alla texts created a scholarly furor not because of the way the discourse of a prophet seized the monumental space of a king, but because of how hard it was to classify their dialect. While one could accuse philologists of focusing on taxonomy to the neglect of meaning (it would hardly be the first time), taxonomy is in fact at the heart of the question of what the Deir Alla texts were for. From the point of view of dialect they are almost alone among texts from the Iron Age IIb in not being in a national language. In fact linguistically, the strongest affinities of these texts do not lie with any standardized form of prose, but with the high poetic register of North-West Semitic best known from biblical prophecy and poetry—especially the prophecies of Balaam himself in Numbers 22–24.

The revelation of sovereign power in Near Eastern empires had always centered on and flowed through the monarch. Assurbanipal, it was said, was chosen by the gods in the womb to represent them. The prophecies received by the West Semitic Zimri-Lim represent the only exception to this pattern. Monuments to royalty were carved in stone, on objects meant to dominate landscapes or situate visitors as subordinates in palatial spaces (A. T. Smith 2003). By contrast the Deir Alla texts present a judgment that has been painted with a brush, not chiseled in stone, on the plaster of a homely interior wall rather than the hard rock of royal inscriptions. They mark not the conquest of space by armies or architects but the circulation of traders or pilgrims, a node in an ancient traditional network of travel. And they command, as part of the divine judgment, that they be read aloud. Like the plaster inscription of Moses' discourse commanded in Deuteronomy 27, they amount to nothing less than prophetic monuments.

The other excavated Iron Age IIb texts that share both this poetic register of language and this form of publication are the plaster inscriptions from Kuntillet Ajrud. These inscriptions, similarly painted on interior walls and located on desert trade and pilgrimage routes, occupy a non-royal, non-monumental space. These also preserve just enough text to confirm that they also described a divine revelation of sovereign power, connected with a catastrophic day of judgment. Earthquakes and storms show that cosmic and social destruction mirror each other, signs of one underlying phenomenon: divine violence for or against a people (e.g., Isaiah 5:25, Deut. 33:2).

> In quaking and blazing light, El [
> Then mountains will melt, those with many peaks be crushed [
> . . .
> (To) bless Baal on the day of bat[tle
> The name of El on the day of bat[tle[81]

The genres of cosmic battle hymns and apocalyptic revelations known from the archaic religious poetry of the Hebrew Bible find their first physical setting in public display on the walls of shrines, located on Iron Age pilgrimage routes. We find here a kind of anti-monumental script, inscribed on interior space rather than dominating a landscape.

The Circulation of Vernacular Texts: Writing with the Mouth, Reading with the Ears

A second pair of inscriptions allows us to examine the new participants of later Iron Age writing from the viewpoint of a more intimate genre: not monuments but letters. The letter of the heartsick soldier Hoshayahu from Lachish (Lachish 3), dated to the end of the Judahite monarchy, has traditionally been used as evidence for Hebrew literacy. But the letter entails a set of values more complex than merely the ability to decipher and create written messages.

Our wronged hero berates his commander in forceful rhetoric and increasingly ragged script for imputing that he cannot read:

> And now, please explain to your servant the meaning of the letter which you sent to your servant yesterday evening. For your servant has been sick at heart ever since you sent (that letter) to your servant. In it my lord said: "You don't know how (to read)—call a scribe!" As the Lord lives, no one has ever tried to read *me* a letter! Moreover, whenever any letter comes to me and I have read it, I can repeat it down to the smallest detail.[82]

What is telling about the letter is not simply Hoshayahu's claim to decode Hebrew script, though this is significant: Frank Moore Cross pointed out years ago that the letter was roughly contemporaneous with the inscriptions of the Assyrian king Assurbanipal, who boasted of his ability to read scholarly texts (1990). That a soldier should be insulted by the insinuation that he lacked

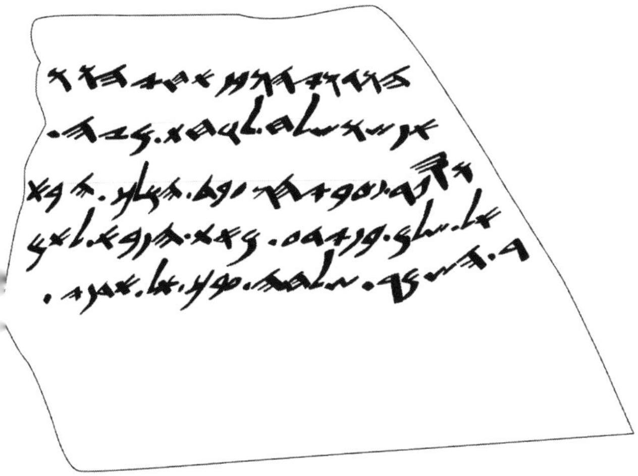

FIGURE 14. Lachish 3, reverse. The "Letter of a Literate Soldier" from Lachish, in Judah, around 587 B.C.E. This part discusses the letter of a prophet that the soldier is sending on to his commander. Drawing courtesy of Christopher Rollston.

a skill that the most powerful human being in the Near East was proud to have represents a remarkable difference. But the nature and intensity of Hoshayahu's relationship with writing is yet more remarkable. The letter, probably in his own hand (Schniedewind 2000b), makes a broader claim about his relationship to texts than merely the ability to decode and encode.

Hoshayahu is asserting a kind of mastery over the circulation of messages: he knows how to proclaim (*qr*ʾ) the letters he receives, he has heard them well and he can repeat their details. Politically meaningful communication is not casually absorbed and forgotten. To read well is to attentively *hear* their contents, so they can be recalled and orally repeated at will. Hoshayahu represents a relationship to writing that is not mere "literacy" in the modern sense of reading and forgetting, but involves the mastery of messages as they move back and forth between media and participants.

To emphasize his own power to receive and circulate messages, this letter about the sender's mastery of letters concludes with a reference to another letter: "I am also sending to my lord the letter of Tobyahu, servant of the king, which came to Shallum son of Yada at the instance of the prophet and which says 'Beware.'"[83]

Hoshayahu asserts the power to participate in the movement of the powerful message par excellence: divine revelation. What is important here is not just the familiarity with writing Hoshayahu claims, but the *direction* in which he circulates the prophecy. The prophet's warning has become a kind of chain letter, serially distributed to at least four writers, each to the next. It seems to have been first written down by the king's servant, but it was then sent to Shallum, and by Shallum to Hoshayahu, and now by Hoshayahu to his commander. The prophet's message does not stop at the palace, and Hoshayahu is not sending it to the king. Lachish 3 is thus of a piece with Deir Alla's public inscription of a narrative with a prophet and his message at the center.

The circulation of written prophecy to people other than the king at Lachish implies a break with patterns elsewhere in the ancient Near East. Martti Nissinen's useful collection (2003) contains 142 references to prophets and prophecy in the Near East, of which most (80) are letters or oracle collections containing prophetic messages, from eighteenth-century Mari and Ekallatum and seventh-century Assyria. In every case where we can tell, the texts are the reports of royal agents (some written by the prophets themselves!) directly to the king, or propaganda directly in the king's service.[84] This was not a coincidence: at Mari, the results of divination were state secrets vital to "national security," and officials swore an oath to transmit them to the king and nobody else. At Assyria recorded oracles were no less the property of the state. On the street, prophets could speak their messages to anybody, but written prophecy could only travel up the chain of command. But Hoshayahu is a node in a different kind of network, one that circulates the prophet's message both up and down the chain of command: a divine word travels horizontally.[85]

Old Babylonian prophecy was not intended for the king alone, but before the Iron Age it had only found a public through performance. A letter from Mari (ARM 26 206) reports a prophet demanding a lamb before the assembly of elders at the gate of his city, in the West Semitic Hana tribal region.[86] Devouring the animal raw, he enacts a disturbing and therefore eminently repeatable pun (he predicts an *ukullu,* in Akkadian both "devouring" and "plague").[87] Such punning actions and images occur repeatedly in the books of the biblical prophets, starting with what is plausibly the earliest collection, that of Amos (e.g., 8:2), where Yahweh shows the prophet summer-fruit (*qāyiṣ*), denoting the end (*qēṣ*) of Israel.[88]

It is widely recognized that the appearance of biblical prophecy in edited books, with the prophets as protagonists, marks a crucial shift in both medium and message from the forms of earlier Near Eastern prophecy. Prophets are not the protagonists of any Mesopotamian literary or historical text. It is also widely recognized that the process of creating the Hebrew prophetic collections was one of accretion, as individual written utterances and narratives were set down, circulated, and brought together. The Deir Alla and Lachish texts represent the inauguration of this new possibility: written prophecy as an independent genre. The collective works found in Isaiah and Jeremiah then carry this process further, as they sediment the extended labor of textual communities around a new kind of object: the prophetic book.[89]

A "secular" example of this broadly felt participation in writing is the harvester's complaint from Mesad Hashavyahu, which he has caused to circulate through the local mediator—a village or military scribe. In this rambling letter, a field worker who never names himself asks a commander to investigate the seizure of his coat by a superior. "Truly," he swears, "all my fellows who work with me in the hot sun will testify for me!"[90] Rather than replacing it, writing extends the force of face-to-face communication: the harvester's petition would have been incomprehensible if the commander did not already know who it was from. While the harvester seems to have gotten a scribe to copy down his words, the soldier from Lachish insists he needs no scribe to use writing.

What the harvester and the soldier share is the sense of *participation* in writing, a sense not captured in what we call "literacy." While only one of the two claims the ability to create and decipher written text-artifacts, both feel empowered to circulate texts through this physical medium. It is this felt power of participation that would have allowed the writings of Isaiah or Jeremiah to matter to them.

Such felt participation in the circulation of texts is beautifully illustrated by a parable about ancient Iran. In reconstructing an ancient Persian ideology of writing, the Iranist Ilya Gershevitch described the seeming paradox of people who could not read or write but participated in a literate society because they could still take advantage of texts. Thus Gershevitch imagines an Elamite love letter:

> An ancient Persian, let us call him Mithradata, wants to write to his girl-friend, let us call her Hutautha, fifty miles away. He dictates to a scribe in Persian, the scribe meanwhile inscribing a clay tablet. At the end of dictation, the scribe reads out to him in Persian the text he had dictated. On receipt of the tablet Hutautha goes to or summons a scribe, who reads to her the message in Persian as often as she asks him or pays him. Neither Mithradata nor Hutautha know or care what the script or language on the tablet is. All that matters to them is that they can "read" and "write." They personally "write" with their mouths and "read" with their ears, but thanks to the ubiquitous presence of scribes they belong to a literate society, a *Persian,* not an Elamite literate society. (Gershevitch 1979:117)

Ancient Hebrew displays an analogous ideology of reading—indeed, one that goes further than the one Gershevitch describes. As in Iran, Iron Age Hebrew writing and reading did not stop at the borders of "literacy." They were tools accessible to anyone who could hire a scribe or listen to an inscription being read. The presence of political inscriptions designed to be "read" aurally is already clear from the Assyrian vassal treaties and their translations into local language (Aramaic) that insisted on being "heard" across a broad geopolitical space.[91] But further biblical and epigraphic evidence suggests that the divide we conceive between "literate" and "non-literate" was not conceived that way by users of ancient Hebrew or their near neighbors in the Levant. As we will see, the ancient Hebrew theory and practice of reading resonates with Gershevitch's notion of writing with the mouth and reading with the ear.

If Israelites did not see literature as confined to writing but as traveling through it, this has further implications for the historical nature of written Hebrew: it means that, first, we do not need to assume an earlier written literature to explain the complexity of Hebrew literary culture. What we have seen of earlier West Semitic literature shows that a highly developed culture of *poiesis,* cultural creation through text-making, must have existed in the early Iron Age and earlier, before there was any desire to set it down in standardized Hebrew. And this idea persists: in prophetic narratives from the late Iron Age, the decisive feature of a text was its communicative power, not its written nature. Texts like First Isaiah (29:18) concur in describing the deaf, not the blind, miraculously "hearing," not "seeing," the words of a book. "Reading" is fundamentally an acoustic performance, and text-reception is imagined as a process of hearing.

The fact that Hebrew texts were not thought of as limited to writing has consequences for our understanding of the historical audience for written Hebrew. Once a text is written down, it is not imagined as confined to or defined by its medium. Isaac Rabinowitz has pointed out that the corresponding opposite of "to hear" was not "to write" but "to compose": "Literary compositions were only written down if intended to serve a purpose that could alone be achieved through such a writing down" (1993:32).

But the Hebrew ideology contrasts with the Iranian one[92] in its distinctly high level of imagined intimacy and intertwining between writing, speech, and presence—as one might expect for a vernacular writing system, as opposed to an alloglottographic one that moves between multiple languages and scripts. Jeremiah is described as creating a scroll (Jeremiah 36) simply to project his presence and voice, and its destruction is incidental to the existence of the prophecy as a composed, preexisting text—the actual prophecy is just reinstantiated in a material form at the end of the chapter. And then in Jeremiah 51:63 he creates a scroll whose whole point is to be read and destroyed. In these passages, texts are forever, but writing is not; the inherent text of the prophecy generates the writing, but the materiality of the writing is merely a theatrical prop for the prophecy's ritual performance, to help it take effect.

In fact, the very term in Hebrew that is translated "read" always also denoted speaking, and connoted a act of public proclamation. As Daniel Boyarin (1993) brilliantly showed, in the overwhelming majority of instances in the Hebrew Bible where someone *qārāʾ*'s a text, the political implications are communal and direct. Even when performed in private, it has public consequences; texts invoke publics, and non-literate people are said to participate in the act of reading (Deuteronomy 31; 2 Kings 22; Jeremiah 36; Nehemiah 8). A strongly related meaning is already attested in Ugaritic literature, where *qra* is used by gods and ritual participants to invoke the presence of other beings, and in inscriptional Phoenician and Aramaic, where it means "call, call upon, invoke, read."[93] We have, then, first a common West Semitic semantic range for *qrʾ* that encompasses the calling together of people and the calling out of texts. And second, for biblical Hebrew in particular, collective communication and political consequences are always entailed in reading's pragmatics.

Thus to read in Hebrew was always also to publish. The root *qrʾ* entailed at once proclamation and circulation—the process never ended with the mere private absorption of written data. It is this ideology that gives written Hebrew prophecy its high stakes.

Imperial Inscriptions in Reverse

Before the Iron Age, almost all written literature in the ancient Near East had been created by palace bureaucracies. What is most distinctive, then, about the new written vernaculars is not the early royal inscriptions, but the second wave of writing, in the eighth century and later, which circulated outside the palace. The historian of religions Cristiano Grottanelli has identified this shift as marking the rise of "non-monarchic ideologies" in writing. In both archaic Greece and the late Iron Age Levant, powers outside kingship mastered writing and turned it to new ends (1999:4).

In the Levant, writing's new political edge came from the way it was used to represent, and transform, an already archaic non-monarchic ideology. This shift has been famously described as part of an "axial age" revolution, but in fact it emerges from a long history.[94] In political structure, this ideology conceived of the people as a political unit separate from the territorial state (Fleming 2004). In political communication, it features a highly marked role for the persuasive use of poetry and rhetoric (Caton 1987).

The critical juncture Grottanelli describes occurs when this non-monarchic ideology is circulated in writing outside of palace scribal bureaucracies, in the context of imperial conquest by Assyria, Babylon, and Persia.[95] It marks "the victory of prophecy in spite of, and contextually with, the institutional victory of universal kingship, because the central theme—and the ideological core—of that body of texts was precisely the direct communication between the national deity and a non-royal member of the nation, chosen by the godhead as the correct mediator between the divine sphere and the human level" (1999:4). This captures the political edge of the Torah: as the texts grew into a canon under the ever more universal empires of the Persian and Hellenistic periods, the imagery of the universal emperor was reframed as that of God, the speaker of the Torah whose law could never truly be mediated by a king. But can we use our results to place it in a more concrete context?

We have seen how local writing in the Levant emerged as a form of imperial learning. Genres of sovereignty were borrowed as royal conquest accounts were put into the voices of local kings speaking to their constituents. Old West Semitic genres not known in Mesopotamia—divine warnings mediated through a prophet to king or people—also entered writing in the wake of this imperial learning. What was most distinctive about the new vernaculars was how West Semitic writers reinterpreted imperial genres of sovereignty to create different views of where power comes from and what texts are for.

A larger-scale comparison can better illuminate the consequences of these new conceptions of participation and political foundation. If we expand our

Iron Age viewpoint to include both contemporary cuneiform monuments and later biblical texts, we can trace the long-term effects of the ways different literary cultures reacted to perhaps the most dominating form of writing the Near East produced: the splendid and terrorizing royal inscriptions of the Neo-Assyrian kings.

A profound lesson about imperial learning is drawn by Peter Machinist (2006) in the contrast between the ways members of two smaller states—Judah and Urartu—responded to Assyrian writing. Soon after the rise of the Neo-Assyrian empire, the Anatolian military kingdom of Urartu began to plagiarize the texts of their major competitor. The first known Urartean monumental inscription is essentially a copy of an Assyrian monumental inscription with the name of the Urartean king, Sarduri, inserted in place of Assurnashirpal III (Zimansky 2006). While the Urartean king eventually began writing inscriptions, however rigidly stereotyped, in Urartean, he used them to liken his kingdom to the Assyrian empire—what Machinist calls a "lateral transfer" of Assyrian political culture (2006:296). Assyrian political culture and writing became a template for the creation of a new empire by ambitious local warlords. The inscriptions offer one answer to the question of where empires come from: from plagiarizing bigger empires.

But if the Assyrian texts were a paradigm for constructing empires, they were also a paradigm for challenging them. Assyrian rhetoric was so susceptible to pirating precisely because of its success: if its discourse was an icon of imperial power, then to use it was to claim to be the equal of the Assyrians. And so different challengers to Assyrian sovereignty mimicked Assyrian discourse differently in the middle of the Iron Age: each challenge was mimetic as well as political.

First Isaiah deals extensively with the imperial thrust of Assyria in the later eighth century B.C.E. The intimate knowledge of Assyrian political rhetoric these texts display must reflect contemporary experience: a century later such propaganda was buried under rubble by the next ruler of the universe, the Babylonian king. Assyrian rhetoric was intended for audition by its intended victims, and it would have reached its audience through multiple channels, including Aramaic translations like the Sefire treaty or threatening pronouncements in Judean such as those of the bilingual Assyrian emissary in 2 Kings 18. Machinist focuses on the poem in Isaiah 10:5–15 beginning (in NRSV):

> Ah, Assyria, the rod of my anger—
> The club in their hands is my fury!
> Against a godless nation I send him,
> And against the people of my wrath I command him,

To take spoil and seize plunder,
and to tread them down like the mire of the streets.
But this is not what he intends, nor does he have this in mind;
but it is in his heart to destroy, and to cut off nations not a few. (10:5–7)

Isaiah turns Assyrian military success upside down: they are not actually victories for the Assyrians but blows struck by the Lord with an empire-shaped weapon: "the rod of my anger." Isaiah's own rhetoric makes a diametrical opposition between what the Assyrian king thinks he is doing and the end he really serves. Yet this inversion is itself based on Assyrian imperial ideology, which describes the hubris of the foe who thinks he can effectively act on his own volition. This critique is brought together with another standard theme of Assyrian inscriptions: the inventory of nations plundered and destroyed. Isaiah's poem fuses these imperial themes:

For he says:
"Are not my commanders all kings?
Is not Calno like Carchemish?
Is not Hamath like Arpad?
Is not Samaria like Damascus?" (10:8–9)

The inventory of conquests and the claims of plundering and destroying nations are clichés of Assyrian propaganda. But Isaiah inverts it on multiple levels, from the choice of vocabulary to its underlying conceptions of power and agency. On a lexical level, the king's own rhetorical question is turned against him, as the term he uses for "king," *melek*, finds its Assyrian cognate in a word for an official (*malku*), while the term he uses for "commander," *śar*, is cognate with the Assyrian word for "king" (*šarru*).[96] The Assyrian king claims that the "generals" who take orders from him are themselves "kings," but he has it backward: as a king, he himself is merely God's general. The Assyrian king is shown in the mirror of his own propaganda:

For he says:
By the strength of my hand I have done it,
and by my wisdom, for I have understanding. (10:13a)

This charge recalls precisely the Assyrian accusation "that the enemies of the Assyrian king fell before him because they trusted in themselves alone, not in the god Ashur" (Machinist 2006:297). Isaiah places the Assyrian king in the very role of the doomed, deluded enemy of Assyrian inscriptions. What is at stake here, then, is not an Urartu-style borrowing but a deliberate inversion of the Assyrian inscriptional tradition. Assyrian royal discourse centers on the king's role as conqueror in service of the imperial god Ashur. The Isaiah poem retains this orientation, but replaces Ashur with the god of Israel. Isaiah 10:5–15 is, from the point of the roles inhabited, "an Assyrian inscription in reverse" (Machinist 2006:298).

Taken together these two written responses to Assyrian texts present two radically different possibilities of political communication. "[The] cases of Urartu and Isaiah in Judah move in opposite directions: the first a lateral or horizontal transfer of Assyrian cultural conventions with no essential differences; the second a vertical transfer, from superior to inferior, with a fundamental inversion" (Machinist 2006:298).

In Judean prophecy, the process of imperial learning comes full circle. The first known extended vernacular texts in the Levant were pirated in the ninth century from Assyrian royal inscriptions, copying the king's self-representation as the speaker and main actor of history: "these are the things I did." Now that very Assyrian self-representation of the king as speaker and actor is reframed: "when you say, 'these are the things I did,' you delude yourself." The genres of power from which history-writing in the Levant emerged are revisited and subverted, their voices taken over by a new double speaker: the prophet and the god he ventriloquizes. If the Urartean king claims to speak as the equal of Assyria and challenges it by imitation, Judean prophecy claims to speak as Assyria's superior, challenging it by both echoing and inverting it.

The fate of each of the three sorts of political rhetoric—Assyrian, Urartean, and Judean prophetic—was bound up with that of its audience. For Urartean, the case is simple: it had no audience. Not until near the end of its life as a state was the slightest effort made to broaden the range of Urartean writing beyond rigidly stereotyped inscriptions. As Zimansky has noted, no texts from Urartu were composed in the name of anyone but the reigning king, giving the impression that he was the only one there (2006). The Urartean state's broader communicative strategy lay in altering the landscape of Urartu itself: as it integrated fortresses into the countryside, Urartean artwork presented these military strongholds as part of the natural world (A. T. Smith 2003). But the result was that Urartu's political existence and historical memory vanished utterly with its military defeat: "A society with no readers is, in the long run, not much influenced by its writers" (Zimansky 2006:269). Assyrian written ideology penetrated far more widely, its rhetoric suffusing that of its challengers and victims. Yet it was a monologue, invoking its audience only as passive subjects, and its victory inscriptions ceased with its downfall.

First Isaiah's rhetoric, by contrast, exemplifies how an Iron Age discourse could address a different kind of audience and gain a different kind of fate from a royal inscription. Here both prophet and god refer to the text's addressees as "my people."[97] Lacking any concrete evidence for Isaiah's distribution before Qumran, we cannot specify its immediate audience or reception. But over the centuries, the text's claim to address "my people" turned out to be true. It is no coincidence that the biblical texts we have to compare with those of Assyria and Urartu are far later: Hebrew manuscripts outlasted cuneiform monuments because writers who considered themselves to be members of this people continued to copy them, in widely varied times and places far exceeding their original contexts. But the early prophetic monuments of Deir Alla and Kuntillet Ajrud suggest that this wider audience was already intended in the Iron Age: by the eighth century vernaculars had been used to rethink whom writing was supposed to address and include.

TOWARD A NEGATIVE POLITICAL THEOLOGY

In inverting the language and ideology of cosmopolitan imperial rule, First Isaiah's discourse imagines a different foundation for power. It implies a rejection of the ground rules of ancient Near Eastern sovereignty, based on intimate familiarity with them. This discourse stands in contrast to a common monarchic political theology, assumed in Iron Age state inscriptions from Assyria to Urartu to the Levant. This common theology is expressed in those standard passages where the king narrates how his patron god enthroned him, granting him victory over his foes. But as much as First Isaiah denigrates the Assyrian emperor, there is no corresponding exaltation of the Judean king. In fact he plays no role in this speech. Indeed, as this imperial genre of sovereignty is inverted, the role of the native king disappears: in Isaiah's conversation between the Lord and the enemy king, the king of Judah is silent.

Mesopotamian-derived imperial ideologies reflected what we would call a positive political theology: Hammurabi was selected by the gods to rule, and his every action reflected their will. By contrast, earlier West Semitic political theory had an ambivalent or contingent political theology. At Mari, the storm god granted the king provisional sovereignty by letting him participate in the cosmic battle with which he won rule. But as we have seen (chapter 2), a threat hangs over this grant: if the king fails to publicly perform the acts of a just judge, the grant will be removed; defeat and loss of sovereignty will follow. The domestication of this provisional grant into an eternal promise is visible in the political theology of the Judean monarchy, expressed in the prose of 2 Samuel 7 and the poetry of Psalms 2 and 89:1–37.[98] But a cultural memory of the storm god's old threat remained.

The replacement of the self-aggrandizing king with a mocking god as the speaker of history implies a new perspective on the otherworldly foundations of earthly order. The storm god's old mythic threat has intensified into a fundamental critique, which we may term a negative political theology.[99] In this view, no ruler can ever be fully "legitimate," in the sense of having a guaranteed otherworldly foundation; any human claim to absolute rule is in fact provisional, and therefore false. In biblical history this negative political theology is held in tension with the archaic positive theology of the Judean royal dynasty.[100] But it is the more distinctive political theory, and it is the one that ultimately structures biblical history, through its Deuteronomistic editing. If we avoid conjectural dating of different strata, treating the Deuteronomistic history typologically as a whole, we can suggest several further implications.

Deuteronomy's very notion that the covenant takes place between the people and God establishes this negative political theology at the ritual basis of the covenant. The Law of the King (Deuteronomy 17), which permits the king no role at all in judgment, formerly the central performance of sovereignty (Levinson 2001) is combined with the old curse of defeat and the loss of sovereignty, now addressed to the people rather than just the ruler. Thus does the West Semitic storm god turn away from the king to the people. At Mari he had threatened the king thus: I granted you power and success through my mythic battle with the sea, but I can abandon you and take it away. In the curses of Deuteronomy just this type of threat—that I established your power and success beginning with the mythic battle with the sea in Exodus, and I can remove it—is now addressed to the collective "you."[101]

This switch is symbolized in history by the Deuteronomistic enthronement of a covenant and a text, rather than a king. It is a well known but astonishing fact of biblical history that no king of Israel or Judah is portrayed as abiding by, or even being aware of, the Law of Moses until near the end of kingship itself in Judah. During the reign of Josiah (640–609 B.C.E.), the Law is said to be discovered accidentally in the course of repairing the Temple (2 Kings 22–23). Shocked at the consequences of their newly revealed disobedience, Josiah has it read before the people, and they make a covenant to follow it. The strongest precedent for this revelation in the Deuteronomistic history is the discovery in the Temple not of a different text but of the king himself—the young heir Joash in 2 Kings 11 (//2 Chron. 22:9–23:21), As Cristiano Grottanelli notes, both are hidden in the Temple, found, revealed, and accepted by the people because warranted by a priest (2 Kings 11) or prophet (2 Kings 22), then bonded to people in a *berît*, a covenant tying people and king to god and people and king together. The covenant is followed by a zealous reign, in which competing places of worship are destroyed (Grottanelli 1999:188–89).

The difference between the two revelations is that the text trumps the king, a passage that correlates suggestively with the inscriptional shift from the presentation of kings to the presentation of texts. This is true on a literal level—the king agrees to abide by the rules of the written law—but also more broadly. The stories reach a crescendo with the discovery of the text, because with the discovery of the king, only a temple of Baal is destroyed, while the discovery of the text causes all other cults in Judah, including those of Yahweh outside Jerusalem, to be swept away. In the first discovery, it is the legitimacy of the king, while in 2 Kings 22–23 it is the legitimacy of the text that is validated. "The book is thus, in our pair of narratives, similar in meaning and function to the king, but more important—more powerful—than the king, because the book rules over the king" (Grotannelli 1999:189). This is part of a larger Deuteronomistic pattern in which the text trumps its transmitter. The Torah, unlike Moses, is able to enter Israel and ensure success in the new land (Josh. 1:8) (Grotannelli 1999:195).

Alongside the concept of the people as a protagonist of history, the vernacular revolution enabled the creation of a negative political theology. It is not just that history can speak for people beyond the state. With the emergence of a divine narrator for history, an eternal political threat became possible: that no history could speak in the voice of the state and be true. Alongside this threat a new promise emerged: a political foundation in which a covenant binds each member of the audience to God—including, without special importance, the king—in a repeated ritual. This emphasis on repeated law, *Deuteros Nomos* in the etymological sense of Deuteronomy, sets up a new capacity for the creation and re-creation of order, beyond the framework of earthly rule, constituted through the circulation of texts.

CONCLUSION

Vernaculars began by pirating the voice of an empire to let a local king speak in a local language, in an attempt to convince an emerging audience that the king's voice was theirs. Taking this process of vernacularization to its logical conclusion, Hebrew writers multiplied the different voices and social locations that could speak in writing. Hebrew's uses reflect an old West Semitic tribal ideology that emphasized discourse as a way of doing politics. People's sense of agency and autonomy were connected to their inclusion in language and their access to words.

This resulted in a historical irony: after multiple attempts to monopolize both communication and coercion, only one of these attempts succeeded, resulting in ancient Hebrew writers bringing about the circulation of a uniform standard of communication in Hebrew with no monopoly on coercion. This dimension of biblical literature has in modern times always stood under the sign of lateness and artifice: the Jews are a nation without a state, the Torah represents the laws of a kingdom without a territory. This lateness has been connected to a fundamental inauthenticity, or a paradoxical and ironic authenticity: the state is only imagined in retrospect, Israel is a creature of ritualized collective memory.

The epigraphy suggests that it may be the other way around. Read against Israel's political history, it indicates that in the case of Israel and Judah we can reverse the expected relationship of priority between coercion and communication. It is precisely in the Iron Age, when the people of Israel and Judah were autonomous in their land, that a local literature created a kind of politics beyond the state. This dimension of Hebrew as written political communication independent of (though usable by) the state made biblical history possible and permitted its remarkable durability. As a history and a politics speaking primarily to and for a people, not a king, it could speak outside of, and live productively beyond, the life of any kingdom.

Conclusion

> It was in the middle of the Middle Ages that Petrarch asked what I see as a fairly astonishing or at least fundamental question. He asked: "Is there nothing more to history than the praise of Rome?" . . . A few centuries after Petrarch, the west saw the appearance or birth of a history that contained the very opposite of the praise of Rome. This was by contrast, a history that sought to unmask Rome as a new Babylon, and which challenged Rome by demanding the lost rights of Jerusalem.
>
> —Michel Foucault

"IS THERE NOTHING MORE TO HISTORY THAN THE PRAISE OF ROME?"

In a remarkable public lecture to the Collège de France, Michel Foucault argued that for most of its career, "history was a ritual that reinforced sovereignty" (2003:69). He called this political storytelling "Roman history." It was a narrative of endless legitimation of the state, and it concealed sovereignty's real source: not divine right but violent conquest. "After all, William the Conqueror did not want to be called 'the conqueror'" because he did not want to remind his subjects who had conquered them (2003:72). But according to Foucault, Roman history had a shadow. There was another way of talking about past public events, drawing at once on a different grammar and a different politics: Foucault called it "biblical history."

> These unjust and biased kings tried to make it look as though they were acting on behalf of all and in the name of all; they certainly wanted people to talk of their victories, but they did not want it to be known that their victories were someone else's defeats: "it was our defeat." (2003:72)[1]

For Foucault, biblical history is a switch in voices, interrupting the litany of the state's triumph and speaking directly to the reader. He presents it as a shift from the third-person history of the state to a first-person plural: "it was *our* defeat." By suddenly becoming personal, this speech turns the spotlight on history's heretofore passive audience. The audience is now implicitly a speaker too (every "us" implies a "you" to whom it speaks) who can play a role that begins by speaking, by becoming a "we."[2] The very claim to defeat breaks the sovereign's monopoly on communication.

There is a message inherent in the language of biblical history: it is indexical, meaning that its very form invokes the people it is speaking to and for, and the context in which it is being spoken. Who is the "us" whose defeat it is? Are you included? Its grammar links political experience to human subjects. The sheer fact of speech from the defeated refutes the sovereign's claim that history is an unbroken succession of his victories. The formal dimension of Roman history, a monologue in the voice of the state, makes it "a ritual that reinforces" sovereignty. But Roman history's form also makes it vulnerable. It can be plagiarized, pirated, or just interrupted: a history that includes "our defeat" is no longer a ritual that reinforces sovereignty. If someone other than the ruler can speak in history, the genre begins to do something new; history can be a ritual that founds something else.

We have asked how the first written vernaculars arose and what they were for. Foucault's idea of biblical history puts a sharp point on our answer. The epigraphic evidence shows how new kinds of history became possible in the ancient Near East. History indeed entered the Levant as a ritual that reinforced sovereignty: during the ninth century, local Levantine kings had their scribes imitate Neo-Assyrian inscriptions, translating imperial genres of power to speak like the most powerful king in the world. But whereas the Assyrian emperor was cosmopolitan, claiming kingship of the universe, kings like Mesha were deliberately local: in Moabite, the "king of the universe" became the "man of Diban." Local kings used these genres to stake a new claim: that they were addressing "their" people in a language they uniquely shared. The possibility of history writing in the Levant emerged as these Levantine kings learned a new trick from Mesopotamian empires: how to make old craft traditions of linear alphabetic writing speak in the voice of a state. Their innovation was to identify this writing with the people whose language it was. Representing local West Semitic speech was a way of imagining a people, locating it in a political space, and laying claim to its loyalty. The new vernaculars were attempts to domesticate West Semitic political culture by materializing and monumentalizing its language.

But local media experts—writers and craftspeople—seemed to take the king at his word: some of the new vernaculars actually became identified with the people they were claimed to represent. The tools of royal history were rethought by writers responsible to communities beyond the royal court. We can see evidence of new discourses being inaugurated in the Iron Age inscriptions. Comparing these with the edited biblical sources suggests that written Hebrew accounts of history and ritual emerged as distinctive in placing the people, alongside the king, as a protagonist of events. This idea is rooted in an old West Semitic political theory in which sovereign decisions for war or peace, allegiance or separation, were made by collective kin groups and negotiated through storytelling and persuasion.

As the only contemporary evidence for Hebrew literary culture, epigraphy has given us a means to begin to specify the changes that made the Hebrew Bible possible. The inscriptions let us outline this new landscape. Yet we cannot use it to portray the whole. Our greatest limiting factor in using the surviving evidence is the peculiar condition of the Bible: the fact that there are no manuscripts of edited Hebrew literary texts remaining from before about 250 B.C.E., but an increasing amount thereafter. How did biblical history develop from the culture we see in the inscriptions?

ON THE POSSIBILITY OF BIBLICAL LITERATURE

We can broaden our view by taking the Bible's actual physical condition as a starting point, not an embarrassing exception. Historically, our problem with biblical texts is that they are so heavily *mediated*: transmitted through multiple, sometimes seemingly innumerable, editors and copyists, rather than archaeologically excavated straight from their original context. It is because the biblical sources represent extended streams of tradition, not Iron Age artifacts, that we cannot date them with our desired level of rigor. But it is precisely because of the discursive power of those traditions—their productivity as tools for talking about the world—that we have the Bible in its current form: a corpus of widely reproduced manuscripts. Rather than authenticating or falsifying biblical texts, this lets us do something more interesting: we can think about the sources of these tools' productivity, the contexts in which these traditions began to achieve their mediating power. Epigraphy does not let us see biblical texts as Iron Age artifacts, but we can read the inscriptions and biblical texts together to help explain key biblical discourses: the inauguration of new ways of writing history, law, and prophecy.

To talk about the inauguration of biblical discourses is a way to imagine the Bible's shift in horizons more concretely. It is a way of comparing the assumptions reflected in inscriptions with the assumptions reflected in biblical genres. It is not to account for the full individuality of each biblical genre, nor the structure and character of each book—and certainly not its precise point of origin. We do not see the specific moment when a brilliant scribe or visionary king decided to inaugurate a new way of writing—if this happened, we do not have the data to say. But looking at the evidence this way can open up new modes of explanation.

History, law, and prophecy are each old Near Eastern genres that circulated in the later Iron Age and appear transformed in the Bible.[3] For each genre, we can epigraphically document a context in which it functioned under certain rules. We then find signs of significant change in those rules during the eighth to sixth centuries: traces of new cultural practices. Much biblical literature consists of rich elaborations of each of these genres. At root, the late Iron Age shift in horizons is a shift in these genres' participants: For whom does the text speak? To whom is it addressed? And who are its protagonists? In each case we see evidence of the genre being reshaped under particular political conditions to meet the assumptions of a new audience. Beginning with traces of previous oral genres or written forms, the newly written discourses use the technology of alphabetic writing to address a West Semitic culture of kinship and political communication transformed by, and transforming, a historical context of imperialism.

History is the first discourse we see inaugurated in the inscriptions. As we have seen, history-writing was long a Mesopotamian royal privilege.[4] But West Semitic speakers told stories about political events long before they wrote history. And the unusual value that kin-based West Semitic societies placed on decisions made in public assemblies made them place a correspondingly high value on storytelling as political persuasion. A West Semitic narrative prose style has been recognized in both the scripture and inscriptions of the first millennium (Parker 1997). The "objective" style of history-writing, told by an anonymous third-person narrator who chronicles events, framing them with a dating formula, appears to be borrowed from Mesopotamian literature; it is not a universal form (M. S. Smith 2007). But the persuasive style of biblical prose, densely plotted and "fraught with background" that forces the audience to engage and interpret the story (Auerbach 1953), is already apparent in the political correspondence of West Semitic writers at Mari. As Jack Sasson (1998) pointed out, this rhetorical style of recounting events is rare or absent in Babylonian letters. In Mesopotamia, the form for extended artful narrative was poetry.[5]

The first known extended West Semitic narrative prose is also the first known West Semitic history-writing. We find it in the narratives of ninth-century royal inscriptions, alongside the first standardized local languages of the first millennium. Indeed, at least four of these "new" languages appear nearly simultaneously in writing (Aramaic, Moabite, Ammonite, and Hebrew), each adapted from Phoenician or a related Canaanite script tradition with no previous trace of their written existence. The earliest substantial examples make their debut on durable monuments—around the same time as ostraca and graffiti in these scripts appear. This fact strongly suggests that these written languages began as tools for the expression of royal courts, created competitively and in awareness of each other. As spoken languages, their ancestries probably extended well into the Late Bronze Age (Izre'el 2003), but as written vernaculars they are new inventions. And the ninth-century royal inscriptions are precisely the kind of thing that royal scribes engineered them to do.

But by the eighth century memorial prose narratives have new heroes. Texts like the Siloam and Deir Alla inscriptions are monuments to prophets and stonecutters, not the king. Rather than identifying themselves with the ruler and addressing an anonymous audience in the king's voice, they identify themselves as texts: *spr* or *dbr.* They tell the stories of independent professionals who mediate images and language: craftsmen and prophets. And it is precisely these mediating professions that best account for the inscriptions; skilled communicators quickly adapted the monumental styles and scripts to represent different types of agents: the collective craft, religious and kin groups to which they themselves belonged.

In the speakers and actors of our eighth-century inscriptions we can glimpse a distinctive organizing element of biblical narrative: kin groups, and their mediators, as the new protagonists of history. Our inscriptions, few and damaged, do not give a full picture of writing's users in the Iron Age. But in the Deir Alla inscription we see the same new protagonists that provide biblical history with an axis from start to finish: the people and the prophets who address them. The Siloam inscription tells the story of a royal building project from the viewpoint of the people who actually built it, without mentioning the king. The eighth-century inscriptions document the new assumption that these people have a central place in written narratives of political events.

The Bible's narrative prose represents a turning point in the history of literary form, as Robert Kawashima (2004) has brilliantly demonstrated. Anonymously narrated literary prose opened up new possibilities in the representation of human viewpoints and actions—possibilities that had not existed in earlier narrative poetry, which directly addresses the audience from the viewpoint of the poet-speaker. Kawashima portrays this event as an almost socially isolated act of genius—but the orchestrated presentation of viewpoints and actions is common to political rhetoric as well as narrative art.

The formal identity of biblical history with Hebrew narrative prose is a terrible problem for historians, and essential to the point it makes. There are few surface features by which we can distinguish contemporary reports from ancient traditions. But this very form fits a long West Semitic practice of political storytelling. Indeed, already by 1800 B.C.E. letters like those of the Amorite warlord Bannum reflect artistic narrative techniques that can be compared with the stories of David's rise. The Iron Age's shift in form brings a move from dialogue—Bannum's letters are addressed to a specific person—to anonymous presentation of political narratives to readers, reflecting the adoption of Mesopotamian history and chronicle traditions. In the Iron Age, only a matter of degree and the fact of editing distinguish the narrative prose form of Deir Alla from the stories of Isaiah or Elijah. Kawashima's crucial insight finds its ground in the history of literary culture: the encounter between alphabetic writing and West Semitic ideals of political communication provides a social context for the Bible's shift in communicative form.

The second discourse whose traces we see is law. Written law also has no known prehistory as a native West Semitic genre. While we have discovered no inscribed West Semitic law collections from before the Persian period,[6] the epigraphic record provides a context for the framing of law in the Bible. The Torah presents law as inaugurated in a series of covenant rituals in which the assembled people participate. These covenants mandate their own reproduction: the first occurs uniquely at Mount Sinai in Exodus, but the second, on the plains of Moab in Deuteronomy, both reiterates the Sinai covenant and commands future ceremonies in Israel.[7] The ceremonies draw on a longstanding cultural ideal: the sovereign collective assembly is documented as both fact and symbol in other West Semitic cultures both before and after the Iron Age, in the later city-states of Phoenicia as well as the earlier ones of Emar and Mari.[8]

But while we can speak of an *ideal* of a sovereign assembly of kin groups persisting in and beyond the Iron Age, its social context in Israel is ambiguous and shifting. During periods of relatively loose central control in Late Bronze and early Iron Age Canaan, kin-based military force thrived. With their cooptation by Judean and then Israelite kings and the subsequent expansion of Assyrian military power to the Levant, the sovereignty of kin-based groups began to decline.

As with the rise of written history in the Levant, here again we see the interplay of old imperial forms with very different audience expectations. It is in the context of West Semitic sovereign assemblies that the Assyrian imposition of collective loyalty oaths invoked a remarkable cultural logic. These covenant ceremonies attempted to co-opt an old tribal notion of rule, making "the people" into a participant in both oral and written rituals. The book of Deuteronomy, framed as the contents of such a collective loyalty oath, represents the transformation of the vassal ceremony into a new written genre. As the tribal assembly became less possible in physical space, the loyalty oath created a written space, both literary and ritual, where it could still happen. The peoples addressed in the ceremony become the public addressed by biblical law and covenant.

A key insight on how law and covenant address their audience appeared in Albrecht Alt's groundbreaking 1934 essay on the indexical aspect of Israelite law—the way these laws point to participants and a context: "The inseparable connection between form and content goes back behind the written records to the period of popular oral composition and tradition, where each form of expression was appropriate to some particular circumstance" (Alt 1966:87). Alt invokes just that impasse of twentieth-century biblical studies that concerns us: by definition, our edited sources cannot satisfy the evolutionist desire to go back to a stage "behind the written records."

The power of Alt's observation increases when we reverse his assumptions: not as a claim about the lost contexts behind the texts, nor even merely about the text's generic form, but about how the text is designed to connect to new contexts.[9] Alt suggests a way to read the connection between form and content in the *present* text. He observed that at structurally significant points biblical laws use pragmatically marked forms: tight, rhythmic lines with commands and norms, regularly using the second person: *lōʾ tignōv*, "thou shalt not steal" (Exod. 20:15; Deut. 5:19). Even the less personal biblical casuistic ("if X, then Y") laws tend to follow this rhythm: *makkēh ʾîš wāmēt, môt yûmāt*, "whoever strikes a man so he dies, he shall be made to die" (Exod. 21:12). Alt called the distinctively Israelite form "apodeictic" and emphasized its stark contrast with the class-stratified and typically casuistic Mesopotamian law: "If a citizen strikes the cheek of another citizen of higher status, he shall be flogged" (Laws of Hammurabi, ed. Roth 1995 pgh 202).

Biblical law has a politically constitutive dimension to the extent that it addresses an audience of readers and hearers who are not yet full subjects, and helps bring about their subjecthood. Alt's point was not that all biblical law was framed in direct address; he was well aware that the major legal sections of the Torah are full of casuistic law. Rather, he argued that apodeictic law's direct addresses and poetic formulas *framed* it as performative, ritually summoning up the people to bind them into a collectivity through a covenant: "It signifies the recalling of the people to the ideals on which its existence is based, a renewed pledging of every member of the nation to the will of Yahweh, without which the welding of the tribes into a national unity could not have come about, nor could endure" (1966:129).[10] It is as a ritual dimension immanent in the text, not buried in tribal prehistory, that the covenant formula has been decisive.

At this point we have entered the world of scribal culture—but without leaving the audience behind. Because now, the speaker who addresses law to the people is not God or the king but the one who mediates law to the people: within the Torah this is Moses; outside the Torah it is the law's scribal and priestly transmitters. Both the Priestly and Deuteronomistic sources frame the legally binding parts of the Torah as authored by God but addressed and published to the assembled people by Moses and his inheritors. After Moses, the scenes of the Torah's rediscovery and republication in 2 Kings 22–23 and Nehemiah 8 name the scribes and Levitical priests.[11] What we know about these laws is that, first, they show substantial influence from Mesopotamian legal traditions that were most widely circulated late in the Neo-Assyrian period (D. Wright 2004, 2006), and second, they were edited by Hebrew scribes in a sophisticated and self-conscious process that proceeded by stages (Levinson 1997, 2004).

As in the shift in history, the role of mediating professions is central, but the mediators fervently imagine an audience as crucial to the success of their work. The editors of the law have transformed the popular assembly that constituted sovereignty in earlier West Semitic political thought, placing it in a new context in which it is not just a literary device but a political theory: the people hear their story and are offered a covenant by Moses. The genres of law and covenant ceremony had never before appeared within the genre of narrative. But now the Priestly and Deuteronomistic editors of the Torah represent the popular assembly as accepting the law within the story itself. This move does not so much "legitimate" the law and its editors as reframe them, and inaugurate their constant reframing. The law is now something that must be repeatedly handed down and accepted in a constituting ritual act. The two great genres of imperial power, law and history, are reconfigured as addressed to a people whose acceptance and performance can constitute them as a public.

Unlike history or law, prophecy was a native genre of performance in West Semitic culture. And prophecy comes to be the most decisive of the three discourses because it provides the frame for the first two. Rather than assuming that the king had the right to speak for a people, we see a different expectation: that the ideal interlocutor for a people is a prophet. Biblical law is handed down by a prophet, and biblical history is framed as the working-out of prophecy. It is as prophecy above all that biblical genres of discourse reflect on, and empower, their own mediation.

Prophetic performance is widely attested in texts from both the Old Babylonian and Iron Age periods. Oracular messages, in the sense of direct discourse quoted from a god and mediated by a prophet, have a long history in the ancient Near East. But literary prophecy, a message circulated to a public in writing, did not exist. As performance, prophecy was always formally independent of kingship because it represented an independent channel of communication from the gods. Its authority comes from the displacement of authorship, from human speaker onto divine author, via the displacement of the human speaker's personhood and responsibility for speech: "this is not my word, it is the word of the god."[12] But as writing, prophecy had always been a state secret. And while there were numerous citations of prophetic actions in writing, there were no narratives with prophets at the center.

Narrative prophecy serves as a kind of meta-genre, framing biblical history and law: it is in the story of Moses' prophecies that the Deuteronomistic source sets out the course of the history of Israel. By itself, literary prophecy provides a narrative framework making the prophet himself a character and a protagonist of events, alongside the publication of prophetic messages. This is why the circulation of prophetic texts that we see at Deir Alla and again at Lachish outside the physical precincts of the royal court is significant. But the further dimension that narrative prophecy adds to edited biblical texts is the subversion of two epigraphic genres of royal sovereignty: history, as an account of the mighty deeds in the past by which the king earned sovereignty, and law, by which his subjects are ritually bound to his present rule. With Deuteronomy's negative political theology the king's history and law themselves become genres of prophecy: speaking to and binding an audience in the present.

The scribal adoption of the prophetic mantle has often been seen as an act of "legitimation," the creation, indeed the forgery, of a basis of authority that did not exist in objective fact.[13] But if we read the biblical discourses of history, law, and prophecy as inaugurated in the transformation of early Iron Age Assyrian-based genres of power into late Iron Age West Semitic-based forms of political communication, we can see them differently: not as legitimation or authority-forging but as taking on a traditional discursive task of summoning and addressing a people. What has changed in the Iron Age is the political condition of sovereignty: it is no longer vested in the military power of the assembled kin or the state. Thus the people are now addressed through the circulation of texts, as a public.

FROM EPIGRAPHY TO SCRIBAL CULTURE

We can do no more than suggest plausible ways that three biblical discourses were inaugurated. For here we encounter one of the most interesting gaps in our record: the total disappearance of Hebrew from the epigraphic record between the Babylonian exile and the Hellenistic period. Writing continues as before, but in Aramaic, with many of the same generic uses: letters, economic documents, and property markers.

This shift finds its cause in the destruction of the Judean political infrastructure in the early sixth century by the Babylonians, combined with the economic devastation and mass deportation of craftspeople and artisans. Written Hebrew's very bond to spoken language created a limit here. It had always been represented as isomorphic with and iconic of speech, and with such an ideology of writing persisting in a time when Aramaic was becoming a main spoken language for much of the Judean population, the switch to Aramaic as the script-language for daily activity seems almost a foregone conclusion.

It is during the exile that the writing of Hebrew becomes the exclusively scribal culture on which Karel van der Toorn and David M. Carr focus. At the same time as written Hebrew completely vanishes from the epigraphic record, we find the most extensive internal evidence of Hebrew texts being edited and rethought, in the allusions to exile and return that pervade later biblical books. The production of extended texts in Hebrew flourished in literature, not daily life.

How did these biblical discourses, which we have contextualized epigraphically, expand into such chronologically extensive, continuous sources? When inscriptions respond to datable events, we can connect them to the same narrow historical moments to which they connect themselves. Even if the Mesha stela is retrospective, its only plausible context is at most a few decades away from the events it describes. Monuments have lives like buildings: their context is a landscape where they stand for years. But when they fall they leave their contexts and are sealed away from them in rubble.

But streams of written tradition look more like our stereotype of oral literature: once they enter the realm of transmission and rewriting, they are no longer limited to responding to a single set of events and circumstances. That may be their major value for their audiences: they can speak to new circumstances. They do not connect themselves to a narrow historical moment, but reconnect with an expandable range of situations. They may be a palimpsest of multiple contexts.

Historical-critical method has traditionally read biblical texts against their grain: scholars look for the original context of a source such as the Deuteronomistic History. We peer under the layers of the palimpsest to the first inscription, then order the layers, more or less successfully. Recent developments in source criticism have begun to see the sources as more continuous flows of discourse, persisting over time.[14] This means less emphasis on pinpointing precise moments of inscription and more emphasis on how a whole discourse was created, then took on new features and intended participants.

We can see biblical sources like the Deuteronomistic History less as strata to date to the decade and more as discourses inaugurated in certain cultural contexts. The ninth century is a time when we see vernacular history-writing inaugurated, but as far as we know it is all in the king's voice. In the eighth century we begin to see another kind of vernacular narrative of events being published: Siloam and Deir Alla are narratives of events from non-royal (not necessarily anti-royal) viewpoints. They have new participants: prophets, peoples, and groups of workers. In the same period, we see local adaptations of Assyrian legal-ritual forms in Sefire. Translated legal-ritual discourse is now being published.

A broader historical reading of the intertextual connections between biblical and epigraphic texts lets us use them as more than forensic evidence: cultures in history, not radiocarbon dates. The immediate consequence of the vernacular revolution for Hebrew literary culture was that biblical law and history become possible by the eighth century, when we have epigraphic evidence of these modes of discourse being configured and where we can see their generic features emerging. They are plausibly integrated into extended, multi-generic texts by an advanced scribal culture in the late seventh and early sixth centuries, just before and after the end of the Judean kingdom. The recent major studies of Schniedewind (2004), Carr (2005), and van der Toorn (2007) all correlate the unusually intense reflection on textual mediation found in biblical texts *about* this period with the peak of dated epigraphic evidence *from* this period. Second Kings 22–23 and Jeremiah 36 present a writing culture meditating on its own increasingly complicated position and activity.[15] We can deemphasize the narrow reconstructive strategy of linking precise texts to precise kings (while using it where plausible and appropriate) and gain a broader, more securely anchored view of Hebrew literary culture in history.

From this point of view it is the second shift in Hebrew literary culture, toward the kind of extended, multi-generic works scholars identify as Deuteronomistic, that was the decisively *biblical* one. Here two epigraphic genres of royal sovereignty, history and law, became literary subgenres of prophecy. History, as an account of the mighty deeds in the past by which the king earned sovereignty, and law, by which his subjects are ritually bound in the present, were subverted to become forms of prophecy, a genre that speaks in the present, directly addressing and thus binding its audience in the here and now: "Not with our ancestors did the Lord make this covenant, but with us, who are all of us here alive today" (Deut. 5:3, NRSV).

It is this prophetic displacement of authorship and personhood, the assimilation of heterogeneous texts and contexts to a notionally unified divine voice, which became the central history-making mechanism of biblical texts. And this very fusion of genres and contexts is what requires source criticism to enact a kind of violence against the text, in order to read against the grain of the foundational scribal editorial principle: "to these many similar words were added" (Jer. 36:32)—a claim that the added words were all actually of a piece with the original text.[16] With the growth of prophecy to encompass history and law, writing gained the capacity to call a new kind of political entity into being.

Reading the Hebrew inscriptions of the late Iron Age together gives us a literary culture in history. It cannot work as radiocarbon dating for specific biblical texts, but it can provide something more interesting. We gain a concrete cultural context for the distinctive and powerful way biblical texts communicate.

FROM PEOPLE TO PUBLIC

Biblical history became possible through the conjuncture between alphabetic writing and West Semitic political theory. But it started to matter when a people began to be addressed through texts as a public.

Over the past half-century of social theory, interest in the interplay between communicative and political forms has blossomed. One phenomenon that the most intellectually interesting social theorists have discovered repeatedly is what Jürgen Habermas and Michael Warner called a public, a political community called into being through the circulation of texts. Texts that address people in a vernacular—a written version of their own local language—enable a distinct kind of recognition in their audience. The texts' addressees can identify the text's language and contents with their own sense of place and belonging. Their own self-recognition as members of the group the text is talking to can actually call that group into existence.[17] Habermas, Warner, and, most famously, Benedict Anderson recognized this process at work in the beginnings of modernity. Perhaps predictably, each discovered it in the materials he knew well and attributed it to the period in which he encountered it. Habermas called it "the public sphere," Warner simply "a public," and Anderson "the nation." Each assumed it was a side effect of the uniquely modern processes with which he was familiar.

But one of the strange things about a public, like a nation, is that nobody has ever met one. That is, like any collectivity beyond the face-to-face, publics never appear in a tangible physical form. Assembled in person, most would not recognize each other. Publics need to be imagined. Today this is easy because we have so many institutions and media to do it for us: in addition to the newspapers, books, and advertising addressed to the U.S. public, there are letters to the editor, weblogs, and polls—whole genres and industries devoted to public opinion. What is typical of modernity is the abundant production of things to represent publics to themselves: surely one of the reasons that Habermas, Anderson, and Warner all recognized them in modernity. But a public is not a matter of technology—or rather, not just one technology.

What made the alphabet's new uses in the Iron Age Levant so important was the new set of assumptions behind them—assumptions about *participation* in written texts: whose language texts can speak, who the protagonists of written accounts can be, and who can circulate texts. It was becoming possible to imagine a group called into being by the circulation of texts, far from modern ideologies of the nation-state. Instead of the capitalist idea of books and newspapers circulating as commodities that everybody might want to buy, there existed then the idea of written texts' circulating through the process of *qr*ʾ, "summoning/reading/ proclaiming," represented repeatedly in the Bible and West Semitic inscriptions as an inherently public and political act.[18] People in the Levant rethought forms of communication to create their own kinds of participation, ones grounded in an old tribal ideology and which entered a new phase with the invention of written Hebrew.

Looking at Hebrew's life on the ground in the late Iron Age suggests a way to see how the Bible's distinctiveness originates in a political context broader and deeper than the history of a state. The features that make the Bible most problematic as a source for ancient Israel's history are precisely the ones that enabled it to survive Israel's demise and serve as a foundation for new communities. It assumes a negative political theology, one in which the human sovereign never has inherent legitimacy before the speaker of the authoritative text. So its predominant viewpoint is not that of a kingdom or king (as most "legitimate" Near Eastern historical sources) but of independent institutions and figures: priests, prophets, and other mediators of texts; it addresses not subjects of a state, in the third person (as, again, most Near Eastern historical sources and all other Near Eastern law) but a people, addressed in the second person as hearers and readers of a revealed text whose authority flows not from state or king but God.

The Deuteronomistic covenant is not intended to constitute a state (let alone a democratic republic) but to imagine a people, constituted by their attention and response to a set of texts (both spoken and written); to the extent that the texts share a goal it is to elicit this attention and response: for addressees to imagine themselves as part of this people. The ideal reader it presupposes is not a member of an already constituted kingdom or polity, but a constituting member. This imagined people, mediated through Hebrew texts, constitutes Israel—the Bible's public.

This book has argued, against Habermas, Anderson, and Warner, that a public is neither the private property nor a unique symptom of modernity. What we have seen suggests that the ideal of a political community grounded in communicative form has a long history. What emerges as remarkable about the Hebrew Bible is not only that it speaks in the voice of God, but how this voice at once directly addresses its audience and represents that audience's responses as both determinative and unpredictable. It speaks in the voice of a God who can inflict terrible punishment, but not coerce obedience. Instead it circulates through and by means of the people it addresses. Epigraphy and linguistics show us that the contest between Foucault's "biblical history" and "Roman history" existed long before Rome.

Lecturing on his deathbed, the historian of religion Jacob Taubes (2004) spoke of an ancient political theology from below, the idea that ultimate claims might not flow down from a ruler but upward from communities constituted by the commandments they encountered in written revelation. By producing the words of an otherworldly sovereign in non-state-sponsored texts, the biblical texts could act as a radical limit on the claims of the human sovereign, what Taubes called the danger of "chaos from above." Thomas Hobbes said the sovereign is simply he whose words are obeyed, but by assigning a sovereignty to words that the ruler by definition cannot produce, political theology from below contests the source of power precisely by contesting its mediation. Rulers can usurp, but never truly speak in, this voice.[19]

The Hebrew Bible is the still-functioning artifact of a vernacular revolution. What we have seen is how this first vernacular revolution opened up a space for a public, as its authors created the Bible to address it. In the course of history such publics have been repeatedly called into being in widely varied languages and contexts: some solidified as churches, some as nations or empires, some as peoples. But each instance implied the formation of further publics, independent of or even against the regimes under which they lived, around the experience of being directly addressed by the text. If we can speak of a characteristically biblical politics, this may be it: an essentially *generative* mode of political communication that helps create its audience by the very means through which it addresses it. This politics, which demands endless translation, was initiated with the invention of Hebrew.

NOTES

PREFACE

1. I thank Tzvi Abusch for introducing me to the world of Babylonian ritual texts as an assistant editor for the *Maqlû* incantation series; Wayne Horowitz gave me the opportunity to learn more as an associate editor of *Cuneiform in Canaan and Israel*, the first complete collection of Babylonian texts found in Israel and Palestine (Horowitz, Oshima, and Sanders 2006).

2. See Landsberger 1926, translated as Landsberger 1976.

3. Hebrew belongs to a family of written languages, including Phoenician, Moabite, Edomite, and Aramaic, which happen to share a relatively close genetic relationship, as varieties of West Semitic. There is no necessary relationship between linear alphabetic writing and West Semitic languages, as is clear by the eighth century B.C.E., when we find the Phoenician script extensively adapted to represent Greek; by the sixth century B.C.E. we also find (East Semitic) Akkadian names written by themselves in Hebrew script (Zorn 2003). Written Aramaic is the most complicated part of this picture, since it begins as a written vernacular but is swiftly repurposed by the Assyrian empire. The earliest Aramaic inscriptions, such as that of Tell Fekheriye, show its origins in local language. Its script is perhaps the first to branch off from Phoenician, but is very quickly adopted for cosmopolitan purposes as a practical language of the Assyrian empire, from which it is inherited by the Babylonian and Persian empires.

4. For the roots of this critique in the religious polemics of late antiquity, see Malcolm 2002.

5. On the shared assumptions of both schools, see the shrewd comments of Gottwald 1997.

6. The minimalists' most effective gesture has been that of debunking, but precisely because of that, their work tended to replicate the categories they critiqued. For a demonstration of Near Eastern archaeology's potential to illuminate, and sometimes dismantle, thinking about the state, see Adam T. Smith 2003.

7. As J. Samuel Preus put it, "no theoretical contribution to the problem of political sovereignty could be made in Spinoza's era without dealing with the claims of religion as the foundation of political legitimacy and order" (Preus 2001:1–2)

INTRODUCTION

1. All Bible translations are mine, except where marked as from the New Revised Standard Version (NRSV) or King James Version (KJV).

2. This question seems especially urgent since it is arguable that the last work within biblical studies to have had an enduring theoretical impact outside of the field was W. Robertson Smith's *Lectures on the Religion of the Semites* (1894). The source criticism of W. M. L. de Wette and Julius Wellhausen had already been deployed in classics.

3. For the obvious but profound point that "cuneiform is a script, not a language," see Van de Mieroop 1999:10.

4. This ideology of difference has been laid out in a preliminary but highly convincing essay by Peter Machinist (1991).

5. They drew very different political conclusions from very similar arguments about biblical authority. While *Leviathan* radically restricts free speech, the *Tractatus Theologico-Politicus* (chap. 20) concludes that its suppression is a far greater threat to peace.

6. For this elegant phrase, see M. S. Smith 2002; for an assessment of the role of this book in the history of scholarship, see Sanders 2002–3.

7. For my identification of a specifically West Semitic political ideology in which a ruler's sovereignty is contingent on the public performance of just judgment, see chapter 2. This pattern is recognizable but significantly different at Ugarit, a society that is imagined in its texts as less kin-based than Mari or Israel. This theme appears at Ugarit in the epic of Kirta, who as a legendary king and dynastic founder, is implicitly a model for the king of Ugarit. The modeling for kings of Mari and Israel is, as we will see, far more explicit.

8. Two amulets from Ketef Hinnom bear a blessing nearly identical with the Priestly Benediction of Numbers 6:24–26. They demonstrate that versions of this text were circulating in the Iron Age, but unfortunately tell us nothing about whether the biblical text was drawing on a preexisting prayer or the other way around.

9. Carr's book is intended to develop a picture of "how people in the ancient world produced and worked with texts" (2005:4, but why is "picture" in the singular?; note similar statements on 5, 11, and passim). Van der Toorn suggests that because scribalism was a profession, it may have been essentially the same across the ancient Near East (2007:52–53). In contrast to Van der Toorn, Carr emphasizes the difficulty of precisely reconstructing pre-Hellenistic scribal culture. Both writers carefully acknowledge diversity and provide nuances, yet these do not always seem to affect the overall picture.

10. In particular, the most complex scribal educational text from Israel is a large ostracon from Kadesh-Barnea listing the hieratic numbers from 1 to 10,000, discussed in chapter 4. This could be used to teach bookkeeping, well attested in the epigraphic corpus, but has no direct bearing on literary texts. In sharp contrast to the various educational texts in Babylonian cuneiform from Late Bronze Age Israel, discussed in chapter 3, there are none from the Iron Age (compare the chart in Horowitz, Oshima, and Sanders 2005:5 with the individual text editions). Carr notes this lack for both Akkadian and Hebrew (2005:59, 123–24).

11. The list Carr provides (2005:122–23) is a useful summary, but note that the Lachish letters, which he cites as a controversial possible example of practice texts copied by a student, cannot be practice texts since the letters from each sender are in different corresponding hands, as noted already by Birnbaum 1939 and reiterated by Na'aman 2003:175.

12. Van der Toorn and Carr acknowledge significant nuances between Hebrew and the scribal cultures of Mesopotamia and Egypt—but perhaps, given their significantly different languages, writing systems, and political structures, this is the least they could do.

13. The two points in time at which we can check our assumptions with adequate epigraphic evidence, comparing ancient Levantine alphabetic scribal cultures with those of Mesopotamia and Egypt (at Ugarit, in the thirteenth century B.C.E., and Qumran, in the second and first) suggests some startling differences. One good way to test for different attitudes would be a comparison of language ideologies: ways that the use of speech and writing is typified in Mesopotamian, Egyptian, biblical, or other West Semitic texts. Unfortunately there are no adequate studies of this topic. For a narrowly focused study of Ugaritic language ideology, see Sanders 2004a; for a useful collection of evidence for Hebrew (with no attempt at synthesis), see Weinberg 1980; the most insightful attempt to characterize biblical attitudes toward language is the rich but uneven work of Rabinowitz 1993.

14. If scribes wrote for scribes, the broad illiterate audience not only does not matter, it practically does not exist. Indeed, the primary source van der Toorn must cite on the illiterate reverence for scribes is himself a Hellenistic scribe, Ben Sira.

15. For a thoughtful and well-informed critique of my methodology, see the article of Allan Millard (2007), to whom I am indebted for both sharpening and nuancing my approach. Every reader interested in what Iron Age alphabetic texts can tell us about Iron Age Levantine cultures would do well to read this piece, which in some cases might apply a fortiori to the Bible—and compare with my brief defense in the body of the text.

16. A perfect example is the newly discovered and not yet published Tel Qeiyafah ostracon, said to date to the tenth century B.C.E. and mention a king, judge, and servant in a language identical or directly ancestral to Hebrew (reportedly diagnosed by the root ʿśh "make/do," supposedly only known from Hebrew, though cognates do in fact exist in Moabite and perhaps Ugaritic). Publication and study of this new evidence will tell whether it pushes back the invention of Hebrew as a standardized language for literature by a century or more, or whether it merely confirms this book's proposal that Hebrew was spoken but not systematically written until it became the subject of a deliberate cultural project in the late ninth century B.C.E.

17. The richly documented and well-rehearsed arguments for an Assyrian imperial model in Deuteronomic covenant-making are mentioned in the conclusion.

18. Fine testimony to the durability of recognition as a political ideal is found in the titles of two major recent works in social and political theory, Elizabeth Povinelli's *The Cunning of Recognition* (2002) and Patchen Markell's *Bound by Recognition* (2003). These two thinkers display great ingenuity in attempting to move beyond the framework of address and recognition as the basis for political agency. Their virtuoso performances, suggesting two irreconcilable new theoretical discourses in themselves, testify to the feeling of being bound by a cunning foe indeed and suggest another potential value to considering how this framework may have been inaugurated.

19. For a classic study of conflicts between this new political theology and an old politics of kinship that was deep-seated in Arabic poetics, see Goldziher 2006. Recent

years have seen exciting new studies of Arabic political communication (Hirschkind 2006; F. Miller 2007) and comparative explorations of Islamic political theory (Buck-Morss 2003), an endeavor to which this book may be able to suggest over two thousand years of further historical depth.

1. MODERNITY'S GHOSTS: THE BIBLE AS POLITICAL COMMUNICATION

1. Martin Yaffe's remark in the preface to his translation of Spinoza's *Tractatus Theologico-Politicus* (Yaffe 2004:vii); this notion is argued in depth by Preus 2001.

2. For examples of this attitude, see, among others, Spinoza's statements in the preface 40, chapter IV:39–43, IV:64, V:2–30.

3. Both Spinoza and Hobbes argued that, even if the Bible's words did come from God, it did not matter precisely because words can only communicate information; they cannot be inherently true or powerful. The Bible's textuality is turned from the source of its cultural dominance (Schniedewind 2004) to its Achilles' heel.

4. This argument is made most clearly and powerfully in S. B. Smith 1997, and the consequences for our understanding of cultural difference as political difference can be drawn by comparing it with Bauman and Briggs 2003.

5. "Modernity is a contrastive historical concept and therefore implies some understanding of what is counted as pre-modern. But much of the work on modernity (from Karl Marx to present-day scholars, such as Anthony Giddens, Jürgen Habermas, Hiklas Luhmann, and so on down the alphabet) offers little in the way of a convincing account of the nature of the 'premodern.'" Pollock 2006a:8.

6. Bauman and Briggs 2003:7. For some earlier scholarly constructions of Language, see Kelly 2006a and Pollock 2006b.

7. A vividly personal introduction to humanists and their ideas is available in Grafton 2002.

8. An illuminating treatment of Valla is that of Ginzburg 1999:54–70.

9. Though apparently not for as long or as consistently as commonly believed. See Fulton 2002.

10. Muir 1997:173. Yet Zwingli's position did not gain broad assent: more influential, in the end, was the Calvinist emphasis on the materiality of the words of the ritual. Drawing on biblical texts such as Ezekiel 3's image of an edible scroll bearing divine writing, Calvinists spoke of "touching" the truth, "digesting" the scriptures, and "tasting" the word of God (Muir 1997, citing Regina Schwartz, 176).

11. Muir 1997:150.

12. Muir 1997:150. The Reformation also changed the religious base of political authority. As David Bell points out, "the Reformation broke the unity of Western Christendom and led to the rise of state churches, which in many cases also functioned as national churches. In the newly Protestant states . . . an identification of the population as a whole as an elect, and as successors to the biblical people of Israel, served as a powerful spur to the development of ethnic and national consciousness" (1996:111). For powerful examples, one need look no further than Herder's use of Israel's *Volk* as an ideal model of the relationship between poetry and politics (cited below).

13. "Christendom" (*Christianitas*), a term first used by Pope John VIII (reigned 872–882), was only briefly a geopolitical reality. Modeled on the Roman empire, it was applied to the Carolingian empire, which by the time of Charlemagne (c. 757–814) covered most of Western Europe; it only lasted until the breakup of that empire in the late ninth century. It was revived as an ideal during the First Crusade and remained a common concept until the eighteenth century. See Guenée 1985:1–2.

14. Indeed, one reason why the Reformation succeeded where earlier heresies had not was that Protestantism was not subversive of the state, only the Church. Indeed, in providing a pretext to throw off the Church's claims to money, land, and allegiance, it provided states with opportunities to strengthen their power. See van Creveld 1999, esp. 67–68.

15. As Sheehan writes, "If the old answer to the old question 'What is the ultimate source of biblical authority?' was 'theological truth,' the new answers were distributed across a variety of humanistic and historical disciplines" (2005:91). When it comes to the old, Sheehan writes of both "old questions" and "old answers," while modernity seems to offer only "new answers." But there were new questions as well, often predicated on the assumption that biblical authority *had* no ultimate source. Indeed, this chapter argues that the greatest change in the Bible's status can be seen as flowing from a repudiation of the old question and its replacement with philological and folkloric ones. The question of whether biblical authority has any legitimate source at all suggests both the title and the center of gravity of Spinoza's *Tractatus Theologico-Politicus*, as Steven B. Smith's 1997 study shows. That Sheehan does not address this issue directly is a weakness of his erudite and interesting book.

16. My phrasing here highlights the extremes of this debate; for a detailed and judicious assessment that perceptively notes the assumptions shared by both sides, see Gottwald 1997.

17. Narrower works such as Richard Simon's *Critical History of the Old Testament* (1678) were also of decisive importance, but I am interested here in those works, chiefly of Hobbes and Spinoza, which stood at the historical juncture where biblical studies and political theory seriously met for the last time. For details of how the Bible's political authority bled away after the fatal blows were struck, resulting in the edifying but ambivalent document Jonathan Sheehan refers to as "the cultural Bible," see Sheehan 2005.

18. All references to *Leviathan* are by Hobbes's chapters, followed by the page number in Richard Tuck's edition (1991).

19. For a more detailed argument on how Hobbes's innovation in biblical criticism resides not in his discussion of sources but his account of communication and authority, see Malcolm 2002. Malcolm provides an extremely rich and insightful account of the history and stakes of source criticism in the early modern period.

20. "For if a man pretend to me, that God hath spoken to him supernaturally, and immediately, and I make doubt of it, I cannot easily perceive what argument he can produce, to oblige me to believe it. It is true, that if he be my Sovereign, he may oblige me to obedience, so, as not by act or word to declare I believe him not; but not to think any otherwise than my reason persuades me. But if one that hath not such authority over me, shall pretend the same, there is nothing that exacteth either belief, or obedience."

21. Hobbes posits the pragmatic basis of semiotics in political disputes: evaluative moral language is "imposed on things in order to indicate either the desire or the aversion of those by whom the things in question are named," but "the desires of men are diverse, depending as they do on the diversity of their temperaments, their customs and their attitudes" and "so long as *good* and *evil* are measured by the mere diversity of present desires . . . those who act in this way will find themselves still living in a state of war" (*De cive*, III.XXXI, cited in the translation of Skinner 1996:318). And, as Quentin Skinner explains, "the only possible remedy is for the sovereign to impose his own definition and use his authority to forbid any further argument" (Skinner 1996:317–18). This sovereign is represented in *Leviathan*, both literally and figuratively, by a Judge: "And therefore, as when there is a controversy in an account, the parties must by their own accord set up for right Reason, the Reason of some Arbitrator, or Judge, to whose sentence they will both stand, or their controversy must either come to blows, or be undecided, for want of a right Reason constituted by Nature" (*Leviathan* I V; cf. discussion of Skinner 1996:341).

22. There is a crucial nuance here. If Hobbes truly believed that all texts, absent coercive authority, were the same then he would hardly have bothered to make such persuasive arguments about what they can and cannot do. In fact, Hobbes and Spinoza were acutely aware that some texts—such as the Bible—actually had the effect of producing a kind of authority in interaction with readers and their expectations. Indeed, this is precisely why they focus on expectations: by attempting to persuade readers that they should not *expect* authority to flow from biblical interpretation—that such authority *should* not be thinkable—they make a gambit to change readers' expectations, undermining the authority that they understood all too well to flow pragmatically, if illegitimately, from biblical interpretation. This slippage by which a descriptive "is" becomes a pragmatic "ought" has been termed the "theory effect" by Pierre Bourdieu (1991).

This is part of a broader problem. For the political philosophers—Hobbes, Spinoza, Niccolo Machiavelli—who instituted modernity as a project, the critique of religion always had a double edge. On the one hand, they debunked religious language as claiming authority regardless of truth; on the other hand, they knew that for their own critiques to claim authority they had to persuade people. As truly political philosophers—philosophers who acted politically—they had to enter the same realm of political communication in which the Bible acted so powerfully. For a discussion of the problem of philosophy's becoming political, see Meier 2006. While these political philosophers had a double-edged view of the poetic, non-rational side of language, the scholarly traditions of philology and folklore that followed them usually held a less complex view.

23. It is in this light that the mid-twentieth-century American enterprise of biblical archaeology assumes a particularly remarkable cast. As Thomas Davis points out in his history of this subdiscipline, "The practitioners of biblical archaeology believed, albeit in different ways, that biblical faith, both Christianity and Judaism, depends on the historical reality of the events that displayed the Hand of God. If the events that the Bible interprets as the intervention of the divine have no basis in reality, then there is no basis for believing in the biblical witness. Thus, any evidence that might

help to buttress the hope of faith is welcome, Here is the ultimate drive for realia" (T. W. Davis 2004:viii). Here, three centuries after the controversies of early modernity, the problem of the authority of scripture reemerges in what would surely have struck Hobbes and his opponents as a debased form. The question is no longer whether the scriptures are the publicly binding word of a sovereign God—there is no longer any political basis for such a claim—but rather whether the events, which one may *choose* to believe signify the past actions of a sovereign God, even happened. Revelation's proponents fight a rear-guard action for vastly shrunken territory.

24. Roger Woolhouse, introduction to Locke 1997:xi.

25. As Bauman and Briggs (2003:38) put it, "discourse produced through explicitly intertextual links is grounded indexically in particular texts, persons, and activities."

26. Bauman and Briggs 2003:72.

27. Blackwell 1970:26.

28. Bauman and Briggs 2003: 92–93, 96.

29. Bauman and Briggs 2003:102.

30. Goody's work seems to be treated as confirmed by Carr 2005:7 and Ong's oral/literate typology is assumed in statements such as "oral cultures dictate a particular style in written texts" by van der Toorn 2007:14–15, 119 (quote on 14). Schniedewind 2004:38, 91–93 challenges the claims of Havelock, Goody, and Ong with ancient evidence.

31. Lowth 1969 1:50.

32. Bauman and Briggs 2003: 217, 153.

33. "Lowth's bold yet premature effort deserves to be resumed on a new level." See Jakobson 1987, where he cites Biblicists, including H. L. Ginsberg and W.F. Albright, and thanks F.M. Cross. The quote is from p. 147. I bracket here the important polemic of Kugel (1981), which is focused more narrowly on biblical exegesis—there is, for example, no reference to Jakobson.

34. These "were the vehicles for the preservation of supernaturalist knowledge and imperfect history; they were instruments of error, within a rhetorical arena of error and truth, of corruption and purity. Functionally, they were the instruments of traditional authority, serving for the socialization of children, the regulation of behavior, the intergenerational transmission of knowledge." Bauman and Briggs 2003:122.

35. Blair 1970a:1–2.

36. Blair 1970b: 3:88.

37. Bauman and Briggs 2003:162, 161.

38. Blair 1970a:33. For Lowth and the Authorized Version as models, see Bauman and Briggs 2003:155n20. The story of Ossian is easy to tell as a scandalous forgery, as is often done in modern scholarship—for two examples, one an extensive retelling in the service of an unmasking of myth as "ideology in narrative form" and the other as a quip, see Lincoln 1999:50–51, and Schama 1995:471 on the eighteenth-century craze for "literary relics" that could be "manufactured by the shrewder entrepreneurs of the sublime." Here Schama is dismissive at the expense of accuracy, jokingly commenting on MacPherson's 1760 *Fragments of Ancient Epic Poetry* that "they always had to be *fragments*, to suggest ruined authenticity"—but the point of MacPherson's 1762 *Fingal*, the first book Schama cites, is precisely that it is not fragmentary but a

complete "Ancient Epic Poem" comparable to Homer, a feature shared with two of MacPherson's three books.

39. Compare the same move by Ernst Renan in his equally significant nineteenth-century essay "What is a Nation?"

40. Herder 1877–1913 12:118–19, 11:230.

41. Herder 1985 2:14; 1877–1913 9:532; 1877–1913 18:387.

42. A project I take up in my forthcoming Brill volume on the morphology of the heavenly journey, *Myths of Revelation*. This major work of Gunkel's (Gunkel 2006) has finally been made available to an English audience.

43. Bauman and Briggs 2003:199, 216.

44. For two diametrically opposed, and therefore symptomatic, views of Albright and his legacy, compare Running and Freedman's reverent study (1975), which sees Albright's philology as flowing naturally from his unique genius, and Long's critique (1997), which painstakingly, and painfully, reduces Albright's scholarship to an exercise of social power. Both reflect the combination of talent, dedication, and strategy by which one man came to dominate American biblical studies for decades.

45. See Cross's meditations on "Alphabets and Pots: Reflections on Typological Method in the Dating of Human Artifacts" in Cross 2003:344–50.

46. Such a three-dimensional study is provided, with rich documentation, by M. S. Smith 2001b.

47. Cf. the "subsurface tradition" discussed by Fishbane 2004.

48. Bauman and Briggs 2003:93.

49. It is important to note that Cross's and Cassuto's Israelite epics were not identical. Cassuto viewed the epic fragments embedded in the Bible as at least formally, if not spiritually, continuous with Canaanite tradition, while Cross claimed that Hebrew epic was fundamentally different in both worldview and genre, what Mark S. Smith (personal communication, August 2005) has described as "a biblical 'anti-epic' posed against Cassuto's." Yet Cross's opposition does not entirely cohere, even with respect to genre. The contrast he offers is actually not between "myth" and "epic" but between two kinds of epic, one that imagines events mythically and one that imagines them historically.

50. The Hebrew publication appeared in 1943. For translation, see Cassuto 1975.

51. Cassuto 1975:74.

52. The addresses appear in Isaiah 51:9–10, 51:17, and 52:1–2. For a verbal parallel between Isaiah 74's splitting and Anat's splitting, see KTU 1.6 II 32. After this chapter was written, Jeremy Hutton shared with me his analysis of these texts, now published as Hutton 2007. He perceptively notes these connections and argues that the intention of Isaiah is to lampoon Judean use of foreign or hostile Canaanite motifs. But there is no evidence of parody, nor any thematization of the image's foreignness, in the text. The most plausible interpretation of the imagery remains that of Fishbane 2003, as in the two exilic psalms Hutton analyzes, Psalms 74 and 89, God's battle is an accepted Israelite myth.

53. Cassuto 1975:98, 103.

54. Again, there are significant differences of nuance and emphasis between Cassuto's and Cross's accounts of the passage from Ugaritic to Israelite folk poetry. For example,

Cross emphasizes that myth was not permanently defeated, referring to the "recrudescence" (etymologically, "becoming raw again," a medical term for the reemergence of a disease) of myth in the Persian and Hellenistic periods (Cross 1973:343).

55. The tenuous reconstructions and nationalist-folkloric agenda of Cassuto's work did not pass unchallenged in Israel, where Shemaryahu Talmon (1981) published a harsh critique.

56. Herder 1985 2:14; 1877–1913 9:532; 1877–1913 18:387.

57. Bauman and Briggs 2003: 221; Lincoln 1999:52–55 is an incisive, even excoriating treatment that leaves unclear Lincoln's own intellectual relationship to the first major exponent of cultural relativism and the close poetic and political reading of the texts of other cultures—tools of every reflexive and progressive comparativist. He admits this contradiction in his conclusion, ending with an unsettling quip that relativizes the book's own critique: "if myth is ideology in narrative form, then scholarship is myth with footnotes" (1999:208). But as Lincoln himself has incisively shown (1991) in the case of George Dumézil's disturbing work "on some fake massacres," the quintessential scholarly gesture—the debunking of myth—can itself be an act of political mystification. Footnotes can narrate their own myths, so we should not rely overmuch on the inherently truth-revealing structures of our own favorite genres.

58. An example of the prevalence of this mode of thinking is the essay of Alexander Joffe (2002, and more briefly and explicitly 2003) precisely because it challenges many other accepted presuppositions in biblical studies and is so sophisticated in other respects that the flatness of his semiotics stands out.

59. For this critique, see Schniedewind 2000a.

60. For the medieval pedigree of the idea that Ezra wrote the Torah, see Malcolm 2002.

61. For the second phenomenon, simply compare William G. Dever's *What did the Biblical Writers Know, and When Did They Know It? What Archaeology Can Tell Us About the Reality of Ancient Israel* with Thomas L. Thompson's *The Mythic Past: Biblical Archaeology and the Myth of Israel.* Was Hobbes right to claim, more than three hundred years ago, that there are no stakes in this debate?

62. The implication seems to be that encounters between the theory and the Bible will not have stakes or consequences for the theory itself. Illustrative examples can be found in books of "applied theory" such as *Levinas and Biblical Studies* (Eskenazi, Phillips, and Jobling 2003), *Mikhail Bakhtin and Biblical Scholarship* (Green 2000; Reed 1993), and *Derrida's Bible* (Sherwood and Hart 2004; Sherwood 2004). Green's introduction is the most raw appraisal of this casting-about for interpretive methods that may be more than interpretive methods. She expresses a symptomatically modern anxiety about foundations: "it is my consistent experience that well-educated, generally sophisticated and faith-seeking individuals and groups . . . often find that the Bible is not very sustaining" (2000:3). Green does not express this as a problem of politics or theology, but of sophistication: "The root of this perception of biblical inadequacy is a presumed naivite of its assertions, not so much now the scientific ones but the moral voices it presents." The epigram that begins the book expresses ambivalence about the solution such seekers might find in a sophisticated theorist: Bakhtinian method "will tell you how to teach, write, live, talk, think" (2000:1): it is Torah for the

secular, without its yoke of obedience or metaphysical foundations. But can nuances of heteroglossia really alleviate anxiety about the claims of revelation? Such a search for sophistication could as easily lead us to continually discard one master thinker for another; jaded scholars might anticipate *Latour and Biblical Studies* or *Agamben's Bible* with fear and trembling.

A central argument in favor of considering Hobbes and Spinoza before Emmanuel Levinas or Bakhtin comes from a principle with which we are perhaps overly familiar: that every thinker reflects the problems of their era. As Steven B. Smith writes, "Only by returning to the early modern expressions of the theologico-political problem can we hope to shed some light on our current dilemmas and controversies. Precisely because the founders of modernity did not live in a world shaped by the separation of church and state and an ethic of toleration, they give us a window on how we have come to arrive at our own self-understanding." Most important, "*The contributors to this debate were not shaped by the forces of modernity*" (S. B. Smith 1997:6, emphasis mine).

63. Bauman and Briggs also note how Lowth's poetics was justly recognized by Jakobson as presaging much of the most important twentieth century on the relationship between linguistic form and social action: as Bauman and Briggs put it, "Lowth is ultimately interested in functional considerations—the religious uses and ritual efficacy of sacred poetry—and his close attention to poetic form is in the service of illuminating form-function interrelationships" (2003:113).

2. WHAT WAS THE ALPHABET FOR?

1. Of the three recent major English works on writing and scribal culture in ancient Israel, only Schniedewind 2004 poses the emergence of Hebrew literary culture as a historical question (Na'aman's 2002 Hebrew work, not mentioned by any of the three English writers, provides the most extensive treatment of this question). Carr 2005 and van der Toorn 2007 seem to assume a fully formed Israelite scribal culture, drawing heavily on Mesopotamian and Egyptian models, without asking how or why this culture was created in the first place. And none of these studies ask a central question of this book: Why create a specifically native literature? What motivated the considerable effort and innovation required in the eighth or ninth century B.C.E. to create local vernaculars like Hebrew? There is little discussion available about what is distinctive about writing produced this way, as opposed to the relatively placeless cosmopolitan literatures of the Assyrian and Babylonian empires.

2. Used here in the minimal sense of "a narrative of political events." To the scholar of religion, the extended debate over what history "really" is, and the need to sharply differentiate it from other people's versions of true narratives (myth, ancestral genealogy, etc.) has self-justifying dimensions suggestive of the old polemical debate over religion versus magic. The critique of history as a form of writing rather than a form of truth was first made by Friedrich Nietzsche, elborated by Roland Barthes, and adapted for an Anglophone audience by Hayden White: see the bibliography in Carolo Ginzburg's insightful response (1999:1–37). The limits of history itself are sug-

gested by its deep ties to the aspirations of the sovereign nation-state, as Constantin Fasolt (2004) has shown.

3. As we will see, in Mesopotamia and the Levant most literate Semitic speakers learned to write by being taught a language no one alive spoke—Sumerian—and then an archaic version of Babylonian, a language only some of them spoke. The alienation between written and spoken language in the Near East resembled that of medieval Europe, but went beyond it. In Europe the literate only had to learn a single dead language, Latin, which many Romance speakers considered it to be close to or even the same as what they spoke (R. Wright 1991).

4. "Judean" is referred to in one late Iron Age instance, the Deuteronomistic account of the Assyrian siege of Jerusalem c. 701 B.C.E., narrated in 2 Kings 18:26, 28 (= Isa. 36:11, 13 = 2 Chron. 32:18 [revision of second instance]). Here, ironically, the concern of the Judean representatives is precisely that the Assyrian representative's Judean speech will *be understood*, and they instead urge him to speak the cosmopolitan language of Aramaic, which they—not the common people of Jerusalem—understand. The goal is to prevent communication in order to protect the citizens of Jerusalem from the intimidating Assyrian propaganda, couched in their local language—proof, incidentally, that Judean is anything but the exclusive property of good Judeans. The one other instance, Nehemiah 13:24, comes from the Persian period and represents a radically changed situation; for the author of Nehemiah, intermarriage between Ashdodites, Ammonites, and Moabites has brought about a situation where "half speak Ashdodite and none can speak Judean." Concerns about linguistic difference along political lines in the Hebrew Bible follow this pattern: discussions of linguistic difference are inconsistenly connected to political boundaries. For a limited discussion, see Weinberg 1980.

5. Arguments have been made in recent decades for the existence of nationalism before the eighteenth century, especially in ancient Israel. As scholarship, this theory is at least as old as Herder (see chapter 1), but the template of the people of Israel as a model nation was already common in early medieval Europe: "the Old Testament contained the sacred history of God's 'people,' a *gens* led by warriors, judges, kings, prophets and priests. Into this ancient past early-medieval authors inserted the histories of their own 'peoples' (*gentes*) and the formation of new kingdoms; Old Testament history thus helped to shape new political identities" (de Jong 2005:112). Thus modern scholarship echoing Herder, or even Charlemagne (Grosby 2002; Goodblatt 2006), can produce a sense of déjà vu: for centuries the idea of Israel as a model nation had been relatively uncontroversial. The contemporary theory that holds that each people in a territory naturally expresses its culture through language appears to be less a universal explanation and more a side effect of the European process of inventing local written languages (see chapter 1). Perhaps a more interesting question is the role of vernacular Bible translation in European communities' self-fashioning as nations (Hastings 1997). Given the Bible's formative influence on European political thought, it is hardly surprising that modern scholars would be able to identify biblical Israel as a nation; the question is whether such theories let us learn anything new from ancient data (Routledge 2003:229).

6. Examples of these broad patterns include the creation of universal written languages with sacred literatures, such as the Latin of medieval Christendom, the Sanskrit

of the medieval Brahmins, the Arabic of medieval Islam, or the Babylonian of the Late Bronze and Iron Ages. These universal languages then enter into relationships with more particular forms of language, such diglossia, in which the "high" prestige forms of languages such as Arabic, Italian, or German, enshrined in standard literatures, exist in a relationship of superiority to spoken vernacular forms.

7. Pollock 2002:16.

8. See the Laws as edited in Roth 1995.

9. Most famously the case of the goring ox in the Laws of Hammurabi pgh 251 and Exodus 21:28–32, 35–36, on which most recently D. Wright 2004.

10. His work thus recapitulates, in a far more sophisticated form, a series of theories in which technology sets the stage for social experience, reaching from Jack Goody and Elizabeth Eisenstein through Marshall McLuhan to, obviously, Karl Marx himself. Dominic Boyer (2007) provides an engaging overview and a fresh approach to this problem.

11. Anderson 1991.

12. For this problem, see John Kelly's critique (2006a), summarized in the rhetorical question, "why is this stuff so useless?" (Sanders 2006:5).

13. For this methodological principle, drawn from a more interesting and useful version of Max Weber than is often perceived, see Kelly 2006a:15.

14. Darnell et al. 2004. The earliest previously proposed date was Sir Alan Gardiner's hypothetical assignment of the proto-Sinaitic inscriptions to the Twelfth Dynasty in Egypt (c. 1991–1783 B.C.E.), cautiously argued for on indirect grounds by Benjamin Sass (1988:135–44; for a sober assessment, see Millard 1992). Sass eventually abandoned this dating for a later one based more on assumptions about new communication technologies (they always spread steadily and quickly) than new evidence (2004–5).

15. The once-obscure alphabetic cuneiform tablet from Beth-Shemesh, written from right to left and originally interpreted as a magical incantation against stuttering in "mirror-writing," was discovered by A. G. Loundin (1987) to be an abecedary written in the *halḥam* order attested a thousand years later in South Arabian texts. The next year, a more complete variant version of this text, written from left to right this time, was unearthed at Ugarit itself (RS 88.2215, edited by Bordreuil and Pardee 2001).

16. Quack 1993, and for a broader discussion with essential bibliography, Kammerzell 2001. I thank Thomas Douza for bringing this evidence to my attention.

17. Bordreuil 1979, 1981, and above all 1983, the consequences of which extend beyond a narrow epigraphic debate. On the implications of the Beth Shemesh abecedary, see Bordreuil and Pardee 2001.

18. Dietrich and Loretz 1988a.

19. In the jargon of Semitic philology, this broad category of Ugaritic texts is "literary," that is, narrative or ritual. There is administrative material in the form of letters, economic documents, and lists, but little legal and diplomatic material. At least in some spheres, Babylonian, not Ugaritic, was the official language of Ugarit. There are no known translations of non-Ugaritic material into Ugaritic, nor is there any known translation of Ugaritic texts into other languages. The Elkunirsa myth known from Hittite uses West Semitic names and themes but we have not yet found an Ugaritic original. The epithet behind the name, which would be expected in the form **il qn arṣ*,

is unknown at Ugarit and perhaps we need not expect it to appear, since the spread of West Semitic myth is far broader than the region of Ugarit (for Egyptian and Hittite texts that reflect myths similar to those in the Baal cycle, see M. S. Smith 1994). In the case of foreign transcriptions the picture is more interesting: there exists a single known continuous Ugaritic text in syllabic cuneiform, KTU 10.1, the content of which is not understood. But KTU2 registers four Akkadian and some thirty Hurrian ritual texts in cuneiform alphabetic script. The Akkadian texts, KTU 1.67, 1.69–70, and 1.73:1–7, consist of unique hymns and incantations, most recently studied by Stanislav Segert (1989). The Hurrian texts are all ritual in nature.

All evidence thus points to the conclusion that Ugaritic scribes were interested in rendering into Ugaritic the sounds, but not the content, of one type of foreign text: rituals. Why an interest in the aural form, but not the content, of this material? These texts embody god-names and other divine language. For Ugaritic ritualists this type of language has the unique property of being pragmatically effective in and of itself: see Sanders 2004a.

20. For an overview, see Cross 1990 and his 1993 postscript to his study of "Early Alphabetic Scripts" (Cross 2003:341–42). For his discussion of how the alphabet made democracy possible, see especially Cross 1990:78, and for a critique of the underlying assumptions Clanchy 1993. The statement appears in slightly bolder form in Albright 1960.

21. This critique was most effectively, if polemically, made in the works of Brian Street; for bibliography and the history of the debate, see Besnier 1995:1–17.

22. Romanticism's groundbreaking theory of culture was itself strongly influenced by biblical poetry as Herder understood it (see chapter 1 and the detailed discussion of Herder in Bauman and Briggs 2003). Romantic theorists of language are well known to biblical studies, which gained its concept of biblical poetry from two of the greatest of them, Herder and Bishop Robert Lowth. See Kugel 1981, esp. 12–15, 283–86, and Olender 1992 *passim*.

23. The correlation of alphabets and ethnic homelands is accurately conveyed by the title of "Die Alphabettafel aus Bet Semes und die ursprüngliche Heimat der Ugariter" ("The Abecedary from Beth Shemesh and the Original Homeland of the Ugaritians") (Dietrich and Loretz 1988b). This model pervades their work on the alphabet; for further examples, see the discussion of possible "ethnic, linguistic, social and political differences" (note the lack of interest in separating these four categories; they are assumed to go together) between two different alphabetic "traditions" carried by two separate "language groups" (Dietrich and Loretz 1989: 110–12). For strong counterarguments, see Knauf 1989 and Pardee 2007.

24. For a critique of the modern ideology of literacy from the point of view of medieval English history, see Clanchy 1993:13–16.

25. A thoughtful methodology for interpreting "ethnicity" in ancient historical writing is developed in Amory 1997:13–39. For a narrower definition, see Hall 2002.

26. For this, see conveniently the arguments and references of Hall 1997 and 2002.

27. The literature on this phenomenon is now vast. The most theoretically interesting viewpoint on how the ideological work of metonymically linking language varieties

with population units is accomplished appears in the work of Susan Gal and Judith Irvine (2000). Professor Gal informs me that a book-length study is in preparation.

28. See the classic article of Carol Kramer (1977) and the broader theoretical statement of Kathryn Kamp and Norman Yoffee (1980).

29. I thank Ryan Byrne for pointing out this analogy to me. For the debate over neo-evolutionism and Yoffee's response, see Yoffee 1993. The debate over evolutionism in politics and epigraphy had already been played out at least a century earlier in the debate between William Dwight Whitney and Ernst Renan over evolutionism in language. See my note below.

30. Yoffee 1993:60.

31. Cross 1990:78. The italics are mine. Here, as well as in the next quote, he echoes many of the claims of his teacher, W. F. Albright.

32. Cross 1990:77–8, slightly softening Albright's assertion, that "since the forms of the letters are very simple, the 22-letter alphabet could be learned in a day or two by a bright student and in a week or two by the dullest" (1960:123). For an example of the way this scholarly folk-theory seems intuitively obvious and continues to be repeated without supporting evidence in popular accounts, see Hoffman 2004:24.

33. See the summary and sources cited in Besnier 1995:1–3.

34. Besnier 1995:1.

35. Cross 1990:78.

36. Besnier 1995:2; Ong 1982:77.

37. Besnier 1995:2.

38. Thomas 1992; the characterization is that of Chambers 1995.

39. It is M. T. Clanchy's thesis that medieval England moved from memory to written record by state decree: people in power made mastery of Latin texts necessary in order to own land, enter into agreements, or go to court, and thus "lay literacy grew out of bureaucracy, rather than from any abstract desire for education or literature" (1993:19). As an observation about the relationship between culture and media in general, this then becomes the central argument of Adrian Johns's pathbreaking *The Nature of the Book* (1998): that many of the features supposed to have flowed *from* the new technology of print (standardization, dissemination, fixity) were in fact conferred on it *by* the cultures that used it (see, e.g., Johns 1998:19, 36, and especially 10 and 10n9, where he notes the similarity between claims made for print and for the invention of writing, a similarity also perceptively noted by Thomas 1992). I have explored the relationship between the semiotics, cultural contexts, and physical media of ancient Aramaic in a talk delivered at the Digital Genres Initiative conference *Semiotic Technologies* conference at the University of Chicago, 2003, which I am preparing for publication as "The Invention of the Signature, November 17, 446B.C.E.: Jewish History and the Ethnography of Writing."

40. Besnier 1995.

41. Macdonald 2005:54–55, summarizing Johansson 1988, who points out three distinctive political and religious features of reading in Sweden: "First, the ability to read gained ground much earlier than the ability to write, whereas these two skills have followed each other closely in most other countries. Second, people were persuaded to learn to read by means of an actual campaign initiated for political and religious

reasons; during the reign of Charles XI, for example, the Church Law of 1686 contained a ruling concerning a religious and Sunday-life reading for every man. Third, this reading campaign was forced through almost completely without the aid of a proper school system in the countryside. The responsibility for teaching children to read was ultimately placed on parents and godfathers. The social pressure was enormous. Everyone in the household and in the village gathered each year to take part in instructions and examinations in reading Gothic letters and biblical texts. The adult who did not succeed for a long time at these meetings would be excluded from both Holy Communion and permission to marry" (1988:137).

42. Tambiah 1968. Tambiah's piece was part of a collection edited by Goody and James Watt in which Goody and Watt's title essay is substantively challenged by nearly every other piece in the book, most prominently those of Tambiah and the Indologist Kathleen Gough.

43. Goody features significantly in each of the recent English-language works on the role of writing in Israel (Schniedewind 2004; Carr 2005; van der Toorn 2007).

44. Mere awareness of writing's existence can actually reinforce existing social hierarchies or create new ones by drawing a line between literates and illiterates. An excellent example is the cultural change around literacy analyzed by Brian Stock (1983). His essential point mirrors Clanchy's, and the work of Johns on later print cultures: neither alphabetic writing nor printing causes social change in itself. Rather, it is the different assumptions and practices around texts: during the eleventh and twelfth centuries, oral discourse "began to function within a universe of communications governed by texts. On many occasions actual texts were not present, but people often thought or behaved as if they were" (3). Thus, "the rules of the game were radically altered when the sole means of establishing a position's legitimacy was assumed to be the discovery of a written precedent" (8) and "oral tradition became associated with illiteracy" (12).

45. For detailed references, see Rollston 2006.

46. Lee, Uttal, and Chen 1995:241, and Venezky 1995.

47. Alan Li (2004) combines statistics on the remarkably high (near 100 percent) literacy rates in Japan and Korea, whose writing systems utilize thousands of Chinese characters, with a striking reversal of common assumptions about the cognitive effects of ideographic writing. He argues forcefully that it is precisely the way ideographs encode abstract concepts that is responsible for the way Japanese and Korean have retained Chinese characters, despite repeated attempts to abolish them.

48. Strictly speaking, it is impossible to differentiate "languages" from "dialects" on a linguistic basis. The problem was already set out lucidly by William Dwight Whitney in 1867: "It will be noticed that we have used the terms 'dialect' and 'language' indifferently and interchangeably, in speaking of any given tongue . . . how vain would be the attempt to establish a definitive and essential distinction between them . . . No form of speech, living or dead, of which we have any knowledge, was not or is not a dialect, in the sense of being the idiom of a limited community, among other communities of kindred but somewhat discordant idiom; none is not truly a language, in the sense that it is the means of mutual intercourse of a distinct portion of mankind" (Whitney 1971:57–58). Most striking is his attack on the evolutionist views of his contemporaries

that saw dialects culminating in national languages, a critique that closely parallels Norman Yoffee's critique of neo-evolutionism in archaeology (Whitney 1971:59). This case was argued again by Edward Sapir in 1931 in his entry under "Dialect" for the *Encyclopedia of the Social Sciences* (reprinted in Sapir 1949:83–88). Without political intervention, the natural tendency is for spoken language varieties to gradually shade into each other, rather than neatly terminating at regional borders. This fact is the basis of the modern linguistic field of dialectology (see Chambers and Trudgill 1998).

Of course "dialect" and "language" retain heuristic value for organizing genetically related varieties sharing a strong family resemblance: Syriac, Mandean, and the main varieties of the Palestinian and Babylonian Talmuds are all meaningfully "Aramaic"; the limits of even this parade example appear at ancient Sam'al and Deir 'Alla. For the heuristic value of "Aramaic" and its limits in understanding relations between North-West Semitic languages, see Huehnergard 1995 and 1991, respectively. The broader problem is the terms' complex and tainted political history: the notion of "dialect" has meant very different things in historical linguistics and popular theories of language. In classic historical linguistics, a "dialect" was, simply and neutrally, a branch on the family tree of languages: thus Assyriologists speak of first-millennium Akkadian as being composed of two dialects, Assyrian and Babylonian. But in wider European culture, "dialects" were thought to be the inferior relatives of "languages," and spoken only by poor, illiterate, rural, or otherwise marginal people. This view came about in the context of the creation of standard registers of state languages, without mastery of which some members of language communities were stigmatized as only speaking "dialect" (as in the California "Ebonics" debate of the 1990s). For a shrewd note on the conceptual and historical situation underlying the whole phenomenon, see Silverstein 1996:140n3, and for a detailed example, see the discussion of Eugen Weber (1976).

49. Weber 1976.

50. Weber's thesis has been challenged prominently by Peter Sahlins (1989), who argued that French national identity appears in a rural context, on the French-Spanish border in the eighteenth century. French identity is asserted to serve local interests well before the state sponsorship of French. However, as David Bell's review (1996) points out, the specificity that makes Sahlins's argument interesting also works against it: self-interested local assertions of Frenchness on the border do not necessarily illuminate nonlocal, ideological assertions of Frenchness across France as a whole.

51. Besnier 1995:7, with references to the programmatic works of Kenneth Basso (1974) and Brian Street (1984).

52. Cooper 2001, esp. 73–74. This diversity of Semitic-speakers hiding behind a single standard Semitic variety includes the native speakers of Eblaite, Ugaritic, and Amorite, as well as the language varieties known from Emar, Taanach, the Phoenician coast, and elsewhere. Most strikingly, it includes the Assyrians, who, it seems, did not set out to write down their own dialect (on this, see Beaulieu 2006). All produced texts in a Babylonian variously influenced by the languages they were speaking; all were more or less captivated by the prestige of Babylonian and none thought to simply write their own languages down in cuneiform.

53. For the spirit attacks, see the edition of MAH 19612 in Garelli 1965:165–67 with translations in Michel 2001 nos. 323–24 (and cf. Michel's note [2001:450] that refer-

ences to spirits of the dead are common in women's correspondence from Kanesh, citing texts no. 313, 316, 324, 348, 383; I thank Gonzalo Rubio for these references). For the pig attack, Pa. 24 edited in Larsen 2002:173. For the grammar (now out of date), Hecker 1968.

54. Lloyd Rudolph's response to Martha Nussbaum's "Patriotism and Cosmopolitanism," *Boston Review* 19.5 (1994): 22, cited in Pollock 2002:49n20.

55. As we will see, there is an important difference between the East Semitic-speaking scribes of Babylonian, who spoke languages close enough to Old or Standard Babylonian that they could misrecognize the written high variety for their own spoken variety with relative ease, and West Semitic-speaking scribes, whose languages had starker structural differences. These salient differences between spoken and written forms may have promoted a situation of linguistic self-consciousness analogous to that of the German-speaking scribes who first asserted the difference, and deadness, of written Latin over against the spoken Romance varieties of their time (see R. Wright 1991). It is to the creative "errors" of these speakers of Canaanite that we owe the remarkble hybrid written language found in the Amarna letters, to which we will turn in chapter 3.

56. On the cosmopolitan status of Hittite and the local role of Luwian during the late Hittite empire, see van den Hout 2006. Written Hittite emerges as a royal heirloom, "the retention of an important dynastic tradition" (Trevor Bryce, cited in van den Hout 2006:234).

57. The dossier of evidence for scribal training at Ugarit is laid out magisterially in van Soldt 1995. The fundamental source for the Hurrian names remains Gröndahl 1967:203–67.

58. For a comprehensive survey of names in the southern Levant, organized by linguistic character and time period, see Zadok 1996. For an in-depth study of the names mentioned in the Amarna letters, see Hess 1993 and for further evidence the sources cited in Horowitz, Oshima, and Sanders 2002.

59. For this material, see the thorough study of Hamilton (2006), especially his explanation on 292–93, which agrees with the more detailed hypothesis of Goldwasser 2006. This situation may change significantly with McCarter's forthcoming decipherment of some of the major proto-Sinaitic inscriptions.

60. Hamilton 2006; Sass 1988. These texts pose major interpretive difficulties connected with their lack of standardization and institutional connections. It is remarkable that a century after their discovery, neither of the two latest comprehensive studies makes so much as a tentative attempt to translate the proto-Sinaitic texts, despite the common agreement that they are in an early variety of West Semitic.

61. For this viewpoint, see, for example, Pollock: "At its borders, every language may appear to merge into something else; the fact that it can be defined, cognitively and discursively, as a *language* in the first place, rather than continuing to exist as unmarked jargon, is largely due to the presence of a body of grammatical, literary, and other texts that provide it with norms and hence stability" (2006b:65).

62. The seal is analyzed by Schaeffer 1956:77–83, with a handcopy on p. 78 and an enlarged photo on p. 80 (note that the seal is incorrectly described as alphabetic on p. 77; the caption on the handcopy, fig. 100, which is obviously syllabic, is correct);

it was found stamped on an alphabetic cuneiform document emancipating a slave (Virolleaud 1957:18).

63. The Ugaritic inventory of twenty-seven consonants is to be contrasted, on the one hand, with the three additional signs, added to indicate different vocalizations of alef and the non-Semitic sibilant, and on the other hand to the texts that show reduction and merger of consonants.

64. It is significant that the earliest actual recorded West Semitic myths predate Ugaritic and are not written in Babylonian but two non-Semitic languages. These are the myth of Elkunirsa, recorded in Hittite, and the story of Seth and Anat, in Egyptian. The source of the Elkunirsa myth must have been West Semitic in language, not just theme, since it shows an escalating parallelism diagnostic of West Semitic poetry in Baal's claim to Asherah that "I have killed your seventy-seven [children], [your] eighty-eight have I killed" (Hoffner 1998:91, section 3; the significance of the parallelism is noted in Hoffner 1965). For translation and discussion of the Hittite text, see Hoffner 1998:90–92; for the Egyptian, see Walls 1992:144–52.

65. KTU 1.1–1.6.

66. Though it is alluded to in the Babylonian texts preserved by the Amorites at Mari (Durand 1993); not coincidentally, it seems, along with the first attestations of the idea of "the people" as a fundamental political and religious unit (see below in this chapter, and in greater detail Fleming 2004).

67. The linguistic magic of this passage was first noted in a remarkable article by Julian Obermann (1947), an Arabist whose insights into Ugaritic were brought to my attention by Mark Smith (2001b). On the significance of the story for Ugaritic views of language, see Sanders 2004a.

68. For this West Semitic political theology of kingship and its manifestations and limits in the Baal cycle, see M. S. Smith 1994:109, and note especially the epithet of Baal as *mlk dn*, "mighty king" (KTU 1.12 II 59). This should be read with Bordreuil and Pardee's caution that there are no explicit references to the divine right of kings at Ugarit, although Baal's patronage of the royal dynasty implies such a right (1993:69). For a more detailed thesis on their relationship, see Wyatt 1996. Nick Wyatt articulates the general thesis that "as the apex of human society, the king represented his people before the gods" (1996:120). As a Pan-Near-Eastern royal claim, this leaves the mechanism of this representation unexplained. It is precisely in the seam between the people being represented and the media that depict them that questions of representation become problems of communication and power.

69. The weapons and their attendant victories are both mythical and real: an administrator announces the arrival of these weapons at the temple of Dagan in Terqa, while another official recounts how the kingship of Mari historically followed Adad's favor. For Adad's march, see the cited portions of the unpublished Zimri-Lim epic conveniently presented in Nissinen 2003:90; for the weapons and their this-worldly location, see Durand's edition of A.1858 (Durand 1993:53).

70. In transliterations and translations, square brackets [ ] indicate broken or damaged text.

71. After the Mari letter A.1968, the theme appears in the Ugaritic epic of Kirta (KTU 1.16 iv 25–end), in the form of a contest between Kirta and his son Yassibu (whose name,

spelled *yṣb*, appears to be based on the West Semitic root *nṣb*, meaning "to stand, set up"—see the evidence surveyed in Pardee 1989–90:407 with the important further analysis of O'Connor 2004:467–68, where the spelling variant within a single Mari text makes the derivation of the name from *nṣb*, with assimilation of the initial *n*, appear very likely). Yassibu accuses his father of not being present to judge the cases of the weak and wronged, and as a consequence he should leave his throne and let Yassibu sit on it. Kirta utters a curse that Yassibu may fall. The theme then surfaces in biblical prayer and narrative. In Psalm 82, God takes his stand (using the same root here as in the Kirta epic), accusing the other gods of not judging the weak and wronged, and saying that as a result they will fall; instead, God will arise to judge the land. Finally, and most remarkably, the same theory of sovereignty stands behind a story with human protagonists, 2 Samuel 15. Here Absalom nearly dethrones David and claims the throne for himself by stationing himself by the road to Jerusalem and telling the aggrieved litigants who pass by that there is no one to hear their case, but that if he were judge of the land they would prevail in court. AfterAbsalom's usurpation nearly succeeds, Joab, David's hatchet man, finally has Absalom cut down to earth (2 Sam. 18:11–17, with two striking plays on the *nṣb* root in 2 Sam. 18:17–18).

72. Bordreuil and Pardee 1984.

73. For a lucid and up-to-date overview, see Pardee 2007.

74. For this view of international political relationships as a kind of virtual village realized by cuneiform scribes, see van de Mieroop 2004:121–60.

75. For the semantics of *ḫabāru*, see Na'aman 1986.

76. See further Liverani 2001.

77. For a comprehensive list, see appendix A of Cross 2003:195–202, to which add the "retainer" named in the arrowhead published by McCarter (1999).

78. The earliest documentation of this statement is apparently at the hands of Max Weinreich (1945) (conveniently reproduced with discussion at http://www.edu-cyberpg .com/Linguistics/armynavy.html).

79. Silverstein's statement is from a personal communication, June 2006. For a detailed theoretical framework for the way that ethnic and national differences are elaborated on the basis of shared *similarities*, see Harrison 2003.

80. Cooper 2001:74, crediting Michalowski 1987:174–75. This fundamental point is made in greater detail by Dietrich 1996, and put in a broader epigraphic context by Millard 1998. For minor exceptions, see Millard 2007, and for a suggested explanation, note 19 above.

81. No texts in the standard Ugaritic alphabet have been found anywhere outside of the close vicinity of Ugarit. Dennis Pardee confirms this, with the following caveat: "Theoretically, a Ugaritic scribe based in a foreign capital could receive and decode messages sent in Ugaritic. It is also thus theoretically possible that some of the incoming texts that we have in Ugaritic, rather than the expected Akkadian, were inscribed by such scribes in the place of origin; only clay tests could tell this and none have been done yet" (personal communication, October 2003).

82. On the division of labor among Ugaritic scribes, see van Soldt 1995.

83. Examples and recent bibliography in Sanders 2004a.

84. See KTU 1.161 with the analysis of Levine and de Tarragon 1984:649–59.

85. These texts are collected, with bibliography, in Dietrich and Loretz 1988a. My own understanding of the underlying social phenomena is laid out in chapter 3.

86. Pardee 2007.

87. For an instructive exploration of nation-ness four hundred years later, see Grosby 1995, which is forced to make do with a single grammatical particle (*kl*, "all" the—territory? administrative district? nation?—of Aram) in the Sefire inscription, written by a vassal king, to gauge native Aramean sentiment.

88. For a critique of this theory as mystifying the unity that shared spoken language produces, see Silverstein 2000.

89. For the Mari example, see Durand 1993; for the mythological heritage of Daniel 7, see Collins 1993 *ad loc.*

90. Pitard 1999:50.

91. "Ihre Gesänge sind das Archiv des Volks" (1877–1913) 9:532. On Herder's role in the creation of "folklore," see chapter 1.

92. This is the title given to the text and English translation in Pardee 2002:77–83. For the full French edition with hand copies and philological commentary, see Pardee 2000:92–142 with fig. 2 (p. 1263).

93. "The relatively large number of texts, reflecting what is basically the same rite is without parallel at Ugarit, while the spread of find-spots and scribal hands . . . shows that the texts were not the product of a single school." Pardee 2002:77–78, and cf. the concurring statement of del Olmo Lete 1999:144. The manuscripts are widely distributed across the site, having been found in the high priest's library on the acropolis, the royal palace, and the House of the Divination Priest on the south side of the tell.

94. The manuscripts are:

KTU 1.84-RS 17.100A+B, replaces king Niqmaddu with the apparently Hurrian *annpgdl* in l. 34, though we do not know whether this is a person or a place. I thank Dennis Pardee for pointing this out to me. The other texts are:

KTU 1.121-RS 24.270A
KTU 1.122-RS 24.270B
KTU 1.154-RS 24.652G+K
KTU 1.153-RS 24.650B

95. For previous work, see the comprehensive bibliography in Pardee 2000.

96. Cf. the eloquent statement of del Olmo Lete 1999:159, with detailed references to previous literature, but without emphasizing the utterly unprecedented nature of such a ritual including whole communities.

97. Here is the one fundamental point of disagreement between del Olmo Lete and Pardee; while Pardee reads the series of phrases beginning *u lp* + [group name] as "according to the statement of," (hyper-literally * *ʾu li-pî*,"or to the mouth of") del Olmo Lete reads them as "(sinning) in the manner of." The difficulty for this second reading is that there is no other evidence that Ugaritic people drew such rigid ethnic boundaries through ritual (as opposed to through literature, which we as have seen was indeed deliberately engineered to be different). This reading implies the stark view that Ugaritic ritual practitioners saw some kinds of religious behavior as sinful in an ethnically specific way, a view not clearly supported by any other Ugaritic text.

98. This section is almost entirely broken away but due to the highly formulaic and repetitive character of the text, in which each of three sections is divided into two

gendered divisions, the first in the second-person masculine plural and the second in the second-person feminine plural, it can be reconstructed with complete confidence. Pardee and del Olmo Lete agree, and there seem to be no plausible alternatives.

99. My translation of lines 19'–24' of the text as edited by Pardee 2000.

100. This statement is based on an informal survey in 2004 of the Assyriologists Walter Farber and Erica Reiner, and the Hittitologist Theo van den Hout, all of the Oriental Institute.

101. In Mesopotamian and Hittite ritual, politically significant rites of atonement and expiation are undertaken on behalf of the king or the army in the case of plague. See the convenient and extensive set of examples organized as parallels to the scapegoat ritual in Milgrom 1991 appendix E, a rich resource that should be used, but with caution because of its lack of historical context.

102. Text: Emar 369:1–3, edited in Fleming 1992:10; compare my looser translation with the more precise version of Fleming 1992:49, who also notes: "It is significant that the Emar rituals are celebrated by the populace of the city as such, not 'the servants of the king,' and note well that at Ugarit the 'sons of Ugarit' identifies the mass of freeborn populace, as opposed to "the servants of the king" (Heltzer 1976:4–6).

103. Of the three places in the Torah where the Day of Atonement is stipulated, only here are the verbal confession and the scapegoat described. By contrast with Numbers 29:7–11, Leviticus 23:26–32, and the text framing the scapegoat ritual, Leviticus 16:29–34, all place it within the ritual calendar and institute a collective fast.

104. As the most far-reaching ritual of sacrifice and purification, Leviticus 16 concludes the establishment of cult and purity law in chapters 1–15 before the second major section, the Holiness code. It thus is at the center of Leviticus thematically and structurally (not quantitatively), as argued most recently by Rendtorff (2003). For an alternative but more superficial treatment (with a fascinating piece of Christian supercessionist theology in place of a conclusion), see Ska 2006:33–35.

105. While we do not have direct evidence for the use of this ritual in the late Iron Age, we can be sure of two points: first, that it came to the Torah's Priestly editors bearing enormous status, which they acknowledged by the prominence they gave this baldly polytheistic ritual in their own rigorously monotheistic work. And second, the first external evidence of the ritual's importance, in Second Temple literature, fits completely with a view of this ritual as absolutely central to Judean religion.

On the first point, scholarship on Leviticus has come to a well-founded consensus that the location of this startling ritual of atonement—at the structural center of the Torah—is deliberate (Rendtorff 2003). The Jubilee year begins with the Day of Atonement, when "you shall return, every one of you, to your property and every one of you to your family" (Lev. 25:9–10). The best explanation of this positioning as the most important annual ritual—the only one described as a *šabbat šabbātôn*, thus corresponding to the Sabbath on a microscopic level and the Jubilee year on a macroscopic level—is that Yom Kippur was the mechanism by which the Priestly center of purity was itself purified and renewed in both space, at the Tabernacle, and time, the new year.

On the second point, early Jewish tradition affirms its centrality, naming the first collection of Halakhic Midrash on Leviticus, *Sifrā*ʾ, "the Book," and the Mishnaic tractate on the Day of Atonement, *Yômā*ʾ, "the Day," and this view may also be reflected in the way New Testament writers allude to the holiday as "the Fast" (e.g., Acts 27:9), assuming that their readers share the assumption of its primacy. That the Day of Atonement was already the Jewish ritual par excellence in the Second Temple period is implied in the Qumran evidence. Scholars of Qumran prayer such as Daniel Falk and Bilhah Niztan have pointed to clear thematic and verbal correlations between old, nonsectarian Qumran texts and early Jewish liturgical poetry, implying that a "broad tradition" of fixed liturgical practice around Yom Kippur was well in place in the Second Temple period. See the summary and assessment of these correlations in Stoekl Ben Ezra 2003:37–46, with comprehensive bibliography.

106. This has been the position of many of the text's classic interpreters, including William Robertson Smith, Yehezkel Kaufman, and Israel Knohl, and it seems to stand behind the avoidance of this text in some recent theories of Priestly ritual (e.g., Geller 1992).

107. These comparisons were explicitly driven by a concern to locate the ritual along the spectrum between religion and magic: James G. Frazier's anthropological classic *The Scapegoat*, part IV of his *The Golden Bough: A Study in Magic and Religion* (1913), argued that, fundamentally, it was all magic, while the contemporary work of Jacob Milgrom takes the more conservative tack that in Israel, and Israel alone, the magical and mythological content has been "eviscerated," is demythologized, morally superior, and hence implicitly religion. For the "evisceration," see Milgrom 1991:1021. For a sweeping and compelling attack on the scholarly tendency to deny myth in the Hebrew Bible as an apologetic move, see Fishbane 2003, especially the positions laid out on pp. 5–9 of the introduction. A similar critique, surprisingly unmentioned in Fishbane's book, was published by Martin Buber in 1916, who argued that "for a long time, both [detractors and apologists] denied the existence of myth in Judaism, . . . And it may well have seemed even to genuine scholarship that anything mythical was alien to the Bible" but now, "scattered veins of the precious ore can be found in all the books of the Bible" (Buber 1967:97).

108. By contrast, the problem for the Israeli historian of Israelite religion Yehezkel Kaufman was the presence of *speaking*. Kaufman had explained that the Priestly system of sacrifice was strictly nonverbal in order to reject "magic" and "idolatrous explanations," so much so that he referred to the Temple as "the sanctuary of silence." Kaufman's great continuator Israel Knohl reinforces this point, explaining that the ritual's verbal nature is in fact a safeguard against its appearing too close to "idolatrous ritual." Knohl (1995:148), with references to Kaufman.

109. Robertson Smith puzzled over the distinctive mechanics of the scapegoat ritual, which escaped his system, based as it was on the forms of communion (both within the community and between the community and their god) provided by blood sacrifice. "There is little trace of any [view connecting the annual sacrifice with sin] in connection with the annual piacula of the heathen Semites; and even in the Old Testament this interpretation appears to be modern. The Day of Atonement is a much less ancient institution than the Passover" (1894:408). "The carrying away of the people's guilt to an isolated and desert region has its nearest analogies, not in ordinary atoning sacrifices, but in those physical methods of getting rid of an infectious taboo which characterize the lowest levels of superstition" (1894:422).

110. In his *Scapegoat* book (1913), Frazer's one reference to the ritual is on page 210; a footnote cites a work of Johannes Buxdorf from 1661 on the continued use of sacrifice by modern Jews. The one reference to Leviticus in Girard's *Scapegoat* (1986) contributes little, since it is a reference to Frazier, asserting that he is wrong (p. 120). As Mary Douglas has shown, the theories of both Frazer and Girard were actually based on the Greek *Pharmakos* ritual, which involves the social approbation and killing of a polluted and despised figure, often a human, during a crisis. See Douglas (2003).

111. Everywhere else in the Torah the term *haqqôdeš* refers to the entire shrine. See Milgrom 1991:1063.

112. See simply Nachmanides' recognition of the problem and richly mythological response in his commentary *ad loc*, as well as Ibn Ezra. As Benjamin Sommer notes (personal communication, June 2007), the ritual's glaringly exceptional character does not mean that the Priestly editors necessarily understood it as contradictory. Indeed, what is intriguing is precisely how they were able to interpret it as coherent with their theology.

113. Gerstenberger 1996:221, who attributes the Priestly edition here to the fifth century B.C.E., a dating that is certainly possible but by no means certain. What even Gerstenberger must concede is that the ritual's Hebrew core must be centuries older.

114. The materialization of "metaphysical" or otherwise non-physically co-present forces is a common, even unremarkable feature of religious ritual. For an influential Western example, consider the Reformation, partly sparked by early modern debates over the Eucharist. In comparative terms these amount to a conflict within native European folk-theory over whether seeing, tasting, or touching a biscuit could communicate authentic experience of the divine (Muir 1997, esp. 150).

115. Milgrom 1991:1073–79. In all, five Hittite and six Mesopotamian rituals are cited, with little discussion of time period or cultural background. This accumulation of data without attention to context limits the power of Milgrom's arguments here, for example, when he uses parallels from a Babylonian New Year's festival as evidence against the "lateness" (1067) of penitential rites on Yom Kippur. This part of the Babylonian festival, known only in manuscripts from Seleucid Uruk, is part of a radically new religious situation in which the priesthood has gained ascendancy over the kingship, which has been politically neutered by Hellenistic rule. This is why the king is humiliated by a priest, something never before seen in official Mesopotamian culture. Nowhere does Milgrom mention the fact that all known copies of this ritual date from the Seleucid period, contemporary with the very latest books of the Bible! For a deliberately provocative study of the Akitu festival in its Hellenistic political context, see J. Z. Smith 1982, surprisingly unmentioned in Milgrom. Sommer 2000 provides a valuable critique of Smith's sources that does not vitiate this central point about the humiliation of the king. The most recent textual evidence is presented in Çagirgan and Lambert 1991–93.

116. Knohl (1995) argues that this speech is in a later stage of Priestly language, that of the Holiness School. This identification would reinforce the idea that the text's editors understood it as working on behalf of the people, since the ritual's implicit role is rendered explicit here.

117. The three terms are: *pešāʿîm* in 16:16, 21 (contrast Num. 15:30–31); *ʾōhel môʿēd* as shrine (16, 17, 20, 23) rather than as in the rest of the Priestly source the whole tent;

and the usual Priestly term for "shrine," *haqqôdeš* (as in Exod. 28:29, 35), here instead designating the innermost part of the sanctuary (2, 3, 16, 17, 20, 23, 27) that the Priestly source designates with *qôdeš haqqôdašîm*. Two more contrasts are that the regular Priestly term for this ceremony, *yôm hakkipurîm*, is not used here; and the other Priestly descriptions of the ceremony (Leviticus 23; Numbers 29) do not mention the scapegoat. "Hence," Milgrom rightly concludes, "vv 2–28 must stem from an earlier source, which was only subsequently incorporated into P" (1991:1063).

118. Contrast the interpretation of Kaufmann, as explicated by Sommer 2001.

119. Most extended Ugaritic rituals refer at multiple points within the text to the time they are to be performed. Because the beginning of KTU 1.40 is not preserved in any existing manuscripts, it is remotely possible that the ritual could, atypically, have contained a rubric with chronological markings only at the beginning.

120. The term Aristotle uses is *polis*, but in apposition with "political association" it seems to have a relatively broad sense: *kaloumenê polis kai hê koinônia hê politikê*.

121. This is true of such a methodologically sophisticated historian as van de Mieroop (2004). The major sections of his history are structured around states, though each is illuminated with significant discussion of the states' others (e.g., pp. 139–40 on the palace dependents and free village population in the Late Bronze Age). Similarly in Kuhrt 1995, the sections are almost entirely based on states (ranging from city-states and kingdoms to empires). Three sections—8a "the 'sea-peoples'" (386–92), 8b "The Arameans" (393–400), and 13b "Persians and Medes" (692–95)—are not based on states or state sources, but are solely devoted to population groups that are thought to have either destroyed states (sea peoples) or founded them (Arameans, Persians, Medes). The single clear exception is 2c, "The Old Assyrian merchants in Anatolia" (90–94), probably due to the presence of a single massive economic archive comparable in scale to the largest state archive of the period. In English, Snell 1997 is an important exception, though it is the most general and impressionistic of the three. In German, there is the collective work on cultural history edited by Klengel (1989). Most detailed in integrating social history with political is the massive Italian (1031 pages) work of Liverani (1988). This book balances an organization around territorial empires with a looser framework based on chronology and region, as well as sections on, for example, "Technology and Ideology in the Late Bronze Age" (449–80).

122. For a brilliant but symptomatic example, Finkelstein and Silberman 2001, and for a thoroughgoing critique Byrne f/c.

123. For a detailed critique, see Yoffee 2005.

124. For an attempt to reconstruct continuities between Yaminites and Benjaminites, see Fleming 1998.

125. I am currently engaged in producing such a study, based on analysis of the West Semitic political lexicon, with funding from the National Endowment for the Humanities.

126. For bibliography, see von Dassow 1999.

127. For richer views of tribal political thought one looked to later periods: tribes are the subject of extensive reflection in Islamic sources, and for Robertson Smith (1894) the tribe is precisely what pre-Islamic Arabia had in common with ancient Israel.

128. The most lucid analysis of this pattern, which amounts to one of the truly great themes in ancient Near Eastern history, is Schwartz 1989.

129. Michael Rowton developed a complex view of tribes as dimorphic, shifting between nomadic and settled. Dominique Charpin and Jean-Marie Durand (1986) first showed that King Zimri-Lim was a member of one of the tribal confederacies he ruled. Fleming's textual work finds corroboration and extension in the archaeological work of Anne Porter on the earlier social frameworks of the middle Euphrates during the third millennium (Porter 2002).

130. This encouraged scholars to see Mari Amorite tribal cultures themselves as fully symmetrical, a received opinion that Fleming seeks to overturn (see 2004: 45–7; 70; for an important revision of the still influential views of Rowton, see 2004:76–80; 89–92; facts like a higher proportion of Akkadian names among Yaminites suggest more extensive ethnic, social, and romantic connections with settled society than Sim'alites).

131. Fleming 2004:103, with full references to the important earlier work of Durand, Jean-Robert Kupper, and others; Malamat 1989:34. Malamat's rich lexical comparison of Hebrew and Amorite political terms (1989:38–47) illustrates both the strengths and weaknesses of an older approach, still strongly influenced by the old "Bible and the ancient Near East" method of searching for parallels that may authenticate biblical documents by illuminating Near Eastern material. By contrast, Fleming's focus on Amorite thought on its own terms and with awareness of the groundbreaking work of Durand and Charpin provides a fresh starting point for English-language studies of ancient tribal societies.

132. The impact of earlier scholars' insights was limited by an approach that did not sufficiently emphasize historical change and cultural specificity. As a result, the Mari texts were sometimes used mainly as "materials for a clearer picture of the tribal organization of the Israelites" (Malamat 1962:143) rather than as evidence for their own cultures first. Compare the insightful comments of Sasson, the most persistent and shrewd critic of these comparisons, on the shared dimensions of the Mari and biblical texts as narratively and rhetorically structured pieces of culture (1998:115).

133. It is worth emphasizing that the Mari evidence does not show any special connection between Amorite and Hebrew, beyond what one would expect from two examples of West Semitic-speaking cultures, a thousand years apart, which nevertheless share some social conditions and ideologies. Rather, these connections show the relationship between a linguistic tradition, a social structure, and a mode of existence. They simply happen to be the two best-preserved bodies of evidence for what has to have been a much more broadly distributed set of cultural features. Mari represents the best evidence for the use of West Semitic social terms and ideology in the Old Babylonian period. Ugarit, with the first actual substantial corpus in West Semitic, shows a drastically more limited range because it has adopted a more standard Late Bronze Age city-state ideology (as Dennis Pardee put it, referring to Ugarit and the later Phoenician cities, "the coast seems to have detribalized first" [personal communication, August 2006]), and these social terms reemerge in the Hebrew Bible partly by virtue of the brute fact that it contains the biggest collection of West Semitic texts

from the Iron Age and Persian periods. We cannot assume a priori that speakers of related languages in the West Semitic group shared political theories, but in this case it is evident that an ancient theory of the people as organizing principle of politics and ritual was transferred and transformed over time, in institutions and language from the Old Babylonian through the Persian period.

134. At Mari, a clan is collectively advised (using plural verbs and pronouns) to "take the hand of your dependents," similarly the laws of Hammurabi 24 speak of the *nišū*, "dependents," of a dead man. A second important population term, *muškēnum*, defines the collective mass of subjects outside the sphere of palace or city-state privilege. Thus in the laws of Hammurabi the term is usually translated "commoner," whose life and property are valued less (sometimes at 33 percent) than those of a citizen (*awīlum*). While marginal, the *muškēnum* manifest frequent agency, speaking, resisting, and even offering sacrifices on their own behalf (Fleming 2004:146). But in general, as Fleming eloquently puts it, "*muškēnum* is a palace word, the terminology of kingship and its economy as its leaders look out on the mass of everything ruled" (2004:145)

135. See Durand 2003:753, with reference to the general pattern laid out in Good 1983.

136. From the fact that there is no such thing as a *gôy YHWH*, only *ʿam YHWH* (true also of non-Israelite gods; Num. 21:29 refers to the *ʿam kemôš*), Speiser draws the significant conclusion that "strictly speaking, therefore, all references to YHWH as a 'national' God at any given time are terminologically inaccurate" (1960:158n5).

137. It is a pragmatic feature of these two early West Semitic terms that most plausibly laid the groundwork for the shift: *liʾmum* and *gāyum* could become marginalized because of their particularity: already at Ugarit *lim* is not "our" tribe anymore; the likelihood is that since the two terms were expressly restricted to their respective confederacies, both "dialect" forms in the sense of being *saliently* partial and local, they were available for resignification as "other's."

138. A.981, edited in Durand 1992, with the comments of Sasson 1998:105 and Fleming 2004:93, 97.

139. Yet what was common knowledge to the West Semitic cultures of Mari (and, as we will see, Israel) still can surprise even the best-informed experts: "That people could shop around for a tribe to which to declare allegiance through a sacrifice is a stunning notion that plays havoc with the anthropologist in us" (Sasson 1998:105). On the contrary: in the ritual of donkey-sacrifice to create tribal allegiance one finds a good illustration of a fairly common notion that is traditional in both anthropology and the ancient Near East: kinship as legal fiction, as Cross discusses below.

140. For detailed theoretical investigations of the fictionality of the state, see Mitchell 1999 and Runciman 2003. First Samuel 8 retells this demand of the assembled people for a king.

141. *Pace* Cross 1998:19, whose illuminating statement on the subject is flawed by an insistence that these forms "survive into the era of the state as vestiges of an earlier society." It is implausible that cultural forms attested, inevitably in state contexts, during the Old Babylonian, Late Bronze, and Iron Age periods are "vestiges" of anything. Indeed, it is only in the biblical representations of Genesis, Judges, and Samuel that we see completely independent pre-state stages portrayed.

142. Fleming 1992: 86.

143. There is wide and varied evidence for collective ideologies in West Semitic cultures of the second millennium. At Mari the Hana "tent-dwellers" can be treated as a single religious-political unit: omens may be taken for them (Fleming 2004:87 and n224), and similarly the *muškēnum* can act as a religious unit offering sacrifices (Fleming 2004:146). Later, in the Late Bronze Age the PḪR, "(divine) assembly," appears as a West Semitic religious institution, to the extent that it has a theological status at Ugarit, where offerings are made to the divinized Assembly of Gods (written in Babylonian translation with the divinity marker, *ᵈpuḫur ilāni*). This entity appears in the same position in four different offering lists (e.g., #29 in KTU 1.47; see the useful parallel edition of Pardee 2002:14–15 and compare the prominence of the *mpḫrt bn il* at the beginning of the list KTU 1.65 and in the ritual KTU 1.40, though here perhaps not as a single divine being). Similarly at Emar we find the divinized "people of Sarta" (using the Amorite term *liʾmum*); see Fleming 2004:61 and n121, who also notes that both *gāyum* [occasionally] and *liʾmum* [frequently] appear in personal names as divine beings).

144. Large states like Babylon may have "dominated regional politics, but their identities followed the fortunes of their rulers, growing and shrinking with the latest victory or defeat. Towns offered a basis for family identity that could go back generations, but families could always move. Tribal identities, on the contrary, accompanied people across every geographical and social boundary" (Fleming 2004:104).

145. "En réalité des appartenances claniques ou tribales ne sont pas, comme nous pourrions le croire, figées de tout éternité et rigides, mais peuvent, au contraire, être le choix d'une decision personelle et ont dû l' être, à un moment ou à un autre" (Durand 1992:116). Though it cut across both time and space, tribal identity was not primordial: membership in the group could be negotiated as well as inherited and was often deployed strategically by its members. Some with tribal heritages made the choice to more fully assimilate to the high-prestige Eastern Mesopotamian state cultural forms. While Hammurabi of Babylon claimed a heritage with the tribes of the *Amnanû* and *Yaḫrurû*, he ended up becoming the territorial emperor par excellence. At the nearby city-state of Larsa, King Warad-Sin refers to his father—but not himself—as "the father of the Amorite land." Each of the Amorite rulers of Mari took different positions, designating themselves in terms that evoked more or less tribal affiliation (Fleming 2004:123–24).

It is the last Amorite king of Mari, Zimri-Lim, who expresses the highest level of tribal connection. Indeed, Zimri-Lim seems to have worked to maintain his tribal authenticity by traveling frequently (Fleming 2004:163), thus maintaining nomadic practices even while ruling a palace. His victory inscription describes nomadic herds arriving at the city gates, which reads like a form of theater (Frayne 1990:623–24). Intriguingly, the Amorite rulers of Mari also chose script styles as signs of political belonging. The texts from before the first tribal kings, known as the Shakkanakku ("governor") period, display the archaic script typical of marginal areas not yet affected by innovations in writing style at centers like Babylon. Under the first tribal king, Yahdun-Lim, the script is modernized to resemble that of the nearest cultural center, Babylon. What we encounter after this is most interesting: a move to regionalize the script under Yasmah-Addu and Zimri-Lim (Durand 1992:121).

146. For the military as a primary mode of relation between Yaminites and Mari government, see Fleming 2004:33. On lineage ideology as "in times of stability, a social structure in reserve"—which can become more salient in times of conflict—see Salzman 1978:626–27 and further sources cited in Fleming 2004:33.

147. See Weeks 1985.

148. Fleming 2004:207.

149. For questions of dating and historical context, see Kupper 1998:24.

150. ARM 28:25 (edited by Kupper 1998:33–34).

151. Tribes are frequently said to assemble for political decisions: Zalmaqqum and Yaminites in A.954, Haneans in A.3567, ARM 26:43, 45, 46 (all edited in Durand 1988); ARM 28:25 (edited by Kupper 1998).

152. "Naturally, some correspondents were better at the task than others. During Zimri-Lim's reign Bannum, Ibal-pi-El, Yamṣum, and Yasim-el were particularly gifted in that regard." Sasson 1998:108–9.

153. "The genre is (debatedly) restricted to pseudo-autobiography (such as those of Idrimi and Adad-Gupi) and to humorous tales (such as the 'The Poor Man of Nippur'). It is practically unrepresented in 'Canaanite' lore (Ugaritic, Phoenician) but it is known in Aramaic (also pseudo-autobiography, e.g. the first part of Ahiqar)" (Sasson 1998:109). It is worth pointing out that the exclusion of Ugaritic and Phoenician, the relatively detribalized West Semitic societies of the late second and early first millennia, and its presence in Aramaic correspond well to the political context in which the verbal art of persuasion was most relevant. Thus Sasson's conclusion that "despite their genre, the Mari letters can open up a window into the art of story-telling among West Semites" (1998:111).

154. Caton 1987:96.

155. From the point of view of political theory, these texts suggest we replace the generic notion of "legitimacy" with persuasion in assembly: absent written law or bureaucracy, military decisions are made in dialogue on the basis of verbal performance. The foundation of power in communication that we witness here suggests an early West Semitic context for the constituting function of narrative prose.

3. EMPIRES AND ALPHABETS IN LATE BRONZE AGE CANAAN

1. The newly discovered Tel Qeiyafa ostracon may provide a perfect illustration of the unsystematic writing of a local spoken variety. If preliminary reports are accurate, this ostracon, dating to the tenth century, shares distinctive lexical features with Moabite and Hebrew but is inscribed in a proto-Canaanite script, against which the known ninth-century Moabite and eighth-century Hebrew scripts have sharply distinguished themselves.

2. No such histories of writing in the Levant seem to exist. The title of Cross's *Leaves from an Epigrapher's Notebook* (2003) suggests its fascinating but fragmentary nature, the single richest source for an archaeology of writing in ancient Israel. The book compiles dozens of epigraphic and philological essays and summaries, returning to

some material and ideas while adding new observations at every turn. As a result, it is more of a source for reconstructing a detailed history of alphabetic writing than such a history in itself. Naveh's *Early History of the Alphabet* (1987) provides the coherence Cross's collection lacks, but its focus is the forms of writing, not its social roles. Thus despite its frequent shrewd insights it is not detailed enough to serve this purpose.

3. See below for Hobbes's demonstration that this is an early concern of Joshua.

4. As Hobbes already pointed out, *Leviathan* xxxiii, 6. Baruch Spinoza and Isaac La Peyrère produced analogous catalogues of signs of temporal distance and intertextuality within the Hebrew Bible; these catalogues are discussed in Strauss 1997:75–77, 264–65. On Hobbes's role in the foundation of biblical criticism, see succinctly Malcolm 2004. In an important recent study of this term, Geoghegan argues that the similarities in the uses of "to this day" in the Tetrateuch (or at least in Genesis, from which all six Tetrateuch examples derive) and Deuteronomistic History "are so marked that they are best explained as deriving from the same person—namely, the Deuteronomistic Historian, who combined northern and southern traditions in both 'works' to give Israel an account of its past and to set a course for its future" (2005:407).

5. For these arguments with up-to-date bibliography, see Bloch-Smith 2003.

6. Bloch-Smith 2003:411.

7. A.D. Smith 2002:442.

8. Exodus and Deuteronomy represent writing as having only one subject: God's words. While the language of these holy inscriptions is never specified, Israelites can read them without difficulty. The only possible biblical representation of pre-monarchic writing from a human source appears in Judges, in the famously difficult passage Judges 8:14. Since there is no reason to believe this story was written down any time before the late Iron Age, it is primary evidence of biblical memory, not actual Late Bronze Age conditions. Scholars do not agree on whether this instance of *ktb* actually denotes writing, and a written list is not necessary to the plot. Gideon captures and interrogates a youth who enumerates (*ktb*) the seventy-seven leaders of Sukkot who refused to help Gideon before he defeated the kings of Midian. Upon victory over Midian, Gideon seizes and flogs these leaders. While the Septuagint uses the term *apograpso* and the New Jewish Publication Society translation follows this with "drew up . . . a list," the King James Version already reads "described," and the New Revised Standard Version has here "he listed." Aaron Demsky's intriguing suggestion (Demsky and Bar-Ilan 1988) that the term for youth, *naʿar*, is here a technical term for junior scribe, as in later texts, remains possible but does not admit of verification on current evidence. Byrne's archaeological and social arguments for the paucity of professional scribes in this period (2007) render it less plausible.

9. Hendel 2001 focuses on "The Exodus in Biblical Memory" while M. S. Smith 2004 addresses *The Memoirs of God: History, Memory, and the Experience of the Divine in Ancient Israel.* It is worth recalling here Ernst Renan's dictum that a feeling of belonging also requires for a group's members to have *forgotten* certain crucial things. For an incisive statement on the role of objects and landscapes in cultural forgetting, see Harrison 2004.

10. EA stands for El-Amarna, using the standard numbering system established by Knudtzon; for a convenient and more up-to-date if bare-bones online edition of the

texts from Canaan, see http://www.tau.ac.il/humanities/semitic/amarna.html. A fully updated edition of all the texts is in preparation by Anson Rainey.

11. This conclusion is suggested, first, by a lack of evidence: we have not discovered in Canaano-Akkadian the distinct school genres, such as Gilgamesh or *Urra=ḫubullu*, which we have found here for Babylonian. But more important, the substantial corpus of Canaano-Akkadian shows such enormous linguistic variation that even if there was any attempt to teach a standard form, it can safely be reckoned a miserable failure (for an excellent introduction to this variation, see Izre'el 2005:3–6). It has been proposed that a unique text from Beth-Shean, the only known example of a cuneiform letter on a cylinder seal, represented a school exercise, but given the text's unclear historical context, multiple possible explanations, and sui generis nature, this is uncertain at best (the proposal is by Rainey 1998:239–42; for edition, discussion, and bibliography, see Horowitz, Oshima, and Sanders 2006:48–49). I thank Leslie Desmangles for raising this question to me.

12. While providing the most detailed and insightful analysis of the linguistic patterns of the texts, Izre'el does not propose a precise bilingual social context in which a mixed language underlying the letters could have arisen (though he emphasizes the school setting as a general context, and points to a long tradition of multiple language use on the part of scribes and officials in Canaan; see especially Izre'el 1995b). The difficulty is that bilingual mixed languages follow one of two patterns: the first is one in which the vocabulary of one language is ordered according to the grammar of another (examples include Media Lingua and Ma'a). The second is one in which there is a grammatical division of labor (thus most verb morphology follows one language, most pronouns follow another; an example is Michif). See Bakker and Matras 2003. As we will see below, Canaano-Akkadian does not seem to fit either. The Semitist A. Gianto (1990) instead described Canaano-Akkadian as an imperfectly learned language, or "interlanguage," produced when speakers of one language, such as a form of Canaanite, only partly learn the rules of a second language, such as Old Babylonian, and thus use rules from both languages to communicate. Again, there is no consideration of the difference between written and spoken language. Study of written language use as a historically and socially embedded phenomenon, pioneered by Roger Wright's "sociophilology" (see, for example, R. Wright 1991), offers the most promising way forward.

13. In fact the alloglottography concept was originally proposed to describe ancient Near Eastern texts in the first place by I. Gershevitch (1979). Ironically Gerschevitch's notion that the Old Persian speech of Darius was translated into Elamite writing and read back in Old Persian has emerged as one of the more controversial proposals. By contrast, there is little room for dispute over a text like the Larsa "ritual" tablet; while the overwhelming number of words are Sumerian, "the total lack of any Sumerian directional elements and the un-Sumerian use of *.meš* beside the abundant use of Akkadian prepositional phrases indicates that this text is written in Akkadian with Sumerian logograms for Akkadian words" (Westenholz and Westenholz 2006:8).

14. Izre'el 1995:118. Izre'el points out that the translation of letters was a diplomatic commonplace in the ancient Near East, citing Ezra 4:7's letter to Artaxerxes "written in Aramaic and translated" (presumably into the king's native Persian). However, this

very same passage of Ezra provides a useful contrast to the situation of Canaano-Akkadian. The story up until Ezra 4:7 is in Hebrew, until it switches to give the words of the letter in Aramaic. But the narrative then remains in the language of the letter until 6:19! Unlike the extremely specialized nature of our evidence for Canaano-Akkadian, which we only know from diplomatic letters, Aramaic had a broad social base: versions were spoken across the Persian empire, and written varieties were used for both official letters and narratives.

15. EA 286:61–64, 287:64–70, 288:62–66, 289:47–51. Of the five Jerusalem letters whose endings are preserved, only one, EA 290, lacks this plea.

16. Recent examples are cited in von Dassow 2004:641n1.

17. The term *litterae francae* comes from Miguel Civil, cited in von Dassow 2004:670n78. Regardless of whether von Dassow's thesis is correct, it ends up following a presupposition common to many philological treatments of ancient texts. This is the notion that a central goal of scholarship should be to uncover the "original" spoken language underlying written artifacts such as *litterae francae*. Thus on the same page she offers the valuable proposition that "in many instances the evidence offers reason to jettison the assumption that writing is a face-value representation of language" but then sets about to show that "the language underlying [the scribes'] communication in cuneiform was not Akkadian but Canaanite" (2004:642 for both). This leads, paradoxically, to the need to create such spoken "originals" through reconstruction (as von Dassow does: see 2004:665–66). But such reconstructed objects are by definition unverifiable since representing spoken language is precisely what the writers of our text-artifacts chose not to do (her reconstruction, presented on p. 664 as a test of her hypothesis, does not necessarily show anything more than that a scholar skilled in comparative Semitics can fill in the texts' universally acknowledged West Semitic syntax with a reconstructed West Semitic vocabulary and morphology). For a critique of this presupposition and an alternative framework, see Silverstein 2006 and, with special reference to the "posthumous life" of Sumerian, Michalowski 2006.

18. Two other very useful books should be noted: Benjamin Sass (1988) collects the linear alphabetic texts from the second millennium, and M. Dietrich and O. Loretz (1988a) bring together the cuneiform alphabetic texts found outside Ugarit, including Israel.

19. On forms of writing and the state, see Kelly 2006a.

20. An absence also pointed out by van der Toorn 2000:108, but note the correction by Byrne 2007:15n16.

21. There is a court record from Hazor that could possibly be dated to the very beginning of the Late Bronze Age (Horowitz, Oshima, and Sanders 2006:69–72). The script and grammar are clearly Old Babylonian, but the language exhibits a few nonstandard forms, including one case of mimation loss. But since none of these is diagnostic, the tablet's late dating is a vague possibility at best and it cannot be included among the confirmed Late Bronze Age texts.

22. On the role of Sumerian writing in producing a political culture, see Michalowski 1991 and more broadly Carr 2005.

23. The fragment is dated to the Late Bronze Age by its parallels to other Western Late Bronze Age versions of Urra (for the date, see Horowitz, Oshima, and Sanders

2006:73; for the parallels see Tadmor's publication [1977]). It is probably part of a student's practice tablet, since the badly effaced opposite side does not seem to continue the Urra series but moves on to a different topic. It should be noted that the Hazor fragment was not archaeologically excavated, but found in the excavation dumps of area A (Yadin 1972:124). It is intriguing that it was found not by an archaeologist but a private individual visiting the site, Oded Golan (see Tadmor 1977), who would later become an antiquities dealer of questionable reputation, indicted for forgery by the Israel Antiquities Authority (though not convicted as of this writing; for a damning analysis of two texts he presented as authentic, see Israel Antiquities Authority 2003). This means that we must at least consider the question of its authenticity. In fact, the text's connections to other regional versions give us a cultural context that helps authenticate it. First, given the miserable condition of the fragment, as well as the difficulty and lack of reward involved in forging such an object, it is implausible that it is not ancient. The nature of its contents and the physical format of the tablet confirm its affinities with both generally western and specifically Palestinian traditions. Tadmor notes that our text omits an introductory line, is written in large script, and somewhat eclectically excerpts from the canonical *Urra=ḫubullu* sequence, all features shared with the Urra excerpt tablets from Ugarit (1977:101 and plate 13, with useful photos of the cut edges of the tablet; the examples from Ugarit were published as "RS 5" and "RS 7" by Thureau-Dangin 1931:234–49). And the Hazor fragment's physical format, with two sets of clay edges cut rather than rounded, is extremely unusual in cuneiform tradition but matches the format of the single known excavated exemplar of Urra from Israel, Ashkelon 1 (Huehnergard and van Soldt 1999:186n2; the rectilinear shape of the edge is clear in the hand copy on 185 figure 2 and confirmed by Huehnergard, personal communication, May 2007).

24. For an exploration of a mystical ideology of Babylonian writing, see Bottéro's analysis of the names of Marduk that close the epic of creation, where he concludes that the hermeneutic procedure is "to analyze words to gain knowledge of things" (1977:26, summarized in Bottéro 1992). For a rich selection of mystical analyses of language from the Neo-Assyrian period, see Livingstone 1986. It is not clear that such mystical ideologies were widespread in the Late Bronze Age or before.

25. For references, see Huehnergard and van Soldt 1999:186n3.

26. This particular text was not taken directly from Mesopotamia, but in its ordering of terms corresponds exactly to a version found at West Semitic-speaking Emar, in Syria on the Euphrates: Emar 541; for references, see Huehnergard and van Soldt 1999:187n5 and 190–91.

27. For this paradigm, see Pollock 2006a.

28. The fragment was found on the surface (Horowitz, Oshima, and Sanders 2006:102) but is datable to the Late Bronze Age by its language, script, and content (George 2003:339–47).

29. There remains the eagerly hoped-for possibility that creative texts in syllabic cuneiform will be excavated in our area and revolutionize our picture of literary life. But it is a methodological error to refrain from consideration of the existing evidence because more might emerge. Indeed, if we postponed analysis until all evidence appeared, we could never begin at all.

30. Our fragment does not directly correspond to the Standard Babylonian version of Gilgamesh, exhibiting a level of divergence from the Babylonian traditions than we find in some other western versions such as those at Boghazkoi. For a detailed characterization of the Boghazkoi fragments, see George 2003:310–11. On the Megiddo tablet George considers it likely that, when complete, it "covered events from Enkidu's dream of doom to his expiry, the events that mark respectively the beginning and end of SB Tablet VII. Nevertheless, concordance between the text of the two versions is rare, a fact that serves to emphasize how much more remotely related [this version] was to the SB text in comparison with the broadly contemporaneous fragments from Babylonia. Moreover, the Megiddo tablet finds no place for much material present in MB Ur and SB Tablet VII" (2003:342).

31. Among the earliest written texts are Egyptian imports at third-millennium Byblos. A statistically significant confirmation of this pattern of literary absence during the Late Bronze Age is found in the 380 texts of the Amarna archive itself; while there is no locally created literature whatsoever, there are versions of three well known Old Babylonian texts (Adapa, Šar Tamḫāri, and Nergal and Erishkegal), each in distinctive versions. What remains to be fully understood is the source of this variation, whether it occurred in the Hittite or Syrian sources of these texts, or by inheritors of this Syrian-Hittite tradition in Canaan or even Egypt. For an up-to-date edition with brief but rich comments on these problems, see Izre'el 1997.

32. The witness list from Schechem (Horowitz, Oshima, and Sanders 2006:123–25) is an exception.

33. One of these is broken, but it fits the structure of the tablet and there are no plausible alternatives. Landsberger 1954:59n123, followed by Zadok 1996:107, reads the first instance as a name, not taking into account the fact that unlike all other names in the tablet, it lacks a number after it and appears after a line that appears to be a tally of the previous numbers. Any more plausible proposal would have to attend to the format of the text, which contains a sequence of lines with NAME, NUMBER, concluded with a summary number followed by a term without a number, which unlike the other names has a phonological shape identical with a Babylonian verb.

34. See CAD "D" volume, q.v.

35. They consist of: the transfer of money (1:8–11) and tribute (5:7–8), luxury items (1:19–25), weapons and soldiers for chariot warfare (2:8–12, 19–20; 5:4–7), captives (5:9–12; 6:23–25), and women for marriage or ransom (1:24–30; 2:22–24).

36. For discussion of the phrase, see Sanders f/c.

37. We find Canaanite blessings (1:5–7; see Horowitz, Oshima, and Sanders 2006:132), syntax (the flexibly coordinating and subordinating uses of *-u-* in all the letters and the relativizing use of *inuma* in 2:5), and even morphosyntax (the enclitic *-mi* particles of 5 and 6).

38. For a concise and insightful grammar, see Izre'el's book with this name (2005). An enormously important, but barely explored, dimension of these letters is that analogous though interestingly different letters do appear at Ugarit in the thirteenth century B.C.E. Studies by Daniel Arnaud of the letters from Tyre and Sidon show two strikingly heterogeneous relationships between cuneiform writing and local language. The Tyre letters (Arnaud 2000) show a mixed language with Canaanite, Akkadian,

and Egyptian elements already visible in the Amarna Tyre letters, which Arnaud terms a *bêche-de-mer*. The Sidon letters could be described as alloglottographic (2001, not Arnaud's term) since the vocabulary, morphology, and even phrases are good Akkadian but the higher-level syntax is Canaanite, a pattern Arnaud explains as the result of a well-trained scribe taking quick dictation from a West Semitic speaker. I am indebted to Dennis Pardee for bringing these studies to my attention.

39. For the linguistic background of these texts, see Rainey 1996, vol. 1. On the possibility of earlier, non-contemporary elements in the Canaanite transmitted by a school tradition, see Izre'el 1991 §6.2.

40. I thank the linguist Robin Shoaps, of the University of Chicago Anthropology Department, for this term (personal communication, August 2007). The interpenetration is highly patterned: typically, we find Canaanite verbal morphology on inflected Babylonian verbal stems, so that the "inner" lexical core is Babylonian and the "outer" grammatical inflection is Canaanite. But these very same verbs may then receive Babylonian pronominal object suffixes (for a table of suffixes, see Izre'el 2005:20; a particularly rich example is the Sumerogram with Canaanite prefix, Babylonian phonetic complement, and Babylonian pronominal object suffix in EA 94:66 discussed by Rainey 1996 vol. 1:32) , and even very rarely a Babylonian noun with a Canaanite suffix (EA 284:19 *qātīhu*, which fuses the Babylonian word for "hand" with a Canaanite third-person masculine singular personal suffix; see Izre'el 2005:22). The idea of a strict barrier between Babylonian lexical material and Canaanite grammatical material cannot be maintained.

41. While the studies of Izre'el (2005) and Rainey (1996) prove that it has been productive to describe the Canaano-Akkadian letters as if they represented one language (or better, in Izre'el's terms, one continuum of lects), compare the statement of Gianto that Canaano-Akkadian "cannot be treated as if it were a language or even a dialect" (2001:126).

42. The most sophisticated characterizations of Canaano-Akkadian grammar, those of Izre'el 2005 and 2007, portray it as having analogies with mixed languages, but do not argue that it completely fits their criteria in terms of origin, social context, or structure. He notes that "clearly, Canaano-Akkadian was not a native tongue, and hence the use of the term creole for it would be inappropriate. But also the use of the term pidgin for this linguistic continuum hardly fits" (2007:1.5). For characterization of Canaano-Akkadian as a pidgin, see Arends, Muysken, and Smith 1995:363; for analogy (not identity) with creoles, see Izre'el 2007:4.1: "Clear cases of continua within a linguistic community which are similar in some respects to the Amarna Canaanite situation may be found in several creole speaking areas where there has been a continuous contact with the model language"; for "mixed language," see the next note.

43. Linguistically, contact-induced languages almost universally have simplified morphology: while nonstandard vocabulary items are the easiest to borrow, inflectional morphology is the most difficult. Yet Canaano-Akkadian displays large portions of the inflectional range of both Babylonian and (what we understand of) fourteenth-century Canaanite (Garrett 2006:55 citing Thomason 2001:70ff.). For a contrary argument emphasizing morphological reduction, see Izre'el 2005:29. None of the recent linguistic analyses of Canaano-Akkadian contain detailed comparison of its grammar

to any languages other than Canaanite or Akkadian. This is also true of the two most sophisticated attempts to categorize it as a language, Izre'el 2007 and von Dassow 2004 (for which, see above). Izreel 2007:1.1 states that Canaano-Akkadian is "a mixed language: Akkadian predominated in its semantic skeleton almost entirely, while the Canaanite language (whatever this might have been), the mother-tongue of the scribes . . . predominated in the domain of grammar. It influenced its syntax and its morphology, and affected the phonology and semantics." Note that Izre'el does not claim that the morphology is straightforwardly Canaanite; almost all grammatical particles and function words, and most of the pronominal suffixes, are in fact Akkadian, and most of the Canaanite morphology that appears is fused with partly inflected Akkadian stems. But contemporary definitions of mixed languages simply do not consider the kind of morphological interpenetration we find in Canaano-Akkadian texts. Canaano-Akkadian fits neither of the two types of mixed language—neither the one that shows a lexical/grammatical split, combining "the grammatical system of one language with the lexicon from another language" (Arends, Muysken, and Smith 1995:47) nor the second type that compartmentalizes different sections of the grammar by language (Bakker and Matras 2003:3–4). For the presence of Akkadian verb morphology, which Izre'el analyzes as confined to exceptional "Akkadianisms," see Izre'el 2007:3.2.3.

44. Thus Bakker and Muysken, ""Media Lengua is essentially the product of replacing the phonological shape of Quechua stems with Spanish forms, maintaining the rest of the Quechua structure" (Arends, Muysken, and Smith 1995:44, with examples on pp. 43–44); for examples of Haitian, see Muysken and Veenstra (in Arends, Muysken, and Smith 1995:154).

45. Garrett 2006.

46. It is not just in the broader scheme of cuneiform literature, but in fact the history of world literature, that the corpus from Late Bronze Age Palestine is unusual: most texts from world empires like those of Mesopotamia or Egypt are written in a standardized form of that empire's official language. Many show the influence of their writers' native languages, but almost none display the radical rearrangement of the cosmopolitan written language by the rules of a second local language that we see here. Even when we find unofficial dialects in writing, we can usually understand what the writers thought they were doing and describe what language the texts are *supposed* to be in. Of the 509 contact languages registered in Norval Smith's list, only Canaano-Akkadian is considered as possibly only written (Arends, Muysken, and Smith 1995:363).

47. For a possible solution to this problem, considering the typology of Canaano-Akkadian, along with Buddhist Hybrid Sanskrit and medieval Romance-inflected Latin, as a new type of written language, see Sanders f/c.

48. For example, at Megiddo we find inscribed ivory plaques from the early twelfth century B.C.E., a cartouche of Ramesses III, and a bronze statue base of Ramesses VI (Weinstein 2001:368), while at Beth Shean there is a fourteenth-century stela of an official in Canaanite style, two basalt royal stelae of Seti I, and a third of Ramesses II, all three dating to the thirteenth century (Mazar 1993:216–17).

49. For a catalogue, see Wimmer 2008.

50. Rollston 2006:20–21.

51. Lemaire and Vernus 1983; Goldwasser 1991. Wimmer 2006 has recently argued against this view.

52. For a detailed scenario of how this transmission could have occurred, see Goldwasser 1991, as well as the less likely alternative of direct transmission during the tenth century (1991:251n2). Goldwasser's scenario is used by Na'aman as evidence for scribal activity in tenth-century Jerusalem (Na'aman 2006:24–25).

53. Robert Miller's careful, archaeologically based social history of Iron Age I Israel finds no evidence for redistribution of goods on a tax basis. Local villages "presented tribute in cash crops or conscripted labor to higher levels of economic centers, although without specialized administrative control apparatus" (2005:08, and compare Byrne 2007).

54. For the findspot, see Kochavi 1977:4. Cross 2003 [1980]:225 gives paleographical arguments that do not diverge widely from Kochavi's date of 1200 B.C.E.

55. The standard Ugaritic order begins *ʾabgḫd*, representing an early twenty-seven plus consonant inventory; Izbet Sarta's *ʾbgd* testifies to a dialect in which at least five of those consonants, including ḫ, have been lost.

56. Compare the discussion of Naveh 1978:31–32. There is only a short scratch where the *mem* is expected, and the letter interpreted *waw* by Kochavi (1977:5) is read as a possible *mem* by Cross (2003 [1980]:220).

57. See Cross 2003[1954]:310–11 and 2003[1967]:323. For a more difficult text from this same place and period, see the Lachish ostracon, which may be interpreted "[for] *Ilib* [the divine Ancestor]" or alternatively "[from] Eliab . . . In the [temple] precinct he installed [this bowl]." This reading, that of Cross 2003[1984]:293–96, is uncertain because it would require interpreting the inscription as boustrophedon, with the first line as right-running and the second line as left-running, despite the fact that the *bets* in both lines face the same direction (a difficulty pointed out by Sass 1988:62 and not mentioned by Cross).

58. The phrase *mʾhb bʿlt*, "beloved of the Lady," spelled three different ways (!) appears in a minimum of three proto-Sinaitic inscriptions, a reading confirmed by a parallel Egyptian inscription, *mry ḥtḥr [nbt] mfkȝt* "Beloved of Hathor [lady of] turquoise" (see Hamilton 2006:332–35). Hamilton reads the phrase in Sinai 345, 353, and 374 (see Hamilton 2006:334, 348, 372.) while Sass considers it possible in up to eight inscriptions (adding 348, 350, 351, 354, and 356; see Sass 1988:12–27).

59. Minimally, this is a complex of large, related coastal sites (comprised of Ugarit, Ras ibn Hani, and Tell Sukkas) in northern Syria. A small number of non-canonical texts are found at Ugarit, but this pattern of distribution is not mutual: there are no canonical texts outside Ugarit's immediate vicinity. Formally, the non-canonical texts found at Ugarit are not consistent with one another and in terms of content they are (with one exception) of the type that could easily have been sent from abroad: economic texts and letters. These texts are analyzed in Bordreuil 1981. The one exception is the abecedary RS 88.2215. The Sukkas text KTU 4.766 is a personnel list characterized on its upper edge as *d bt mlk*, "of the royal household" (kindly brought to my attention by Alan Millard). Because it was found at a port close to Ugarit it does not significantly change the profile: the king's household extends to the immediate vicinity of Ugarit.

60. For the site's role in trade networks, see Bunimovitz and Lederman 1993; for comprehensive bibliography on the tablet, see Horowitz, Oshima, and Sanders 2006:157.

61. The linear alphabetic ostracon was discovered in a residential area, which the site's excavators, Bunimovitz and Lederman (1993), date to the same stratum as the alphabetic cuneiform tablet. The ostracon's inscription runs from left to right, as in Ugaritic and a number of the early linear alphabetic texts, and may be dated to the twelfth century B.C.E. I follow Cross (2003:324) in the twelfth-century date and the reconstruction of the legible names.

62. Identification suggested in Jerusalem by Takayoshi Oshima, April 2004, and confirmed on the basis of the author's hand copy by the archaeologist and metallurgist Aslahan Yener at the Oriental Institute, October 2004. Compare the inscribed Ugaritic axes KTU 6:6–8, 6.10 and the adze KTU 6.9 (listed together as "axes" in KTU).

63. The most complete order is, according to Irvine and Beeston (1988) known from Qatabanian. For epigraphic and linguistic treatment of the Beth Shemesh abecedary, see my edition in Horowitz, Oshima, and Sanders 2006:157–60.

64. Recall the title of Dietrich and Loretz (1988b), "Die Alphabettafel aus Bet Semes und die ursprüngliche Heimat der Ugariter." Cf. their discussion of possible "ethnic, linguistic, social and political differences" (four categories assumed to go together) between two different alphabetic "traditions" carried by two separate "language groups" in (1989:110–12). For important counterarguments, see Sass (1991), primarily, "the fact that the Sabaeans chose the *hlḥ* and not the *ʾbg* order is in itself no confirmation of the former being South Semitic in Palestine" (p. 319); Knauf 1989; and Pardee 2007.

65. That is, while it shares a common proto-Semitic sound inventory and a few probable letterforms with later epigraphic South Arabian, there is no evidence of any broader structural correspondence. Loudin could not find the *b, s, ḫ,* or *ḏ* in their expected places, and he did not even look for the *ẓ* or *ś* that are preserved in forms of epigraphic South Arabian but not in Ugaritic. In fact there does not seem to be any place for either of these consonantal phonemes in any ancient alphabetic cuneiform text. Most important, the distinctive South Arabian sibilant s_2, corresponding to Hebrew ś but unattested in Ugaritic, as well as the *ẓ* phoneme, are both absent. Attempts to directly connect this text with any specific South Arabian language, let alone ethnic identity, are therefore dubious. Furthermore, a closely similar sequence of consonants is found in Egyptian: see Quack 1993.

66. The text discovered in 1988, RS 88.2215, is an abecedary written in a more canonical scribal form. It is inscribed from left to right on a tablet of common type, at the hands of a better scribe than the Beth Shemesh tablet. It allows us to reconstruct the entire contents of the Beth Shemesh text (first publication Bordreuil and Pardee 1995, full edition Bordreuil and Pardee 2001).

67. For analysis of the non-canonical alphabetic cuneiform texts, see Bordreuil 1979, 1981, 1983. Indeed, it is entirely possible that at least the graphic, and perhaps the linguistic, tradition underlying the two abecedaries is neither Canaanite nor Phoenician in origin, as Pardee and Bordreuil have argued (2001, summarized on p. 348). Features of the letters accord with "non-canonical" texts found both south of Ugarit and in Ugarit itself, such as RS 22.003, also written with various consonantal neutralizations. But major aspects are unique in alphabetic cuneiform, such as the 90 degree rotation of all four sibilants, a phenomenon also visible in the Bet Shemesh text and known from later linear alphabetic scripts. Pardee and Bordreuil (2001, esp. pp. 344–45) provide a detailed analysis of the Ras Shamra text's complex graphic affinities.

68. See Kaufman 1997:119.

69. Recently, with Richard Steiner's groundbreaking analysis of Papyrus Amherst 63, and the light it casts on older theories of Hebrew phonemes in place-names preserved in Septuagint transcription, it has emerged that *ǵ* and *ḫ* were also still productive, independent phonemes in varieties of fourth- and third-century Hebrew and Aramaic. "The Israelites adopted unchanged a twenty-two-sign version of the alphabet current in their area, even though they had preserved *more than twenty-two* [NB not twenty-three-SLS] of the twenty-nine Proto-Semitic consonants. Consequently, they were forced to use some signs with more than one value. Only one instance of such polyphony survived long enough to be recognized by the Masoretes" (1997:148). For the full argument, see Steiner 2005.

70. For further bibliography, see the treatment in Sanders 2006.

71. The blade is inscribed from right to left, lacks word dividers, and displays the symmetrical formation of the *bet*, like the *dalet* of the Beth Shemesh abecedary. It appears, as Weippert first argued (1966), that the *ṣ* sign here stands for *s*, implying a neutralization of the emphatic/voiceless distinction in the scribe's language variety.

72. The assimilation is specifically of final *n* to the initial, non-laryngeal, consonant of the following word. For more on the linguistic issues, see Sanders 2006.

73. While there is no reason to believe that the Tabor knife originates in the place it was found (pointed out by Alan Millard, personal communication, May 2004), its only plausible place of manufacture and use is within the southern Levant because it belongs to a type—prestige artifacts inscribed in non-canonical alphabetic cuneiform—known only from this region (Dietrich and Loretz 1988a:244).

74. For the distinctively proto-Phoenician elements of the Sarepta jar, see Greenstein 1976 with the additional comments of Bordreuil 1979. For the probable proto-Phoenician elements of the Hala Sultan Tekke bowl, see Bordreuil 1983, with the significant criticisms of Puech 1986:208–11; and for a defense of Bordreuil's reading, see Sanders f/c.

75. Because this suggestion is made on the basis of isolated features, it should not be taken too far: these differences could be limited to variation in local vocabulary and expression of a few consonants, without sweeping differences in language structure. But Izre'el (2003:90–95) has noted further evidence, especially in Canaano-Akkadian letters from Megiddo, suggesting that there was complex linguistic variation on the morphological and syntactic level as well.

76. For bibliography, see Horowitz, Oshima, and Sanders 2006:161. Since the original of the text is now lost (see Sanders 2006:161n1), the reading here is based on Cross's hand copy and does not claim epigraphic confidence.

77. Unlike our other two examples from Israel, this text is written from left to right. But it shares the absence of word dividers; paleographic distinctions, such as the symmetrical writing of the *b* (both also found in the Tabor knife); a symmetrical *d*, found in the Beth Shemesh tablet; and a *ṯ* sign to be read *š*, with the phonological merger found in some southern alphabetic cuneiform texts.

78. For evidence of itinerant craft production between Canaan and Egypt, see Bietak 1998, and for its connection to the origins of the alphabet, see Goldwasser 2006.

79. The bookkeeping texts in Egyptian hieratic are the exception that proves the rule here.

80. I was gratified to realize that this thesis was original with Franz Rosenthal, who already in his review of the first Ugaritic grammar wrote: "I doubt more and more whether it is necessary at all to look far afield for the explanation of the three aleph signs in Ugarit. If we understand that the alphabet employed in Ugarit was a blending of the cuneiform method of writing and the alphabetic principle, we must acknowledge that this process must have been a phonetic as well as a mechanically orthographic one, and inconsistencies are not at all surprising. The Accadian signs expressing a mere vowel might indeed have attracted the attention of the inventor, because in spelling often enough they took the place of aleph. This peculiarity of Accadian orthography might account sufficiently for the fact that the aleph was viewed differently from the other consonants" (Rosenthal 1942:172).

While Rosenthal's theory seems to have fallen out of the literature, not cited in any modern grammar, the citation may be found along with a description of the current, unconvincing, theory in M. S. Smith's deeply researched history of Ugaritic studies (2001b:55). Bordreuil and Pardee make a narrower proposal, that the vocalic *alefs* may have been developed to transcribe Akkadian words (2004:36–37, also noting a problem with this proposal, that there are very few transcribed Akkadian texts). This is, of course, different from the proposal being made here (and first by Rosenthal) that the Ugaritic scribes' experience with syllabic writing affected the very way they conceived of writing an *alef*. Shlomo Izre'el (personal communication, August 2008) has pointed out a further question to be explored in this theory: the asymmetrical value of the three *alefs*, where the *ʾa* and *ʾu* signs stand for the *alef* followed by a realization of the *a* or *u* value, long or short, while the *ʾi* sign has the additional value of standing for *ʾ*, a syllable-closing *alef*. What structural distinction motivated the *ʾi* sign's role as the unique marker for the bare *ʾ* phoneme?

81. On the prestige of standardized Phoenician, see also Cross 2003:226.

4. THE INVENTION OF HEBREW IN IRON AGE ISRAEL

1. In contrast to the urban coastal Phoenician script that we find on monuments and valuable objects, the Gezer and Tel Zayit inscriptions suggest that a less elaborate inland tradition existed by the tenth century, perhaps the more rural, low-budget tribal fringe of the Phoenician-derived scribal craft network.

2. As we will see, the City of David seals imply that most linear alphabetic writing in this period may well have been done on papyrus and in Phoenician.

3. Liverani 2005:38.

4. The non-weapon inscriptions that Benjamin Sass describes with some confidence as dating from the Iron Age I consist of the Lachish bowl fragment, Lachish bowl, Beth Shemesh ostracon, Izbet Sartah ostracon, Qubur el-Walaida bowl, Zarephath sherd (reading uncertain), Byblos cones A and B, Manahat sherd, Tekke bowl, Nora fragment—some ten texts (1988:62–95).

5. For a maximal catalogue of the ninth- and tenth-century inscriptions from Israel and presentation of three discovered at Tel Rehov, see Mazar 2003. For a critical paleographic discussion of these inscriptions and presentation of the latest discovery, the tenth-century Tel Zayit inscription (discussed below), see Tappy et al. 2007. Most

of the tenth- and ninth-century seals and impressions are not yet published, but the excavators' analysis makes the consequences clear. For a preliminary discussion and eight photos of the City of David seals and impressions, see Reich, Shukron, and Lernau 2007:156–63. Amihai Mazar states that "at Tel Rehov we have about thirty seals and seal impressions on jar handles. In only a few cases we have sealings on lumps of clay which could seal jars or other commodities—no clear evidence for bullae that sealed papyri" (personal communication, January 2008). See also briefly the statement of Mazar 2007.

6. The seals and bullae from the late ninth- to early eighth-century City of David were used to seal both papyrus documents and containers of imported goods. Since they are not preserved, we cannot be sure whether the documents were in Phoenician, Hebrew, Aramaic, or another written language. But the preliminary publication emphasizes two telling facts about the bullae: first, the ones that sealed papyri are broken along the string that wrapped the document, meaning they are "incoming mail," received from elsewhere (Reich, Shukron, and Lernau 2007:156). Second, the iconography of the seals is Phoenician: motifs include palmettes, pomegranites, Phoenician vessels, and pseudo-hieroglyphic designs. And a very large number and variety of fish bones at the site indicate the presence of a fishmarket (Reich, Shukdron, and Lernaus 2007, esp. 160–61). Thus all signs point to the Phoenician coast as the documents' place of origin.

7. Indeed, when it comes to the only reliable corpus—that of archaeologically excavated seals and impressions—there are now far more uninscribed seals than inscribed ones. Nahman Avigad and Benjamin Sass count some eighty-six unique provenanced seals and bullae in their 1997 handbook, of which all dated instances come from the eighth through sixth centuries, as opposed to the two hundred uninscribed items from the tenth through early eighth centuries counted by Reich and Mazar!

8. P. Kyle McCarter argues that the dating of each is reliable because four of the six texts come from secure archaeological contexts, and the script of each matches the others closely. The four texts from well-stratified contexts are (1) the Tel Zayit abecedary, (2) the Tel Amal storage jar, (3) the Tel Batash rim sherd and (4) the Rehov body sherd; the two texts of uncertain stratification whose scripts tightly fit the first four are (5) the Gezer calendar and (6) the Beth Shemesh gaming board (see Tappy et al. 2007:28 with stratification and bibliography). For a similar but not identical list of tenth-century inscriptions, with similar content, see Renz and Röllig 1995 1:29–39.

9. For this argument (though without comparative script charts), see Tappy et al. 2007. For an argument to the contrary, see Rollston 2008 with McCarter's response.

10. Sass (2005) has provided a valuable and clearly argued reassessment of the dating of the tenth-century Phoenician texts, pointing out that the absolute dating of two important inscriptions is dependent on evidence that only proves a terminus post quem, not a date (2005:15–17). But his arguments are themselves dependent on art-historical considerations that are far from decisive (2005:75–77), rely on unprovenanced material (2005:32–33), and contradict the paleographic analysis of provenanced texts (Tappy et al. 2007). Even if one accepts Sass's arguments, they are of limited consequence for the discussion here. While they would push the Phoenician texts into the ninth century, they do not affect the major historical shifts for which this chapter argues,

since Sass himself accepts the late ninth-century date of the first Aramaic, Moabite, and Ammonite royal inscriptions.

11. Except for KAI 5, where a reference to the object is the most plausible and widely accepted reconstruction, given the rigidly stereotyped genre and the pervasive parallels: [*mš z y]b*ʾ ʾ*bb* ʿ*l*,"[The statue(?) that] Abi-Baal broug[ht]." The others begin ʾ*rn z*, "The sarcophagus that . . ." (KAI 1), *bt z*, "The temple that . . ." (KAI 4), *mš z*, "The statue(?) that . . ." (KAI 6), *qr z* ,"The wall that . . ." (KAI 7). For a more detailed presentation, see Sanders 2008.

12. For detailed treatment of all known Mesopotamian calendars, see M. E. Cohen 1993.

13. For analysis of these differing systems, see Lemaire 1998.

14. The lack of fit between the physical 365+ day year and the 360 days postulated by the lunisolar ritual calendar requires systematic bureaucratic adjustment; otherwise after a few decades of 12 30-day months the "month of summer-fruit" would be solidly in the middle of winter. This is not a difficulty for the Gezer calendar, which lists seasons, not evenly measured time units.

15. While the texts' content definitely does not fit a "curriculum," it is possible that they are secondarily related to a curriculum: the Gezer calendar could represent an experiment with literizing, an attempt to put a "folksong" or "almanac" into writing. Indeed elsewhere—in early modern France, for example—almanacs of folk wisdom were put in writing not by peasant farmers but precisely when intellectuals become interested in recording and distributing the ideas of the "folk" (see Davis 1975).

16. Despite the academic presupposition that written culture must have as its ideal endpoint a ponderous, decades-long enculturation, Michael C. A. Macdonald (2005) brings copious evidence that writing's main role in ancient South Semitic Safaitic written culture, and modern Berber-speaking Touareg culture, is amusement and momentary diversion.

17. Accepting McCarter's convincing argument that the *l-k* order is a mistake (Tappy et al. 2007).

18. It should be recalled here that the *peh-ayin* order, which in the existing evidence was actually the most popular Iron Age alphabetical order, is unknown in the standard Ugaritic abecedaries and may well have arisen through influence from a completely different alphabetic tradition that was known at Ugarit and in Israel, the southern *halḥam* order, which orders the letters *samekh-alef-peh-ayin*. As noted in chapter 3, the presence of the *samekh* before *peh* and *ayin* could well have triggered the reversal.

19. Again, while its content definitely does not fit a "curriculum," it is possible that it is secondarily related to a curriculum: the Zayit abecedary could be the work of a particularly bad writer, the reversals his first attempts at engraving a more standard alphabet. But the closest and strongest Semitic parallels point in the opposite direction: to writing as pure play, not educational discipline (Macdonald 2005:74–92, on Safaitic). But these arguments are not anchored in evidence; to go any further we would first need at least some sign of a state curriculum in tenth-century Israel.

20. For arguments that we should take the text's claim that David had a single scribe at face value, see Byrne 2007.

21. We should not be surprised that these royal victory inscriptions appear full-

blown. For such a genre, prior evolutionary phases are not only unnecessary—they are hard to imagine. Could a king have successfully presented such long-winded speeches, taking pesonal responsibility for every military victory, in an assembly of self-assertive tribal leaders who had conducted most of the actual fighting? Of what use would such a genre, expressly designed for public display on prominent and durable monuments, have been if it was written only on perishable material? Neither does the concept of royal victory graffiti seem compelling. Surely the phrases, tropes, and subgenres of which these inscriptions are composed had West Semitic precursors, spoken and perhaps written. Yet these precursors are difficult to find in Ugaritic, and the best-understood subgenre, the "Danklied" in the Zakkur stela (illuminated by Greenfield 1969), has clear parallels in Assyrian as well as biblical literature. From a literary point of view the inscriptions are best understood as hybrids of local West Semitic and common imperial cultures.

22. The biblical depiction of Moab as both "people of Kemosh" and a territory belonging to a king is best exemplified by Numbers 21:29; 22–24; 2 Kings 3.

23. Thus the inscription speaks of "the land of Madaba" in 7–8, "the land of Atarot" (line 10), and implicitly when he refers to the conquest of territory as "annexing it to Dibon" (20–21, and 28–29 when cities are "annexed to the land" of Dibon).

24. The third difference, the presence of the Gt form in *lḥm*, "do battle," is, like the feminine singular noun form, an archaic retention (cf. the form's presence in Ugaritic).

25. "Strange as it may seem, the first distinctive features of Hebrew writing can be discerned in the scripts of the ninth-century Moabite inscriptions . . . Although their language is Moabite . . . their script is Hebrew" (Naveh 1987: 68).

26. Zakkur's emphasis on pure divine election implies that he became king not by inheriting the throne from his father, whom he avoids mentioning, but through usurpation and conquest.

27. For edition and full bibliography, see Ahituv 2004:329–333. Not part of this genre is the Bar-Hadad inscription, probably datable to the late ninth century (detailed epigraphic and historical treatment in Pitard 1999). This short inscription thanks the god Melqart, otherwise known as a Phoenician deity, for "hearing" the king's "voice," a trope common to votive inscriptions (e.g., for healing the king from an illness or granting him an heir). The stela could represent gratitude for military victory (as in Zakkur's song of thanks, illuminated by Greenfield 1969), but it narrates no conquest or other political events.

28. He characterizes this unifying intention, following the linguist Hans Heinrich Hock, as linguistic nationalism, "the conscious attempt to produce a language characteristic of one political/social group as opposed to another" (1993:57). But as Routledge (2003, 2005) notes about the use of "national" terminology for early Iron Age kingdoms, this may be anachronistic. We find neither an explicit kinship dimension nor a unified territory in view in the ninth-century texts, and Israel is not consistently the enemy.

29. For the linguistic evidence, see Young 1993:54–58, which notes that "a great deal of the early history of the southern Aramean states . . . is filled with political self-definition against the constant enemy and sometimes overlord, Israel."

30. The epigraphic evidence, as well as the later legacies of Standard Aramaic and Hebrew, suggests the wider use of narrative prose in these languages by the early eighth century. Interesting linguistic and historical arguments have been made for ninth-century Hebrew historical narratives as sources in the book of Samuel, for example, Halpern 2001, but note the counterarguments of Na'aman 2002.

31. For discussion, see Hawkins 2000:2–3.

32. Written in a language closely related to Hittite, the Luwian inscriptions are in form and content direct descendents of the monumental inscriptions of Hittite kings, using the same conventionalized dialect, rhetoric, and graphic techniques, which change little over the course of five hundred years. Fascinatingly, a single group—the Hittite royal dynasty, probably a linguistic minority in their empire, used Luwian exclusively for monuments to address the broad audience that recognized Luwian, while restricting Hittite to uses within their royal court. This phenomenon, in which a single group uses one written language for one purpose and a completely different language for a socially different goal, is a fascinating example of that rigid division of linguistic labor that Pollock (2006a) has termed "hyperglossia." Van den Hout's detailed analysis of Hittite-Luwian hyperglossia reveals a striking relationship between culture and power in written language, as the Hittite dynasts adopt the radically different writing system of hieroglyphic Luwian to address the linguistically similar Luwian-speaking (or at least -identified) majority that they rule (van den Hout 2006). At the beginning of the Iron Age, Luwian rulers themselves repossess the Luwian writing tradition and use it to talk about themselves. Yet Luwian rulers had no interest in projecting any kind of simple local identity. At the same time one of these kings borrows the most prestigious West Semitic alphabet of the early Iron Age to produce the elaborate bilingual Luwian-Phoenician inscription of Karatepe. In an irony typical of the history of writing, the Karatepe inscription, commissioned for a governor with the good Luwian name of Azatiwada, happens to be the longest extant text in Phoenician.

33. This conflict, fundamentally based on shared features rather than difference, is of course what Sigmund Freud called "the narcissism of small differences." It has been connected to issues of language and ethnic identity by the anthropologist Simon Harrison: people use the same tools to assert their difference from each other in a process of "denied resemblance." Harrison points out that two of the most insightful scholars of nationalism, Ernest Gellner (1983) and Benedict Anderson (1991), "both note how the strongly 'modular' character of nationalism made it readily 'pirated' . . . by new nationalist movements. The borrowing of other nations' ways of defining or individuating themselves does seem to be a widespread feature of nationalism. For example [in] the use of language to symbolize national identity" (Harrison 2003:351). Distinct states such as Israel and Moab are, when it comes to national script-languages, "connected to each other by shared principles of individuation. They are related and alike in the respects in which they create dissimilarities among themselves" (Harrison 2003:352).

34. Claudius Marius Victor, *Alethia* 3 line 274, cited in Bartlett 1993:198. For background on Victor, see Hudson-Williams 1964.

35. The drastic shift in the political situation between the expanding city-states of the pre-Hammurabi Old Babylonian period and the great powers of the Late Bronze

Age explains the presence of Mesopotamian-style monuments at West Semitic Mari; here Amorite kings used a Mesopotamian scribal apparatus to produce imperial inscriptions because they aspired to the power of Mestopotamian-style emperors. The most successful of these Amorite kings was, of course, Hammurabi, who became the Mesopotamian emperor par excellence and destroyed Mari.

36. Even in the Old Babylonian period, the only West Semitic-speaking ruler at Mari from whom we have a chronicle was Shamshi-Adad, who seems to have modeled himself to an unusual degree on Northern Mesopotamian rulers, to the extent that his chronicle has been classified as an Assyrian genre. For the text, translation, and categorization as Assyrian, see Glassner 2004:160–65 (and for a suggestion to characterize the text's affiliation as "Northern Mesopotamian" instead, see Brinkman 1995:670).

37. Frayne 1990:602–4.

38. It is very plausible that the Baal epic was read before an audience (its poetic techniques are difficult to explain without a performance tradition, though see the cautionary note of Hillers and McCall 1976). But the fact that it exists in a single manuscript shows that what we have was not designed to circulate to that audience in writing.

39. Na'aman points out that "the earliest Assyrian stelae are dated to the beginning of the second third of the ninth century B.C.E. and, thus, antedate by about a generation the earliest alphabetic display inscriptions" (2006:212). He argues that "the sudden appearance of royal inscriptions in alphabetic script arose from an emulation of the Assyrian custom. The kings of Syria and Palestine had taken note of the Assyrian custom of erecting stelae to commemorate their victories and to display their achievements and began to imitate it" (2006:175–76). For the historical relations between Shalmaneser III and Israel, see Younger 2007, and for a detailed list of ninth-century Assyrian inscriptions located in or discussing the Levant, see D. Wright 2003.

40. This question has occupied even the most richly documented and sensitively argued studies of Assyrian-West Semitic cultural contact, such as Machinist 1983, without producing an entirely satisfying or concrete answer.

41. There appear to be actual translation techniques at work, signs that the Assyrian empire had enough interest in these wealthy northern outposts to have a scribe or two working in both languages (though the script itself seems to be a backward, local variety with enough archaisms to separate it from the Aramaic national script in which Zakkur and Hazael wrote; on the attempts to standardize Aramaic, see Greenfield 1978:93–99).

42. The earliest preserved Assyrian vassal treaty dates from c. 823–820 B.C.E. (Parpola and Watanabe 1988: xxvi). As a major instrument of Assyrian policy, the treaties were thus in circulation by the late ninth century B.C.E., though later, better-preserved examples help illustrate the forms. For the most extensive example, see Esarhaddon's succession treaty, which refers to the vassal throughout in the second-person plural and includes a first-person plural oath (Parpola and Watanabe 1988 text 6); see also the treaty of Assurbanipal phrased as a first-person plural oath (text 9) and the treaty with the entire tribe of Qedar (text 10).

43. For a list of parallels between Sefire and a Neo-Assyrian vassal treaty, see Parpola and Watanabe 1988:xxvii–xxviii.

44. The double publication, visual and aural, of the Sefire treaty (KAI 222, with parallels in KAI 223 and 224; latest edition Fitzmeyer 1995) is indicated in I A 13 (visual), B 8–9 (aural), C 1–3 (both). Dating from the eighth century, it is indicative of an imperial process of translation already attested in the Tel Fekheriye inscription.

45. The Hebrew religious and linguistic character of the second of these inscriptions is clear from the use of the divine name YHWH and the plural verb forms *wyšbʿw* and *ytnw* marked with the final *mater w*, never found in Phoenician orthography (Renz and Röllig 1995 1:57–59).

46. McCarter (1987) makes the important point that these texts could be the result of the Israelite conquest of Judean territory described in 2 Kings 14. The texts would then have northern features because Israelite soliders and scribes, not necessarily Hebrew writing in general, had flowed through state barriers. But this makes the same point in a different way. While the texts' writers may have arrived from Samaria as part of a military conquest, it is certain that their techniques, adopted and retained in Judah, outlasted the kingdom in which they may have originated.

47. For discussion, see Rainey and Notley 2006:221–22.

48. The fundamental article is Stager 1985, updated and nuanced by Schloen 2001.

49. Rollston's work confirms and extends the earlier important study of Renz 1997.

50. Rollston provides a thorough survey of the debate on the scribal character of written Hebrew. He cites the claim of Weeks that "there is nothing in the development of the [Hebrew] script which demands the existence of schools or of lengthy schooling." This claim is based on the assertion that "it is simply a fallacy to suppose that it [the Iron Age Hebrew script] was uniform: it went through periods of very rapid development, and different styles certainly existed side by side." Rollston points out that this argument is a straw man, since no paleographers of Iron Age Hebrew argue that the Iron Age Hebrew script was completely "uniform," or that different styles did not "exist side by side." But the argument is also wrong: Rollston shows that the standardized script, spelling, and numerals of Hebrew epigraphic texts do indeed demand the existence of formal training (Weeks 1994:152). He also refutes David W. Jamieson-Drake's similar claim that the alphabetic script is "simple enough that functional knowledge of it could be passed on from one person to another in a comparatively short time." Jamieson-Drake states further that "schools would hardly have been necessary, unless other skills that demanded an educational setting were being taught alongside literacy." But the issue is not merely the ability to write in roughly the same style of linear alphabet (as we see in the early Iron Age) but the *uniform* writing of this alphabet (Jamieson-Drake 1991:154).

51. Rollston 1999; f/c.

52. The consistent regional differences in orthography between Israel and Judah in the eighth century represent two closely related, coherent and uniform dialects: diphthongs are always uncontracted in the south, as reflected in Judahite *yyn* as opposed to Northern Israelite *yn*. Other words reflect differences in phonology or vocabulary, for example, Judahite *šnh*, compared with Northern Israelite *št*, as in Phoenician. Because these dialectal differences are consistent within Northern Israelite and Judahite Hebrew, they are a further sign of standardization: it is highly implausible that spoken linguistic features would in fact have been distributed so neatly within political boundaries. For this issue, see Garr 1985:1–13 and chapter 2, above.

53. Cross and Freedman 1952:50.

54. Abou-Assaf, Bordreuil, and Millard 1982. Cf. also Kaufman 1982, esp. 155–56.

55. Cross and Freedman 1952:57.

56. Walter Aufrecht (1989:355) argues that hieratic numerals were used in Ammonite (Heshbon I, IV, XII), but the hieratic paleographer Stefan Wimmer (2006) rejects these readings.

57. Rollston 2006:66. Both Hebrew letters and hieratic numerals are apparent on this ostracon; see the text and photographs in Aharoni 1981:98–99. For the latest assessment of this stratum's date, from the mid-ninth to mid-eighth centuries, see Herzog 2002.

58. Gilula 1976: 107.

59. R. Cohen 1981; the hieractic ostracon is published as a supplement to the article on pp. 98–99.

60. It is also possible, though implausible, to argue that these ostraca were produced by Egyptian scribes capable of writing Hebrew.

61. Lemaire 1981:7–33. Not all of Lemaire's examples are certain. For example, Lemaire considered an ostracon from Aroer with the letters *qr* to be a possible abecedary. But this sequence could simply be part of a word, as noted by Puech 1988:191 in his detailed and sober analysis of proposals on school texts in ancient Israel. Lemaire also argued that several Arad ostraca (50–57) were produced by school children practicing the writing of their names. Although this is possible, neither the script, nor the presence of a personal name, necessitates it. Moreover, sometimes Lemaire assigns problematic readings to faded and fragmentary ostraca (cf. Lemaire 1976: 109–10, where the editor, Aharoni, added a critical note at the conclusion of Lemaire's article).

62. Friedemann Golka, for example, asserted that "as the scribal office was hereditary, schools for training were unnecessary." Golka 1993:9.

63. Ed Greenstein provides the caveat that "the sites where one expects the largest concentration of writing and of schools are Samaria and Jerusalem, both destroyed with limited material remains" (personal communication, March 2008). Yet as noted above, excavations of ninth- and tenth-century strata at Tel Rehov and the City of David are uncovering more writing-related material that implies relatively narrow early uses: not the tip of the iceberg but its middle, if not its base.

64. It shares this lack of deliberate differentiation with the eighth-century dialect of Deir Alla, which also lacked the crucial changes by which the national script-languages of Israel, Moab, and Aram (Huehnergard 1991) were identified against each other,

65. Naveh 1968.

66. Excavations have produced around ninety seals and bullae inscribed in Hebrew, almost all of which date to the Iron Age IIb. The task for future study of the provenanced seals is to actually date them according to their archaeological contexts, a desideratum that Avigad and Sass's handbook (1997) disappointingly often avoids. I have produced, with the assistance of Shira Wallach (now of Jewish Theological Seminary), a provisional database of archaeological dates during an National Endowment for the Humanities research fellowship at the Albright Institute in Jerusalem in 2006–7, which I will be happy to send upon request. The removal of probable forgeries may or may not change the broad picture (we cannot be sure how many seals in the Assyrian corpus are forgeries as well, for example), but a statistical analysis (Vaughn and

Dobler 2006) provides a disturbing suggestion that the corpus of unprovenanced seals deviates significantly from the corpus of provenanced seals, suggesting a significant portion of the unprovenanced ones are forged.

67. In Greece this monopoly can be explicitly defended when it comes to writing. Greek laws at Crete include provision for "exclusive right" to write in a town (Gagarin 2002:66–67). Compare Zaccagnini 1983 on ancient Near Eastern craft circulation within a palace economy and the incisive work of Moyer 2006 on the economic bases of cultural exchange between Greece and the Near East.

68. It is a matter of debate whether this was a deliberate and brilliant innovation, as Powell 1991 argues, or, like the much more restricted vowel system of the Ugaritic *alefs,* a productive misunderstanding. The latter was the position of L. H. Jeffery: "The reactions of the Etruscans, the Romans, and later inheritors from the Roman indicate that, unless the Greeks were exceptions from the usual rule, they too accepted their alphabet in the beginning uncritically from their teachers, making changes, indeed, from their very inability to pronounce exactly the Semitic names, but with no conscious desire to improve the set of letters" (1990:22). Jeffery's argument has been strengthened by Peter Daniels, who finds that cross-historically, major transformations of preexisting writing systems are linked to misunderstanding: "only when a community attempts to imitate an existing writing system without having mastered it through a traditional course of scribal training does something new and different appear" (2007:59, 60–61).

69. The translations are from Powell 1991, where editions and bibliography can be found. The inscriptions are 63A (Powell's numbering, pp. 172–73) and 65C (pp. 175–76). I thank Martha Risser for bringing these texts, whose very existence is all but censored under Jeffery's term "remarks" (Jeffery 1990:318, 323), to my attention.

70. Powell no. 66 (p. 177). Powell notes how the inscriptions are continuous with, but go beyond, other Greek combinations of dance, performance, and sexuality: "The surprising confluence of agonistic dance, *poiesis,* hexametric expression, and early alphabetic writing found on the Dipylon oinochoe and on the Cup of Nestor reappears here, but interestingly amplified by explicit reference to homosexual *charis* served by excellence in the dance" (1991:172).

71. This dating is confirmed by a convergence of Greek historical tradition and epigraphic evidence (Thomas 1992:66).

72. Svenbro 1993:17; for his interpretation 1993:8–25.

73. A large number of studies have nuanced the essential work of Alt 1966 (for a useful contribution see Watts 1999) but the value of his essential formal insight into the shift in person remains.

74. From Samaria: Ahituv 2004:245, from the Ophel Ahituv 2005:21–23, from the City of David Ahituv 2004:20–21, and now a new fragment from the City of David, Reich and Shukron 2008. For a thoughtful argument that this absence is in fact part of a significant pattern, see Rendsburg 2007, with the caveat that the latest City of David fragment may contain a king's name.

75. Translating with Parker 1997:37. The presence of a smoothed area of stone above the current inscription is open to various explanations: a planned relief-carving or historical preamble, a misjudgment of the space that would be required for the cur-

rent inscription. What it cannot plausibly represent is the first part of a standard royal monument, of which the present text is the continuation. It is the king or his god who assumes responsibility for all the kingdom's actions in the existing Iron Age West Semitic royal inscriptions.

76. I am aware of one exception in the entire corpus of ancient Near Eastern cuneiform and alphabetic inscriptions: the foundation brick from Seleucid Uruk, dated to the time of Antiochus IV (175–64 B.C.E.), in which the administrator Anu-uballit-Kephalon claims to have rebuilt a temple that was originally built by the semidivine sage Adapa. For discussion, see Doty 1998.

77. McCarter insightfully characterizes the language as a local instantiation of the "common literary vehicle" of Israel, Judah, Moab, and Ammon (1980:51)—though he does not make the distinction, relevant here, between the grammar and register of poetry and those of narrative prose. He notes that, by contrast, the two pedestrian stone inscriptions from the site may be simply Aramaic, if one may judge by the relative pronoun and definite article (1980:50–51).

78. Reading *[zh] spr [bl]ʿ[m brbʿ]r ʾš ḥzh ʾlhn hʾ* with Ahituv 2004:385–407. Ahituv's reading of the deictic is the most plausible reconstruction, given that the text refers to itself again as a *spr* in line 17 of combination II (Ahituv 2004:400). The most convenient English treatment, that of Seow in Nissinen 2003, should be used with some caution. Despite the linguistic skill of the translator, the critical first line presents a typographical error and an epigraphically uncertain reading, neither of which the reader can check. For the context, McCarter's characterization of rubrics as "for passages referring to the inscription itself, its composition, its utilization, and so on" is apposite (1980:49). These are precisely what linguists would call *metapragmatic* uses, ones that tell the reader what to do with the text.

79. My translation of the text as edited in Ahituv 2004:385–407.

80. I owe this point to Ryan Byrne, discussed in Byrne, N.D.

81. For biblical parallels, see Ahituv 2004:242–44, whose epigraphic reading is followed here, translating the four best-preserved lines (2'–3', 5'–6'), and avoiding Ahituv's plausible but uncertain emendation of line 4'.

82. The translation follows the fluid rendering of Pardee 2002:79, with alteration of the divine name. On the significance of the letter, see the study of Schniedewind 2000b on what he terms the letter of a "literate" (in scare quotes) soldier. Though based on some uncertain arguments (his description of the letter as "scrawled" [2000b:157] bolsters the claim that the soldier himself wrote it but contradicts Cross's characterization of the script [2003:132] as "skilled and elegant"), his point is well made by the title's typography. The scare quotes emphasize that the letter's composer is not literate in the way we would understand it. His nonstandard grammar and formulas suggest that the proud soldier's familiarity with writing is not that of the first ideal type of user of writing detailed above, but tends toward the farther end of the spectrum in which a pragmatic use of writing, confined to a narrow spectrum of genres, is the norm. Hoshayahu's skills and attitude are illuminating examples of the broad *ideological* base of writing in late Iron Age Israel.

83. The translation follows Pardee but avoids his explanation (2002:76n14) for the three parties connected to the prophet's letter, which seems convoluted. The suggestion

of Cross (2003:132) that the letter was a record made by Tobyahu of an oral prophecy is more straightforward and in line with attested Near Eastern practice. Cf. Jeremiah 29 for the idea that a letter's content can be shortened in reporting.

84. In the Assyrian collection of oracles supporting the king, there is a single address to a collective human audience, SAA 9 3.2, which begins, "[List]en, O Assyrians!" but the content is straightforwar pro-monarchic political propoganda. For the text, see Nissinen, ed. 2003:119.

85. To be more precise, the letter's circulation describes an arc in terms of status: while the prophecy seems to have been delivered to the king's servant, thus entering writing at a high level, it has presumably moved downward with its distribution to the untitled Shallum, and has certainly reached a middle or lower level in Hoshayahu, who sends it back up to his commander.

86. The events of the letter occur in the territory of the Hana "tent-dwellers" near Mari, at either Saggaratum or the Saggaratum gate of Terqa (for these issues, see Nissinen 2003:39).

87. For the analysis, see Charpin 1992:22.

88. For further, more physical examples of these "object lessons," see, for example, Isaiah 8:1–4; Hosea 1–3; Jeremiah 13, 18:1–17, 19; Ezekiel 4, 5.

89. A rich exploration of the intellectual world of such a community can be found in Benjamin Sommer's study (1998) of how the thinkers behind Second Isaiah read other Hebrew texts, including early elements of the Torah and Jeremiah, which they already considered sacred.

90. Ahituv 2004:143–149.

91. For the succession oath of Essarhaddon's direction at a broad listening audience of citizenry, see the text edited in Parpola and Watanabe 1988.

92. As reconstructed by Gershevitch, at least.

93. See the references in del Olmo Lete and Sanmartín 2004 q.v., and for the Levantine context of proclamations, see Millard 1999b.

94. On the axial age, see, for example, Eisenstadt 1986, and for a critique Pollock 2005.

95. Following results that were popular in European biblical criticism but completely lacking in empirical anchoring, Grottanelli dates this shift to the Persian periods. But as the Mari texts show, this form of political communication does not arise ex nihilo in the Persian period, and it is already attested in the Iron Age contact between West Semitic poetic tradition and alphabetic writing. Yet it only entered the cuneiform archives by accident, when one of these West Semitic tribes conquered an Old Babylonian state.

96. Machinist's presentation builds on his previous work (1983, with reference to Wildberger's independent notice of some of the wordplay). He has further noted (orally, February 2005, at the Margins of Writing conference) that First Isaiah may be playing on a widespread hybrid political consciousness, in which local rulers have one status in their own vernacular political system and language, and a second, reversed status in the larger cosmopolitan framework of empire. Thus Isaiah is on the one hand *recognizing* a situation like the one at Tell Fekeriye where the local vassal, Hadad-Yis'i, is *mlk*, "king," in the local Aramaic text but merely *šakinmātu*, "governor," in the As-

syrian text. But at the same time he is exploiting this translational logic through a play on two cognates with different political meanings in Hebrew and Assyrian. To elaborate Machinist's interpretation further: First Isaiah's implication is that the true framework is one in which what are *melakîm*, "kings," for the Assyrians are really God's *malku*'s "officials" (subordinate to the king) and the Assyrian *šarru*'s, "kings" merely serve as God's *śarîm*, "commanders."

97. For the Lord's address to "my people," see Isaiah 10:24; Isaiah, or perhaps the unified speaking voice of Isaiah and the Lord, addresses them as "my people" in the previous utterance (10:2), which does not refer to Assyria.

98. A more positive version of this participation in the storm god's victory is evident at Ugarit and in the archaic political theology of Psalms 2 and 89:1–37; for a provocative overview, see Wyatt 1996.

99. The theory is derived from Jacob Taubes's exegesis of St. Paul (2004), following in the footsteps of Karl Barth, Franz Rosenzweig, and perhaps ultimately Paul (for negative political theology in Barth and Rosenzweig, simpler than Isaiah's because it dismisses all earthly power without political evaluation, see Lilla 2007:270–76). Taubes never elaborated the theory fully, and I take the term from the interpretation of his work by Marin Terpstra and Theo de Wit (1997).

100. In seeing the political theology of the Judean monarchy as having archaic roots known from West Semitic culture of the Late Bronze Age, I follow the Cross school, which must be correct at least from a typological point of view. A critique, more common in Europe, which sees this theology as exilic or later, appears on the surface to have two major weaknesses: first is that a precise dating requires acceptance of a network of unverifiable assumptions (this difficulty is, by itself, no more or less problematic than the Cross school's early dating), none of which can be confirmed or denied with currently available data. On the problems inherent to this network of assumptions, see the judicious overview of Römer and de Pury 2000, esp. 72–74. The second, more serious one is that it is inadequate to explain the long-term history of culture in Israel from which the text inevitably springs. The existence of an old West Semitic myth of kingship with a claim to cosmic foundation in the storm god's victory over the sea is not in doubt, nor is the idea that the replication of this victory on the earthly level represented the re-foundation of kingship (in addition to Cross 1973, see M. S. Smith 1994 and Wyatt 1996). Thus, while the particular date at which texts such as 2 Samuel 7, Psalm 2, and Psalm 89 were configured is important, a late dating has precisely the same explanatory problem as an early dating: to account for the myth's transmission in a political context. Judean royal ritual is not the only possible context of transmission for this myth, but it is the most plausible, and quite difficult to deny completely.

101. It should be emphasized that this implied collective is not merely a grammatical effect of the second-person plural address. In fact the grammatical number of this second-person is irregular, does not correspond to any commonly agreed-upon editorial stream, and may well be at least partly poetic or rhetorical (see the pioneering work of Minette de Tillesse 1962 and the useful summary of Römer and de Pury 2000). The morphology of the addressee should be read alongside other indicators such as the descriptions of the collective audience in the narrative scenes of lawgiving and covenant-making in Deuteronomy.

CONCLUSION

1. Petrarch was actually speaking in favor of Rome. He made his original comment, *Quid est enim aliud omnis historia, quam Romania laus?* ("For what is all of history but the praise of Rome?") (Petrarca 2003:416–17) in an invective defending Italy. Foucault makes him ask a more interesting question to set up Foucault's claims about Roman history ending at the dawn of modernity. Ironically, Petrarch was arguably the first to see an end to antiquity. He famously set up a distinction between antiquity and what would follow it: an irrational "ancient history," in which he still saw himself living, and an enlightened "new history" yet to come.

2. The linguist Emile Benveniste (1971) made the groundbreaking analysis of the difference between the first and second persons, which are mutually entailing, and the third person, which does not entail interlocutors (leading Benveniste to refer to it as a "nonperson").

3. These three ideal types are used here heuristically, and with a note of irony. In the Protestant history of biblical studies, they sometimes played the role of a dialectical trinity, with a vital nationalistic history being ossified into a merely formal law and then redeemed by the corrective spiritual impulse of prophecy. As T. Römer and A. de Pury point out (2000:72–74), this Protestant historiography, or theology of history, is neatly replicated in the redaction-critical theory that posits DtrH, DtrN, and DtrP—an original history, with later nomistic and prophetic redactions. The typology is nonetheless useful for three reasons: (1) they were real genres, in that their designations actually name well-attested patterns of evidence in the ancient Near East; (2) these patterns also appear in the Bible, in recognizable but meaningfully new ways; (3) their very familiarity makes them both easy to grasp and suitable to turn in a new direction.

4. In this way it is separate from the writing of chronicles, lists of events without narrative form, which were also produced in Mesopotamian temples.

5. West Semitic culture, of course, hardly lacked distinctive narrative poetry, as Ugarit abundantly attests. The point is that epic, as a broad generic form, was common to most of the ancient Near East.

6. Texts like the Xanthos inscription, showing a Persian royal edict translated into Aramaic, Greek, and Lydian, suggest the possibility of earlier imperial legal monuments in West Semitic. Similarly, the Punic Marseilles tariff, with its fees for ritual sacrifice, shows that priestly monuments could have been possible.

7. Fraade 2006.

8. The simultaneously ideal and real dimension of this practice is exemplified by the way that the assembly unites the two bases of kinship: the discourse of consanguinity (stories of shared genealogy and ancestors) and the experience of consociation (living and talking with one another).

9. Thus critiques like that of Weinfeld 1973 add useful parallels but limit their value by concentrating on decontextualized similarities in generic form (and skipping freely over periods of more than five hundred years, from Hittite instructions to Neo-Assyrian and Hellenistic Babylonian ordinances).

10. In n120 Alt explains that the covenant renewal ceremony he imagines is essentially identical with the one reconstructed as happening on Sukkot by Sigmund Mowinckel (and still held by Frank Moore Cross forty years later) and observes that

even at the time of Ezra the reading and pledge to obey takes place at the feast of Tabernacles (Nehemiah 8).

11. For the framing of Moses as speaker of law in Torah, see the intricate analysis by Polzin 1993; for the scribes and Levitical priests as tradents, see van der Toorn 2007 with bibliography.

12. For this theme in Mesopotamian incantations, see Sanders 2001.

13. Van der Toorn describes Jeremiah 36, the story of the publication, destruction, and rewriting of prophecy, as "designed to legitimize a scroll containing prophecies attributed to Jeremiah" (2007:77). He also describes the editing of Deuteronomy as done, in the first pre-exilic edition around 622, "to legitimize the measures taken by the king" (that is, Josiah; van der Toorn 2007:153) then immediately after the exile, to claim "privileged information . . . available to [the scribes] in the form of a written text . . . to legitimize the leadership they aspired to" (2007:159–60).

14. For a useful introduction, see Dozeman and Schmid 2006; in more depth, Blum 1990; Schmid 1999.

15. The forthcoming University of Chicago dissertation work of Edward Silver, "The Prophet and the Lying Pen: Jeremiah's Poetic Challenge to the Deuteronomic School," with its synthesis of linguistic anthropology and critical exegesis, promises a fuller engagement of this complexity than has been previously possible.

16. A claim explored in the greatest depth by Bernard Levinson (2008).

17. The political theorist Louis Althusser termed this event "interpellation," when an individual recognizes himself or herself as part of a social order by responding to an address from a representative of that order (the "hey, you!" moment). See the groundbreaking essay by Althusser (1997, in a usefully provocative edited volume).

18. The best exposition of the biblical ideology of reading is Boyarin 1993; a useful overview of the practice of proclamation is Millard 1999b. The richest West Semitic epigraphic example is the double publication, visual and aural, of the eighth-century Aramaic Sefire vassal treaty, which commands the parties, "Let not one word of this text be silent," and concludes, "thus we have said and thus we have written" (Sefire I A 13, B 8–9, C 1–3).

19. One could even read the history of Christendom (e.g., van Creveld 1999) from the time of Constantine to the beginnings of modern politics, as the history of the state's attempt to tip the scales between the Bible's positive Davidic and negative Deuteronomistic political theologies.

BIBLIOGRAPHY

Abou-Assaf, Ali, Pierre Bordreuil, and Alan R. Millard. 1982. *La Statue de Tell Fekheryé et son inscription bilingue assyro-araméenne.* Paris: Editions Recherche sur les civilizations.

Aharoni, Yohanan. 1981. *Arad Inscriptions.* Jerusalem: Israel Exploration Society.

Ahituv, Shmuel. 2004. *HaKetav VeHaMiktav: Handbook of Ancient Inscriptions from the Land of Israel and the Kingdoms Beyond the Jordan from the Period of the First Commonwealth.* Biblical Encyclopedia Library 21. Jerusalem: Bialik. [in Hebrew]

Albright, William F. 1934. The Cuneiform Tablet from Beth-Shemesh. BASOR 53: 18–19.

———. 1945. Some Publications Received by The Editor. BASOR 99:21–23.

———. 1960. Discussion. In *City Invincible: A Symposium on Urbanization and Cultural Development in the Ancient Near East,* ed. C. H. Kraeling and Robert M. Adams, 94–123. Chicago: University of Chicago Press.

———. 1964. The Beth Shemesh Tablet in Alphabetic Cuneiform. BASOR 173:51–53.

Alt, Albrecht. 1966. The Origins of Israelite Law. In *Essays on Old Testament History and Religion,* trans. R. A. Wilson, 79–132. Oxford: Basil Blackwell.

Althusser, Louis. 1997. Ideology and Ideological State Apparatuses: Notes Toward an Investigation. In *Mapping Ideology,* ed. Slavoj Zizek, 100–140. London: Verso.

Amadasi, Guzzo, Maria Giulia, Johannes Friedrich, and Wolfgang Röllig, with Werner Mayer. 1999. *Phönizisch-Punische Grammatik.* Analecta Orientalia 55. Rome: Pontificio Istituto Biblico.

Amory, Patrick. 1997. *People and Identity in Ostrogothic Italy, 489–554.* Cambridge: Cambridge University Press.

Anderson, Benedict. 1991. *Imagined Communities: Reflections on the Origin and Spread of Nationalism.* London: Verso. [1st ed. 1983]

Arends, Jacques, Pieter Muysken, and Norval Smith, eds. 1995. *Pidgins and Creoles: An Introduction.* Creole Language Library 15. Amsterdam and Philadelphia: J. Benjamins.

Arnaud, Daniel. 2000. Une bêche-de-mer antique, La langue des marchands à Tyr à la fin du XIIIe siècle. *Aula Orientalis* 17–18:143–66.

———. 2001. Lettres, et annexe: le jargon épistolaire de Sidon. In Yon and Arnaud, eds. 2001:257–322.

Aubet, Maria Eugenia. 2001. *The Phoenicians and the West: Politics, Colonies and Trade,* trans. Mary Turton. New York: Cambridge University Press.

Auerbach, Erich. 1953. *Mimesis: The Representation of Reality in Western Literature,* trans. Willard Trask. Garden City, NY: Doubleday.

Aufrecht, Walter. 1989. *A Corpus of Ammonite Inscriptions.* Lewiston: Edwin Mellen.

Avigad, Nahman, and Benjamin Sass. 1997. *Corpus of West Semitic Stamp Seals*. Jerusalem: Israel Academy of Sciences and Humanities; Israel Exploration Society; Institute of Archaeology, the Hebrew University of Jerusalem.

Bakker, P., and Y. Matras, eds. 2003. *The Mixed Language Debate*. Berlin: Mouton De Gruyter.

Balentine, Samuel E. 2002. *Leviticus*. Louisville, KY: John Knox.

Bartlett, Robert. 1993. *The Making of Europe*. Princeton: Princeton University Press.

Barton, G. A. 1933. Notes on the Ain Shems Tablet. BASOR 52:5–6.

Basso, Keith. 1974. The Ethnography of Writing. In *Explorations in the Ethnography of Speaking*, ed. Richard Bauman and Joel Sherzer, 425–32. London and New York: Cambridge University Press.

Bauman, Richard, and Charles Briggs. 2003. *Voices of Modernity: Language Ideologies and the Politics of Inequality*. Cambridge: Cambridge University Press.

Baurain, C., et al., eds. 1991. *Phoinikieia Grammata: lire et écrire en Méditerranée*. Namur: Société des etudes classiques.

Beaulieu, Paul-Alain. 2006. Official and Vernacular Languages: The Shifting Sands of Imperial and Cultural Identities in First-Millennium B.C. Mesopotamia. In Sanders, ed. 2006:187–216.

Bell, David. 1996. Recent Works on Early Modern French National Identity. *Journal of Modern History* 68:84–113.

Benveniste, Emile. 1971. The Nature of Pronouns. In *Problems in General Linguistics*, 217–22. Coral Gables, FLA: University of Miami Press.

Besnier, Niko. 1995. *Literacy, Emotion, and Authority: Reading and Writing on a Polynesian Atoll*. Cambridge: Cambridge University Press.

Bietak, Manfred. 1998. Gedanken zur Ursache der ägyptisierenden Einflüsse in Nordsyrien in der Zweiten Zwischenzeit. In *Stationen, Beiträge zur Kulturgeschichte Ägyptens* [Festschrift R. Stadelmann], ed. H. Guksch and D. Polz, 165–76. Mainz: P. von Zabern.

Biran, Avraham, and Joseph Naveh. 1995. The Tel Dan Inscription: A New Fragment. IEJ 45:1–18.

Birnbaum, S. 1939. The Lachish Ostraca I. PEQ 71:20–23.

Blackwell, Thomas. 1970. *An Enquiry into the Life and Writings of Homer*. New York: Garland. [1735]

Blair, Hugh. 1970a. *A Critical Dissertation on the Poems of Ossian, Son of Fingal*. New York: Garland. [1765]

———. 1970b. *Lectures on Rhetoric and Belles-Lettres*. New York: Garland. [1785]

Bloch-Smith, Liz. 2003. Israelite Ethnicity in Iron I: Archaeology Preserves what is Remembered and what is Forgotten in Israel's History. JBL 122:401–25.

Blum, Erhard. 1990. *Studien zur Komposition des Pentateuch*. Beihefte zur Zeitschrift für die alttestamentliche Wissenschaft 189. Berlin and New York: Walter de Gruyter.

Bourdieu, Pierre. 1991. *Language and Symbolic Power*, trans. Gino Raymond and Matthew Adamson. Cambridge, MA: Harvard University Press.

Bordreuil, Pierre. 1979. L'inscription phénicienne de Sarafand en cunéiformes alphabétiques. UF 11:63–68.

———. 1981. Cunéiformes alphabétiques non canoniques I: La tablette alphabétique senestroverse RS 22.03. *Syria* 58:301–10.

———. 1983. Cunéiformes alphabétiques non canoniques II: A propos de l'épigraphe de Hala Sultan Tekké. *Semitica* 33:7–15.
———, and Dennis Pardee. 1984. Le Sceau Nominal de ʿAmmīyiḏtamrou, Roi d'Ougarit. *Syria* 61:11–14.
———, and Dennis Pardee. 1993. Le Combat de Balu avec Yammu d'apres les textes ougaritiques. MARI 7:63–70.
———, and Dennis Pardee, 1995. Un abécédaire du type sud-sémitique découverte en 1988 dans les fouilles archéologiques françaises de Ras Shamra-Ougarit. *Comptes rendus de l'Académie des Inscriptions et Belles-lettres*:855–860.
———, and Dennis Pardee. 2001. Textes Aphabétiques en ougaritique: 8. Abécédaire. In Yon and Arnaud, eds. 2001:341–48.
———, and Dennis Pardee. 2004. *Manuel d'ougaritique*. 2 vols. Paris: Geuthner.
Bottéro, Jean. 1977. Les Noms de Marduk, l'ecriture et la 'logique' en Mesopotamie ancienne. In *Essays on the Ancient Near East in Memory of Jacob Joel Finkelstein*, ed. Maria De Jong Ellis, 5–28. Memoirs of the Connecticut Academy of Arts and Sciences XIX. Hamden, CT: Archon.
———. 1992. Writing and Dialectics, or the Progress of Knowledge. In *Mesopotamia: Writing, Reasoning and the Gods*, 87–102. Chicago: University of Chicago Press.
Boyarin, Daniel. 1993. Placing Reading: Ancient Israel and Medieval Europe. In *The Ethnography of Reading*, ed. Jonathan Boyarin, 10–37. Berkeley: University of California Press.
Boyer, Dominic. 2007. *Understanding Media: A Popular Philosophy*. Chicago: Prickly Paradigm.
Brettler, Marc Zvi. 1995. *The Creation of History in Ancient Israel*. London: Routledge.
Brinkman, J. A. 1995. Glassner's Mesopotamian Chronicles. JAOS 115:667–70.
Buber, Martin. 1967. Myth in Judaism. In *On Judaism*, 95–107. New York: Schocken.
Buck-Morss, Susan. 2003. *Thinking Past Terror: Islamism and Critical Theory on the Left*. London and New York: Verso.
Budd, Philip J. 1996. *Leviticus: Based on the New Revised Standard Version*. London: M. Pickering; Grand Rapids, MI: Eerdmans.
Bunimovitz, Shlomo, and Zvi Lederman. 1993. Beth-Shemesh. In Stern, ed. 1993 1:249–53.
Burkert, Walter. 1992. *The Orientalizing Revolution: Near Eastern Influence on Greek Culture in the Early Archaic Age*, trans. Walter Burkert and Margaret E. Pinder. Cambridge, MA: Harvard University Press.
Byrne, Ryan. 2007. The Refuge of Scribalism in Iron I Palestine. BASOR 345:1–31.
———. f/c. *Statecraft in Ancient Israel: An Archaeology of the Political Sciences*. Winona Lake, IN: Eisenbrauns.
———. N.D. Apiru, Hebrew, and the Discourse of Patrimony. Unpublished manuscript.
Çagirgan, Galip, and W. G. Lambert. 1991–93. The Late Babylonian Kislimu Ritual for Esagil. *Journal of Cuneiform Studies* 43–45:89–106.
Carr, David M. 2005. *Writing on the Tablet of the Heart: Origins of Scripture and Literature*. New York: Oxford University Press.
Cassuto, Umberto. 1943. The Israelite Epic. *Keneset* 8:21–142. [in Hebrew]
———. 1975. *Biblical and Oriental Studies*. 2 vols. Jerusalem: Magnes.

Caton, Steven C. 1987. Power, Persuasion, and Language: A Critique of the Segmentary Model in the Middle East. *International Journal of Middle East Studies* 19:77–101.

———. 1990. *"Peaks of Yemen I Summon": Poetry as Cultural Practice in a North Yemeni Tribe.* Berkeley: University of California Press.

Chambers, James T. 1995. Review of Thomas 1992. *History of Reading News* 19. http://www.historyliteracy.org/scripts/search_display.php?Article_ID=69.

Chambers, J. K., and Peter Trudgill. 1998. *Dialectology.* 2nd ed. Cambridge: Cambridge University Press.

Charpin, Dominique. 1992. Le contexte historique et géographique des prophéties dans les texts retrouvés à Mari. *Bulletin of the Canadian Society for Mesopotamian Studies* 23:21–31.

———. 2004. Histoire politique du Proche-Orient Amorrite (2002–1595). In *Mesopotamien: Die altbabylonische Zeit,* ed. Dominique Charpin, Dietz Otto Edzard, and Marten Stol, 5–480. Fribourg: Academic; Göttingen: Vandenhoeck & Ruprecht.

Charpin, Dominique, and Jean-Marie Durand. 1986. 'Fils de Sim'al': Les origins tribales des rois de Mari. *Revue d'assyriologie* 80:141–81.

Clanchy, M. T. 1993. *From Memory to Written Record: England 1066–1307.* Oxford: Blackwell. [1st ed. 1983]

Cohen, Mark E. 1993. *The Cultic Calendars of the Ancient Near East.* Bethesda: CDL.

Cohen, Rudolph. 1981. Excavations at Kadesh-barnea 1976–78. BA 44:93–105.

Collins, John J. 1993. *Daniel: A Commentary on the Book of Daniel.* Minneapolis: Fortress.

Cooper, Jerrold. 2001. Sumerian and Semitic Writing in Most Ancient Syro-Mesopotamia. In van Lerberghe and Voet, eds. 2001:61–77.

Cross, Frank Moore. 1968. The Canaanite Cuneiform Tablet from Taanach. BASOR 190:41–46.

———. 1973. *Canaanite Myth and Hebrew Epic.* Cambridge, MA: Harvard University Press.

———. 1990. The Invention and Development of the Alphabet. In *The Origins of Writing,* ed. Wayne M. Senner, 77–90. Lincoln: University of Nebraska Press.

———. 1998. *From Epic to Canon.* Cambridge, MA: Harvard University Press.

———. 2003. *Leaves from an Epigrapher's Notebook: Collected Papers in Hebrew and West Semitic Palaeography and Epigraphy.* Winona Lake, IN: Eisenbrauns.

———, and David Noel Freedman. 1952. *Early Hebrew Orthography: A Study of the Epigraphic Evidence.* American Oriental Series 36. New Haven: American Oriental Society.

———, and David Noel Freedman. 1975. *Studies in Ancient Yahwistic Poetry.* Society of Biblical Literature Dissertation series 21. Missoula, MT: Scholars Press.

———, and Thomas O. Lambdin. 1960. An Ugaritic Abecedary and the Origins of the Proto-Canaanite Alphabet. BASOR 160:21–26.

Daniels, Peter T. 2007 *Littera ex occidente*: Toward a Functional History of Writing. In C. Miller, ed. 2007:53–68.

Darnell, J., F. W. Dobbs-Allsopp, M. Lundberg, P. K. McCarter, and B. Zuckerman. 2004. *Two Early Alphabetic Inscriptions from the Wadi el-Ḥ ˇôl, AASOR* 59.2. Boston: American Schools of Oriental Research.

Davies, G. I. 1995. Were there Schools in Ancient Israel? In *Wisdom in Ancient Israel: Essays in Honour of J. A. Emerton*, ed. John Day, Robert P. Gordon, and H. G. M. Williamson, 199–211. Cambridge: Cambridge University Press.

Davila, James. 1994. Dialectology in Biblical Hebrew: A North Israelite Dialect? Synchronic and Diachronic Considerations. SBL seminar paper http://www.st-andrews.ac.uk/divinity/hebrew_dialectology_94.htm.

Davis, Natalie Zemon. 1975. *Society and Culture in Early Modern France*. Stanford: Stanford University Press.

Davis, Thomas W. 2004. *Shifting Sands: The Rise and Fall of Biblical Archaeology*. Oxford and New York: Oxford University Press.

de Jong, Mayke. 2005. Charlemagne's Church. In *Charlemagne: Empire and Society*, ed. Joanna Story, 103–35. Manchester and New York: Manchester University Press.

de Moor, J. C., and P. Sanders. 1991. An Ugaritic Expiation Ritual and its Old Testament Parallels. UF 23:283–300.

Demsky, Aaron. 1990. The Education of Canaanite Scribes in the Mesopotamian Cuneiform Tradition. In *Bar-Ilan Studies in Assyriology*, ed. Jacob Klein and Aaron Skaist, 157–70. Jerusalem: Bar-Ilan University Press.

Demsky, Aaron, and Meir Bar-Ilan. 1988. Writing in Ancient Israel and Early Judaism. In *Mikra: Text, Translation, Reading and Interpretation of the Hebrew Bible in Ancient Judaism and Early Christianity*, ed. Martin Jan Mulder, 2–38. Assen: Van Gorcum; Philadelphia: Fortress.

Dietrich, M. 1996. Aspects of the Babylonian Impact on Ugaritic Literature and Religion. In *Ugarit, Religion and Culture, ed.* N. Wyatt et al., 33–47. Münster: Ugarit-Verlag.

———, and O. Loretz. 1988a. *Die Keilalphabete: Die phönizisch-kanaanäischen und altarabischen Alphabete in Ugarit*. ALASP 1. Münster: Ugarit-Verlag.

———, and O. Loretz. 1988b. Die Alphabettafel aus Bet Semes und die ursprüngliche Heimat der Ugariter. In *Ad bene et fideliter seminandum* [Fs. Deller], ed. Gerlinde Mauer and Ursula Magen, 61–85. Neukirchen: Butzon & Bercker Kevalaer.

———, and O. Loretz. 1989. The Cuneiform Alphabets of Ugarit. UF 21:110–12.

Diringer, David, with Reinhold Regensburger. 1968. *The Alphabet: A Key to the History of Mankind*. 3rd ed. London: Hutchinson. [1st ed. 1948]

Doty, L. T. 1998. Nikarchos and Kephalon. In *A Scientific Humanist: Studies in Memory of Abraham Sachs*, ed. E. Leichty, Maria de J. Ellis, and Pamela Gerardi, 95–118. Occasional Publications of the Samuel Noah Kramer Fund 9. Philadelphia: University Museum.

Douglas, Mary. 2003. The Go-Away Goat. In *The Book of Leviticus: Composition and Reception*, ed. Rolf Rendtorff and Robert Kugler, 121–41. VTSupp. 93. Leiden: Brill.

Dozeman, Thomas B., and Konrad Schmid, eds. 2006. *A Farewell to the Yahwist?: The Composition of the Pentateuch in Recent European Interpretation*. Atlanta: Society of Biblical Literature.

Driver, G. R. 1960. Abbreviations in the Massoretic Text. *Textus* 1:112–31.

Durand, J.-M. 1988. *Archives épistolaires de Mari* 1/1. ARM 26/1. Paris: Éditions Recherche sur les Civilisations.

———. 1992. Unité et diversités au Proche-Orient à l'époque ammorite. In *Le circulation des biens, des personnes et des idées dans le Proche-Orient ancient,* ed. Dominique Charpin and Francis Joannès, 97–128. CRRAI 38. Paris: Éditions Recherche sur les Civilisations.

———. 1993. Le mythologème du combat entre le dieu de l'orage et la mer en Mésopotamie. M.A.R.I. 7:41–61.

———. 2003. Assyriologie. *Annuaire du Collège de France* 2001–2:741–61.

Ellison, John Lee. 2002. *A Paleographic Study of the Alphabetic Cuneiform Texts from Ras Shamra/Ugarit.* PhD diss., Harvard University.

Emerton, John A. 2006. The Kingdoms of Judah and Israel and Ancient Hebrew History Writing. In *Biblical Hebrew in Its Northwest Semitic Setting: Typological and Historical Perspectives,* ed. Steven E. Fassberg and Avi Hurvitz, 33–50. Winona Lake, IN: Eisenbrauns; Jerusalem: Magnes.

Eskenazi, Tamara Cohn, Gary A. Phillips, and David Jobling, eds. 2003. *Levinas and Biblical Studies.* Society of Biblical Literature Semeia Studies 43. Atlanta: Society of Biblical Literature.

Fasolt, Constantin. 2004. *The Limits of History.* Chicago: University of Chicago Press.

Finkelstein, Israel, and Neil Asher Silberman. 2001. *The Bible Unearthed: Archaeology's New Vision of Ancient Israel and the Origin of its Sacred Texts.* New York: The Free Press.

Finkelstein, J. J. 1966. The Genealogy of the Hammurapi Dynasty. *Journal of Cuneiform Studies* 20:95–118.

Fishbane, Michael. 1985. *Biblical Interpretation in Ancient Israel.* New York: Oxford University Press.

———. 2003. *Biblical Myth and Rabbinic Mythmaking.* New York: Oxford University Press.

———. 2004. Textuality and Subsurface Traditions. *Jewish Quarterly Review.* 94:3–5.

Fitzmyer, Joseph. 1995. *The Aramaic Inscriptions of Sefire.* Rev. ed. Rome: Editrice Pontificio Istituto Biblico.

Fleming, Daniel. 1992. *The Installation of Baal's High Priestess at Emar: A Window on Ancient Syrian Religion.* Harvard Semitic Studies 42. Atlanta, GA: Scholars Press.

———. 1998. Mari and the Possibilities of Biblical Memory. RA 92:41–78.

———. 2004. *Democracy's Ancient Ancestors: Mari and Early Collective Governance.* Cambridge: Cambridge University Press.

Foucault, Michel. 2003. *Society Must Be Defended: Lectures at the Collège de France, 1975–76,* ed. Mauro Bertani and Alessandro Fontana; trans. David Macey. New York: Picador.

Fraade, Steven. 2006. Deuteronomy and Polity in the Early History of Jewish Interpretation. *Cardozo Law Review* 28:245–58.

Frayne, Douglas. 1990. *Old Babylonian period 2003–1595 BC.* Royal inscriptions of Mesopotamia. Early periods vol. 4. Toronto and Buffalo: University of Toronto Press.

Frazer, James G. 1913. *The Scapegoat.* Part IV, vol. IX of *The Golden Bough.* 2nd ed. London: Macmillan.

Friedman, Richard Elliott. 1997. *Who Wrote the Bible?* New York: HarperCollins.

Fukuyama, Francis. 1989. The End of History? *National Interest* 16:3–18.

Fulton, Rachel. 2002. *From Judgment to Passion: Devotion to Christ and the Virgin Mary, 800–1200*. New York: Columbia University Press.

Gagarin, Michael. 2002. Letters of the Law: Written Texts in Archaic Greek Law. In *Written Texts and the Rise of Literate Culture in Ancient Greece*, ed. Harvey Yunis, 59–77. Cambridge: Cambridge University Press.

Gal, Susan, and Judith Irvine. 2000. Language Ideology and Linguistic Differentiation. In Kroskrity, ed. 2000:35–83.

Garelli, Paul. 1965. Tablettes cappadociennes de collections diverses (*suite*). RA 59:149–76.

Garr, Randall. 1985. *Dialect Geography of Syria-Palestine 1000–586 B.C.E.* Philadelphia: University of Pennsylvania.

Garrett, Paul B. 2006. Language Contact and Contact Languages. In *A Companion to Linguistic Anthropology*, ed. Alessandro Duranti, 46–72. Malden, MA: Blackwell.

Gelb, I. J. 1980. *Computer-Aided Analysis of Amorite*. Assyriological Studies 21. Chicago: Oriental Institute of the University of Chicago.

Geller, Stephen A. 1992. Blood Cult: An Interpretation of the Priestly Work of the Pentateuch. *Prooftexts* 12:99–124.

Gellner, Ernest. 1983. *Nations and Nationalism*. Ithaca: Cornell University Press.

———. 1995. Tribe and State in the Middle East. In *Anthropology and Politics: Revolutions in the Sacred Grove*, 180–201. Oxford and Cambridge, MA: Blackwell.

———. 1996. Ernest Gellner's Reply: 'Do Nations Have Navels?' *Nations and Nationalism* 2:366–70.

Geoghegan, Jeffrey C. 2005. Additional Evidence for a Deuteronomistic Redaction of the 'Tetrateuch.' *Catholic Biblical Quarterly* 67:405–21.

George, Andrew R. 2003. *The Babylonian Gilgamesh Epic: Introduction, Critical Edition and Cuneiform Texts*. Vol. 1. Oxford: Oxford University Press.

Gershevitch, I. 1979. The Alloglottography of Old Persian. *Transactions of the Philological Society*: 114–90.

Gerstenberger, Erhard S. 1996. *Leviticus: A Commentary*, trans. Douglas W. Stott. Louisville, KY: Westminster John Knox.

Gianto, Agustinus. 1990. *Word Order Variation in the Akkadian of Byblos*. Studia Pohl. Series maior. 15. Roma: Pontificio Istituto Biblico, 1990.

———. 2001. Amarna Akkadian as a Contact Language. In Van Lerberghe and Voet, eds. 2001:123–32.

Gilula, Mordechai. 1976. An Inscription in Egyptian Hieratic from Lachish. *Tel Aviv* 3:107–8.

Ginzburg, Carolo. 1999. *History, Rhetoric, and Proof: The Menachem Stern Lectures in History*. Hanover, NH: University Press of New England.

Girard, Rene. 1986. *The Scapegoat*. Baltimore: Johns Hopkins University Press.

Gitin, S., T. Dothan, and J. Naveh. 1997. A Royal Dedicatory Inscription from Ekron. IEJ 47:1–16.

Glassner, Jean-Jacques. 2004. *Mesopotamian Chronicles*. Writings from the Ancient World 19. Atlanta: Scholars.

Goldwasser, O. 1991. An Egyptian Scribe from Lachish and the Hieratic Tradition of the Hebrew Kingdoms. *Tel Aviv* 18:248–53.

———. 2006. Canaanites Reading Hieroglyphs. Horus is Hathor?—The Invention of the Alphabet in Sinai. *Ägypten und Levante* 16:121–60.

Goldziher, Ignaz. 2006. The Arabic Tribes and Islam. In *Muslim Studies*, ed. S. M. Stern and C. R. Barber; trans. S. M. Stern, 45–97. New Brunswick, NJ: Aldine Transaction.

Golka, Friedemann. 1993. *The Leopard's Spots*. Edinburgh: T & T Clark.

Good, Robert M. 1983. *The Sheep of his Pasture: A Study of the Hebrew Noun ʿAmm and Its Semitic Cognates*. Harvard Semitic Monographs 29. Chico, CA: Scholars.

Goodblatt, David. 2006. *Elements of Ancient Jewish Nationalism*. New York: Cambridge University Press.

Goody, Jack, ed. 1968. *Literacy in Traditional Societies*. Cambridge: Cambridge University Press.

Goren, Yuval, Israel Finkelstein, and Nadav Naʾaman. 2002. The Seat of Three Disputed Canaanite Rulers. *Tel Aviv* 29:221–37.

———. 2004. *Inscribed in Clay: Provenance Studies of the Amarna Tablets and other Ancient Near Eastern Texts*. Tel Aviv: Emery and Claire Yass Publications in Archaeology.

Gorman, F. H. 1990. *The Ideology of Ritual: Space, Time and Status in the Priestly Theology*. Sheffield: JSOT.

Gottwald, Norman K. 1997. Triumphalist versus Anti-Triumphalist Versions of Early Israel: A Response to Articles by Lemche and Dever in Volume 4 1996. *Currents in Research: Biblical Studies* 5:15–42.

Grafton, Anthony. 2002. *Bring Out your Dead*. Cambridge, MA: Harvard University Press.

Grant, Elihu. 1933. Beth Shemesh in 1933. BASOR 52:3–5.

———. 1934. *Rumeileh being Ain Shems Excavations*. Part III. Haverford: Haverford College.

Green, Barbara. 2000. *Mikhail Bakhtin and Biblical Scholarship: An Introduction*. Atlanta: Society of Biblical Literature.

Greenfield, Jonas. 1969. The Zakir Inscription and the Danklied. In *Proceedings of the Fifth World Congress of Jewish Studies*, vol. 1, 174–91. Jerusalem: World Union of Jewish Studies.

———. 1974. Standard Literary Aramaic. In *Actes du premier Congrès international de linguistique sémitique et chamito-sémitique, Paris, 16–19 juillet 1969*, ed. André Caquot and David Cohen, 280–89. The Hague: Mouton.

———. 1978. The Dialects of Early Aramaic. JNES 37:93–99.

———. 1991. Of Scribes, Scripts and Languages. In Baurain et al., eds., 1991:173–85.

———, and Aaron Shaffer. 1983. Notes on the Akkadian-Aramaic Bilingual Statue from Tell Fekheriye. *Iraq* 45:109–16.

Greenstein, Edward. 1976. A Phoenician Inscription in Ugaritic Script? JANES 8:49–57.

———. 1996. The Canaanite Literary Heritage in the Writings of Hebrew Scribes. *Michmanim* 10:19–38. [in Hebrew]

Gröndahl, Frauke. 1967. *Die Personennamen der Texte aus Ugarit*. Studia Pohl 1. Rome: Typis Pontificiae Universitatis Gregorianae.

Grosby, Steven. 1995. *ᵓRM KLH* and the Worship of Hadad: A Nation of Aram? *Aram* 7:337–52.
———. 2002. *Biblical Ideas of Nationality: Ancient and Modern.* Winona Lake, IN: Eisenbrauns.
Grottanelli, Cristiano. 1999. *Kings and Prophets: Monarchic Power, Inspired Leadership, and Sacred Text in Biblical Narrative.* Oxford: Oxford University Press.
Guenée, Bernard. 1985. *States and Rulers in Later Medieval Europe,* trans. Juliet Vale. Oxford: Blackwell.
Gunkel, Hermann. 2006. *Creation and Chaos in the Primeval Era and the Eschaton: A Religio-historical Study of Genesis 1 and Revelation 12,* with contributions by Heinrich Zimmern; trans. K. William Whitney, Jr. Grand Rapids, MI: Eerdmans.
Habermas, Jürgen. 1989. *The Structural Transformation of the Public Sphere: An Inquiry into a Category of Bourgeois Society,* trans. Thomas Burger with Frederick Lawrence. Cambridge, MA: MIT Press.
Hall, Jonathan. 1997. *Ethnic Identity in Greek Antiquity.* Cambridge: Cambridge University Press.
———. 2002. *Hellenicity: Between Ethnicity and Culture.* Chicago: University of Chicago Press.
Halpern, Baruch. 2001. *David's Secret Demons: Messiah, Murderer, Traitor, King.* Grand Rapids, MI: Eerdmans.
Hamilton, Gordon J. 2006. *The Origins of the West Semitic Alphabet in Egyptian Scripts.* CBQMS 40. Washington, DC: Catholic Biblical Association of America.
Haran, Menachem. 1988. On the Diffusion of Literacy and Schools in Ancient Israel. SVT 40:81–95.
Harrison, Simon. 2003. Cultural Difference as Denied Resemblance: Reconsidering Nationalism and Ethnicity. *Comparative Studies in Society and History* 45: 343–61.
———. 2004. Forgetful and Memorious Landscapes. *Social Anthropology* 12:135–51.
Hastings, Adrian. 1997. *The Construction of Nationhood: Ethnicity, Religion, and Nationalism.* Cambridge: Cambridge University Press.
Hawkins, J. D. 2000. *Corpus of Hieroglyphic Luwian Inscriptions.* Vol. 1: Inscriptions of the Iron Age. Berlin: Walter de Gruyter.
Hawley, Robert. 2008. On the Alphabetic Scribal Curriculum at Ugarit. In *Proceedings of the 51st Rencontre Assyriologique Internationale, Held at the Oriental Institute of the University of Chicago, July 18–22, 2005,* ed. Robert D. Biggs, Jennie Myers, and Martha T. Roth, 57–68. CRRAI 51. Chicago: The Oriental Institute.
Hecker, K. 1968. *Grammatik der Kültepe-Texte.* Analecta Orientalia 44. Rome: Pontificium Institutum Biblicum.
Heltzer, Michael. 1976. *The Rural Community in Ancient Ugarit.* Wiesbaden: Reichert Verlag.
———. 2003. Comments on the Rise of Secondary States in the Iron Age Levant. JESHO 46:525–28.
Hendel, Ron. 2001. The Exodus in Biblical Memory. JBL 120:601–22.
Herder, Johann Gottfried. 1877–1913. *Sämtliche Werke,* ed. Bernhard Suphan. 33 vols. Berlin: Weidmannsche Buchhandlung.

———. 1985. *Schriften zum Alten Testament*, ed. Rudolf Smend; *Werke in Zehn Bänden, ed.* Gunter Arnold et al. Frankfurt: Deutscher Klassiker Verlag.
Herdner, A. 1946–48. A-t-il existé une variété palestinienne de l'écriture cunéiforme alphabétique? *Syria* 25:165–68.
Herzog, Ze'ev. 2002. The Fortress Mound at Tel Arad: An Interim Report. *Tel Aviv* 29:1–103.
Hess, Richard. 1993. *Amarna Personal Names*. American Schools of Oriental Research Dissertation Series 9 Winona Lake, IN: Eisenbrauns.
Hetzron, Robert, ed. 1997. *The Semitic Languages*. New York: Routledge.
Hillers, Delbert R. 1964. An Alphabetic Cuneiform Tablet from Taanach TT 433. BASOR 173:45–50.
Hillers, Delbert R., and Marsh McCall, Jr. 1976. Homeric Dictated Texts: A Reexamination of Some Near Eastern Evidence. *Harvard Studies in Classical Philology* 80:19–23.
Hirschkind, Charles. 2006. *The Ethical Soundscape: Cassette Sermons and Islamic Counterpublics*. New York: Columbia University Press.
Hobbes, Thomas. 1991. *Leviathan*, ed. Richard Tuck. Cambridge: Cambridge University Press.
Hodder, Ian. 1982. *Symbols in Action: Ethnoarchaeological Studies of Material Culture*. Cambridge: Cambridge University Press.
Hoffman, Joel M. 2004. *In the Beginning: A Short History of the Hebrew Language*. New York: New York University Press.
Hoffner, Harry. 1965. The Elkunirsa Myth Reconsidered. *Revue Hittite et Asianique* 76:5–16.
———. 1998. *Hittite Myths*. 2nd ed. Atlanta: Scholars.
Hoftijzer, J., and K. Jongeling, eds. 1995. *Dictionary of the North-West Semitic Inscriptions*. Handbuch der Orientalistik I/21. 2 vols. Leiden: Brill.
Hoftijzer, J., and G. van der Kooij, eds. 1991. *The Balaam Text from Tell Deir ʿAlla Re-evaluated*. Leiden: Brill.
Horowitz, Wayne, Takayoshi Oshima, and Seth L. Sanders. 2002. A Bibliographical List of Cuneiform Inscriptions from Canaan, Palestine/Philistia, and the Land of Israel. JAOS 122:753–66.
———. 2006. *Cuneiform in Canaan and the Land of Israel: Cuneiform Sources from the Land of Israel in Ancient Times*. Jerusalem: Israel Exploration Society and The Hebrew University.
Hudson-Williams, A. 1964. Notes on Claudius Marius Victor. *Classical Quarterly* 14:296–310.
Huehnergard, John. 1991. Remarks on the Classification of the Northwest Semitic Languages. In Hoftijzer and van der Kooij, eds. 1991:282–93.
———. 1995. What is Aramaic? *Aram* 7:261–82.
Huehnergard, John, and W. H. van Soldt. 1999. A Cuneiform Lexical Text from Ashkelon with a Canaanite Column. IEJ 49:184–92.
Huizinga, Johan. 1936. A Definition of the Concept of History. In *Philosophy and History: Essays Presented to Ernst Cassirer*, ed. Raymond Klibansky and H. J. Paton, 1–10. Oxford: Clarendon.

Hutton, Jeremy M. 2007. Isaiah 51:9–11 and the Rhetorical Appropriation and Subversion of Hostile Theologies. JBL 126:271–303.

Irvine, A. K., and A. F. K. Beeston. 1988. New Evidence on the Qatabanian Letter Order. PSAS 18:35–38.

Israel Antiquities Authority. 2003. Final Report Of The Examining Committees For the Yehoash Inscription and James Ossuary http://www.antiquities.org.il/article_Item_eng.asp?module_id=&sec_id=17&subj_id=175&id=266.

Izre'el, Shlomo. 1991. *Amurru Akkadian: A Linguistic Study With an Appendix on the History of Amurru by Itamar Singer.* 2 vols. Harvard Semitic Studies 40–41. Atlanta: Scholars.

———. 1995. The Amarna Glosses: Who Wrote What for Whom? Some Sociolinguistic Considerations. IOS 15:101–22.

———. 1995b. The Amarna Letters from Canaan. In *Civilizations of the Ancient Near East,* ed. Jack M. Sasson, 4:2411–19. 4 vols. New York: Scribners.

———. 1997. *The Amarna Scholarly Tablets.* Cuneiform Monographs 9. Groningen: Styx.

———. 2003. Canaanite Varieties in the Second Millennium BC: Can We Dispense with Anachronism? *Orient* 38:66–104.

———.2005. *Canaano-Akkadian.* Languages of the World / Materials, 82. Corrected Second Printing. München: Lincom Europa. [1st ed. 1998]

———. 2007. Canaano-Akkadian: Some Methodological Requisites for the Study of the Amarna Letters from Canaan, online at http://www.tau.ac.il/humanities/semitic/canakk2007.pdf.

Jakobson, Roman. 1987. Grammatical Parallelism and Its Russian Facet. In *Language in Literature,* 145–79. Cambridge, MA: Harvard University Press.

Jamieson-Drake, David W. 1991. *Scribes and Schools in Monarchic Judah: A Socio-Archaeological Approach.* Sheffield: Almond.

Jeffery, L. H. 1990. *The Local Scripts of Archaic Greece: A Study of the Origin of the Greek Alphabet and its Development from the Eighth to the Fifth Centuries B.C.* Rev ed., with a supplement by A. W. Johnston. Oxford: Clarendon Press; New York: Oxford University Press.

Joffe, Alexander. 2002. The Rise of Secondary States in the Iron Age Levant. JESHO 45:425–67.

———. 2003. On the Language of Complex Societies: Reply to Michael Heltzer. JESHO 46:530–32.

Johansson, Egil. 1988. Literacy Campaigns in Sweden. *Interchange* 19:135–62.

Johns, Adrian. 1998. *The Nature of the Book: Print and Knowledge in the Making.* Chicago: University of Chicago Press.

Kammerzell, Frank. 2001. Die Entstehung der Alphabetreihe: Zum ägyptischen Ursprung der semitischen und westlichen Schriften. In *Hieroglyphen, Alphabete, Schriftreformen,* ed. Dörte Borchers et al. 117–57. Göttingen, Seminar für Ägyptologie und Koptologie.

Kamp, Kathryn, and Norman Yoffee. 1980. Ethnicity in Ancient Western Asia During the Early Second Millennium B.C.: Archaeological Assessments and Ethnoarchaeological Perspectives. BASOR 237:85–104.

Kaufman, Stephen A. 1982. Reflections on the Assyrian-Aramaic Bilingual From Tell Fakhariyeh. *Maarav* 2:137–75.

———. 1997. Aramaic. In Hetzron, ed. 1997:114–30.

Kawashima, Robert. 2004. *Biblical Narrative and the Death of the Rhapsode.* Bloomington: Indiana University Press.

Kelly, John 1996. What Was Sanskrit For? Metadiscursive Strategies in Ancient India. In *Ideology and Status of Sanskrit: Contributions to the History of the Sanskrit Language,* ed. Jan Houben, 87–107. Leiden: Brill.

———. 2006a. Writing and the State: India, China and General Definitions. In Sanders, ed. 2006: 15–32.

———. 2006b. Who Counts? Imperial and Corporate Structures of Governance, Decolonization and Limited Liability. In *Lessons of Empire,* ed. C. Calhoun et al., 157–74. New York: New Press.

Kleinig, John W. 2003. *Leviticus.* St. Louis, MO: Concordia.

Klengel, Horst, ed. 1989. *Kulturgeschichte des alten Vorderasien.* Berlin: Akademie-Verlag.

Kletter, Raz. 1998. *Economic Keystones. The Weight System of the Kingdom of Judah.* Journal for the Old Testament Studies Supplement Series 276. Sheffield: Sheffield Academic Press.

Knauf, E. A. 1989. The Migration of the Script and the Formation of the State in South Arabia. PSAS 19:79–91.

Knohl, Israel. 1995. *The Sanctuary of Silence.* Minneapolis: Fortress.

Kochavi, M. 1977. An Ostracon of the Period of the Judges from Izbet Sartah. *Tel Aviv* 4:1–13.

Kramer, Carol. 1977. Pots and Peoples. In *Mountains and Lowlands: Essays in the Archaeology of Greater Mesopotamia,* ed. L. D. Levine and T. C. Young, Jr., 91–112. Bibliotheca Mesopotamica 6. Malibu, CA: Undena.

Kroskrity, Paul, ed. 2000. *Regimes of Language: Ideologies, Polities, and Identities.* Santa Fe: School of American Research Press.

Kugel, James L. 1981. *The Idea of Biblical Poetry.* New Haven: Yale University Press.

Kuhrt, Amélie. 1995. *The Ancient Near East, c. 3000–330 BC.* London and New York: Routledge.

Kupper, Jean-Robert. 1998. *Lettres royales du temps de Zimri-Lim.* ARM 28. Paris: Éditions Recherches sur les Civilisations.

Kutscher, E. Y. 1974. *The Language and Linguistic Background of the Isaiah Scroll IQIsa[a].* Leiden: Brill.

Landsberger, Benno. 1926. Die Eigenbegrifflichkeit der babylonischen Welt. *Islamica* 2:355–72.

———. 1954. Assyrische Königsliste und "Dunkles Zeitalter." *Journal of Cuneiform Studies* 8:31–45, 47–73; 106–33.

———. 1957. *Materials for the Sumerian Lexicon V.* Rome: Pontifical Bible Institute.

———. 1976. *The Conceptual Autonomy of the Babylonian World,* trans. Thorkild Jacobsen, Benjamin R. Foster, and Heinrich von Siebenthal. Sources and Monographs, Monographs on the Ancient Near East 1/4. Malibu, CA: Undena.

Larsen, Mogens Trolle. 2002. *The Assur-nada Archive.* Old Assyrian Archives 1. Leiden: Nederlands Instituut voor het Nabije Oosten.

Latour, Bruno. 1993. *We Have Never Been Modern*, trans. Catherine Porter. Cambridge, MA: Harvard University Press.

Lee, Shin-Ying, David H. Uttal, and Chuansheng Chen. 1995. Writing Systems and Acquisition of Reading in American, Chinese and Japanese First-graders. In Taylor and Olson, eds. 1995:247–64.

Lemaire, André. 1976. A Schoolboy's Exercise on an Ostracon at Lachish. *Tel Aviv* 3:109–10.

———. 1981. *Les Écoles et la formation de la Bible dans l'ancien Israël*. Fribourg: Editions universitaires; Göttingen: Vandenhoeck & Ruprecht.

———. 1995. Les Inscriptions Arameennes de Cheikh-Fadl Egypte. In *Studia Aramaica: New Sources and New Approaches*, ed. Markham J. Geller et al., 77–132. Oxford: Oxford University Press.

———. 1998. Les formules de datation en Palestine au premier millénaire avant J.-C. In *Temps vécu, temps pensé*, ed. F. Briquel-Chatonnet and H. Lozachmeur, 53–82. Etudes Sémitiques 3. Paris: Editions Maisonneuve.

———, and P. Vernus. 1983. L'ostracon paléo-hébreu no. 6 de Tell Qudeirat Qadesh-Barnéa. In *Fontes atque Pontes: eine Festgabe für Hellmut Brunner*, ed. M. Görg, 302–26. Wiesbaden: Harrassowitz.

Levine, Baruch, and J.-M. de Tarragon. 1984. Dead Kings and Rephaim: The Patrons of the Ugaritic Dynasty. JAOS 104:649–59.

Levinson, Bernard. 1997 *Deuteronomy and the Hermeneutics of Legal Innovation*. Oxford and New York: Oxford University Press.

———. 2001. The Reconceptualization of Kingship in Deuteronomy and the Deuteronomistic History's Transformation of Torah. VT 51:511–34.

———. 2004. Is the Covenant Code an Exilic Composition? A Response to John Van Seters. In *In Search of Pre-Exilic Israel: Proceedings of the Oxford Old Testament Seminar*, ed. John Day, 272–325. Edinburgh: T. & T. Clark.

———. 2008. *Legal Revision and Religious Renewal in Ancient Israel*. New York: Cambridge University Press.

Li, Alan. 2004. A Reexamination of Protoliteracy through an Analysis of Modern Chinese Character Use. *Written Communication* 21:111–40.

Lilla, Mark. 2007. *The Stillborn God: Religion, Politics, and the Modern West*. New York: Alfred A. Knopf.

Lincoln, Bruce. 1991. Myth and History in the Study of Myth: An Obscure Text of Georges Dumézil, Its Context and Subtext. In *Death, War, and Sacrifice: Studies in Ideology and Practice*, 259–68. Chicago: University of Chicago Press.

———. 1994. *Authority: Construction and Corrosion*. Chicago: University of Chicago Press.

———. 1999. *Theorizing Myth: Narrative, Ideology, and Scholarship*. Chicago: University of Chicago Press.

Liverani, Mario. 1988. *Antico Oriente: storia, società, economia*. Roma: Laterza.

———. 2001. The Fall of the Assyrian Empire: Ancient and Modern Interpretations. In *Empires: Perspectives from Archaeology and History*, ed. Susan E. Alcock et al., 374–91. Cambridge: Cambridge University Press.

———. 2005. *Israel's History and the History of Israel*, trans. Chiara Peri and Philip R. Davies. London and Oakville, CT : Equinox.

Livingstone, Alasdair. 1986. *Mystical and Mythological Explanatory Works of Assyrian and Babylonian Scholars.* Oxford: Clarendon.

Locke, John. 1997. *An Essay Concerning Human Understanding.* New York: Penguin.

Long, Burke O. 1997. *Planting and Reaping Albright: Politics, Ideology, and Interpreting the Bible.* University Park: Pennsylvania State University Press.

Loundin, A. G. 1987. L'abécédaire de Beth Shemesh. *Le Muséon* 100:243–50.

Lowth, Robert. 1969. *Lectures on the Sacred Poetry of the Hebrews.* 2 vols. Hildesheim: Georg Olms Verlag. [1787]

Macdonald, Michael C. A. 2005. Literacy in an Oral Environment. In *Writing and Ancient Near Eastern Society. Papers in Honour of Alan R. Millard,* ed. P. Bienkowski, C. B. Mee, and E. A. Slater, 49–118. Journal for the Study of the Old Testament. Supplement 426. Harrisburg, PA: T. & T. Clark.

Machiavelli, Niccolo. 1996. *Discourses on Livy,* trans. Harvey Mansfield and Nathan Tarcov. Chicago: University of Chicago Press.

Machinist, Peter. 1983. Assyria and its Image in the First Isaiah. JAOS 103:719–37.

———. 1991. The Question of Distinctiveness in Ancient Israel: An Essay. In *Ah, Assyria. . .,* ed. Mordechai Cogan and Israel Eph'al, 196–212. Scripta Hierosolymnitana 33. Jerusalem: Magnes.

———. 2006. Final Response: On the Study of the Ancients, Language, Writing, and the State. In Sanders, ed. 2006:291–300.

Malamat, Abraham. 1962. Mari and the Bible: Some Patterns of Tribal Organization and Institutions. JAOS 83:143–50.

———. 1989. *Mari and the Early Israelite Experience.* Oxford: Oxford University Press.

———. 1995. A Word for "Clan" in Mari and its Hebrew Cognate. In *Solving Riddles and Untying Knots: Biblical Studies in Honor of Jonas C. Greenfield,* ed. Z. Zevit et al., 177–79. Winona Lake, IN: Eisenbrauns.

Malcolm, Noel. 2002. Hobbes, Ezra, and the Bible: The History of a Subversive Idea. In *Aspects of Hobbes,* 383–431. Oxford: Oxford University Press.

———. 2004. *Leviathan,* the Pentateuch, and the Origins of Modern Biblical Criticism. In *Leviathan after 350 Years,* ed. Tom Sorell and Luc Foisneau, 241–64. Oxford: Oxford University Press.

Mayer, Arno. 2000. *The Furies: Violence and Terror in the French and Russian Revolutions.* Princeton: Princeton University Press.

Mazar, Amihai. 1993. Beth-Shean. In Stern, ed. 1993 1:214–23.

———. 1994. The Northern Shephelah in the Iron Age: Some Issues in Biblical History and Archaeology. In *Scripture and Other Artifacts: Essays in the Bible and Archaeology in Honor of Philip J. King,* ed. M. Coogan, J. C. Exum, and L. Stager, 247–67. Louisville: Westminster John Knox.

———. 2003. Three 10th–9th Century B.C.E. Inscriptions From Tel Rehov. In *Saxa loquentur: Studien zur Archäologie Palälastinas/Israels—Festchrift für Volkmar Fritz,* ed. Cornelis G. den Hertog, 171–84. Münster: Ugarit-Verlag.

———. 2007. Response to article Precarious Scholarship: Problems with Proposing that the Seal of Yzbl was Queen Jezebel's. American Schools of Oriental Research website http://www.asor.org/mazar.htm.

McCarter, P. Kyle. 1980. The Balaam Texts from Deir ʿAlla: The First Combination. BASOR 239:49–60.

———. 1987. Aspects of the Religion of the Israelite Monarchy: Biblical and Epigraphic Data. In Miller, Hanson, and McBride, eds. 1987:137–55.

———. 1999. Two Bronze Arrowheads with Archaic Alphabetic Inscriptions. EI 26:123*–28*.

McLean, Mark David. 1982. *The Use and the Development of Palaeo-Hebrew in the Hellenistic and Roman Periods.* PhD diss., Harvard University.

McNutt, Paula. 1990. *The Forging of Israel: Iron Technology, Symbolism and Tradition in Ancient Society.* Sheffield: Almond.

Meier, Heinrich. 2006. *Leo Strauss and the Theologico-political Problem.* trans. Marcus Brainard. New York: Cambridge University Press.

Michalowski, Piotr. 1987. Language, Literature and Writing at Ebla. In *Ebla 1975–1985,* ed. L. Cagni, 165–75. Naples: Istituto Universitario Orientale.

———. 1991. Charisma and Control: On Continuity and Change in Early Mesopotamian Bureaucratic Systems. In *The Organization of Power: Aspects of Bureaucracy in the Ancient Near East,* ed. R. D. Biggs and M. Gibson, 45–58. Chicago: University of Chicago Press. [1st ed. 1987]

———. 2006. The Lives of the Sumerian Language. In Sanders, ed. 2006:157–82.

Michel, Cécile. 2001. *Correspondance des marchands de Kaniš au début du IIe millénaire avant J.-C.* Paris: Cerf.

Mieroop, Marc van de. 1999. *Cuneiform Texts and the Writing of History.* London and New York: Routledge.

———. 2004. *A History of the Ancient Near East, ca. 3000–323 B.C.* Malden, MA: Blackwell.

Milgrom, Jacob. 1991. *Leviticus 1–16.* The Anchor Bible. New York: Doubleday.

Milik, J. T. 1956. An Unpublished Arrow-head with Phoenician Inscription of the 11th–10th Century B.C. BASOR 143:3–6.

Millard, Alan. 1992. Review of Sass 1988. *BiOr* 59 5/6:691–95.

———. 1998. Books in the Late Bronze Age in the Levant. IOS 18:171–81.

———. 1999a. Owners and Users of Hebrew Seals. EI 26:129*–33*.

———. 1999b. Oral Proclamation and Written Record: Spreading and Preserving Information in Ancient Israel. In *Michael: Historical, Epigraphical and Biblical Studies in Honor of Prof. Michael Heltzer,* ed. Y. Avishur and R. Deutsch, 237–42. Tel Aviv: Archaeological Center Publications.

———. 2007, Alphabetic Writing, Cuneiform and Linear, Reconsidered. *Maarav* 14:83–93.

Miller, Cynthia, ed. 2007. *Studies in Semitic and Afroasiatic Linguistics Presented to Gene B. Gragg.* Chicago: Oriental Institute Press.

Miller, Flagg. 2007. *The Moral Resonance of Arab Media: Audiocassette Poetry and Culture in Yemen.* Cambridge, MA: Harvard Center for Middle Eastern Studies.

Miller, Patrick D., Paul Hanson, and S. Dean McBride, eds. 1987. *Ancient Israelite Religion: Essays in Honor of Frank Moore Cross.* Philadelphia: Fortress.

Miller, Robert D., II. 2005. *Chieftains of the Highland Clans: A History of Israel in the 12th and 11th Centuries B.C.* Grand Rapids, MI: Eerdmans.

Millet Alba, Adelina. 2004. La localisation des terroirs Benjaminites du royaume de Mari. In *Nomades et sédentaires dans le Proche-Orient ancient,* ed. Christophe Nicolle, 225–34. *Amurru* 3. Paris: Éditions recherche sur les civilisations.

Minette de Tillesse, Georges. 1962. Sections "tu" et sections "vous" dans le Deuteronome. VT 12:29–87.

Mitchell, Timothy. 1999. Society, Economy, and the State Effect. In *State/Culture: State-Formation after the Cultural Turn,* ed. George Steinmetz, 76–97. Ithaca: Cornell University Press.

Moran, William. 1992. *The Amarna Letters.* Baltimore: Johns Hopkins University Press.

Moyer, Ian. 2006. Golden Fetters and Economies of Cultural Exchange. *Journal of Ancient Near Eastern Religions* 6:225–56.

Muffs, Yochanan. 1969. *Studies in the Aramaic Legal Papyri from Elephantine.* Leiden: Brill.

Muir, Edward. 1997. *Ritual in Early Modern Europe.* Cambridge: Cambridge University Press.

Na'aman, Nadav. 1986. Habiru and Hebrews: The Transfer of a Social Term to the Literary Sphere. JNES 45:271–88.

———. 2002. *The Past that Shapes the Present: The Creation of Biblical Historiography in the Late First Temple Period and After the Downfall.* Jerusalem: Arna Hess. [in Hebrew]

———. 2003. The Distribution of Messages in the Kingdom of Judah in Light of the Lachish Ostraca. VT 53:169–80.

———. 2006. *Ancient Israel's History and Historiography: The First Temple Period.* Collected Essays. Vol. 3. Winona Lake, IN: Eisenbrauns.

Naveh, Joseph. 1968. A Palaeographic Note on the Distribution of the Hebrew Script. HTR 61:68–74.

———. 1971. Hebrew Texts in Aramaic Script in the Persian Period? BASOR 203: 27–32.

———. 1978. Some Considerations on the Ostracon from 'Izbet Sartah. IEJ 28:31–35.

———. 1987. *Early History of The Alphabet.* 2nd ed. Jerusalem: Magnes.

Nebes, Norbert, and Peter Stein. 2004. Ancient South Arabian. In *The Cambridge Encyclopedia of the World's Ancient Languages,* ed. Roger D. Woodard, 454–87. Cambridge: Cambridge University Press.

Nissinen, Martti, with C. L. Seow and Robert K. Ritner. 2003. *Prophets and Prophecy in the Ancient Near East,* ed. Peter Machinist. Atlanta: Society of Biblical Literature.

Obermann, Julian. 1947. How Baal Destroyed a Rival: A Mythological Incantation Scene. JAOS 67:195–208.

O'Connor, Michael. 2004. The Onomastic Evidence for Bronze-Age West Semitic. JAOS 124:439–70.

Olender, Maurice. 1992. *The Languages of Paradise: Race, Religion, and Philology in the Nineteenth Century,* trans. Arthur Goldhammer. Cambridge, MA: Harvard University Press.

del Olmo Lete, Gregorio. 1999. *Canaanite Religion: According to the Liturgical Texts of Ugarit,* trans. Wilfred G. E. Watson. Bethesda, MD: CDL. [1st ed. 1992]

———, and Joaquín Sanmartín, 2004. *A Dictionary of the Ugaritic Language in the*

Alphabetic Tradition. 2nd rev. ed., ed. and trans. Wilfred G. E. Watson. 2 vols. Handbook of Oriental Studies 1/67. Leiden: Brill.

Ong, Walter J. 1982. *Orality and Literacy: The Technologizing of the Word.* London: Methuen.

Pardee, Dennis. 1989–90. Ugaritic Proper Nouns. *Archiv für Orientforschung* 36–37: 390–513.

———. 2000. *Les Textes Rituels.* Ras Shamra-Ougarit XII. Paris: Éditions Recherche sur les Civilisations.

———. 2002. *Ritual and Cult at Ugarit.* Atlanta: Society of Biblical Literature.

———. 2007. The Ugaritic Alphabetic Cuneiform Writing System in the Context of Other Alphabetic Systems. In C. Miller, ed. 2007:181–200.

Parker, Simon B. 1997. *Stories in Scripture and Inscriptions: Comparative Studies on Narratives in Northwest Semitic Inscriptions and the Hebrew Bible.* New York: Oxford University Press.

———, ed. 1997. *Ugaritic Narrative Poetry.* Atlanta: Society of Biblical Literature.

Parpola, Simo, and Kazuko Watanabe. 1988. *Neo-Assyrian Treaties and Loyalty Oaths.* State Archives of Assyria 2. Helsinki, Finland: Helsinki University Press.

Peckham, Brian. 1987. Phoenicia and the Religion of Israel. In Miller, Hanson, and McBride, eds. 1987:79–99.

Petrarca, Francesco. 2003. *Invectives,* ed. and trans. David Marsh. I Tatti Renaissance Library 11. Cambridge, MA: Harvard University Press.

Pitard, Wayne. 1999. The Alphabetic Ugaritic Tablets. In *Handbook of Ugaritic Studies,* ed. Wilfred G. E. Watson and Nicolas Wyatt, 46–57. Handbuch der Orientalistik 39. Leiden: Brill.

Pollock, Sheldon. 1998. The Cosmopolitan Vernacular. *Journal of Asian Studies* 57: 6–37.

———. 2002. Cosmopolitan and Vernacular in History. In *Cosmopolitanism,* ed. Carol Breckenridge et al., 15–53. Durham: Duke University Press.

———., ed. 2003. *Literary Cultures in History: Reconstructions from South Asia.* Berkeley: University of California Press.

———. 2005. Axialism and Empire. In *Axial Civilizations and World History,* ed. Johann Arnason, 397–450. Leiden: E.J. Brill.

———. 2006a. Response for Third Session: Power and Culture Beyond Ideology and Identity. In Sanders, ed. 2006:277–87.

———. 2006b. *The Language of the Gods in the World of Men: Sanskrit, Culture, and Power in Premodern India.* Berkeley: University of California Press.

Polzin, Robert. 1993. *Moses and the Deuteronomist: A Literary Study of the Deuteronomic History.* Bloomington: Indiana University Press.

Porter, Anne. 2002. The Dynamics of Death: Ancestors, Pastoralism, and the Origins of a Third-Millennium City in Syria. BASOR 325:1–36.

Powell, Barry B. 1991. *Homer and the Origin of the Greek Alphabet.* Cambridge and New York: Cambridge University Press.

Preus, J. Samuel. 2001. *Spinoza and the Irrelevance of Biblical Authority.* Cambridge: Cambridge University Press.

Puech, E. 1986. Origine de L'alphabet. RB 93:161–213.

———. 1988. Les Ecoles dans l'Israël prèexilique: donnèes épigraphiques. SVT 40: 189–203.

———. 1991. La tablette cunéiforme de Beth Shemesh. Premier témoin de la séquence des lettres du sud-sémitique. In Baurain, ed. 1991:315–26.

Quack, Joachim Friedrich. 1993. Ägyptisches und südarabisches Alphabet. *Revue d'Égyptologie* 44:141–51.

Rabinowitz, Isaac. 1993. *A Witness Forever: Ancient Israel's Perception of Literature and the Resultant Hebrew Bible*, ed. Ross Brann and David I. Owen. Bethesda, MD: CDL.

Rainey, Anson F. 1996. *Canaanite in the Amarna Tablets: A Linguistic Analysis of the Mixed Dialect Used by Scribes from Canaan*. 4 vols. Leiden: Brill.

———. 1998. Syntax, Hermeneutics, and History. IEJ 48:239–51.

———. 1999. Taanach Letters. EI 26 [Fs. Cross] 153*–162*.

———, and R. Stephen Notley. 2006. *The Sacred Bridge: Carta's Atlas of the Biblical World*. Jerusalem: Carta.

Reed, Walter L. 1993. *Dialogues of the Word: The Bible as Literature According to Bakhtin*. Oxford: Oxford University Press.

Reich, R., and E. Shukron. 2008. A Fragmentary Palaeo-Hebrew Inscription from the City of David, Jerusalem. IEJ 58:48–50

Reich, R., E. Shukron, and O. Lernau. 2007. Recent Discoveries in the City of David, Jerusalem. IEJ 57:153–69.

Rendsburg, Gary. 2002. *Israelian Hebrew in the Book of Kings*. Bethesda, MD: CDL.

———. 2007. No Stelae, No Queens: Two Issues Concerning the Kings of Israel and Judah. In *The Archaeology of Difference: Gender, Ethnicity, Class and the Other in Antiquity: Studies in Honor of Eric M. Meyers*, ed. D. R. Edwards and C. T. McCullough, 95–107. Annual of the American Schools of Oriental Research 60–61. Boston: American Schools of Oriental Research.

Rendtorff, Rolf. 2003. Leviticus 16 als Mitte der Tora. *Biblical Interpretation* 11: 252–58.

Renz, Johannes. 1997. *Schrift und Schreibertradition: Ein Paläographische Studie zum kulturgeschichtlichen Verhältnis von israelitischem Nordreich und Südreich*. Wiesbaden: Harrassowitz.

Renz, Johannes, and Wolfgang Röllig, 1995. *Handbuch der Althebräischen Epigraphik*. Darmstadt: Wissenschaftliche Buchgesellschaft.

Richter, Thomas. 2005. Qatna in the Late Bronze Age: Preliminary Remarks. In *General Studies and Excavations at Nuzi 11/1*, ed. David I. Owen and Gernot Wilhelm, 109–26. Studies on the Civilization and Culture of the Hurrians 15. Bethesda: CDL.

Robertson Smith, William. 1894. *Lectures on the Religion of the Semites*. London: A&C Black.

Rollston, Christopher. 1999 *The Script of Hebrew Ostraca of the Iron Age: 8th–6th Centuries BCE*. PhD dissertation, Johns Hopkins University.

———. 2003. Non-Provenanced Epigraphs I: Pillaged Antiquities, Northwest Semitic Forgeries, and Protocols for Laboratory Tests. *Maarav* 10:135–94.

———. 2004. Non-Provenanced Epigraphs II: The Status of the Non-Provenanced Epigraphs within the Broader Corpus of Northwest Semitic. *Maarav* 11:57–79.

———. 2006. Scribal Education in Ancient Israel: The Old Hebrew Epigraphic Evidence. BASOR 344:47–74.
———. 2008. The Phoenician Script of the Tel Zayit Abecedary and Putative Evidence for Israelite Literacy. In *Literate Culture and Tenth-Century Canaan: The Tel Zayit Abecedary in Context*, ed. R. E. Tappy and P. Kyle McCarter, 61–96. Winona Lake, IN: Eisenbrauns.
———. f/c. Northwest Semitic Cursive Scripts of Iron II. In *An Eye for Form: Epigraphic Essays in Honor of Frank Moore Cross*, ed. Jo Ann Hackett and Walter Aufrecht. Winona Lake, IN: Eisenbrauns.
Römer, T., and A. de Pury. 2000. Deuteronomistic Historiography (DH): History of Research and Debated Issues. In *Israel Constructs Its History: Deuteronomistic Historiography in Recent Research*, ed. A. de Pury, T. Römer, and J.-D. Macchi, 24–141. Sheffield: Sheffield Academic Press.
Rosenthal, Franz. 1942. Review of Cyrus Gordon, *Ugaritic Grammar. Or* 11:171–79.
Roth, Martha T. 1995. *Law Collections from Mesopotamia and Asia Minor.* Atlanta: Scholars.
Routledge, Bruce. 2000. The Politics of Mesha: Segmented Identities and State Formation in Iron Age Moab. JESHO 43:221–56.
———. 2003. The Antiquity of the Nation? Critical Reflections from the Ancient Near East. *Nations and Nationalism* 9:212–32.
———. 2005. Review of Grosby 2002. *Nations and Nationalism* 11:175–77.
Rubio, Gonzalo. 2006. Writing in Another Tongue: Alloglottography in the Ancient Near East. In Sanders, ed. 2006:33–52.
Runciman, D. 2003. The Concept of the State: The Sovereignty of a Fiction. In *States & Citizens: History, Theory, Prospects*, ed. Q. Skinner and B. Stråth, 28–38. Cambridge: Cambridge University Press.
Running, Leona Glidden, and David Noel Freedman. 1975. *William Foxwell Albright, a Twentieth-Century Genius.* New York: Two Continents.
Ryckmans, Jacques. 1988. A. G. Lundin's Interpretation of the Beth Shemesh Abecedary: A Presentation and Commentary. PSAS 18:123–29.
Sahlins, Peter, 1989. *Boundaries: The Making of France and Spain in the Pyrenees.* Berkeley: University of California Press.
Salzman, Philip Carl. 1978. Ideology and Change in Middle Eastern Tribal Societies. *Man* 13:618–37.
Sanders, Seth L. 2001. A Historiography of Demons: Preterit-Thema, Para-Myth and Historiola in the Morphology of Genres. In *Proceedings of the XLV Rencontre Assyriologique Internationale: Historiography in the Cuneiform World.* ed. Tzvi Abusch, 429–40. Bethesda, MD: CDL.
———. 2002. Old Light on Moses' Shining Face. VT 52:400–407.
———. 2002–3. Review of Mark S. Smith's *The Early History of God. Journal of Hebrew Scriptures* 4 http://www.arts.ualberta.ca/JHS/reviews/review119.htm.
———. 2004a. Performative Utterances and Divine Language in Ugaritic. JNES 63:161–81.
———. 2004b. What was the Alphabet for? The Rise of Written Vernaculars and the Making of Israelite National Literature. *Maarav* 11:25–56.

———, ed. 2006. *Margins of Writing, Origins of Cultures: New Approaches to Writing and Reading in the Ancient Near East.* Chicago: Oriental Institute Press.

———. 2008. Writing and Early Iron Age Israel: Before National Scripts, Beyond Nations and States. In *Literate Culture and Tenth-Century Canaan: The Tel Zayit Abecedary in Context*, ed. R. E. Tappy and P. Kyle McCarter, 97–112. Winona Lake, IN: Eisenbrauns.

———. f/c. Empires and Alphabets: The Political Economy of Writing in Late Bronze Age Palestine. In *The History of Writing in Israel*, ed. Ryan Byrne. Atlanta and Boston: Society of Biblical Literature/Brill.

Sapir, Edward. 1949. *Selected Writings in Language, Culture, and Personality*, ed. David G. Mandelbaum. Berkeley: University of California Press.

Sass, Benjamin. 1988. *The Genesis of the Alphabet and its Development in the Second Millennium B.C.* Ägypten und Altes Testament 13. Wiesbaden: Harrassowitz.

———. 1991. The Beth Shemesh Tablet and the Early History of the Proto-Canaanite, Cuneiform and South Semitic Alphabets. UF 23:315–26.

———. 2004–5. The Genesis of the Alphabet and its Development in the Second Millennium B.C.—Twenty Years Later. *De Kemi à Birit Nari* 2:137–56.

———. 2005. *The Alphabet at the Turn of the Millennium: The West Semitic Alphabet ca. 1150–850 BCE, The Antiquity of the Arabian, Greek and Phrygian Alphabets.* Tel Aviv: Emery and Claire Yass Publications in Archaeology.

Sasson, J. M. 1998. About 'Mari and the Bible.' RA 92:453–70.

Schaeffer, Claude F.-A. 1956. *Ugaritica III: Sceaux et cylindres hittites, épée gravée du cartouche de Mineptah, tablettes chypro-minoennes et autres découvertes nouvelles de Ras Shamra.* Paris: Geuthner.

Schama, Simon. 1995. *Landscape and Memory.* New York: Vintage.

Schloen, David. 2001. *The House of the Father as Fact and Symbol: Patrimonialism in Ugarit and the Ancient Near East.* Winona Lake, IN: Eisenbrauns.

Schmid, Konrad. 1999. *Erzväter und Exodus: Untersuchungen zur doppelten Begründung der Ursprünge Israels innerhalb der Geschichtsbücher des Alten Testaments.* Wissenschaftliche Monographien zum Alten und Neuen Testament. Bd. 81. Neukirchen-Vluyn: Neukirchener Verlag.

Schniedewind, William. 1996. The Tel Dan Stele: New Light on Aramaic and Jehu's Revolt. BASOR 302:75–90.

———. 2000a. Orality and Literacy in Ancient Israel. *Religious Studies Review* 26:327–32.

———. 2000b. Sociolinguistic Reflections on the Letter of a "Literate" Soldier. *Zeitschrift für Althebraistik* 13:157–67.

———. 2004. *How the Bible Became a Book: The Texualization of Ancient Israel.* Cambridge: Cambridge University Press.

———. 2006. Aramaic, The Death of Written Hebrew, and Language Shift in the Persian Period. in Sanders, ed. 2006:137–47.

———, and Daniel Sivan. 1997. The Dialect of the Elisha-Elijah Narratives: A Case Study in Northern Hebrew. *Jewish Quarterly Review* 137:303–37.

Schwartz, Glenn. 1989. The Origins of the Arameans in Syria and Northern Mesopotamia: Research Problems and Potential Strategies. In *To the Euphrates and Beyond: Archaeological Studies in Honour of Maurits N. van Loon*, ed. O. M. C. Haex et al., 275–91. Rotterdam: A. A. Balkema.

Segert, Stanislav. 1989. Die Orthographie der alphabetischen Keilschrifttafeln in akkadischer Sprache aus Ugarit. *Studi epigrafici e linguistici* 5:189–205.

Sheehan, Jonathan. 2005. *The Enlightenment Bible: Translation, Scholarship, Culture.* Princeton: Princeton University Press.

Sherwood, Yvonne. 2004. *Derrida's Bible: Reading a Page of Scripture with a Little Help from Derrida.* Palgrave Macmillan.

Sherwood, Yvonne, and Kevin Hart, eds. 2004. *Derrida and Religion: Other Testaments.* New York and London: Routledge.

Shiloh, Yigael. 1987. South Arabian Inscriptions from the City of David, Jerusalem. PEQ 119:9–18.

Silver, Edward. N.D. Entextualization and Prophetic Action: Jeremiah 36 as Literary Artifact. Paper presented at 2008 Society of Biblical Literature meeting.

Silverstein, Michael. 1996. Encountering Language and Languages of Encounter in North American Ethnohistory. *Journal of Linguistic Anthropology* 6:126–44.

———. 2000. Whorfianism and the Linguistic Imagination of Nationality. In Kroskrity, ed. 2000:85–138.

———. 2006. Writing at the Chronotopic Margins of Empires. In Sanders, ed. 2006:149–55.

Sivan, Daniel. 1984. Grammatical Analysis and Glossary of the Northwest Semitic Vocables in Akkadian Texts of the 15th–13th C.B.C. from Canaan and Syria. Alter Orient und Altes Testament 214. Kevelaer: Butzon & Bercker; Neukirchen-Vluyn: Neukirchener Verlag.

Ska, Jean-Louis. 2006. *Introduction to Reading the Pentateuch,* trans. Pascale Dominique. Winona Lake, IN: Eisenbrauns.

Skinner, Quentin. 1996. *Reason and Rhetoric in the Philosophy of Hobbes.* Cambridge: Cambridge University Press.

Smith, Adam T. 2003. *The Political Landscape: Constellations of Authority in Early Complex Polities.* Berkeley: University of California Press.

Smith, A.D. 2002. Authenticity, Antiquity and Archaeology. *Nations and Nationalism* 7:441–49.

Smith, Jonathan Z. 1982. A Pearl of Great Price and a Cargo of Yams: A Study in Situational Incongruity. In *Imagining Religion: From Babylon to Jonestown,* 90–101. Chicago: University of Chicago Press.

———. 2002. Religion Up and Down, In and Out. In *Archaeology and the Religions of Israel,* ed. Barry Gittlen, 3–10. Winona Lake, IN: Eisenbrauns.

Smith, Mark S. 2001a. *The Origins of Biblical Monotheism: Israel's Polytheistic Background and the Ugaritic Texts.* New York: Oxford University Press.

———. 2001b. *Untold Stories: The Bible and Ugaritic Studies in the Twentieth Century.* Peabody, MA: Hendrickson.

———. 2002. *The Early History of God: Yahweh and the Other Deities in Ancient Israel.* 2nd ed. Grand Rapids, MI: Eerdmans; Dearborn, MI: Dove.

———. 2004. *The Memoirs of God: History, Memory, and the Experience of the Divine in Ancient Israel.* Minneapolis: Fortress.

———. 2007. Recent Study of Israelite Religion in Light of the Ugaritic Texts. In *Ugarit at Seventy-Five, its Environs and the Bible,* ed. K. Lawson Younger, 1–26. Winona Lake, IN: Eisenbrauns.

———, ed. 1994. *The Ugaritic Baal Cycle.* Vol. 1. VT Supp. 55. Leiden: E. J. Brill.

Smith, Steven B. 1997. *Spinoza, Liberalism, and the Question of Jewish Identity.* New Haven: Yale University Press.

Snaith, N. H. 1967. *Leviticus and Numbers.* London: Thomas Nelson & Sons.

Snell, Daniel C. 1997. *Life in the Ancient Near East, 3100–332 B.C.E.* New Haven: Yale University Press.

Soldt, W. H. van. 1995. Babylonian Lexical, Religious and Literary Texts and Scribal Education at Ugarit and its Implications for the Alphabetic Literary Texts. In *Ugarit: Ein ostmediterranes Kulturzentrum im Alten Orient,* ed. Manfried Dietrich and Oswald Loretz, vol. 1, 171–93. ALASP 7 Münster: Ugarit-Verlag.

Sommer, Benjamin D. 1998. *A Prophet Reads Scripture: Allusion in Isaiah 40–66.* Stanford: Stanford University Press.

———. 2001. Conflicting Constructions of Divine Presence in the Priestly Tabernacle. *Biblical Interpretation* 9:41–63.

———. 2000. The Babylonian Akitu Festival: Rectifying the King or Renewing the Cosmos? JANES 27:81–95.

Speiser, E. A. 1960. 'People' and 'Nation' of Israel. JBL 79:157–63.

———. 1962. *Genesis.* The Anchor Bible. New York: Doubleday.

Spiegel, Gabrielle. 1997. *The Past as Text: The Theory and Practice of Medieval Historiography.* Baltimore: Johns Hopkins University Press.

Stager, Lawrence. 1985. The Archaeology of the Family in Ancient Israel. BASOR 260:1–35.

Steiner, Richard L. 1997. Ancient Hebrew. In Hetzron, ed. 1997:145–73.

———. 2005. On the dating of Hebrew Sound Changes **ḫ*>*ḥ* and **ǵ*> ʿ and Greek Translations 2 Esdras and Judith. JBL 124:229–67.

Stern, Ephraim, ed. 1993. *New Encyclopedia of Archaeological Excavations in the Holy Land.* Ayelet Lewinson-Gilboa, assistant editor; Joseph Aviram, editorial director. 4 vols. Jerusalem: Israel Exploration Society & Carta; New York: Simon & Schuster.

Stock, Brian. 1983. *The Implications of Literacy: Written Language and Models of Interpretation in the Eleventh and Twelfth Centuries.* Princeton: Princeton University Press.

Stoekl Ben Ezra, Daniel. 2003. *The Impact of Yom Kippur on Early Christianity: The Day of Atonement from Second Temple Judaism to the Fifth Century.* Wissenschaftliche Untersuchungen zum Neuen Testament 163. Tübingen: J. C. B. Mohr.

Strauss, Leo. 1997. *Spinoza's Critique of Religion.* Chicago: University of Chicago Press.

Street, Brian. 1984. *Literacy in Theory and Practice.* Cambridge: Cambridge University Press.

Svenbro, Jesper. 1993. *Phrasikleia: An Anthropology of Reading in Ancient Greece,* trans. Janet Lloyd. Ithaca: Cornell University Press.

Sznycer, M. 1975. L' 'assemblée du peuple' dans les cités puniques d'après les témoignages épigraphiques. *Semitica* 25:47–68.

Tadmor, Hayim. 1977. A Lexicographical Text from Hazor. IEJ 27:98–102.

Talmon, Shemaryahu. 1981. Did There Exist a Biblical National Epic? In *Proceedings of the Seventh World Congress of Jewish Studies,* 41–61. Jerusalem: World Union of Jewish Studies.

Tambiah, Stanley J. 1968. Literacy in a Buddhist Village in North-East Thailand. In Goody, ed. 1968:85–131.

Tappy, Ron E., P. Kyle McCarter, Jr., Marilyn Lundberg, and Bruce Zuckerman. 2007. An Abecedary of the Mid-Tenth Century B.C.E. from the Judaean Shephelah. BASOR 344:5–46.

Taubes, Jacob. 2004. *The Political Theology of Paul.* Stanford: Stanford University Press.

Taylor, Insup, and David R. Olson, eds. 1995. *Scripts and Literacy: Reading and Learning to Read Alphabets, Syllabaries and Characters.* Dordrecht: Kluwer.

Terpstra, Marin, and Theo de Wit. 1997. 'No spiritual investment in the world as it is': Die negative politische Theologie Jacob Taubes. *Etappe* 13.

Thomas, Rosalind. 1992. *Literacy and Orality in Ancient Greece.* New York: Cambridge University Press.

Thomason, Sarah G. 2001. *Language Contact.* Washington, DC: Georgetown University Press.

Thureau-Dangin, F. 1931. Vocabulaires de Ras-Shamra. *Syria* 12:225–66.

van den Hout, Theo. 2006. Institutions, Vernaculars, Publics: The Case of Second-Millennium Anatolia. In Sanders, ed. 2006:217–56.

van der Toorn, Karel. 2000. Cuneiform Documents from Syria-Palestine: Texts, Scribes, and Schools. *Zeitschrift des Deutschen Palästina-Vereins* 116:97–113.

———. 2007. *Scribal Culture and the Making of the Hebrew Bible.* Cambridge, MA: Harvard University Press.

Trabazo, Jose Virgilio Garcia. 2002. *Textos religiosos hititas: Mitos, plegarias y rituals.* Madrid: Editorial Trotta.

Valdman, Albert. 1970. *Basic Course in Haitian Creole.* Bloomington: Indiana University Press; The Hague: Mouton.

van Creveld, Martin. 1999. *The Rise and Decline of the State.* Cambridge: Cambridge University Press.

Van Lerberghe, K., and G. Voet, eds. 2001. *Languages and Cultures in Contact: At the Crossroads of Civilizations in the Syro-Mesopotamian Realm.* CRRAI 42. Leuven: Peeters.

Vanstiphout, Herman. 2003. *Epics of Sumerian Kings: The Matter of Aratta.* Atlanta: Society of Biblical Literature.

Vaughn, Andrew, and Carolyn Dobler. 2006. A Provenance Study of Hebrew Seals and Seal Impressions. In *I Will Speak the Riddles of Ancient Times: Archaeological and Historical Studies in Honor of Amihai Mazar on the Occasion of His Sixtieth Birthday,* ed. Aren M. Maeir and Pierre de Miroschedji, 757–71. Winona Lake, IN: Eisenbrauns.

Venezky, Richard L. 1995. How English is Read: Grapheme-Phoneme Regularity and Orthographic Structure in Word Recognition. In Taylor and Olson, eds. 1995:111–29.

Virolleaud, Charles. 1957. *Le Palais royal d'Ugarit II: Textes en cunéiformes alphabétiques des archives est, ouest et centrals.* Paris: Imprimerie Nationale.

———. 1960. L'alphabet sénestrogyre de Ras Shamra Ugarit. *Comptes rendus de l'Académie des Inscriptions et Belles-Lettres*:85–90.

von Dassow, Eva. 1999. On Writing the History of Southern Mesopotamia. ZA 89: 227–46.

———. 2003. What the Canaanite Cuneiformists Wrote. Review of Rainey 1996. IEJ 53:196–217.

———. 2004. Canaanite in Cuneiform. JAOS 124:641–74.

Walls, Neal. 1992. *The Goddess Anat in Ugaritic Myth*. Atlanta: Scholars.

Warner, Michael. 2002. Publics and Counter-Publics. *Public Culture* 14:49–90.

Watts, James D. 1999. *Reading Law: The Rhetorical Shaping of the Pentateuch*. Sheffield: Sheffield Academic Press.

Weber, Eugen. 1976. *Peasants into Frenchmen: The Modernization of Rural France, 1870–1914*. Stanford: Stanford University Press.

Weber, Max. 1952. *Ancient Judaism*. New York: The Free Press.

———. 1978. *Economy and Society*, ed. Guenther Roth and Claus Wittich. 2 vols. Berkeley: University of California Press.

———. 1992. Politik aus Beruf. In *Gesamtausgabe*, ed. Horst Baier et al., 157–252. Part I, vol. 17. Tübingen: J. C. B. Mohr.

———. 1994. The Profession and Vocation of Politics. In *Political Writings*, ed. Peter Lassman and Ronald Speirs, 309–69. Cambridge: Cambridge University Press.

Weeks, N. 1985. The Old Babylonian Amorites: Nomads or Mercenaries. *Orientalia Lovaniensia Periodica* 16:49–57.

Weeks, Stuart. 1994. *Early Israelite Wisdom*. Oxford: Oxford University Press.

Weinberg, Werner. 1980. Language Consciousness in the OT. *Zeitschrift für die Alttestamentliche Wissenschaft* 92:185–204.

Weinfeld, Moshe. 1973. The Origin of the Apodictic Law: An Overlooked Source. VT 23/1:63–75.

Weinreich, Max. 1945. YIVO and the Problems of our Time. *Yivo-bleter* 25/1:13. [in Yiddish]

Weinstein, James. 2001. Byblos. In *The Oxford Encyclopedia of Ancient Egypt*, ed. Donald B. Redford, 1:219–21. 4 vols. New York: Oxford University Press.

Weippert, M. 1966. Archäologischer Jahresbericht. *ZDPV* 82:274–330.

———. 1967. Zur Lesung der alphabetischen Keilschrifttafel vom Tell Ta'annek. ZDPV 83:82–83.

Wells, Bruce. 2006. The Covenant Code and Near Eastern Legal Traditions: A Response to David P. Wright. *Maarav* 13:85–118.

Westenholz, Joan, and Aage Westenholz. 2006. *Cuneiform Inscriptions in the Collection of the Bible Lands Museum Jerusalem: The Old Babylonian Inscriptions*. Cuneiform Monographs 33. Leiden and Boston: Brill.

White, Hayden. 1978. *The Tropics of Discourse: Essays in Cultural Criticism*. Baltimore: Johns Hopkins University Press.

———. 1989. 'Figuring the nature of the times deceased': Literary Theory and Historical Writing. In *The Future of Literary Theory*, ed. Ralph Cohen. New York: Routledge.

Whitehead, Neil L. 1992. Tribes Make States and States Make Tribes: Warfare and the Creation of Colonial Tribe and State in Northeastern South America, 1492–1820. In *War in the Tribal Zone: Expanding States and Indigenous Warfare*, ed. R. B. Ferguson and N. L. Whitehead, 127–50. Santa Fe: School of American Research Press, with the University of Washington Press.

Whitney, William Dwight. 1971. *Whitney on Language,* ed. Michael Silverstein. Cambridge, MA: MIT Press.

Wilks, Ivor. 1968. The Transformation of Islamic Learning in the Western Sudan. In Goody, ed. 1968:161–97.

Wimmer, Stefan. 2006. Egyptian Hieratic Writing in the Levant in the First Millennium B.C. *Abgadiyat* 1:23–28.

———. 2008. A New Hieratic Ostracon from Ashkelon. *Tel Aviv* 35:65–72.

Wright, David. 2003. The Laws of Hammurabi as a Source for the Covenant Collection Exodus 20:23–23:19. *Maarav* 10:11–87.

———. 2004. The Compositional Logic of the Goring Ox and Negligence Laws in the Covenant Collection Ex 21:28–36. *Zeitschrift für Altorientalische und Biblische Rechtsgeschichte* 10:93–142.

———. 2006. The Laws of Hammurabi and the Covenant Code: A Response to Bruce Wells. *Maarav* 13:211–60.

Wright, Roger, ed. 1991. *Latin and the Romance Languages in the Early Middle Ages.* London and New York: Routledge.

Wyatt, Nick. 1996. *Myths of Power: A Study of Royal Myth and Ideology in Ugaritic and Biblical Tradition.* Münster: Ugarit-Verlag.

Yadin, Yigael. 1972. *Hazor.* London: Oxford University Press for the British Academy.

Yaffe, Martin D., ed. 2004. *Spinoza's Theologico-Political Treatise.* Newburyport, MA: Focus.

Yeivin, S. 1945. A New Ugaritic Inscription from Palestine. *Kedem* 2:32–41. [in Hebrew, English Summary p. viii]

Yoffee, Norman. 1993. Too Many Chiefs? or, Safe Texts for the 90's. In *Archaeological Theory: Who Sets the Agenda?* ed. Norman Yoffee and A. Sherratt, 60–78. Cambridge: Cambridge University Press.

———. 2005. *Myths of the Archaic State: Evolution of the Earliest Cities, States and Civilizations.* Cambridge: Cambridge University Press.

Yon, M., and D. Arnaud, eds. 2001. *Études ougaritiques I. Travaux 1985–1995.* Ras Shamra-Ugarit 14. Paris: Éditions Recherche sur les Civilisations.

Young, Ian. 1993. *Diversity in Pre-Exilic Hebrew.* Tubingen: J. C. B. Mohr Paul Siebeck.

———. 2002. The Languages of Ancient Sam'al. *Maarav* 9:93–105.

Younger, K. Lawson. 2007. Neo-Assyrian and Israelite History in the Ninth Century: The Role of Shalmaneser III. In *Understanding the History of Ancient Israel,* ed. H. G. M. Williamson, 243–77. Proceedings of the British Academy 143. Oxford: Oxford University Press.

Zaccagnini, Carlo. 1983. Patterns of Mobility among Ancient Near Eastern Craftsmen. JNES 42:245–64.

Zadok, Ran. 1996. A Prosopography and Ethno-Linguistic Characterization of Southern Canaan in the Second Millennium B.C.E. *Michmanim* 9:97–145.

Zimansky, Paul. 2006. Writing, Writers, and Reading in the Kingdom of Van. In Sanders, ed. 2006:257–76.

Zorn, Jeffrey R. 2003. Tell en-Nasbeh and the Problem of the Material Culture of the Sixth Century. In *Judah and the Judeans in the Neo-Babylonian Period,* ed. Oded Liptschits and Joseph Blenkinsopp, 413–47. Winona Lake, IN: Eisenbrauns.

INDEX

Page numbers in italics refer to illustrative material or tables.

Aaron (high priest), 62–63, 65
abecedaries, 93–97, *94*, 129–30. *See also* alphabetical orders
  Beth Shemesh, 40, 92–*93*, 95–97, 107
  Izbet Sartah, 90–*91*, 95, 97
  Tel Zayit, 109–*12*
ʾ*abgad* order. *See* alphabetical orders
Akkadian language group and texts, 74, 145, 173n3, 185n19. *See also* Canaano-Akkadian, as language and as writing; multilingualism
  alloglottographic writing of, 202n13
  in Canaano-Akkadian, 207n43
  as cosmopolitan culture, 47–49
  dialects of, 188n48
  influence on Ugaritic writing, 211n80
Albright, William F., 23–24, 28–29, 180n44
alloglottography, 81–82, 202n13
Alphabet, The (Diringer), 41–42
alphabetic writing systems, 44–45, 102. *See also* Aramaic language and script; Greek alphabet/writing; Hebrew alphabet/writing; Hebrew language and literature; Phoenician language and script; Ugaritic alphabetic writing system
  cuneiform. *See* cuneiform writing systems: alphabetic
  evolutionism and neo-evolutionist theory of, 43–44, 186n32
  history of, 39–42, 99–101, 184–85n19
  Iron Age, 6–9, 113–14, 168–69, 174nn15–16
  Late Bronze Age, 5, 49–57, 106–7
  models, 42–43, 185n22
  persistence and diffusion of, 132–37
  political aspects, 51–53, 57, 118, 149
  political communication and, 34–35, 38, 158, 160, 162
  social hierarchies and, 97–98, 105, 123, 187n44
  standardization of, 54–57, 136
alphabetical orders, 40, 92–*94*, 111–12, *123*, 129, 213n18
Alt, Albrecht, 163
Amarna letters, 81–82, 99, 101
Ammonite language, 116–17
Amorite language, 5, 69–70, 119, 197n133
Anderson, Benedict, 32–34, 39, 58, 168–70
animal sacrifices, 71. *See also* atonement and unity rituals
anthropology
  cultural, 78–79
  linguistic, 34–35
  models, 43–46, 56
Arad ostraca, 129–30
Aramaic language and script, 6, 121–22, 128, 166
  diversity, 95–96, 116–18
  standardization of, 116–17, 136
archaeology and archaeological evidence, 37, 43, 77–79, 107–8, 178–79n23
arrowhead inscriptions, 55, 107–*8*
artisans. *See* craftsmen and craft networks
Ashkelon fragment, 85
Assyria, 6, 149–52. *See also* inscriptions: royal/conquest
  influence on alphabetic writing, 102, 120–21, 167, 216n39
  loyalty oaths and vassal treaties, 121–22, 162–63
atonement and unity rituals, 59–66, 193n105, 194n107, 195n115
  Judean, 61–64
  Ugaritic, 59–60, 64, 192n93
audiences for texts, 2–4, 104–7, 117–19, 151–52. *See also* alphabetic writing systems: political communication and; "people, the" (concept)

addressing, 13–14, 33–34, 38–39, 168–71
the Bible and, 1, 7–11, 147
participatory, 137, 158–66
authority. *See* Bible, the; kings and kingship; power; sovereignty
authority of texts, 14, 21, 178n22
Azazel, 61–63

Baal epic, 50–53, 52, 58
Babylonian creation epic, 51–52, 71–73
Babylonian language and texts, 5, 119, 203n21, 204n24, 205n31. *See also* Amarna letters; cuneiform writing systems; *Enuma Elish*; Gilgamesh epic; Hammurabi; *Urra = ḫubullu*
in Canaano-Akkadian, 81–82, 88–89, 189n55, 206n40, 207n43
as cosmopolitan culture, 47–49, 54, 83–86, 188n52
as dialect, 188n48
influence on Judean calendar, 110
at Mari, 68–69, 190n66
New Year's ritual, 195n115
at Ugarit, 50–51, 56, 184n19
Balaam (prophet), 139–42
Balaam inscription. *See* Deir Alla inscription
Bauman, Richard, 15, 24, 32, 34, 182n63
Besnier, Niko, 44–45
Beth Shemesh tablet, 40, 92–93, 95–97, 107
Bible, the, 4, 7, 78, 80. *See also* history: views and configuring of; Torah
audiences for, 8–10
authority, 13–14, 17–21, 32, 177n15, 178n22
history and, 13–14, 178–79n23. *See also* history: biblical
political aspects, 1–2, 13, 19, 170–71
biblical studies, 13–21, 181–82n62. *See also* Bible, the; source criticism
Hobbes, Thomas and, 19–21, 177n19
minimalist and maximalist schools, xiii, 18, 34
nationalism/national identity and, 25–26
oral/literate divide and, 23–25, 32
social theory and, xiii–xiv
bilingualism. *See* multilingualism
Blackwell, Thomas, 22–23, 30–31
Blair, Hugh, 25–26
Bloch-Smith, Elizabeth, 79
Bourne, Henry, 22
Brand, John, 22
Briggs, Charles, 15, 24, 32, 34, 182n63
bureaucracy, 90, 98, 186n39
and alphabet, 124–25, 129–30, 148
control over time, 109–12
bureaucratic lists. *See* genres: administrative

calendars, 66, 109–11, 213n12, 213n14
Canaano-Akkadian, as language and as writing, 81–84, 98–99, 202nn11–12
contact languages and, 88–90, 206nn42–43, 207n46
texts, 83–86
Carr, David, 8–9, 166–67, 174n9, 174n11, 203n22
Cassuto, Umberto, 23–24, 30–32, 34, 180n49
Christendom, 17–19, 176n12
circulation of texts, 140–48, 154–55, 164, 224n18
absence of, 58
political aspects, 168–70
prophetic messages and, 144, 164–65
city-states, 67. *See also* Emar (city-state); Mari (city-state and texts); Ugarit (city-state)
collective governance and ideologies, 72, 199n143
collective redemption, 102. *See also* atonement and unity rituals
communication, 2–3, 7, 140, 177n19, 190n68. *See also* audiences for texts; political communication
and coercion, 107, 124–26, 155
of divine Word, 16–17, 19–21
and empire, 86
exclusion from, 10, 158, 183n4
mass vs. ancient forms, 58
state and, 109–11, 120
contact languages, 88–90, 206nn42–43, 207n46
cosmopolitan cultures, languages, and writing systems, 47–49. *See also* Akkadian language group and texts; Assyria; Babylonian language and texts; cuneiform writing systems; Egypt; genres: imperial; Ugarit (city-state); Ugaritic language and literature
Hittite, 189n56
local language and, 82, 89–90, 98, 102

Qur'anic Arabic as, 10–11
vs. vernacular cultures, 5, 56–57, 64, 89–91, 120–21
covenants and covenantal law, 153–54, 167–68
Assyrian vassal treaties and, 121, 163
Torah and, 162–64
tribal and vassal basis of, 10, 71
craftsmen and craft networks, 127, 131–34, 159
alphabetic writing systems and, 97–98, 107
role of, 100, 161
creation epic (Babylonian), 51–52, 71–73
Critical Dissertation on the Poems of Ossian (Blair), 26
Cross, Frank M., 23, 27–31, 34, 43–44, 82, 180n49
"Culture Area" hypothesis, 78–79
cuneiform writing systems, 54, 102. *See also* Akkadian language group and texts; Sumerian language and texts
alphabetic, 40–41, 50, 92, 99–100, 211n80
disappearance of, 106
Late Bronze Age, 4–5, 77, 80–84
mystical ideology and, 84, 204n24
Semitic languages and, 47–48
syllabic, 47, 53–56, 77, 80–86, 97–100, 106–7

David (king), 71, 113, 162
Day of Atonement (*yôm hakkipurîm*). *See* atonement and unity rituals
Deir Alla inscription, 130, 139–42, 161–62, 167
Deuteronomistic history and editor, 38–39, 153–54, 164–67, 201n4. *See also* source criticism
dialects, 46, 95–96, 187–88n48
Aramaic. *See* Aramaic language and script
Hebrew, 37, 95, 217n52
West Semitic, 100, 141–42, 208n55
Dietrich, Manfred, 42
diplomatic letters
Canaano-Akkadian, 81
Egyptian/Babylonian exchange, 86–88, *87*, 205–6n38
Diringer, David, 41–42

educational/school texts, 81, 83–85, 98, 129, 174n10, 202n11
Megiddo Gilgamesh fragment, 49, 85, 205n30
Urra = ḫubullu, 84–85, 203n23
Egypt, 8
alphabetic writing and, 40, 82, 91, 102
cuneiform texts and, 5–6, 83, 86–88, *87*
letters and lists, 98. *See also* diplomatic letters
Egyptian hieratic numerals. *See* hieratic numeral system
Emar (city-state), 55, 60, 72, 193n102, 199n143, 204n26
Enuma Elish epic, 51–52, 71–73
epic poetry, 29–30
Greek, 23
Hebrew, 29–32, 180n49
Scottish, 26
epics
Baal, 50–53, *52*, 58
Enuma Elish, 51–52, 71–73
Gilgamesh, 49, 85, 91
Zimri-Lim, 53
epigraphy and epigraphers, 23, 67, 122, 159–60, 166–67
evidence/models, 33–37, 39–43, 77, 104–6, 131
techniques, 28–29
ethnicity, 56, 78–79, 215n33
and alphabet, 40, 42–43, 185n23, 209nn64–65
in Late Bronze Age Levant, 87
in Ugaritic ritual, 59–60, 192n97
evolutionism and neo-evolutionist theory of writing, 27–28, 33, 43–44, 95, 186n32
expiation rituals. *See* atonement and unity rituals

folklore and folklorists, 22, 27–28, 58
forgetting, cultural. *See* memory
Foucault, Michel, 32, 157–58, 223n1

genres, 77, 104–5, 160, 168
administrative, 83, 86, 99. *See also* tax documents
alphabetic versus syllabic, 98
biblical, 65, 160, 165
diplomatic letters, 81, 86–88, *87*, 205–6n38
educational/school texts. *See* educational/school texts
epic, 223n5. *See also* epics
graffiti, 134

historical narrative, 36–37, 113–16, 120, 164, 182n2
history, 102, 164–65, 167, 223n3
imperial, 102, 120–22, 148, 152
law and covenant, 102, 162–65, 167, 223n3
oral. *See* oral/literate divide; poetry
political, 158, 165, 169
prophecy, 141–45, 151, 164–65, 167–68, 223n3
Gershevitch, Ilya, 146
Gezer calendar, 109–11
Gilgamesh epic, 49, 85
Goody, Jack, 23, 44–45
graffiti, 134, 161
Greek alphabet/writing, 133–36
Greek poetry, 23
Greenfield, Jonas, 117
Grimm brothers (Wilhelm and Jacob), 27–29
Grottanelli, Cristiano, 148, 153–54
Gunkel, Hermann, 27–29

Habermas, Jürgen, 32–33, 168–70
halḫam order, 40, 93–94
Hammurabi, 38, 68, 119, 199n145, 215–16n35
Hazor *Urra = ḫubullu* fragment, 84, 203n23
hearing, reading and, 146–47
Hebrew alphabet/writing, 95, 108–9. *See also* alphabetic writing systems; Hebrew language and literature
divided monarchy period, 116–18
hieratic numeral system and, 128–29
Iron Age, 122–26, *123*, *125*
letters, *143–44*
non-monarchic, 136
orthography and spelling, 127–28
paleography and script style, 109, 126–27, 133, 217n50
standardization and localization of, 108, 116–17, *123–33*, *125*
united monarchy period, 113
Hebrew Bible. *See* Bible, the
Hebrew language and literature, 3, 13, 76–77, 103–55, 161. *See also* Bible, the; Hebrew alphabet/writing; poetry: Hebrew
audiences for, 146–47
Babylonian exile and, 166
biblical history and, 162, 167–68
biblical politics and, 171
dialects, 37, 217n52
history of, 137
invention of, 37, 80
participation and, 137
political communication and, 34–35, 155
political context and, 169–70
standardization of, 46–47, 126–33
Hebrew poetry, 3, 24–27, 29–30
Herder, Gottfried, 3, 29–32, 34–36, 42
folk literature, 58
literary theory, 26–27
hieratic numeral system, 90, 99, 128–29
historical narratives, 36–37, 113–16, 120, 164, 182n2
historical veracity, 25
the Bible and, 178–79n23
Hebrew poetry and, 25
history, 41–42. *See also* Deuteronomistic history and editor
biblical, 103–4, 162, 167–68
as genre, 102, 164–65, 167, 223n3. *See also* genres: historical narrative
"Roman" (Foucault), 157–58
views and configuring of, 157–61, 164, 170
Hittite empire and people, 56, 60
Hittite language and culture, 48–49, 184n19, 189n56, 190n64, 215n32
Hobbes, Thomas, 2–3, 170
biblical criticism and, xiv, 19–21, 32, 177n19
Leviathan, 17–21, 178nn21
Hodder, Ian, 78
Homer, 22–23
Hoshayahu (soldier), *143–45*

imitation of texts and inscriptions, 10, 47, 102
innovative aspects, 219n68
political aspects, 119–22, 149–51, 158
"imperial imitation" (concept), 120–22, 151
imperialism, 149–50, 157–58. *See also* genres: imperial; inscriptions: royal/conquest; kings and kingship
inscriptions, 107, 158–61
alphabetic, 40, *50*
Arad, 129–30
Aramaic, 116–17
Assyrian, 149–51
audiences for, 114, 140. *See also* audiences for texts
Beth Shemesh, 92, *93*, 95–97, 107
biblical history and, 103–4
Deir Alla, 130, 139–42, 161–62, 167
Greek, 134–36

Hebrew, 2, 137–39, 168
Kadesh-barnea, 128–29
Kuntillet Ajrud, *123–26*, 142
Lachish, 91, 97, 127–29, 133, *143–45*
Luwian, 117, 215n3
Mesha stela, 72, 114–16, *115*
Phoenician, 72, 109, 117, 119
royal/conquest, 113–14, 117, 120–22, 149–51, 213–14n21
Sefire, 122
Siloam, 130, 138–*39*, 161, 167
Taanach, 49, 86–*87*, 96–97
Tabor, 96–97
Tel Dan, 116
Tel Fekheriye, 121, 128
interpenetration (morphological), 88–89, 206n40
Isaiah (First), 149–52
Israel (northern kingdom), 124, 217n46, 217n52. *See also* Judah (southern kingdom)
Israel (people), 1. *See also* Judah (southern kingdom); "people, the" (concept)
connection to Ugarit, 4
as distinctive culture, 8, 77
endurance of, 155, 170
Izbet Sartah abecedary, 90–91, 95, 97
Izre'el, Shlomo, 81

Jakobson, Roman, 25
Judah (southern kingdom), 149–51, 217n52, 222n100. *See also* Israel (northern kingdom); "people, the" (concept)

Kadesh-barnea ostraca, 128–29
Kawashima, Robert, 161
Kilamuwa of Zinjirli (king), 215n32
kings and kingship, 105, 109. *See also* genres: imperial; inscriptions: royal/conquest; *and individual names and polities*
absence in Hebrew texts, 152–54, 169
authority of, 19, 53, 57, 71, 149–53, 158
historical narratives and, 113–16, 120
subversion of, 165
tribal connections, 199n145
kinship and kin-based groups, 104, 118. *See also* tribes; West Semitic cultures: political theory
political aspects, 67, 69–72, 75, 118, 175n19
sovereignty and, 162

Kothar-wa-Hasis, 51–52
KTU 1.40 text. *See* atonement and unity rituals
Kuntillet Ajrud texts, *123–26*, 142

Lachish inscriptions, 127–29, 133
ewer, 91, 97
letter 3, *143–45*
language and languages, 14–16. *See also* alphabetic writing systems; contact languages; dialects; mixed languages; semiotics; *and individual languages*
nationalism/national identity and, 118
political aspects, 14, 27
representation of, 79, 201n8
standardization of, 46–47, 54–57, 100, 130–33
theories of, 21, 95
language/writing gap. *See* writing/language
law, 19–21, 159–60. *See also* covenants and covenantal law; genres: law and covenant; Torah
biblical, 137–38, 162–64, 167
mediating, 7, 38–39, 148, 164
Mesopotamian, 163–64. *See also* Hammurabi
reframing, 164
Laws of Hammurabi. *See* Hammurabi
legitimacy and legitimation, 157, 165, 224n13
biblical, 9, 18–19
royal, 19, 53, 153
of text and its mediators, 154, 169
"Letter of a Literate Soldier" (Hoshayahu) (=Lachish letter 3), *143–45*
letters, 143. *See also* diplomatic letters; Lachish inscriptions; messages; Taanach texts
Levant, the, 1–8, 77, 79–83, 101–2, 105–9, 118–22
Leviathan (Hobbes), 18–21, 178nn21
Leviticus (chapter 16), 61–66
linear scripts. *See* alphabetic writing systems
linguistics. *See* language and languages; philology and philologists
literacy, 15–16, 98–99, 186n39. *See also* circulation of texts; multilingualism; writing/language: gap
oral/literate divide, 29, 42–45, 187n44
political aspects, 45–46
Liverani, Mario, 106, 124
Locke, John, 22

Loretz, Oswald, 42
Lowth, Robert (bishop), 3, 22–24, 26–27
loyalty oaths, Assyrian, 121–22, 162–63. *See also* covenants and covenantal law
Luwian inscriptions, 117, 215n32

Machinist, Peter, 149–51
MacPherson, James, 26, 179n38
Mari (city-state and texts), 4–5, 53, 67–75, 197–98nn133–34
mass communication, 58
maximalist school (biblical studies), 18, 34
Megiddo Gilgamesh fragment, 49, 85, 205n30
memory, 78, 80, 201n9
Mesha stela, 72, 114–16, *115*
Mesopotamian law, 163–64. *See also* Hammurabi
messages, 83, 88, 138
  circulation of, 140–41, 144–46
  divine, 80, 141
  prophetic, 144–45, 165
minimalist school (biblical studies), xiii, 18, 34
mixed languages, 81, 88–89, 202n12, 205n38, 206nn42–44. *See also* multilingualism
Moabite inscription. *See* Mesha stela
Moabite language and script, 116
modernity/pre-modernity, xiv, 15–16, 23–24, 27, 29, 42–45
monarchs. *See* kings and kingship
monuments. *See* inscriptions
Moses, 27, 164–65
Mowinckel, Sigmund, 25
multilingualism, 49, 81, 84–85, 202n12. *See also* mixed languages
mystical ideology, 84, 203n24
myths and mythology, 4, 27, 31–32, 190n64. *See also* epic poetry; epics
  rituals and, 65–66
  West Semitic, 52–54

Na'aman, Nadav, 120–21, 216n39
narrative prose, 73–75, 113–16, 161, 200n153. *See also* genres: historical narrative; Hebrew language and literature
nationalism/national identity, 58, 183n5. *See also* atonement and unity rituals
  biblical studies and, 25–26
  languages and, 118
Neo-Assyrian empire. *See* Assyria
nomadism. *See* tribes

oaths, loyalty. *See* covenants and covenantal law; loyalty oaths, Assyrian
Ong, Walter J., 44
oracular messages. *See* messages: prophetic
oral/literate divide, 15–16, 22
  biblical studies and, 23–25, 29
  poetry, Hebrew and, 29–30
oral traditions, 162–63. *See also* oral/literate divide
Ossian (bard), 26, 179n38
ostraca. *See* inscriptions

parallelism (poetic), 25–26, 190n64
participation in writing, 58, 104, 145–46. *See also* circulation of texts
"people, the" (concept), 104, 118, 197–98n133. *See also* Israel (people); Judah (southern kingdom); public, the (concept)
  audiences for texts, 122, 130, 153
  communication and, 10
  participant in history, 161
  participant in politics, 67–72, 75, 148, 159
  participant in ritual and covenant, 58–66, 163, 197–98n133
  participant in ritual and politics, 4–6
  vernacular literature and, 27
persuasion, political. *See* political communication; storytelling
Petrarch, 157, 223n1
philology and philologists, 15–16, 22–24, 27–35. *See also* language and languages
Phoenician language and script, 96, 100–102, 111–13, 116–17, 128
  adaptation and diffusion of, 79, 133–36
  inscriptions, 109
  prestige of, 132
  standardization of, 127
Phrasikleia funerary marker, 135–36
poetry, 23–27, 58. *See also* epic poetry; epics
  Hebrew, 3, 24–27, 29–30
political communication, 38, 148, 154–55
  alphabetic writing systems and, 33, 158, 160, 171
  cuneiform writing systems and, 80–81
  imitation of texts and inscriptions, 119–22, 149–51, 158

as persuasion, 73–74, 118–19, 200n155
shift to non-monarchic, 105, 137–40, 148
texts and/as, 10, 13–27, 32–35, 168
political communities, 168–71
political theology, 11, 17–21, 170–71
Babylonian, 51–52, 152
Judean monarchy and, 222n100
negative, 153–54, 165, 169, 222n99
positive, 152
Ugaritic, 60
West Semitic mythology and, 52–54
politics. *See also* political communication; political communities; political theology; West Semitic cultures: political theory
religion and, 2–3, 174n5, 186–87n41
tribal, 67–75, 196n127, 197n129
Pollock, Sheldon, 38–39, 102, 122
power, 13–21, 32, 74–75, 152–54. *See also* kings and kingship; sovereignty
pre-modernity. *See* modernity/pre-modernity
Priestly source and priests, 61–66, 104, 164
prophecy and prophets, 130, 159–60. *See also* Balaam (prophet); genres: prophecy; Isaiah (First); Moses
challenges to Assyria, 149–51
literary/narrative, 141–47, 164–65
subversion of history and law to, 167–68
public, the (concept), 2, 27, 32–34, 58, 147, 163–64, 168–70. *See also* audiences for texts; "people, the" (concept); political communities
public events. *See* history

Qur'an, 10–11

reading, 146–47, 186–87n41
Reformation, the, 16–17, 176n12, 176n14
religion and politics, 2–3, 174n5, 186–87n41
rhetoric, 74, 149
ritual and history. *See* history: views and configuring of
rituals, 4–7. *See also* atonement and unity rituals
collective redemption, 102
covenant (law), 162–65, 167–68
public/political, 57–67, 75
tribal and kinship, 70–72
Rollston, Christopher, 125–28, 217n50
Romantic theory of writing, 42–43, 78–79, 185n22
royal seals, 50–51, 54
rulers. *See* kings and kingship; sovereignty

sacred texts, 14–21, 24, 159–60. *See also* Bible, the; Hebrew language and literature; Torah
salvation, national, 59–66
scapegoat ritual. *See* atonement and unity rituals
Schniedewind, William, 7
school texts. *See* educational/school texts
scribes and scribal culture/education, 5–9, 81–86, 164–65, 174–75nn9–14, 182n1
Hebrew, 126–33, 166–67
Hittite, 48–49
international/local, 56–57, 112–13
Phoenician, 132
Semitic, 119, 189n55
Ugaritic, 51–57, 184–85n19
Scripture. *See* Bible, the; sacred texts
seals, inscribed, 105–6, 108, 211–12nn5–7, 218–19n66. *See also* royal seals
Sefire inscriptions, 122, 167
semiotics, 178n21
Siloam tunnel inscription, 130, 138–39, 161, 167
Smith, Anthony D., 79
social hierarchies, 97–98, 105, 123, 187n44
social theory, 2, 124, 168
biblical studies and, xiii–xiv, 13–15
modernity/pre-modernity, xiv, 29
philology and, 32
source criticism, 13–14, 18, 30, 103–4, 164–68. *See also* Deuteronomistic history and editor; Priestly source and priests
sovereignty, 20, 67, 164, 178n21. *See also* Assyria; genres: imperial; kings and kingship
challenges to, 149, 165
foundation of, 13, 152–54, 165
history and, 157–58
kin-based groups and, 73, 162
speech/writing gap. *See* writing/language: gap
spelling, Hebrew, 127–28
Spinoza, Baruch, xiv, 2–3, 13–14, 18, 178n22
state, the, 71–72, 123. *See also* Ugarit (city-state); writing

and coercion, 19, 21
communication and, 109–11, 120
as foundation of politics, xiii, 67–68, 196n121
storytelling, 73–74, 159–62, 200n153. *See also* narrative prose
Studies in Ancient Yahwistic Poetry (Cross and Friedman), 28
Sumerian language and texts, 47–49, 84–85, 105. *See also* multilingualism
syllabic writing systems, 47, 56, 77, 80–86, 97–102, 106–7
Symbols in Action (Hodder), 78

Taanach texts, 49, 86–*87*, 96–97
Tabor knife inscription, 96–97
tax documents, 83–84, 109–10. *See also* hieratic numeral system
Tel Dan inscription, 116
Tel Fekheriye inscription, 121, 128
Tel Zayit abecedary, 109–*12*
Torah, 10, 31, 65–66, 162–64. *See also* Deuteronomistic history and editor; Priestly source and priests
Tractatus Theologico-Politicus (Spinoza), 13–14, 18
tribes, 118–19, 198n139. *See also* kinship and kin-based groups
identification with, 199nn144–45
political aspects, 67–75, 196n127, 197n129
trilingualism. *See* multilingualism

Ugarit (city-state), 60, 66, 71–72, 108, 174n7
connection to Israel (people), 4
vernacular literature and, 41, 54–58, 92, 102
Ugaritic alphabetic writing system, 40–41, 92, 99–100, 184–85n19
Ugaritic expiation ritual. *See* atonement and unity rituals
Ugaritic language and literature, 4, 50, 105
communal aspects, 59, 192n93
localization and standardization of, 50, 54–58
Urartu, 149–51
Urra = ḫubullu, 84–85, 203n23

Valla, Lorenzo, 16
van der Toorn, Karel, 8, 166–67
vassal treaties. *See* covenants and covenantal law; loyalty oaths, Assyrian
vernacular literatures, 2–4, 66, 154, 167–68
audiences for, 8–10, 122–23, 149–52, 158–59
Late Bronze Age, 76–77
political aspects, 10, 26, 38
political theology and, 154
rise of, 54–58, 102–8
social hierarchies and, 123
Voices of Modernity (Bauman and Briggs), 15
von Dassow, Eva, 81, 203n17
vowels, 127–28, 134

warlords, *87*, 96, 107, 149
Warner, Michael, 32–33, 168–70
weapons, 51–53, 96–*97*, 107
Weber, Max, 19
weight system, Judean, 132–33
Weinreich, Max, 36, 43
Wellhausen, Julius, 14, 28–29, 121–22
West Semitic cultures, 67
languages, 4–6, 173n3. *See also individual languages*
political culture, 33, 104, 158, 160–61
political theory, 52–54, 72–75
Wood, Robert, 22–23
writing, 140. *See also* alphabetic writing systems; cuneiform writing systems; participation in writing
as entertainment, 111, 213n16
non-scribal use, 133
state and, 68–69, 109–11, 120, 123–25, 130–32, 135–36
writing/language
gap, 79–81, 95, 98
interplay in Canaano-Akkadian, 82–83

yôm hakkipurîm (Day of Atonement). *See* atonement and unity rituals
Young, Ian, 117

Zaccagnini, Carlo, 131–32
Zimri-Lim epic, 53, 199n145

SETH L. SANDERS is an assistant professor of religion at Trinity College and the editor of the *Journal of Ancient Near Eastern Religions*. He edited *Margins of Writing, Origins of Cultures* and coedited *Cuneiform in Canaan.*

TRADITIONS

Baby and Child Heroes in Ancient Greece
Corinne Ondine Pache

Assyrian and Babylonian Medicine:
Diagnostic Texts
Translated and with commentary by
Jo Ann Scurlock and Burton R. Andersen

Homer's Text and Language
Gregory Nagy

Indo-European Sacred Space:
Roman and Vedic Cults
Roger D. Woodard

The Invention of Hebrew
Seth L. Sanders

C. P. Cavafy: The Economics of Metonymy
Panagiotis Roilos

The University of Illinois Press
is a founding member of the
Association of American University Presses.

UNIVERSITY OF ILLINOIS PRESS
1325 South Oak Street
Champaign, IL 61820-6903
www.press.uillinois.edu